ArtScroll® Series

Rabbi Nosson Scherman / Rabbi Meir Zlotowitz
General Editors

הגדה של פסח

CHAYIL Haggadah

Rabbi Dov Weller

THE PANETH EDITION

The EISHES

Published by
ArtScroll®
Mesorah Publications, ltd

FIRST EDITION
First Impression ... March 2016
Second Impression ... April 2016
Third Impression ... January 2017
Fourth Impression ... February 2021
Fifth Impression ... January 2022

Published and Distributed by
MESORAH PUBLICATIONS, LTD.
313 Regina Avenue / Rahway, N.J. 07065

Distributed in Europe by
LEHMANNS
Unit E, Viking Business Park
Rolling Mill Road
Jarow, Tyne & Wear, NE32 3DP
England

Distributed in Australia and New Zealand
by **GOLDS WORLDS OF JUDAICA**
3-13 William Street
Balaclava, Melbourne 3183
Victoria, Australia

Distributed in Israel by
SIFRIATI / A. GITLER — BOOKS
POB 2351
Bnei Brak 51122

Distributed in South Africa by
KOLLEL BOOKSHOP
Northfield Centre, 17 Northfield Avenue
Glenhazel 2192, Johannesburg, South Africa

ARTSCROLL® SERIES
THE EISHES CHAYIL HAGGADAH
© Copyright 2016, by MESORAH PUBLICATIONS, Ltd.
313 Regina Avenue / Rahway, N.J. 07065 / (718) 921-9000 / FAX (718) 680-1875 / www.artscroll.com

---

ALL RIGHTS RESERVED
The text, prefatory and associated textual contents and introductions
— including the typographic layout, cover artwork and ornamental graphics —
have been designed, edited and revised as to content, form and style.

No part of this book may be reproduced
IN ANY FORM, PHOTOCOPYING, OR COMPUTER RETRIEVAL SYSTEMS
— even for personal use without written permission from
the copyright holder, Mesorah Publications Ltd.
except by a reviewer who wishes to quote brief passages
in connection with a review written for inclusion in magazines or newspapers.

THE RIGHTS OF THE COPYRIGHT HOLDER WILL BE STRICTLY ENFORCED.

To contact the author with questions and comments:
eisheschayilhaggadah@gmail.com

ISBN 10: 978-1-4226-1720-5 / ISBN 13: 1-4226-1720-3
ITEM CODE: HECH

Typography by CompuScribe at ArtScroll Studios, Ltd.
Bound by Sefercraft, Quality Bookbinders, Ltd. Rahway, NJ

This volume is dedicated in memory of
our beloved mother

Perel Paneth ע"ה
פערל בת הרב חיים יהודה ע"ה
24 Av, 5775

On her hundredth birthday, someone said, "The holy *sefarim* tell us that the number 100 represents completion."

Our mother was complete in every way. She loved Hashem. She loved Torah. She loved *talmidei chachamim*. She loved her family. She loved every Jew she could help — and there were many. When it was time for her to marry, there was one absolute prerequisite: she was determined that her partner in life and the father of her children "must be a *ben Torah, a shomer Torah u'mitzvos par excellence.*" She found him.

She and our father Yaakov Chaim ז"ל raised and guided us through good times and hard. Their ideals never changed. Always they remained true to the teachings of their sainted parents and grandparents ז"ל.

After our father was called to the *Yeshivah Shel Maalah,* our mother was alone for the next 46 years, but *we* were never alone. She was father and mother, role model and inspiration, living embodiment of the spiritual grandeur of her forebears.

Her great nachas was to sit at the Seder table and listen to the *divrei Torah* of her children, grandchildren, and great-grandchildren. They were the fulfillment of her dreams, the reward for her selflessness, the testimony to her success in carrying on the legacy of our father ז"ל and past generations, and building a Torah-true future.

It is fitting, therefore, that this Haggadah is dedicated in her memory. It will enrich thousands of Seder tables and tens of thousands of Jewish parents and children — as her memory will always continue to guide and warm us.

Chesky and Sheindy Paneth
and family

בס"ד

HaRav Doniel Neustadt
216-287-0376
dneustadt@cordetroit.com

ESTABLISHED 1871 · 15400 West Ten Mile Road · Oak Park, Michigan 48237 · 248-967-3969

Adar II 5776

The efforts expended by women in preparation for Pesach far exceed those of any other holiday on the Jewish calendar. The lion's share of cleaning, cooking, clothes shopping, planning, and myriad other preparations has traditionally been shouldered by Jewish women. The fruits of this labor result in the enjoyable and meaningful *yom tov* that families cherish and remember.

In reality, women's Pesach preparations have a much more profound influence. Women are the עקרת הבית, the backbone of the home, the ones who directly impact its atmosphere. Indeed, it was the merit of the righteous women, and their staunch *emunah* during the most turbulent times, which uplifted their families and accelerated the Jewish nation's redemption from Egypt.

In our times, the task of infusing Jewish homes with *emunah* and *bitachon* is more vital than ever, since we live in a world that challenges many of the principles that were bestowed upon us at Yetziyas Mitzrayim and Matan Torah. The sole beacon for us is our relationship with Hashem, which casts a guiding light on our uncertain and confusing world. Pesach and Seder night is the special time when all this comes to center stage. The Haggadah is the platform for instilling an awareness of Hashem's unconditional love for us, a love which is constantly demonstrated through *hashgachah pratis* even in the smallest facets of our lives.

The Eishes Chayil Haggadah, meticulously and lovingly compiled by Rav Dov Weller *shlita*, offers women of all ages and backgrounds the opportunity to spiritually prepare for Pesach and to tap into the Haggadah's repositories of treasured wisdom and inspiration. The moving, down-to-earth lessons and stories contained in this Haggadah will both captivate and inspire, spurring women to growth far beyond the seven days of Pesach.

For presenting Klal Yisrael with such a wonderful gift, we are indebted to Rav Weller, and we are honored to have the opportunity to wish him much success with this endeavor and all of his future undertakings on behalf of the *tzibbur*.

יישר חילך לאורייתא!

Rabbi Doniel Neustadt
Detroit

PUBLISHER'S PREFACE

The Sages declare that our ancestors were redeemed from Egypt in the merit of the righteous women of that generation. For this reason, the Sages teach that the righteous women of every generation are equal partners in all the mitzvos of the Seder. We are proud, therefore, to present this new Haggadah written especially for women.

The **Eishes Chayil Haggadah** offers a commentary designed to enhance appreciation for the women's role in the miracles of *Yetzias Mitzrayim*. It offers a rich commentary and an abundance of stories that emphasize the role of women in the Exodus and in Jewish life throughout the ages.

We are grateful to **Rabbi Dov Weller**, the author of this volume, and we are confident that countless readers — men and women alike – will join us in thanking him for this important Haggadah.

This Haggadah is dedicated by **Chesky and Sheindy Paneth**. Their quiet support of Torah education and Torah projects, and their *chesed* to individuals have earned them the respect and admiration of their entire community. They recognized that this volume is not just "one more Haggadah," but a unique service that will enrich the Seder of wives, mothers, and daughters everywhere. We applaud their vision and generosity, and thank them for their friendship.

Rabbi Michoel Levi, principal of Bais Yaakov d'Rav Meir in Brooklyn, New York, is one of the most distinguished educators of our time. He has been a loyal friend of ArtScroll/Mesorah since its inception, and a close personal friend for many years before that. His guidance and help are always available and are much appreciated.

We thank the entire ArtScroll staff, in America and Israel, who devotedly and effectively brought this work to fruition. Countless Sedarim will be enriched because of them.

Rabbi Meir Zlotowitz / Rabbi Nosson Scherman

II Adar 5776 / March 2016

Acknowledgments

In his introduction to the Haggadah, the Malbim writes that 10 measures of elucidation of Torah through *sefarim* were sent down to this world in order to explain, understand, and disseminate the Torah. Nine of the measures were used to explain the *Haggadah Shel Pesach* and the remaining single measure was reserved for the balance of the entire Torah. With thousands of Haggados in print and dozens more printed each year, the Jewish nation has taken to heart and to pen the Haggadah's dictum of *Kol Hamarbeh L'Sapeir B'Yitzias Mitzrayim Harei Zeh M'Shubach*.

I thank Hashem for granting me the privilege of publishing this Haggadah whose goal is to afford women an opportunity to have a deeper insight and appreciation for one of the holiest nights of the year: a night whose purpose is to instill in every Jew the pillars of *emunah* and *bitachon*. I daven that the Eishes Chayil Haggadah should serve as a vehicle for helping all those who read this Haggadah to come closer to Hashem, closer to their fellow Jew, and to gain a greater understanding of Pesach and its themes. Having the merit of benefiting the public is an unbelievable *zechus*, one that I approach with anticipation and emotion.

The Shulchan Aruch (472:2) writes that one should adorn the Seder table with כֵּלִים נָאִים — one's finest dining accoutrements. Rav Hillel of Kalami, a student of the Chasam Sofer, had the custom to decorate his Seder table with the various *sefarim* that he had authored. When asked for an explanation of this novel practice, he explained, "Dovid Hamelech writes in Tehillim (119:72) טוֹב לִי תוֹרַת פִּיךָ מֵאַלְפֵי זָהָב וָכָסֶף *Better for me is the Torah of Your mouth than thousands in gold and silver*. Hence, through displaying my Torah manuscripts on the table I fulfill the halachah of setting my table with the finest tableware as these *sefarim* are more valuable than gold and silver." I thank Hashem for the privilege and the merit of presenting a Haggadah which I hope will, likewise, be a כְּלִי נָאֶה — a beautiful adornment to the Seder table of all its readers.

Two years ago, we were visiting my brother several days before Pesach and my sister in-law, a Bais Yaakov teacher, mentioned that she was looking for a Haggadah that could serve as a means of inspiring and educating her class. After thinking for a few moments about several options I said to her, "There must be a women's Haggadah that you can use." That statement and the subsequent realization that no such Haggadah was available to the English-speaking public launched the Eishes Chayil Haggadah that sought to fill this void. The *sefarim* (*Maagid D'Varav L'Yaakov* §222) write that all those with whom we come in contact with, everything that we hear, and all that we see are direct messengers from Hashem crossing our paths so that we can learn some lesson. This encounter was a prime example of this teaching and serves as the inspiration for this Haggadah.

Despite their enormously busy schedules there were a number of dedicated Rabbanim, Rebbetzins, and others who played a vital role in this Haggadah coming to fruition. Their interest, guidance, and knowledge are deeply appreciated. **Rav Dovid Braunfeld**, author of *Moznei Tzedek* (a guidebook to the intricate *halachos* of *shiurim*), generously gave of his time and expertise. We are sincerely grateful for his support. **Rav Mordechai Frankel** and **Rav Dovid Heber**, both members of the Star-K team and renowned *poskim*, reviewed many parts of the *halachos* and made many valuable comments. **Rav Avrohom Kleinkaufman**, a senior editor at ArtScroll and a Rebbi in Yeshiva of Far Rockaway, was instrumental in helping this project get up and running and was a continuous source of wise counsel. **Rav Dovid Ribiat**, author of the famed *sefer* on the 39 *melachos,* gave of his time and expertise that were vital to the project.

I would like to thank **Rebbetzin Miriam Feldman** of Atlanta for reading the Haggadah and providing guidance and insight that truly helped shape it. Thank you to **Rebbetzin Debbie Greenblatt** for taking time from her busy schedule to read the Haggadah and to make valuable suggestions. Thank you to **Mrs. Miriam Zakon** of ArtScroll whose literary vision saw the potential of this Haggadah. You supported this project from its initiation through its completion ensuring that every detail was attended to and deftly assembled a great team of editors and designers, including **Dr. Emmy Zitter, Mrs. Suri Brand, Rabbi Avrohom Biderman, R' Mendy Herzberg, Mrs. Judi Dick, Mrs. Faygie Weinbaum,** and **Mrs. Estie Dicker,** each of whom contributed in their area of expertise. In addition, my profound appreciation to **R' Eli Kroen** for the great cover.

To my parents **Dr. Judah and Harriet Weller**, thank you for your continuous love, support, and encouragement. Your committed drive to influence the *klal*, no matter the circumstances, has inspired your children to likewise want to fulfill a dream of זִכּוּי הָרַבִּים.

To my in-laws **Dr. Eli and Feige Mayer**, thank you for seeing the potential of this project from its inception and for constantly providing us your all-encompassing support and confidence.

To my wife, **Rochel**, for the past two years we certainly fulfilled the mitzvah of recalling the Exodus each day and night. Spring, summer, fall, winter, Yamim Noraim, Chanukah, Purim, Shavuos and Shabbos were all laced with a taste of Pesach. Thank you for reviewing and editing the Haggadah countless times, providing a listening and ever-intuitive ear, being a springboard for ideas, and for never ceasing to lend your encouragement throughout this journey. This Haggadah is truly a joint venture. May we merit to see much *nachas* from our family and be a source of *nachas* to *Klal Yisrael*.

Dov Weller

Adar Beis 5776

The author dedicates his work to the memory of:

אברהם יצחק בן יחזקאל הכהן ע"ה – כ"ט ניסן תשל"ג

ואשתו חנה מלכה בת משה ע"ה – ג' חשון תש"מ

דוב בן אברהם יואל ע"ה – י"ד אייר תשמ"ה

הרה"ג ר' אברהם בן ר' חיים מנחם בן ציון ע"ה – ד' אדר תשס"ז

יוסף צבי בן שמעון ע"ה – י"ג אדר תשע"ג

נעכא פריידה בת אברהם צבי ע"ה – טז אדר א תשע"ד

מיכל אריאלה בת אברהם יצחק ע"ה – כ"ז תמוז תשע"ה

יהושע שלום בן בנימין דוד ע"ה – י' אלול תשע"ה

ר' משה בן ר' דוד ע"ה – ט' שבט תשע"ו

ת. נ. צ. ב. ה.

INTRODUCTION

Leil haSeder — Seder night. The family is seated around the elegantly set table, ready to begin one of the most memorable and majestic nights of the year. Preparations for this moment have taken front and center for weeks. The house has been turned inside out in the search for the most minuscule crumb of *chametz,* and now it sparkles from the basement to the attic. For weeks, the whole family has been busy: cleaning and scrubbing, buying new clothing and new dishes, ordering or baking matzos, stocking up on wine and grape juice, and, of course, preparing *divrei Torah* for the Seder. The warm and familiar aroma of Pesach cooking has filled the air for days.

We prepare our homes and ourselves for every holiday, but no Yom Tov demands the kind of effort we put into our Pesach preparations. And that's not all that makes this holiday unique. In addition to the many weeks that we prepare for Pesach, there is a special obligation to retell the story of our Exodus from Egypt.

The truth is, we recall the story of the Exodus all year long, every single day of our lives! So many of our mitzvos remind us of the Exodus: we remember the story when we daven, when we *bentch*, and at the Friday-night Kiddush.

What makes Pesach and the story of our redemption from Egypt so central to our lives as Jews? What exactly will we be celebrating at the Seder for which we have expended so much effort?

Chag HaEmunah — the Holiday of Faith

On Pesach we recall how in Egypt Hashem demonstrated His *hashgachah pratis*, His Divine Providence, over this world and over each and every person living in it. Six hundred thousand Jewish men and millions of Jewish women and children witnessed Hashem performing miracles that defied nature. They saw how the Egyptians were punished "measure for measure" for their cruelty to Hashem's people. Ten devastating plagues confirmed Hashem's absolute control over all aspects of creation, from the waters to the earth, from animals to people, from the tiniest to the mightiest of His creatures.

The *Zohar* says that the Exodus from Egypt is mentioned in the Torah no less than 50 times, and we are commanded to recall our miraculous redemption from slavery every day and night (*Zohar Chadash, Yisro* 5–6). All these commemorations of the Exodus reinforce our *emunah* in Hashem and His *hashgachah*.

Emunah is the breath of life to every Jew. Like a constant flow of oxygen, our faith in Hashem gives us the ability to face life's challenges. Tonight, on the night of the Seder, Hashem grants us a special opportunity and *siyatta d'Shmaya* to strengthen our *emunah*. The Nesivos Shalom (Vol. 2, p. 335) calls Pesach the "Rosh Hashanah for *emunah*" — a time to renew our faith for the entire year. Pesach is a wellspring of *emunah*, a magical time when we're given the opportunity to step away from all the distractions of life and to tap into eternity.

Right before the Exodus, when the Jewish people stood on the brink of nationhood and began to march out of Egypt, Hashem commanded them to eat matzah and to take care that it didn't become *chametz*. Thousands of years later, refraining from eating *chametz* on Pesach reminds us of that Exodus and the miracles Hashem performed. Each act of cleaning, vacuuming, sweeping, scrubbing, mopping, and ridding the home of *chametz* demonstrates our *emunah* in Hashem and strengthens His connection to each and every one of us.

It's no surprise, then, that the first commandment of the Ten Commandments — the mitzvah to believe in Hashem — enjoins us to remember that Hashem took us out of Egypt, to recall Hashem's *hashgachah pratis* that the Jewish people witnessed then. Rav Shamshon Refael Hirsch explains (*Shemos* 20:2) that the mitzvah of *emunah* is not merely about believing that there is God in the world. The mitzvah is to infuse into our very essence the concept that Hashem is the God over *me*, and has a direct connection to *me*, and loves *me* like a father loves his firstborn child, as it says, בְּנִי בְכֹרִי יִשְׂרָאֵל, My firstborn son is Yisrael! (*Shemos* 4:22).

The Tur (*Orach Chaim* 429) quotes his brother Rabbi

Yehudah, who says that each of the three biblical Yamim Tovim corresponds to the three patriarchs: Pesach to Avraham, Shavuos to Yitzchak, and Succos to Yaakov. Avraham was the only one in his generation to understand that there is a God Who created and runs the world. Hence Pesach, *Chag HaEmunah*, corresponds to Avraham, the first person to come to the realization of Hashem's presence and of His constant involvement in our lives.

> *In the 1920s, the Chofetz Chaim visited a doctor who said that after the tragedy of World War I, when thousands of Jews were killed, he could no longer believe in Hashem. The Chofetz Chaim said, "Well, I don't believe that you're a licensed doctor."*
>
> *"Excuse me, Rabbi," said the doctor, "but here on the wall is my diploma. It proves that I graduated medical school and received my license to practice."*
>
> *The Chofetz Chaim went over to the wall, looked at the diploma, and said, "It says here that you received your diploma and license nearly 40 years ago. How do I know you're still capable of practicing now?"*
>
> *"Rabbi, once you receive your diploma and medical license, you're allowed to practice forever without taking new examinations and receiving new diplomas."*
>
> *"Exactly," said the Chofetz Chaim. "When Hashem took us out of Egypt, He demonstrated to us hashgachah pratis through His incredible miracles. We saw clearly His infinite ability to impact our individual lives. This was Hashem's 'diploma,' confirming His absolute control over the world and over our lives. Hashem is not required to renew this 'diploma' in each and every generation."*
>
> *On the night of Pesach, we take another look at this "diploma," so to speak, strengthening our and our children's faith in Hashem. Similarly, Ramban (Shemos 13:16) explains that Hashem doesn't perform open miracles in each generation. Rather, the miracles He performed when taking us out of Egypt serve as testimony to His constant presence in our daily lives.*

On Pesach night we have a unique mitzvah to view ourselves as having been released from slavery. Imagine someone wrongly convicted of murder who has sat in jail for 25 years, never thinking he would be exonerated. Unexpectedly, new DNA evidence is found that clearly points the finger of guilt at someone else. He's cleared! He's free! What a feeling of indescribable joy! Of renewed life!

When the Jewish people left Egypt, they experienced the same feelings of renewed life and joy. But the joy we feel on the night of the Seder goes further than the happiness of a slave released from servitude. The *Chovos HaLevavos* (Introduction to *Sha'ar HaBitachon*) tells us that we can live life happily without worry only if we trust in Hashem. Tonight, the night of Pesach, we recline and dine like kings, not just because we are no longer slaves, but because we have revitalized ourselves with strengthened *emunah* and *bitachon* in Hashem. Unlike the released prisoner, who still has to face the anxieties of starting a new life, we know we don't have to worry because we have a Father Who loves us dearly and will take care of our needs.

Rambam writes, מִצְוָה לְהַרְאוֹת אֶת עַצְמוֹ כְּאִילוּ הוּא בְּעַצְמוֹ יָצָא **עַתָּה** מִשִּׁיעְבּוּד מִצְרַיִם, *Every person is commanded to see himself as if he himself just left Egypt* (Hilchos Chametz U'Matzah 7:6). On the night of Pesach we have a mitzvah to strengthen ourselves with *emunah* and *bitachon*, with faith that releases us from all our worries. With such faith, we can feel free to serve Hashem and live life with joy.

The Love Between Hashem and His People

When Hashem redeemed the Jewish people from Egypt, they had sunk to the lowest spiritual point possible. We are told that the ministering angels were baffled, asking why the Jewish people should be freed at all. Yet Hashem redeemed us anyway! We became בְּנִי בְכֹרִי יִשְׂרָאֵל, *My firstborn son, Yisrael*, a term of endearment and love. We became the Chosen Nation at a point when we were totally devoid of merit and far from Hashem. Through this, Hashem demonstrated to us that His love for us is like the love a father has for his child, a bond so deep and intense that even when the child sins, the father's love remains.

Rav Tzadok HaKohen (*Pri Tzaddik*) writes that the mitzvah to recall the Exodus from Egypt includes the remembrance of how Hashem redeemed us when we were so far from Him, since this strengthens our understanding of how much Hashem truly loves us. When we internalize that Hashem loves us unconditionally, we in return will want to love Him unconditionally.

The Mishnah in *Avos* (5:19) states that love that is unconditional will last forever. When Hashem redeemed us from Egypt despite our sins, He proved that His love for us is unconditional and absolute. Hence, the Jewish people are the only religion and people to have survived for thousands of years — a people who continue to believe in Hashem and to love Him as He loves us.

In the weeks before Pesach, children observe their fathers and mothers preparing for a Yom Tov that is the foundation of the Jewish nation; the Haggadah calls Pesach "*rosh kol mo'ados,*" the "chief festival" (in "*VaAmartem Zevach Pesach*"), since Pesach, the *chag* of *emunah,* is the key to the rest of the Jewish calendar. But sometimes the day-to-day preparations and stresses involved in cleaning the house, cooking the food, and getting everyone ready for the Yom Tov can cause us to forget why we are sweating, running around, and working so hard. When we see all these preparations as a means of fortifying our faith in Hashem's love for us, our preparations become less onerous and more joyous.

When our children see us prepare for Pesach with joy, they will also internalize the resonant message of faith that scrubbing and shopping and cooking for the right reasons can transmit. Then our homes, our families, and we ourselves are transformed into bastions of *kedushah* and faith. The best lesson a mother can teach her child comes from real-life demonstrations of how she works to be close to Hashem and to perform His will. Pesach and all its preparations are a proven wonderful and opportune time for such *chinuch*.

A Woman's Role on Pesach — So Much More Than Cleaning!

It's well known that the Jewish nation was redeemed from Egypt in the merit of righteous women (*Sotah* 11b). What was the specific merit of the Jewish women?

The answer is, *emunah,* faith. The faith of the women in Hashem's promise of redemption was so beloved to Hashem that He redeemed the Jewish nation before the designated time. This was the faith of women who encouraged the broken men not to allow their backbreaking slave labor to cause them to despair. This was the faith of the young girl Miriam encouraging her parents to remarry, faith that brought about the birth of Moshe, who would lead the people out of Egypt. This was the faith of women who brought drums with them as they prepared to leave Egypt, knowing with full *emunah* that they would soon be singing Hashem's praises as they left the land of slavery forever.

Women's strength. Women's faith. These were evident in ancient Egypt, but the pattern of Jewish women fortifying and sustaining hope among the Jewish nation can be seen in any review of our long and rich history.

Shifrah and Puah, whom Chazal tell us were Yocheved and Miriam, overtly defied Pharaoh's command to kill every Jewish baby boy, risking their own lives.

When Moshe went up to Heaven to receive the Torah and didn't return, the people made the golden calf, ascribing godly powers to it and crediting it for taking them out of Egypt. But the women didn't take part, proving their *emunah* and devotion to Hashem. By contrast, when it came to serving Hashem properly, the women were the first to wholeheartedly pledge their jewelry and services toward the construction of the Mishkan and its vessels.

Women and their strength, courage, and faith are central to so many stories in *Navi*: Devorah, prophetess and judge; Yael, the courageous woman who stabbed Sisera, the enemy of Israel to death; Chanah, the mother of Shmuel HaNavi, whose prayers became the model of prayer to Hashem; Michal, the daughter of King Shaul, who saved her husband David's life; Rus, Naomi, Avigayil, the *ishah haShunamis*... The list goes on. It's no wonder that Hashem proudly refers to His people, the Jewish nation, as "Daughters of Zion," "Daughter of Jerusalem," "Daughter of Yehudah," and "Daughter of My People." There is no greater praise than the title of "Jewish woman" (*Collected Writings of Rav Hirsch*, Vol. 8, p. 117).

What was true of women in earlier times remains true today. The Torah refers to the Jewish woman as the *akeres habayis*, "the mainstay of the home." Women are the backbone of the Jewish family. The Talmud (*Bava Metzia* 59a) tells us that women bring *berachah* to the home. The Jewish mother can infuse the home with good spirit, joy, calmness, and a Torah and mitzvah value system.

Women create the excitement of Shabbos and Yom Tov in the home. The lit candles, the beautifully set table, the special dishes and desserts — indeed, the serenity — these create the Shabbos and Yom Tov memories that remain with their offspring forever. Preparations for Pesach and the Seder itself are particularly memorable times for a child. It's this spirit that every one will replicate in their own homes when they become parents themselves.

> At a bris attended by a broad spectrum of gedolim spanning both the Chassidic and Litvish worlds, Rav Yechezkel Sarna rose to speak. "Each of the Admorim and Roshei Yeshivah sitting here today undoubtedly feels that it was his father, or his Rebbe, or other great Rabbeim who were the most influential personages of the last century. Yet I tell you that the most influential person of the last century of Jewish life never learned a page of Talmud." The crowd was stunned. Yet, when he continued and declared that he was referring to Sara Schenirer, the mother of the Bais Yaakov movement, they all agreed. "Without her the Admorim would very likely not have any Chassidim and the Roshei Yeshivahs any students!" (Eim HaDerech, p. 45; Carry Me in Your Heart, page 17).

How did Sarah Schenirer create such a dramatic revolution in Jewish girls' education while she faced fierce challenges from the Reform movement? By teaching her students fundamental principles of *emunah*, and instilling the knowledge that Hashem loves them so dearly, she successfully transformed a bleak future for Jewish girls into a vibrant Bais Yaakov school system spanning the entire world. In fact, Rav Shamshon Refael Hirsch's *Nineteen Letters*, which discusses the foundations of *emunas Hashem*, was an integral part of the curriculum in the early Bais Yaakov school system.

Rav Shach would point out that the Hebrew word for mother, *eim* (אֵם), is derived from the word *emunah* (אֱמוּנָה). The mother builds her home and instills her family with *emunah* in Hashem. The mother wakes up her children with "*Modeh Ani*" and puts them to sleep with "*Shema Yisrael*."

The Chassid Yosef Yaavetz, who lived in the time of the

Spanish Inquisition, witnessed the terrible persecution and forced conversions of the Jews. Who was capable of withstanding the ultimate test to their faith? Who sacrificed their lives *al kiddush Hashem*, for the sake of God? Not those philosophers who deduced the presence of God analytically. No, it was the women who had *emunah peshutah*, simple faith, who remained strong and unwavering (*Bnei Yissaschar*, Sivan 5).

We expend extensive efforts in physically preparing for Pesach, but this shouldn't come at the expense of spiritually preparing ourselves for this special *chag*. This Haggadah is the springboard for inspiring, educating, and preparing us for Pesach. It is my hope that the *divrei Torah*, stories, and messages found in these pages will connect us to the holiday, to our families and fellow Jews, to ourselves, and to Hashem.

On an airplane the flight attendant's routine safety instructions include telling passengers that in the event the plane loses cabin pressure, oxygen masks will descend. When traveling with younger children, the flight attendant adds, parents should remember to first attach their own oxygen masks and then those of their children. The reason is obvious: parents struggling to breathe will have great difficulty helping their children don their own oxygen apparatus.

The same is true in the spiritual realm. Women must ensure that as spouses, parents, daughters, and as women blessed with the vital responsibility of transmitting our *mesorah,* we are fully breathing our life source: *emunah*. This Haggadah seeks to infuse in its readers the ability to breathe in the beauty of Pesach night, to inhale the wonders of our closeness to Hashem — and to then safely pass this "breath of life" to those relying on them.

The message of Pesach is a message of faith. This is the message behind the weeks of Pesach preparation, and it is the message of the Pesach Seder. Moreover, this is the message that a woman transmits every day in a home whose foundation is belief in Hashem, His love for His people, and the unending *hashgachah pratis* that He evinces to us every day of our lives.

The Midrash says (*Yalkut Shimoni, Rus* 606; *Kav HaYashar* 82) that just as the Jewish nation was redeemed from Egypt in the merit of the righteous women, the Jewish nation's ultimate and final *geulah* will come about in the *zechus* of that Jewish woman whose every act proclaims her faith in Hashem.

ערב פסח

Erev Pesach

Selected Laws of Erev Pesach

On *erev Pesach*, beginning from *chatzos* (midday) there are several restrictions regarding what type of work may be done. The reason for these work restrictions is that when the *Beis HaMikdash* was standing, the *pesach* sacrifice was brought at this time, giving the day the status of a Yom Tov. We are, therefore, forbidden to perform certain types of work (*Mishnah Berurah* 468:1). There are a few *halachos* that pertain to this restriction:

- The work restrictions of *erev Pesach* after midday are similar but more lenient than those of Chol HaMo'ed. Therefore, whatever is permitted on Chol HaMo'ed is certainly permitted on *erev Pesach* (*Mishnah Berurah* 468:7).
- Work restrictions after midday on *erev Pesach* apply only to a Jew and not to a non-Jew working on behalf of a Jew. Thus, a woman may ask her cleaning help to wash laundry or sew clothing needed for Yom Tov (*Mishnah Berurah* 468:7).
- All laundry done by a Jew must be completed before midday. Spot cleaning a garment is permitted all day.
- Insignificant and simple sewing jobs needed for Yom Tov, such as replacing a button or sewing a small tear, may be done after midday even by a Jew (*Mishnah Berurah* 468:8).
- Clothing may be picked up from the tailor and cleaners even after midday (*Shulchan Aruch* 468:10).
- Polishing shoes on *erev Pesach* after midday is permitted (*Shemiras Shabbos K'Hilchasah*, Ch. 42, n. 143).
- All haircuts must be taken prior to midday; in the event that one was delayed, a haircut may be taken even after midday but only if done by a non-Jewish barber (*Mishnah Berurah* 468:5).
- Women may tweeze and shave other parts of the body, except for the head, even after midday (*Shulchan Aruch* 546:5 and *Beur Halachah* there).
- Nails should be cut before midday; if one was delayed, one can cut them even after this time (*Mishnah Berurah* 468:5).
- All food preparation is permitted the entire *erev Pesach*.
- When *erev Pesach* falls on Shabbos, various *halachos* apply on Friday. One should consult one's rabbi for guidance.

Erev Pesach Checklist

- ☐ Adjust timers controlling lights, air conditioning, or heat to remain on for the duration of the Seder.
- ☐ Make the *eiruv tavshilin* (when *erev Pesach* occurs on Wednesday — see "Laws of *Erev Pesach*" below).
- ☐ It may be practical to light a multi-day candle before Yom Tov. This candle will remain lit to provide a flame to light candles on the second night of Yom Tov (or before the onset of Shabbos if the first day of Chol HaMo'ed falls out on Shabbos). This is done because one may not strike a match on Yom Tov to start a new fire; a fire may be taken only from a preexisting flame. One can also use the flame on the stove to light the candle.
- ☐ Prepare *charoses* before Yom Tov. The classic Ashkenazic ingredients for the *charoses* are grated apples, almonds, nuts, dates, cinnamon, ginger, and red wine. Everyone should follow their family custom.
- ☐ Prepare a vegetable to be used for *Karpas*.
- ☐ Wash and check the *maror* leaves — usually Romaine lettuce — to inspect them for insects.
- ☐ If you use fresh horseradish for *maror*, it's preferable to grate it before Yom Tov and cover it tightly in a container. If you forgot to grate the horseradish before Yom Tov, you may grate it on Yom Tov in an unusual manner — a *shinui* — such as grating it onto the table as opposed to a plate. When the Seder falls on Shabbos, the *maror* must be grated beforehand.
- ☐ Prepare the salt water for *Karpas*.
- ☐ Roast the *zero'a*. The shank bone may not be eaten on the Seder night, since there is a prohibition of eating roasted meat at the Seder.
- ☐ Boil and then roast an egg to be placed on the Seder plate.
- ☐ Prepare prizes and treats for the children. They're the most important people at the Seder table!
- ☐ Set the Seder table. Everything should be ready so the Seder can begin immediately without delay. The Seder table should be set with your finest dishes and cutlery.

- ☐ Prepare comfortable cushions for those who will be reclining.
- ☐ Prepare a bag or pillowcase cover for the *afikoman*.

Care should be taken that Pesach preparations should be completed in a timely manner to allow family members (especially mothers!) to rest and be refreshed for the Seder. An *erev Pesach* nap does wonders for the whole family!

EREV YOM TOV

A Time for Peace

The Gemara (*Gittin* 52a) relates that every week, on *erev Shabbos*, the Satan would come and instigate a quarrel between two Jews. Week after week, the fighting continued until just before Shabbos began, and then finally Rav Meir prevailed upon them to make peace. The Satan, we are told, said in despair, "Woe that Rav Meir threw me out of the house!"

Shabbos is a time of peace and rest, a time of *menuchah*; it is "*me'ein Olam HaBa*" — a foretaste of the World to Come, where only peace reigns. That's a challenge to the Satan. And that's why, right before Shabbos, the Satan makes one last-ditch attempt to inject disharmony and stress into the home (*Sichos Mussar* 33).

There is just so much to do on *erev Shabbos* and *Yom Tov*! The house must be cleaned, the children bathed and dressed. Food has to be cooked, the hot water urn plugged in, Shabbos clocks set, the *blech* prepared…and generally most of the work falls on the mother. The Satan wants nothing more than for us to come into Shabbos or Yom Tov haggard, annoyed, upset, and sullen. Knowing his devious plan, we can make an effort to avoid stress and enter Shabbos and Yom Tov in a state of *simchah* and harmony, greeting the Shabbos Queen in the way a queen should be treated.

Setting the Shabbos or Yom Tov table a few hours before candle-lighting (or even the night before), or bringing in Shabbos or the holiday a little earlier (if it doesn't add to the pressure), can work wonders in turning the usually stressful moments before Shabbos or Yom Tov into a peaceful time. Sometimes, it can bring great *berachah* to the home.

> Rav Refael Dovid Auerbach once visited Rav Yechezkel Abramsky's house on a Friday morning. He was surprised to see that the Shabbos table was already set, down to the last glass and napkin. Rav Yechezkel explained that setting the Shabbos table early Friday morning was the custom in his home.
>
> "It started a generation before, when the rebbetzin's grandfather, the rav of Slutzk (known as the Ridvaz) became deathly ill," Rav Yechezkel said. "I stood by his bedside and heard him say quietly, in a near whisper, 'Hashem, what do You want from me? I learn Your Torah, I toiled to author a sefer on Talmud Yerushalmi. Do You want me to write a sefer on Bavli as well, when so many have already been printed?'
>
> "The Ridvaz then drifted back to sleep. A short while later he awoke, called his wife over, and told her, 'I know what Hashem wants from us. Please, every Friday morning when I return from Shacharis, can you have the Shabbos table set? This, and only this, will bring about my recovery.'
>
> "The rebbetzin began setting the Shabbos table early each Friday morning, and the Ridvaz made a full recovery. My rebbetzin and I have also undertaken this practice and set our Shabbos table early every Friday morning" *(Mekadshei Shevi'i, p. 48)*.

The town of Lakewood was reeling. Week after week, tragedy after tragedy had befallen the city. As the months passed, the severity of the tragedies only worsened. Families were grief-stricken, and the community was at a loss as to how to dam the tide of misfortune.

At this difficult time, Rav Aharon Leib Steinman visited the United States to strengthen Torah and mitzvah observance there. Rav Steinman visited Lakewood and was asked by its leaders what they could do to stem the wave of misfortune that had beset the city. In a speech he delivered to the yeshivah, Rav Steinman said, "Shabbos is the source of berachah. Shabbos brings peace to the world. Accept Shabbos 30 minutes early, and you will bring berachah into your homes and community. This will stop the flow of misfortune you've been having."

The entire Lakewood community heeded the venerable gadol's words and accepted Shabbos 30 minutes early that week.

After Shabbos, the rosh hayeshivah, Rav Malkiel Kotler, called Rav Steinman, full of excitement. "The Hatzolah members of the community are in shock. On a regular Shabbos they get between 30 and 40 calls for medical assistance, and they're kept busy all Shabbos. This Shabbos, there were hardly any incidents. It was a quiet and peaceful Shabbos. We merited seeing the unique berachah that Shabbos has showered on us" (Gadol B'Kirbecha, p. 256).

— Think About It —

The Meaning of Mo'ed-Yom Tov

The Torah uses the word *mo'ed* to describe the Yamim Tovim. (*Parashas Emor* 23:2) What's the meaning of the word *mo'ed*?

The Maharal explains (*Chiddushei Aggados, Makkos* 23a) that the word means "meeting place." He relates the word to the Torah's description of the meetings between Hashem and the Kohen Gadol in the *Kodesh HaKodashim* of the Mishkan, in front of the *Aron*. In a verse that uses the same root as *mo'ed*, the Torah tells us, וְנוֹעַדְתִּי לְךָ שָׁם, *It is there that I will set My meetings with you* (*Shemos* 25:22). By the holiest vessel in the holiest place — at the spot where Hashem's presence was most concentrated, so to speak — the Kohen Gadol would *meet* Hashem. *Mo'ed*, then, suggests a meeting place, a connecting point between us and Hashem.

The Maharal goes on to cite the Mishnah (*Avos* 3:11), which states that someone who doesn't respect the Yamim Tovim won't merit a portion in the World to Come — even if he studied Torah and performed mitzvos. The punishment is harsh because someone who disrespects Yamim Tovim demonstrates a disregard for this point of connection between us and Hashem. How could such a person merit a portion in Olam HaBa?

All the Yamim Tovim are a "*zecher liyetzias Mitzrayim*" — a commemoration of the Exodus. Upon miraculously redeeming us from Egypt, despite our lowly spiritual level, Hashem demonstrated that His love for us was unconditional, the love of a father to a child, pure and unrestricted. On Yom Tov, then, we break away from the day-to-day grind and reinvigorate ourselves with the knowledge that Hashem loves each and every one of us dearly and wants to form a close relationship with us.

Each *mo'ed* offers us a unique opportunity to connect with Hashem in a special way; each Yom Tov offers its own particular and peerless point of connection. Pesach connects us through *emunah* and *bitachon*, Succos through joy, Shavuos through the Torah. When we prepare for Yom Tov, we hope to improve ourselves, our homes, and our families in order to greet Hashem, so to speak, at the meeting place that the *mo'ed* represents. We can then receive the abundant wellsprings of *berachah* that Hashem apportions at each Yom Tov.

Much more than seven days of celebration, a Yom Tov is a seven-day meeting with Hashem that can transform our lives through our connection to Him. This transformation lasts long after the Yom Tov is over. This is why the other name for the *chagim* is *regalim*, "feet," since the Yom Tov can help us move forward and climb spiritually higher throughout the year.

בְּדִיקַת חָמֵץ

Some say this declaration of intent before searching for *chametz*:

הִנְנִי מוּכָן וּמְזוּמָן לְקַיֵּם מִצְוַת עֲשֵׂה וְלֹא תַעֲשֶׂה שֶׁל בְּדִיקַת חָמֵץ. לְשֵׁם יִחוּד קוּדְשָׁא בְּרִיךְ הוּא וּשְׁכִינְתֵּיהּ, עַל יְדֵי הַהוּא טָמִיר וְנֶעְלָם, בְּשֵׁם כָּל יִשְׂרָאֵל: וִיהִי נֹעַם אֲדֹנָי אֱלֹהֵינוּ עָלֵינוּ, וּמַעֲשֵׂה יָדֵינוּ כּוֹנְנָה עָלֵינוּ, וּמַעֲשֵׂה יָדֵינוּ כּוֹנְנֵהוּ:

The *chametz* search is initiated with the recitation of the following blessing:

בָּרוּךְ אַתָּה יהוה אֱלֹהֵינוּ מֶלֶךְ הָעוֹלָם, אֲשֶׁר קִדְּשָׁנוּ בְּמִצְוֹתָיו, וְצִוָּנוּ עַל בִּעוּר חָמֵץ.

Upon completion of the *chametz* search, the *chametz* is wrapped well and set aside to be burned the next morning and the following declaration is made. The declaration must be understood in order to take effect; one who does not understand the Aramaic text may recite it in English, Yiddish, or any other language. Any *chametz* that will be used for that evening's supper or the next day's breakfast or for any other purpose prior to the final removal of *chametz* the next morning is not included in this declaration.

כָּל חֲמִירָא וַחֲמִיעָא דְּאִכָּא בִרְשׁוּתִי, דְּלָא חֲמִתֵּהּ וּדְלָא בִעַרְתֵּהּ וּדְלָא יְדַעְנָא לֵהּ, לִבָּטֵל וְלֶהֱוֵי הֶפְקֵר כְּעַפְרָא דְאַרְעָא.

> **≈§ Important Times for Erev Pesach**
>
> - Searching for *chametz*: The search for *chametz* takes place on 14 Nissan, the night preceding Pesach, immediately after nightfall. When Pesach begins on Motza'ei Shabbos, the search for the *chametz* is performed on the preceding Thursday night. After searching for the *chametz*, the first "Kol Chamira" — nullifying all *chametz* of which one is unaware — is recited.
> - Eating *chametz*: One may eat *chametz* until the end of the fourth halachic hour of the day. These times change depending on the time of year and location, so consult a calendar or your rabbi for clarification.
> - Burning and selling the *chametz*: The *chametz* must be burned or sold by end of the fifth halachic hour of the day (again, consult a calendar or rabbi for the exact time). After the *chametz* is burned, the second "Kol Chamira", nullifying all *chametz*, is recited.
> - The beginning of Yom Tov: Yom Tov begins at sundown. One should refrain from doing any *melachah* forbidden on Yom Tov starting several minutes before sundown.

BEDIKAS CHAMETZ

Some say this declaration of intent before searching for chametz:

Behold, I am prepared and ready to fulfill the positive and prohibitive mitzvos of searching for *chametz*. For the sake of the unification of the Holy One, Blessed is He, and His presence, through Him Who is hidden and inscrutable — [I pray] in the name of all Israel. May the pleasantness of the Lord, our God, be upon us, and may He establish our handiwork for us; our handiwork may He establish.

The chametz search is initiated with the recitation of the following blessing:

Blessed are You, HASHEM, our God, King of the universe, Who has sanctified us with His commandments, and commanded us concerning the removal of *chametz*.

Upon completion of the chametz search, the chametz is wrapped well and set aside to be burned the next morning and the following declaration is made. The declaration must be understood in order to take effect; one who does not understand the Aramaic text may recite it in English, Yiddish, or any other language. Any chametz that will be used for that evening's supper or the next day's breakfast or for any other purpose prior to the final removal of chametz the next morning is not included in this declaration.

Any *chametz* which is in my possession which I did not see, and remove, nor know about, shall be nullified and become ownerless, like the dust of the earth.

BEDIKAS CHAMETZ / בדיקת חמץ

The rabbi was puzzled. A member of his Canadian congregation, a nonreligious Holocaust survivor, didn't keep Shabbos or kashrus. Yet in the weeks before Pesach, he spent hours cleaning and preparing his home like the most devout and observant Jew. The rabbi respectfully asked the man, "Why Pesach?"

The man responded that his mother was killed in the war when he was very young. His one memory of her was the devotion and effort she put into cleaning her house before Pesach.

"I keep this one mitzvah because of my love for my mother. I keep Pesach as a remembrance of her!" (Chashukei Chemed Haggadah p. 2).

Such is the power of a mother's toil and dedication to mitzvos!

ביעור חמץ

The following declaration, which includes all *chametz* without exception, is to be made after the burning of leftover *chametz*. It should be recited in a language which one understands. When Pesach begins on Motza'ei Shabbos, this declaration is made on Shabbos morning. Any *chametz* remaining from the Shabbos-morning meal is flushed down the drain before the declaration is made.

Some have the custom to recite the following declaration of intent:

הִנְנִי מוּכָן וּמְזוּמָן לְקַיֵּם מִצְוַת עֲשֵׂה וְלֹא תַעֲשֶׂה שֶׁל שְׂרֵיפַת חָמֵץ, לְשֵׁם יִחוּד קוּדְשָׁא בְּרִיךְ הוּא וּשְׁכִינְתֵּיהּ עַל יְדֵי הַהוּא טָמִיר וְנֶעְלָם בְּשֵׁם כָּל יִשְׂרָאֵל: וִיהִי נֹעַם אֲדֹנָי אֱלֹהֵינוּ עָלֵינוּ, וּמַעֲשֵׂה יָדֵינוּ כּוֹנְנָה עָלֵינוּ, וּמַעֲשֵׂה יָדֵינוּ כּוֹנְנֵהוּ:

כָּל חֲמִירָא וַחֲמִיעָא דְּאִכָּא בִרְשׁוּתִי, דַּחֲזִתֵּהּ וּדְלָא חֲזִתֵּהּ, דַּחֲמִתֵּהּ וּדְלָא חֲמִתֵּהּ, דְּבִעַרְתֵּהּ וּדְלָא בִעַרְתֵּהּ, לִבָּטֵל וְלֶהֱוֵי הֶפְקֵר כְּעַפְרָא דְאַרְעָא.

עירוב תבשילין

It is forbidden to prepare on Yom Tov for the next day even if that day is Shabbos. If, however, Shabbos preparations were started before Yom Tov began, they may be continued on Yom Tov. The *eiruv tavshilin* constitutes this preparation. A matzah and any cooked food (such as fish, meat, or an egg) are set aside on the day before Yom Tov to be used on Shabbos and the blessing is recited followed by the declaration [made in a language understood by the one making the *eiruv*]. If the first days of Pesach fall on Thursday and Friday, an *eiruv tavshilin* must be made on Wednesday.

In Eretz Yisrael, where only one day Yom Tov is in effect, the *eiruv* is omitted.

> **◈§ Selected Laws of Eiruv Tavshilin**
>
> Only one *eiruv tavshilin* is needed per household.
> - The food items used for the *eiruv tavshilin* must remain intact until all the Shabbos preparations have been completed. Ideally one should not eat the *eiruv tavshilin* until after the Friday-night candle lighting (*Shulchan Aruch* 527:16). Therefore, one should keep the *eiruv tavshilin* in a place where it will not get eaten, spoiled, or thrown out.

BURNING THE CHAMETZ

The following declaration, which includes all *chametz* without exception, is to be made after the burning of leftover *chametz*. It should be recited in a language which one understands. When Pesach begins on Motza'ei Shabbos, this declaration is made on Shabbos morning. Any *chametz* remaining from the Shabbos-morning meal is flushed down the drain before the declaration is made.

Some have the custom to recite the following declaration of intent:

Behold, I am prepared and ready to fulfill the positive and prohibitive mitzvos of burning *chametz*. For the sake of the unification of the Holy One, Blessed is He, and His presence, through Him Who is hidden and inscrutable — [I pray] in the name of all Israel. May the pleasantness of the Lord, our God, be upon us, and may He establish our handiwork for us; our handiwork may He establish.

Any *chametz* which is in my possession which I did or did not see, which I did or did not remove, shall be nullified and become ownerless, like the dust of the earth.

THE EIRUV TAVSHILIN

It is forbidden to prepare on Yom Tov for the next day even if that day is Shabbos. If, however, Shabbos preparations were started before Yom Tov began, they may be continued on Yom Tov. The *eiruv tavshilin* constitutes this preparation. A matzah and any cooked food (such as fish, meat, or an egg) are set aside on the day before Yom Tov to be used on Shabbos and the blessing is recited followed by the declaration [made in a language understood by the one making the *eiruv*]. If the first days of Pesach fall on Thursday and Friday, an *eiruv tavshilin* must be made on Wednesday.

In Eretz Yisrael, where only one day Yom Tov is in effect, the *eiruv* is omitted.

- Many have the commendable custom to use the *eiruv tavshilin* matzah as part of the *lechem mishneh* at all the Shabbos meals: Friday night, again at the Shabbos-afternoon meal, and finally at *seudah shelishis* (Mishnah Berurah 527:48).
- If one forgot to prepare the *eiruv tavshilin*, or if the *eiruv tavshilin* was eaten or lost before the Shabbos preparations were completed, one should consult a rabbi.

The *eiruv* foods are held while the following blessing
and declaration are recited.

בָּרוּךְ אַתָּה יהוה אֱלֹהֵינוּ מֶלֶךְ הָעוֹלָם, אֲשֶׁר
קִדְּשָׁנוּ בְּמִצְוֹתָיו, וְצִוָּנוּ עַל מִצְוַת עֵרוּב.

בְּהָדֵין עֵרוּבָא יְהֵא שָׁרֵא לָנָא לַאֲפוּיֵי
לְבַשּׁוּלֵי וּלְאַצְלוּיֵי וּלְאַטְמוּנֵי
וּלְאַדְלוּקֵי שְׁרָגָא וּלְתַקָּנָא וּלְמֶעְבַּד כָּל צָרְכָּנָא,
מִיּוֹמָא טָבָא לְשַׁבַּתָּא לָנָא וּלְכָל יִשְׂרָאֵל הַדָּרִים
בָּעִיר הַזֹּאת.

הדלקת נרות

The candles are lit and the following blessings are recited. When Yom
Tov falls on Shabbos, the words in parentheses are added.

בָּרוּךְ אַתָּה יהוה אֱלֹהֵינוּ מֶלֶךְ הָעוֹלָם, אֲשֶׁר
קִדְּשָׁנוּ בְּמִצְוֹתָיו, וְצִוָּנוּ לְהַדְלִיק נֵר
שֶׁל (שַׁבָּת וְשֶׁל) יוֹם טוֹב.

בָּרוּךְ אַתָּה יהוה אֱלֹהֵינוּ מֶלֶךְ הָעוֹלָם,
שֶׁהֶחֱיָנוּ וְקִיְּמָנוּ וְהִגִּיעָנוּ לַזְּמַן הַזֶּה.

✥ Selected Laws of Candlelighting on Erev Yom Tov

- Women should be dressed in their Yom Tov clothing prior to lighting the Yom Tov candles (*Kitzur Shulchan Aruch* 75:6; *Mishnah Berurah* 262:11).
- According to many opinions, the Yom Tov candles should be lit before the onset of Yom Tov, which begins at *shekiah*, sundown. The son of the Sma quotes his mother as saying that this is the proper time to light, and many authorities follow this ruling. Others hold that the Yom Tov candles should be lit immediately before the start of the Seder. Every woman should follow her family custom. If one does not have a family custom, she should follow the first opinion and light candles prior to the onset of Yom Tov (*Siddur Yaavetz*, Laws of *Erev Pesach* 4; *Mateh Efraim* 625:33). When Pesach falls on Shabbos, however, the candles **must** be lit prior to *shekiah*.
- All opinions agree that on the second night of Yom Tov, the candles may only be prepared and lit after *tzeis hakochavim*, nightfall (consult a calendar or your rabbi for the exact time).

The eiruv foods are held while the following blessing and declaration are recited.

Blessed are You, HASHEM, our God, King of the universe, Who sanctified us by His commandments and commanded us concerning the commandment of *eiruv*.

Through this *eiruv* may we be permitted to bake, cook, fry, insulate, kindle flame, prepare for, and do anything necessary on the Festival for the sake of the Shabbos — for ourselves and for all Jews who live in this city.

⁌LIGHTING THE CANDLES⁍

The candles are lit and the following blessings are recited. When Yom Tov falls on Shabbos, the words in parentheses are added.

Blessed are You, HASHEM, our God, King of the universe, Who has sanctified us through His commandments, and commanded us to kindle the flame of the (Shabbos and the) Festival.

Blessed are You, HASHEM, our God, King of the universe, Who has kept us alive, sustained us, and brought us to this season.

- On Shabbos, women light the candles and then recite the *berachah*. On Yom Tov, however, many opinions state that it is better to first recite the *berachah* and then to light the candles, while some have the custom to light the candles and then recite the *berachah* as is done when lighting the Shabbos candles (*Mateh Efraim* 625:33). One should follow her family custom or consult a rabbi.
- The prevalent custom is for women to recite the *berachah* of *Shehecheyanu* when lighting candles for Yom Tov, although some communities have the custom that women do not recite the blessing of *Shehecheyanu* at this time, but wait to hear it at Kiddush. Even if a woman recited *Shehecheyanu* when lighting the candles, she may answer Amen to the *berachah* of *Shehecheyanu* when it is recited at Kiddush (*Shemiras Shabbos K'Hilchasah*, Vol. 2, Ch. 44, n. 18).
- After lighting candles, it is an auspicious time for women to daven, especially for the success of their children in Torah and mitzvos (*Rabbeinu Yonah, Iggeres HaTeshuvah* 81; *Rabbeinu Bachya, Shemos* 19:3).
- The act of lighting Shabbos and Yom Tov candles is the first mitzvah to usher in Shabbos and Yom Tov and therefore carries with it great merit and *berachah* (*Kedushas Levi*, Chanukah, *Kedushah Sheniyah*).

It is customary to recite the following prayer after the kindling. The words in brackets are included as they apply.

יְהִי רָצוֹן לְפָנֶיךָ, יהוה אֱלֹהַי וֵאלֹהֵי אֲבוֹתַי, שֶׁתְּחוֹנֵן אוֹתִי [וְאֶת אִישִׁי, וְאֶת בָּנַי, וְאֶת בְּנוֹתַי, וְאֶת אָבִי, וְאֶת אִמִּי] וְאֶת כָּל קְרוֹבַי; וְתִתֶּן לָנוּ וּלְכָל יִשְׂרָאֵל חַיִּים טוֹבִים וַאֲרוּכִים; וְתִזְכְּרֵנוּ בְּזִכְרוֹן טוֹבָה וּבְרָכָה; וְתִפְקְדֵנוּ בִּפְקֻדַּת יְשׁוּעָה וְרַחֲמִים; וּתְבָרְכֵנוּ בְּרָכוֹת גְּדוֹלוֹת;

LIGHTING THE CANDLES / הדלקת הנרות

Why We Light

What are some of the reasons for the mitzvah of lighting candles on *erev Shabbos* and *erev Yom Tov*?

- ☐ *Kavod* — lighting candles is a means of honoring Shabbos and Yom Tov (*Rambam, Hilchos Shabbos* 30:5).
- ☐ *Oneg* — having light increases one's "*oneg Shabbos*," enjoyment of Shabbos and Yom Tov, since one can see and thereby enjoy his food (*Shulchan Aruch* 263:1).
- ☐ *Shalom bayis* — having light prevents people from stumbling in the dark and becoming irritated, so lighting candles promotes peace in the home (*Shabbos* 25b).

A Special Mitzvah for Women

Candlelighting before Shabbos and Yom Tov is a special mitzvah given to women. Why were women given this mitzvah?

One reason is that Chavah convinced Adam to eat from the *eitz hada'as*, the tree of knowledge. As a result, death was introduced into the world: Hashem decreed that people would no longer live forever. A person is compared to a candle. As a means of attaining forgiveness for Chavah's "extinguishing the candle of the world," and bringing death to mankind, Jewish women throughout the generations light candles on *erev Shabbos*

> It is customary to recite the following prayer after the kindling.
> The words in brackets are included as they apply.
>
> May it be Your will, HASHEM, my God and God of my forefathers, that You show favor to me [my husband, my sons, my daughters, my father, my mother] and all my relatives; and that You grant us and all Israel a good and long life; that You remember us with a beneficent memory and blessing; that You consider us with a consideration of salvation and compassion; that You bless us with great blessings;

and *erev Yom Tov* (*Tur O.C.* 263).

Another reason women were given this mitzvah is that women are the ones most usually found in the home and are responsible for household duties. They therefore merit receiving the mitzvah of *hadlakas neiros*, which ensures that there will be ample light in the home (*Shulchan Aruch O.C.* 263:3).

In the Merit of the Candles

Sometimes the light of the Shabbos candles can make smoke disappear....

> *Rav Yitzchak Zilberstein recently told of a woman who became observant, though her husband refused to take on the mitzvos. She tried to get her husband to at least stop smoking in the house on Shabbos, telling him that it disturbed the atmosphere of Shabbos that she was trying to create, but her husband adamantly refused. Her rabbi came up with a suggestion for a compromise: the husband should refrain from smoking for as long as the Shabbos candles were lit. The husband agreed.*
>
> *At first the wife used standard candles, but eventually she began using thicker candles, which burned longer. The husband, true to his word, refrained from smoking as long as the candles burned. As the weeks went by, the woman used thicker and thicker candles until eventually she began using candles that lasted 24 hours, the entire duration of Shabbos. The husband dutifully kept to his pledge, and as result of his wife's Shabbos candles, he increased his observance of Shabbos.*

וְתַשְׁלִים בָּתֵּינוּ; וְתַשְׁכֵּן שְׁכִינָתְךָ בֵּינֵינוּ. וְזַכֵּנִי לְגַדֵּל בָּנִים וּבְנֵי בָנִים חֲכָמִים וּנְבוֹנִים, אוֹהֲבֵי יהוה, יִרְאֵי אֱלֹהִים, אַנְשֵׁי אֱמֶת, זֶרַע קֹדֶשׁ, בַּיהוה דְּבֵקִים, וּמְאִירִים אֶת הָעוֹלָם בַּתּוֹרָה וּבְמַעֲשִׂים טוֹבִים, וּבְכָל מְלֶאכֶת עֲבוֹדַת הַבּוֹרֵא. אָנָּא שְׁמַע אֶת תְּחִנָּתִי בָּעֵת הַזֹּאת, בִּזְכוּת שָׂרָה וְרִבְקָה וְרָחֵל וְלֵאָה אִמּוֹתֵינוּ, וְהָאֵר נֵרֵנוּ שֶׁלֹּא יִכְבֶּה לְעוֹלָם וָעֶד, וְהָאֵר פָּנֶיךָ וְנִוָּשֵׁעָה. אָמֵן.

With the candles lit and the cigarettes extinguished, the holy atmosphere of Shabbos shone in their home (Aleinu L'Shabei'ach, vol. 2, p. 537).

A Mother's Prayers

The time immediately after lighting Shabbos and Yom Tov candles is considered a special time for women to daven and, specifically, to pray for their children's spiritual welfare. The Talmud (*Shabbos* 23b) tells us that the Torah is referred to as "*ohr*," a light, and someone who fulfills the mitzvah of *hadlakas neiros* will merit having children who light up the world with their Torah.

> Rav Aharon Shmuel Kaidanover was a great rav and Torah scholar, but his mother was a simple woman and unlearned. She didn't even know how to read Hebrew, let alone daven. Yet after lighting the Shabbos candles each week, she would pray in her native Russian that her son Shmuel grow up to be a Torah scholar. These heartfelt tefillos of a simple mother were answered in her son's immense achievements in Torah learning (Da'as Moshe, Terumah, quoting his father the Maggid of Kozhnitz).

A more recent story illustrating the immense power of a mother's *tefillos* at *hadlakas neiros* was told by an outstanding Torah scholar who came from a family that had not been religious for generations. Asked how someone without a background in Torah studies could attain such heights in learning, the *talmid chacham* attributed his success in Torah to his grandmother.

that You make our households complete; that You cause Your Presence to dwell among us. Privilege me to raise children and grandchildren who are wise and understanding, who love HASHEM and fear God, people of truth, holy offspring, attached to HASHEM, who illuminate the world with Torah and good deeds and with every labor in the service of the Creator. Please, hear my plea at this time, in the merit of Sarah, Rivkah, Rachel, and Leah, our mothers, and cause our light to illuminate that it not be extinguished forever, and let Your countenance shine so that we are saved. Amen.

My grandmother wasn't religious, but she always lit candles on Friday night before sundown and davened for the success of her children and grandchildren, remembering that her mother had done so. What kind of success did she have in mind? Well, her husband, my grandfather, worked for then–Prime Minister David Ben-Gurion. He would come home every day praising his boss's talents, skills, and brilliance. Impressed by these stories, my grandmother would daven every Friday night after lighting candles that her children and grandchildren should grow up to be like Prime Minister Ben-Gurion.

One day the prime minister met with the Chazon Ish in a well-publicized meeting. After the meeting, Prime Minister Ben-Gurion called all of his staff together, including my grandfather, telling them how he had never met someone like the Chazon Ish, a man with such brilliance and deep perception.

My grandfather came home that day, and as usual reported everything that Ben-Gurion had said at the office. Upon hearing how Ben-Gurion said that he had never met such a man as the Chazon Ish, my grandmother said that if Prime Minister Ben-Gurion said that the Chazon Ish was a man like no other, she would start davening Friday night after candlelighting that her children and grandchildren should be like the Chazon Ish, and not like the prime minister!

It appears that the awesome power of a woman's tefillos at the time of candle lighting made all the difference for me! (L'ha'er, p. 20; HaMechanech, p. 200).

Today, Jewish mothers around the world daven for their children's growth in Torah and mitzvos. We can never underestimate the power of a mother's prayers!

Ten-year-old Moshe was struggling in school. He tried very hard to pay attention and follow what was being taught in class, but he just wasn't getting it. Why was it so easy for his friends to learn Torah, and for him it was so hard? Why couldn't he understand what the rebbi was saying?

Moshe's parents did what they could; they hired private tutors, consulted with teachers and learning-disability specialists, but to no avail. No one knew why, but Moshe just wasn't succeeding.

Not succeeding, that is, until the middle of the year, when Moshe's rebbi noticed some positive changes. Suddenly, Moshe seemed to be able to sit and listen. A few days later, he asked a question on the sugya; a week later, he answered one. Was all the extra help that Moshe was getting beginning to pay off?

The rebbi called Moshe's parents to share the wonderful news of their son's progress and find out what had finally made him turn the corner. Moshe's mother explained the near-miraculous turnaround in her son's learning.

"For months, Moshe came home crying, pouring out his heart to me. He wanted so much to learn Torah, to understand what was being taught, but nothing seemed to help him. How long can a mother see her son in such excruciating pain? I knew I had to do something.

"A few weeks ago, I told Moshe that when a mother lights candles on erev Shabbos, there's a special zechus in her prayers for her children's achievements in Torah study. I explained that I had always davened for his success, but that from now on I would daven with even greater concentration and intensity. I suggested that the next time I lit Shabbos candles, he should stand next to me, and we would daven together, in the hopes that both of our tefillos would be heard by Hashem.

"The next Friday, at hadlakas neiros time, Moshe stood by my side as I lit the Shabbos candles. We then began to daven together, and I heard Moshe, my little 10-year-old tzaddik, cry out to Hashem, pleading for success in his learning. Moshe's tefillos and tears mingled with mine in a harmonious plea to Hashem. This has been going on for the last few weeks, and,

baruch Hashem, our *tefillos* are being answered" (*Barchi Nafshi*, vol. 4, p. 352).

The Power of Women's Tefillos

The *tefillos* of a woman are particularly effective and dear to Hashem. When Rachel Imeinu died, Yaakov Avinu didn't bury her in Me'aras HaMachpeilah, where he would later be buried with his forefathers. Instead, he buried Rachel on the outskirts of the city so that generations later, when the Jewish people would pass by her grave as they were sent to exile, she would cry out to Hashem for their salvation: the heartfelt prayer of a mother for her suffering children.

Another woman in *Tanach*, Chanah, is held up as an example of how we pray. The Talmud (*Berachos* 31a) deduces many essential laws of *tefillah* from Chanah's heartfelt *tefillah* to Hashem that she should merit a child, a prayer that was answered with the birth of Shmuel HaNavi. On Rosh Hashanah, we read the chapter describing Chanah's *tefillah* in the haftarah, teaching us that in the merit of the Jewish women's *tefillos* we can merit a favorable judgment.

The Eish Das asks why we read the Torah portion that focuses on the merits of our foremothers on the first day of Rosh Hashanah, leaving the Torah portion regarding the merits of our forefathers for the second day. He explains that when a child falls, a father picks him up, dusts him off, and helps him get back on his feet. A mother, with her *tefillos* and actions, prevents the child from falling in the first place. On Rosh Hashanah, then, the foremothers' great merits are recalled even before those of our forefathers.

> The first Belzer Rebbe, Rav Shalom Rokeach, would only daven in a shul that housed a women's section. He would say that the tear-laden tefillos of the women enable all the tefillos in the shul to go up to Hashem (Margoliyas HaShas, Bava Metzia, p. 446).
>
> Similarly, when the Chozeh of Lublin first entered the new beis midrash built for him, he said, "There is still something missing here." He explained that there was no women's section in the beis midrash. "The tears and tefillos of the women are vital for the acceptance of all the tefillos!" (HaLekach V'Halibuv Haggadah, p. 50).
>
> In Ponevezh, too, they learned the importance of women's

tefillos. The Ponevezh Yeshivah is particularly crowded on Rosh Hashanah and Yom Kippur, since both current students and alumni flock to the yeshivah to daven among their great roshei yeshivah and rebbeim. One year the expected crowd was going to be too large for the beis midrash. Those in charge of the seating suggested that they open the women's section and use it for additional men's seating. When they went to the rosh hayeshivah, Rav Shach, to ask his opinion, he flatly refused. "You may not take away the women's section. We need the tears and tefillos of the women davening there!" (Orchos HaBayis, p. 396).

Rav Yosef Shaul Nathansohn, the rav of Lemberg and a great posek, was asked if it was permitted to make the men's section of the synagogue smaller in order establish a women's section. He wrote, "I don't see any reason for this to be prohibited. On the contrary, this [establishing a women's section] is a great mitzvah...for they [Chazal] have said it was in the merit of the Jewish women of the generation that the Jewish nation merited redemption" (Shaul U'Meishev 2:22).

The Talmud says that ten portions of "*sichah*," speech, were sent down to this world; women took nine shares, and men took one (*Kiddushin* 49b). The plain meaning of this is that innately women are more inclined to talk than men. Rav Shimshon Dovid Pincus gives a deeper explanation of this Talmudic teaching. The word *sichah* specifically refers to *tefillah* (*Berachos* 26b). Women didn't take a greater portion of ordinary talk and chitchat; they took a greater portion of *tefillah*. Women were given a unique and exceptional ability to connect to Hashem through *tefillah*. Moreover, the word *sichah* implies an informal conversation; we can speak to Hashem at any time and in any place about anything that's on our minds (*Nefesh Chayah*, p. 38).

The Chazon Ish writes that one can daven to Hashem in any language in which he is comfortable, and he should pray to Hashem "as one speaks to his friend." You can talk to Hashem on a moment-to-moment basis, in any language, without any formal preparations (*Kovetz Igros* 2:2; *Mesillas Yesharim* 19). Whether you're cooking supper, driving, taking care of the children, or shopping for groceries, you can always converse with Hashem.

Rebbetzin Shoshana Aliza Zilberstein, the daughter of Rav Yosef Shalom Elyashiv, and the wife of Rav Yitzchak Zilberstein, was once at home when a neighbor came to ask her a question. The neighbor was about to knock on the door when she heard the rebbetzin speaking to someone. Not wanting to disturb, the neighbor left.

Fifteen minutes later the neighbor returned, and again she heard the rebbetzin talking to someone. The neighbor waited a few more minutes until the conversation stopped. Finally, she knocked.

Rebbetzin Zilberstein opened the door, and the neighbor was surprised to see that the rebbetzin was alone, and she wasn't on the phone. It turned out that the rebbetzin had been davening, and when she davened she spoke to Hashem with ease, simplicity, and directness, as one would speak to a friend (Shoshanas HaAmakim, p. 8).

הסדר
The Seder

Seder Night / ליל הסדר

A Special Night

On Seder night, we follow a clearly demarcated progression of mitzvos, commencing with *Kaddesh* and ending in *Nirtzah*. Many of these mitzvos can only be fulfilled properly in the specific sequence instructed by Chazal; hence the name *Leil HaSeder*, literally, "Night of Order."

Seder night is a night like no other. We set the table with our best dishes and dress in our finest clothing. We recline and drink wine like royalty. The Shelah points out that on the night of Pesach a man and his wife should conduct themselves like a king and queen, and their children should be treated like princes and princesses (*Kitzur Shelah*, p. 182).

It's also an auspicious time for *tefillah*. The Midrash says (*Pirkei D'Rebbe Eliezer* 32) that Yitzchak gave the *berachos* to Yaakov on Pesach. Yitzchak said, "Tonight all the people recite Hallel, and the storehouses of *berachah* are open."

Since the lofty nature of Pesach makes it a propitious time for the acceptance of *tefillos*, many have the custom of blessing their children on the night of Pesach (*Vayaged Moshe*, p. 67, quoting the *Chaim L'Rosh Haggadah*).

— *Think About It* —

Night of Order

Try to find your way in an unfamiliar dark room. You'll probably stumble on the smallest object and become upset over the room's lack of organization and order. But then light a candle, and you will discover that the room had actually been organized and was in good order all along. Only the darkness caused you to stumble.

The *Zohar* (see the Chida's *Simchas HaRegel*) tells us that on the night of Pesach, לַיְלָה כַּיּוֹם יָאִיר, *night was illuminated like the day itself.* Upon miraculously redeeming us from Egypt and punishing the Egyptians, Hashem revealed to us His guiding hand. On this night, His *hashgachah pratis* was illuminated for us, and we could see the order in what had seemed like disorder.

This is why the night of Pesach is called "*Leil HaSeder*" — the Night of Order.

On the night of Pesach, we strengthen our *emunah* in Hashem, understanding that there is a *seder*, an order, to everything that happens. We can see that everything comes from Hashem, the One Who loves us and Who knows what is truly best for us.

This explains what we say at the end of *Maggid*: we thank Hashem for taking us out of Egypt, from אֲפֵלָה לְאוֹר גָּדוֹל, *from darkness to bright light.* Faith in Hashem provides order and clarity to our lives, illuminating our path in life (*Rav Tzvi Hirsch Meisels, Mekadshei Hashem*, Vol. 2, p, 73; see also *Mahari Steif Haggadah*, p. 309, and *Rav Tzadok HaKohen, Tzidkas HaTzaddik* 261).

An Unbreakable Chain of Tradition

Rav Eliyahu Lopian told of meeting a descendant of the Malbushei Yom Tov, Rav Betzalel, who described how his grandfather would begin his Seder:

> *We are sitting here tonight conducting our Seder, and so are all the Jews of this city. Not only are the Jews in this city conducting a Seder, Jews throughout the country and throughout the world are also sitting down to a Seder. Jews all over the world are having a Seder with four cups of wine and three matzos, and all are reciting the Haggadah.*
>
> *Where did every Jew learn how to conduct a Seder? We all received the tradition from our fathers when we participated in their Seder. And where did our fathers learn how to conduct a Seder like the one we're having today? From their fathers, and their fathers from their fathers, all the way back, generation upon generation, back to the time period of the Rishonim. And the Rishonim received the tradition from the Geonim, who*

received it from the earlier Sages back to the Amoraim, who received it from the Tannaim to the Anshei Knesses HaGedolah, who received it from the prophets who received the tradition from the elders, all the way back to Moshe and Aharon and the Jewish people who actually experienced the Exodus.

The Torah says, אַתֶּם רְאִיתֶם אֲשֶׁר עָשִׂיתִי לְמִצְרָיִם, *You saw what I did to Egypt* (*Shemos* 19:4). Our Seder tradition, the mitzvos we perform, is built on a firm foundation of undeniable *mesorah*. It is up to us to impart that *mesorah*, in turn, to our children and those present at our Seder (*Lev Eliyahu, Va'eschanan*).

The Names of Seder Night

Seder night is referred to by several names including *Leil HaSeder* and *Leil Shimurim*. What is the reason for these names?

- ☐ *Leil HaSeder* — this night is called "Night of Order" because on this night we saw that there is order in the universe. Also, at the Seder, we follow a specific sequence of steps formulated by Chazal (see above).

- ☐ *Pesach* — The *korban pesach* was sacrificed on the 14th day of Nissan (*Vayikra* 23:5). The word *pasach* means jump or skip, referring to Hashem skipping over the Jewish homes, whose mezuzos were marked by the blood of the *korban pesach*. As a result only the homes of the Egyptians were struck from the plague of *Makkas Bechoros* and the firstborn sons of the Jews were spared.

- ☐ *Leil Shimurim* — As is written in the Torah, לֵיל שִׁמֻּרִים הוּא לַה' לְהוֹצִיאָם מֵאֶרֶץ מִצְרָיִם הוּא הַלַּיְלָה הַזֶּה לַה' שִׁמֻּרִים לְכָל בְּנֵי יִשְׂרָאֵל לְדֹרֹתָם, *It is a night of anticipation for Hashem to take them out of the land of Egypt; this was the night for Hashem, a protection for all the children of Israel for their generations* (*Shemos* 12:42). The word *shimurim* here means "anticipation" because on this night we "anticipated" the redemption. The word is plural in the *pasuk* because when Hashem's children, the Jewish people, are in pain and are suffering, Hashem suffers too, as it says, עִמּוֹ אָנֹכִי בְצָרָה, *I [Hashem] am with him in distress* (*Tehillim* 91:15). Hence, Hashem too anticipated our redemption: our pain is His pain; our joy is His joy (*Yalkut Shimoni* 200).

Hashem protected the Jewish nation on the night that all the Egyptian firstborns were killed. Likewise, this night is a special night of protection for all generations (Rosh Hashanah 11b). It is for this reason that many have the custom not to lock their doors the night of Pesach (where doing so will not pose a danger) and we do not recite the parts of the bedtime *Krias Shema* that were established for protection.

The *Ibn Ezra* explains that *shimurim* connotes safe-guarding. Pesach night is called *Leil Shimurim*, a guarded night, since we stay up late into the night telling the story of the Exodus, like guards who remain awake all night.

☐ *Leil Hiskadesh Chag* — The *navi* Yeshayahu refers to the night of Pesach when he says, הַשִּׁיר יִהְיֶה לָכֶם כְּלֵיל הִתְקַדֶּשׁ חָג, *The song will be yours like the night of the festival's consecration* (*Yeshayahu* 30:29). Rav Tzadok HaKohen explains (*Pri Tzaddik*, Pesach 16) that Pesach is the first of all the Yamim Tovim (see Talmud, *Rosh Hashanah* 4a), and it is the Yom Tov from which all other Yamim Tovim receive their holiness. In that sense, Pesach is "*hiskadesh chag*" — the *chag* that gives holiness to all the other Yamim Tovim.

The 15 Simanim

Seder night is divided into 15 "*simanim*," or steps, beginning with *Kaddesh* and ending with *Nirtzah*. It is customary to recite all 15 *simanim* at the start of the Seder and then each *siman* before it begins.

Why are there precisely 15 *simanim*?

Fifteen steps led up to the courtyard of the *Beis HaMikdash*. These 15 steps brought a person closer to Hashem and to the *Shechinah*, which dwelled in the Mikdash.

Likewise, on Pesach night we strengthen our *emunah* and *bitachon* in Hashem by speaking of our miraculous redemption and fulfilling His mitzvos. The evening culminates with our joyous singing of Hallel and reciting *Shir HaShirim*, demonstrating our love for Hashem and remembering His love for us. The 15 *simanim* of the Seder have elevated us, just as the 15 steps leading into the *Beis HaMikdash* drew His people closer to Hashem.

We feel closer and closer to Hashem as we perform each *siman* until we finally declare, אֶחָד מִי יוֹדֵעַ אֶחָד אֲנִי יוֹדֵעַ אֶחָד אֱלֹהֵינוּ שֶׁבַּשָּׁמַיִם וּבָאָרֶץ, *Who knows One? I know One! One is our God in the heavens and the earth!*

The Four Cups

On Seder night, it's a mitzvah for each individual to drink four cups of wine. Why four cups?

- ☐ The four cups of wine stand for the four terms in the Torah used to describe the redemption from Egypt: **וְהוֹצֵאתִי** אֶתְכֶם מִתַּחַת סִבְלֹת מִצְרַיִם **וְהִצַּלְתִּי** אֶתְכֶם מֵעֲבֹדָתָם **וְגָאַלְתִּי** אֶתְכֶם בִּזְרוֹעַ נְטוּיָה וּבִשְׁפָטִים גְּדֹלִים: **וְלָקַחְתִּי** אֶתְכֶם לִי לְעָם, *I shall take you out from under the burdens of Egypt; I shall rescue you from their service; I shall redeem you with an outstretched arm and with great judgments; I shall take you to Me for a people* (*Shemos* 6:6–7; *Yerushalmi, Pesachim* 10:1).

- ☐ The four cups of wine are symbolic of the four matriarchs: Sarah, Rivkah, Rachel, and Leah. In the merit of these holy women's modesty, the Jews were redeemed from Egypt, despite the nation's sins. David HaMelech compares women to a vine, stressing their modest nature: אֶשְׁתְּךָ כְּגֶפֶן פֹּרִיָּה בְּיַרְכְּתֵי בֵיתֶךָ, *Your wife will be like a vine, fruitful in the **inner** chambers of your home* (*Tehillim* 128:3). On the night of Pesach, we drink four cups of wine — the fruit of the vine to which women are compared — reminding us of the special merits of the four matriarchs (*Midrash Rabbah, Shemos* 6:26; *Maharal, Gevuros Hashem* 60).

- ☐ The four cups of wine correspond to the four decrees Pharaoh passed against the Jewish nation in Egypt: the edict that the Jews would labor as slaves, the demand that the midwives Shifrah and Puah murder Jewish newborn boys, the law that all baby boys should be thrown into the river, and finally the command that Jews search for their own straw for bricks, though their set building quota would not be reduced (*Midrash Rabbah, Shemos* 6:26).

- ☐ The halachah mandates that when one is saved from four types of danger, he is required to recite *birkas hagomel*, the *berachah* of thanksgiving to Hashem. These include one who was imprisoned and released, one who safely crosses the sea, one who successfully travels through a wilderness, and one who recovers from a life-threatening sickness. The Jewish people were saved from all four types of danger. They were released from Egyptian imprisonment, they safely crossed the Yam Suf and the wilderness, and upon arriving at Har Sinai, all those with ailments were healed. We drink four cups of wine on Pesach night as an expression of thanks to Hashem for saving us from these four dangers throughout the exile and during the Exodus (*Vilna Gaon; Maharsha, Berachos* 54b).

Why specifically wine?

- It is not possible to graft a grapevine together with other fruits to form a new variety. The vine will always remain exclusive, isolated, pure, and unadulterated. Similarly, despite living in Egypt for more than 200 years, the Jewish people retained their identity by not changing their names, clothing, or mode of speech, and in this merit they were redeemed. We celebrate our redemption, then, by drinking wine, the fruit of the grape that remains true to its origin (*Mateh Moshe*).

- When the Jewish nation left Egypt, they departed with just the matzos they carried on their backs and no other food or drink. Millions of men, women, and children traveled into the barren wilderness with no idea of how long they would be wandering in the wilderness. The Jewish people didn't question Moshe or Hashem about their lack of bread and water; instead, they marched out of Egypt filled with *bitachon* that Hashem would care for all their needs. No questions were asked; no calculations were made: the Jews left, propelled by their incredible *bitachon* in Hashem, an act of faith that went beyond all logical or rational thought.

    In a *pasuk* that we read every Rosh HaShanah, we hear how Hashem recalls this awesome demonstration of trust in Him: כֹּה אָמַר ה' זָכַרְתִּי לָךְ חֶסֶד נְעוּרַיִךְ אַהֲבַת כְּלוּלֹתָיִךְ לֶכְתֵּךְ אַחֲרַי בַּמִּדְבָּר בְּאֶרֶץ לֹא זְרוּעָה, *So said Hashem: "I recall for you the kindness of your youth, the love of your nuptials, your following Me into the wilderness, into an unsown land"* (*Yirmiyahu* 2:2).

Drinking wine suspends one's ability to think logically. To recall the Jewish nation's awesome display of *bitachon* in Hashem and how they asked no questions, made no calculations, and suspended all rational thinking upon leaving Egypt and traveling into the wilderness, wine, which likewise suspends all logical thinking, is drunk on this night (*Shem MiShmuel*).

It is generally preferable that the wine for the four cups be red. Why?

- ☐ The Torah praises wine whose color is red as being of superior quality (*Mishlei* 23:31).
- ☐ Red wine recalls the hundreds of children slaughtered daily for Pharaoh to bathe in their blood (*Taz* 472:9).
- ☐ Red wine recalls the blood of the *pesach* sacrifice and the blood of *bris milah*. It was through these two mitzvos the Jewish nation was redeemed (*Ohr Zarua* 256).
- ☐ Red wine recalls the plague of blood (*Pri Megadim* 472:13)
- ☐ Red wine recalls the blood that the Jewish people placed on their doorposts prior to the plague of the slaying of the Egyptian firstborn.

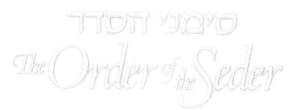

The Order of the Seder

KADDESH	**Sanctify** the day with the recitation of Kiddush.	קדש
URECHATZ	**Wash** the hands before eating Karpas.	ורחץ
KARPAS	Eat a **vegetable** dipped in salt water.	כרפס
YACHATZ	**Break** the middle matzah. Put away larger half for Afikoman.	יחץ
MAGGID	**Narrate** the story of Yetzias Mitzrayim.	מגיד
RACHTZAH	**Wash** the hands prior to the meal.	רחצה
MOTZI	Recite the blessing, **Who brings forth**, over matzah as a food.	מוציא
MATZAH	Recite the blessing over **matzah**.	מצה
MAROR	Recite the blessing for the eating of the **bitter herbs**.	מרור
KORECH	Eat the **sandwich** of matzah and bitter herbs.	כורך
SHULCHAN ORECH	The **table prepared** with the festive meal.	שלחן עורך
TZAFUN	Eat the Afikoman which had been **hidden** all during the Seder.	צפון
BARECH	Recite Bircas HaMazon, the **blessings** after the meal.	ברך
HALLEL	Recite the **Hallel** Psalms of praise.	הלל
NIRTZAH	Pray that God **accept** our observance and speedily send the Messiah.	נרצה

THE EISHES CHAYIL HAGGADAH

Kiddush should be recited and the Seder begun as soon after synagogue services as possible; however, not before nightfall. Each participant's cup should be poured by someone else to symbolize the majesty of the evening, as though each participant had a servant.

Some have a custom to say the following declaration of intent:

הִנְנִי מוּכָן וּמְזֻמָּן לְקַדֵּשׁ עַל הַיַּיִן וּלְקַיֵּם מִצְוַת כּוֹס רִאשׁוֹן מֵאַרְבַּע כּוֹסוֹת. לְשֵׁם יִחוּד קֻדְשָׁא בְּרִיךְ הוּא וּשְׁכִינְתֵּיהּ, עַל יְדֵי הַהוּא טָמִיר וְנֶעְלָם, בְּשֵׁם כָּל יִשְׂרָאֵל. וִיהִי נֹעַם אֲדֹנָי אֱלֹהֵינוּ עָלֵינוּ, וּמַעֲשֵׂה יָדֵינוּ כּוֹנְנָה עָלֵינוּ, וּמַעֲשֵׂה יָדֵינוּ כּוֹנְנֵהוּ.

On Friday night begin here:

(וַיְהִי עֶרֶב וַיְהִי בֹקֶר)

יוֹם הַשִּׁשִּׁי וַיְכֻלּוּ הַשָּׁמַיִם וְהָאָרֶץ וְכָל צְבָאָם. וַיְכַל אֱלֹהִים בַּיּוֹם הַשְּׁבִיעִי מְלַאכְתּוֹ אֲשֶׁר עָשָׂה, וַיִּשְׁבֹּת בַּיּוֹם הַשְּׁבִיעִי מִכָּל מְלַאכְתּוֹ אֲשֶׁר עָשָׂה. וַיְבָרֶךְ אֱלֹהִים אֶת יוֹם הַשְּׁבִיעִי וַיְקַדֵּשׁ אֹתוֹ, כִּי בוֹ שָׁבַת מִכָּל מְלַאכְתּוֹ אֲשֶׁר בָּרָא אֱלֹהִים לַעֲשׂוֹת.[1]

On all nights other than Friday, begin here;
on Friday night include all passages in parentheses.

סַבְרִי מָרָנָן וְרַבָּנָן וְרַבּוֹתַי:

בָּרוּךְ אַתָּה יהוה אֱלֹהֵינוּ מֶלֶךְ הָעוֹלָם, בּוֹרֵא פְּרִי הַגָּפֶן.

> **The Four Cups**
> - Women are obligated to fulfill the mitzvah of drinking the four cups of wine at the Seder.
> - Women are not required to lean while drinking the four cups, or any of the mitzvos of Seder night, although they may if they wish. Many women who follow the Sephardic tradition have the custom to lean (*Rema* 472:4; *Kaf HaChaim* 472:28).

KADDESH

Kiddush should be recited and the Seder begun as soon after synagogue services as possible; however, not before nightfall. Each participant's cup should be poured by someone else to symbolize the majesty of the evening, as though each participant had a servant.

Some have a custom to say the following declaration of intent:

Behold, I am prepared and ready to recite the Kiddush over wine, and to fulfill the mitzvah of the first of the Four Cups. For the sake of the unification of the Holy One, Blessed is He, and His Presence, through Him Who is hidden and inscrutable — [I pray] in the name of all Israel. May the pleasantness of the Lord, our God, be upon us, and may He establish our handiwork for us; our handiwork may He establish.

On Friday night begin here:

(And there was evening and there was morning)

The sixth day. Thus the heaven and the earth were finished, and all their array. On the seventh day God completed His work which He had done, and He abstained on the seventh day from all His work which He had done. God blessed the seventh day and hallowed it, because on it He abstained from all His work which God created to make.[1]

On all nights other than Friday, begin here; on Friday night include all passages in parentheses.

By your leave, my masters and teachers:

Blessed are You, HASHEM, our God, King of the universe, Who creates the fruit of the vine.

---
1. *Bereishis* 1:31-2:3.

> ### ⋦ The Shehecheyanu Blessing
> - Women who already recited the *berachah* of *Shehecheyanu* during candlelighting do not recite it here again, but they may answer Amen to the one reciting the berachah.

בָּרוּךְ אַתָּה יהוה אֱלֹהֵינוּ מֶלֶךְ הָעוֹלָם, אֲשֶׁר בָּחַר בָּנוּ מִכָּל עָם, וְרוֹמְמָנוּ מִכָּל לָשׁוֹן, וְקִדְּשָׁנוּ בְּמִצְוֹתָיו. וַתִּתֶּן לָנוּ יהוה אֱלֹהֵינוּ בְּאַהֲבָה (שַׁבָּתוֹת לִמְנוּחָה וּ)מוֹעֲדִים לְשִׂמְחָה חַגִּים וּזְמַנִּים לְשָׂשׂוֹן אֶת יוֹם (הַשַּׁבָּת הַזֶּה וְאֶת יוֹם) חַג הַמַּצּוֹת הַזֶּה, זְמַן חֵרוּתֵנוּ (בְּאַהֲבָה) מִקְרָא קֹדֶשׁ, זֵכֶר לִיצִיאַת מִצְרָיִם. כִּי בָנוּ בָחַרְתָּ וְאוֹתָנוּ קִדַּשְׁתָּ מִכָּל הָעַמִּים, (וְשַׁבָּת) וּמוֹעֲדֵי קָדְשֶׁךָ (בְּאַהֲבָה וּבְרָצוֹן) בְּשִׂמְחָה וּבְשָׂשׂוֹן הִנְחַלְתָּנוּ. בָּרוּךְ אַתָּה יהוה, מְקַדֵּשׁ (הַשַּׁבָּת וְ)יִשְׂרָאֵל וְהַזְּמַנִּים.

קַדֵּשׁ / Kaddesh

Proud to Be a Jew

אֲשֶׁר בָּחַר בָּנוּ מִכָּל עָם וְרוֹמְמָנוּ מִכָּל לָשׁוֹן
Who has chosen us from all nations, exalted us above all tongues

Rav Yekusiel Yehudah Halberstam, the Klausenberger Rebbe, went through the concentration camps, under conditions too appalling for words. He lost his wife and 11 children to the Holocaust. One day a broken and disheartened fellow Jew came to him.

"Rebbe," the man said, "please tell me, under such inhumane conditions, such torture, oppression, and starvation, how can we still proudly proclaim, אֲשֶׁר בָּחַר בָּנוּ מִכָּל עָם, Who has chosen us from all the nations?"

"On the contrary," the Rebbe responded, "it's at such a time, when I see the subhuman and barbaric behaviors of the non-

Blessed are You, HASHEM, our God, King of the universe, Who has chosen us from all nations, exalted us above all tongues, and sanctified us with His commandments. And You, HASHEM, our God, have lovingly given us (Shabbasos for rest,) appointed times for gladness, feasts and seasons for joy, (this Shabbos and) this Feast of Matzos, the season of our freedom (in love), a holy convocation in commemoration of the Exodus from Egypt. For You have chosen and sanctified us above all peoples, (and Shabbos) and Your holy festivals (in love and favor), in gladness and joy have You granted us as a heritage. Blessed are You, HASHEM, Who sanctifies (Shabbos,) Israel, and the festive seasons.

Jews, behaviors that we as Jews would never dream of doing to another human being, that I can proudly say with all my heart, Who has chosen us from all the nations!" (Imrei Yatziv, p. 335; Lapid Eish, Vol.1, p. 184).

Impossible to Express

וְרוֹמְמָנוּ מִכָּל לָשׁוֹן
Exalted us above all tongues

Rav Simchah Bunim of Peshischa writes that וְרוֹמְמָנוּ מִכָּל לָשׁוֹן, [He] *exalted us above all tongues*, means that Hashem has such unbounded love for us it's impossible to describe it in words. No tongue, no language, no idiom or expression a human can utter can accurately convey the deep love and care Hashem has for the Jewish nation (*Kol Mevasser*, p. 156).

The Baal Shem Tov would say, "The love that we have for the biggest *tzaddik* in the nation can't rival the love Hashem has for the biggest *rasha* in the nation!"

On Motza'ei Shabbos, add the following two paragraphs.
Two candles or wicks with flames touching are held and the following blessings are recited.

בָּרוּךְ אַתָּה יהוה אֱלֹהֵינוּ מֶלֶךְ הָעוֹלָם, בּוֹרֵא מְאוֹרֵי הָאֵשׁ.

Hold the fingers up to the flame to see the reflected light.

בָּרוּךְ אַתָּה יהוה אֱלֹהֵינוּ מֶלֶךְ הָעוֹלָם, הַמַּבְדִּיל בֵּין קֹדֶשׁ לְחוֹל, בֵּין אוֹר לְחֹשֶׁךְ, בֵּין יִשְׂרָאֵל לָעַמִּים, בֵּין יוֹם הַשְּׁבִיעִי לְשֵׁשֶׁת יְמֵי הַמַּעֲשֶׂה. בֵּין קְדֻשַּׁת שַׁבָּת לִקְדֻשַּׁת יוֹם טוֹב הִבְדַּלְתָּ, וְאֶת יוֹם הַשְּׁבִיעִי מִשֵּׁשֶׁת יְמֵי הַמַּעֲשֶׂה קִדַּשְׁתָּ, הִבְדַּלְתָּ וְקִדַּשְׁתָּ אֶת עַמְּךָ יִשְׂרָאֵל בִּקְדֻשָּׁתֶךָ. בָּרוּךְ אַתָּה יהוה, הַמַּבְדִּיל בֵּין קֹדֶשׁ לְקֹדֶשׁ.

On all nights conclude here:

בָּרוּךְ אַתָּה יהוה אֱלֹהֵינוּ מֶלֶךְ הָעוֹלָם, שֶׁהֶחֱיָנוּ וְקִיְּמָנוּ וְהִגִּיעָנוּ לַזְּמַן הַזֶּה.

The wine should be drunk without delay while reclining on the left side. It is preferable to drink the entire cup, but at the very least, most of the cup should be drained.

— Think About It —

A Holiday of Freedom

אֶת יוֹם חַג הַמַּצּוֹת הַזֶּה זְמַן חֵרוּתֵנוּ
This Feast of Matzos, the season of our freedom

Considering the lengthy and intense preparations required for Pesach, how is this Yom Tov an expression of freedom? Indeed, what is the true meaning of "*zeman cheiruseinu*"?

To answer that question, we have to ask the larger question:

On Motza'ei Shabbos, add the following two paragraphs.
Two candles or wicks with flames touching are held and the following blessings are recited.

Blessed are You, HASHEM, our God, King of the universe, Who creates the illumination of the fire.

Hold the fingers up to the flame to see the reflected light.

Blessed are You, HASHEM, our God, King of the universe, Who distinguishes between sacred and secular, between light and darkness, between Israel and the nations, between the seventh day and the six days of activity. You have distinguished between the holiness of Shabbos and the holiness of a Festival, and have sanctified the seventh day above the six days of activity. You distinguished and sanctified Your nation, Israel, with Your holiness. Blessed are You, HASHEM, Who distinguishes between holiness and holiness.

On all nights conclude here:

Blessed are You, HASHEM, our God, King of the universe, Who has kept us alive, sustained us, and brought us to this season.

The wine should be drunk without delay while reclining on the left side. It is preferable to drink the entire cup, but at the very least, most of the cup should be drained.

---

what is freedom? A person can be physically free to move around, but he may feel powerless to accomplish things and enjoy life because of his worries. True freedom is freedom from worry and an ability to rise above the stresses created by society, peer pressure, and what is sometimes called the "rat race" of life.

The word *Mitzrayim* comes from the word *metzer*, "boundary." When the Jews were enslaved in Egypt, they were imprisoned with nowhere to turn, physically, spiritually, emotionally. At the time of redemption, the Jewish nation was enveloped by Hashem's loving and protective embrace. He demonstrated

וּרְחַץ

The head of the household — according to many opinions, all participants in the Seder — washes his hands as if to eat bread [pouring water from a cup, twice on the right hand and twice on the left], but without reciting a blessing.

---

to them through countless miracles and His exact measure-for-measure retribution that He controls this world and all that occurs in it.

On Pesach we inject ourselves with the same feelings the Jewish nation felt upon leaving Egypt: clear *emunah*, a deep love for Hashem, and the knowledge of Hashem's love for us. These feelings allow us to break through the boundaries that immobilize us and cause us to worry, boundaries that stifle our ability to grow closer to Hashem and accomplish what we're truly capable of. These feelings make us free!

The *Chovos HaLevavos* (*Sha'ar HaBitachon*) says that one can only be freed from life's worries if he strengthens his *bitachon*, his faith in Hashem. Only *bitachon*, the knowledge that Hashem is watching over us and knows what's best for us, can give us a calm and worry-free life and bring us to true freedom, no matter how much work we have waiting for us in the kitchen.

Rav Moshe Aharon Stern illustrated this with a parable. Every young child is taught that when crossing the street he needs to look both ways and proceed with caution. But when that same child holds his father's hand, he crosses the street without looking and without worry. Why? Because he's holding the hand of his father, the one he trusts wholeheartedly to protect him. This is the level of trust we should strive to have in Hashem (*Bayis U'Menuchah*, p. 110).

When we trust in Hashem and understand how deep His love

> ### ⇜§ Selected Laws of Urechatz
> - Women should remove their rings before washing.
> - After washing the hands, it is preferable that one not speak about matters unrelated to *Urechatz* and *Karpas* until the *Karpas* vegetable has been eaten.

URECHATZ

The head of the household — according to many opinions, all participants in the Seder — washes his hands as if to eat bread [pouring water from a cup, twice on the right hand and twice on the left], but without reciting a blessing.

---

is for us, we can relax, throw off our worries, and experience true freedom. Pesach is called "*zeman cheiruseinu*" because Hashem demonstrated this deep love for us and His immutable ability to take care of us in all circumstances — something that gives us freedom.

> *Upon his marriage, Rav Yitzchak Zev Soloveitchik received a block of buildings in Warsaw as a dowry, a fortune of valuable real estate. Shortly after, the estate was lost and his dowry vanished. When asked if he was worried about the future, he said, "People think that a wealthy person is someone who owns properties in Warsaw. They're wrong. A wealthy person is someone who has 'sha'ar habitachon,' the gate of faith, in his heart" (Avodas V'Hanhagos L'Beis Brisk, Vol.1, p. 73).*

The Mishnah says, אֵין לְךָ בֶּן חוֹרִין אֶלָּא מִי שֶׁעוֹסֵק בְּתַלְמוּד תּוֹרָה, *Only one who attaches himself to Hashem and His Torah can experience true freedom* (Avos 6:2). That's why we recline like kings and queens on the Seder night; on this night of strong *emunah* in Hashem, we really do feel free.

URECHATZ / ורחץ

Why We Wash

Before eating a vegetable or fruit that is wet, one is required to wash his hands. Although during the year we do not wash hands before eating wet vegetables, we do so on this night as a means of encouraging the children to question why we wash our hands (*Chok Yaakov*).

[61] **THE EISHES CHAYIL HAGGADAH**

All participants take a vegetable other than *maror* and dip it into salt water. A piece smaller in volume than half an egg should be used. The following blessing is recited [with the intention that it also applies to the *maror* which will be eaten during the meal] before the vegetable is eaten.

בָּרוּךְ אַתָּה יהוה אֱלֹהֵינוּ מֶלֶךְ הָעוֹלָם, בּוֹרֵא פְּרִי הָאֲדָמָה.

The head of the household breaks the middle matzah in two. He puts the smaller part back between the two whole matzos, and wraps up the larger part for later use as the *afikoman*. Some briefly place the *afikoman* portion on their shoulders, in accordance with the Biblical verse recounting that Israel left Egypt carrying their matzos on their shoulders, and say בְּבֶהָלוּ יָצָאנוּ מִמִּצְרָיִם, "In haste we went out of Egypt."

Also, since the night of Pesach is an extraordinarily holy night, it is fitting to fulfill even stringent practices, such as this one (*Levush*).

KARPAS / כרפס

Why We Eat Karpas

Vegetables are not usually eaten prior to a meal. On the night of Pesach, a vegetable dipped in salt water is eaten before the meal begins so that the children will be inspired to ask questions regarding the uniqueness of this night (*Pesachim* 114b).

Also, the letters in the word *karpas* form the words *samech parech* (ס' פרך). The numerical value of the letter *samech*, 60, alludes to the 600,000 Jews who were forced by the Egyptians into "*parech*," backbreaking labor (*Avudraham*; *Magen Avraham* 473:4).

☙KARPAS☙

All participants take a vegetable other than *maror* and dip it into salt water. A piece smaller in volume than half an egg should be used. The following blessing is recited [with the intention that it also applies to the *maror* which will be eaten during the meal] before the vegetable is eaten.

Blessed are You, HASHEM, our God, King of the universe, Who creates the fruits of the earth.

☙YACHATZ☙

The head of the household breaks the middle matzah in two. He puts the smaller part back between the two whole matzos, and wraps up the larger part for later use as the *afikoman*. Some briefly place the *afikoman* portion on their shoulders, in accordance with the Biblical verse recounting that Israel left Egypt carrying their matzos on their shoulders, and say בְּבְהִלוּ יָצָאנוּ מִמִצְרָיִם, *"In haste we went out of Egypt."*

YACHATZ / יחץ

Why We Break the Middle Matzah

- ☐ A poor person generally only has broken pieces of bread, or he divides his bread and saves a part for later since he is unsure where or when his next meal will come from. Tonight we recall the Jewish nation's poverty and servitude in Egypt, and so we recite the Haggadah over a broken piece of matzah (*Beis Yosef* 473; *Pesachim* 115b).

- ☐ Breaking the matzah reminds us of the miracle Hashem performed when He split the Yam Suf (*Da'as Zekeinim, Shemos* 12:8).

- ☐ The *Rambam (Devarim* 16:2) explains that matzah has a

dual symbolism. The Egyptians fed the Jews matzah during their time of slavery since it is digested slowly, precluding the need to feed them often. Hence, the matzah recalls the Jewish slavery in Egypt. But the matzah also recalls the redemption, since the Jewish people were redeemed in a hurry and were thus unable to allow the dough on their shoulders to rise. In order to mark the dual symbolism innate in the matzah, it is broken in two. One part fills its role during the first part of the Seder, when we recall the slavery and persecution. The other half of the matzah is set aside and used later, at the second part of the Seder, which is dedicated to recalling the redemption and our freedom.

☐ The three matzos represent the three branches that comprise the Jewish nation: Kohen, Levi, and Yisrael. Of all the tribes forced into Egyptian servitude, only the tribe of Levi was never enslaved. We might think that the tribe of Levi didn't suffer in the time of slavery, but we would be mistaken. The middle matzah representing Levi is broken to demonstrate that although the tribe of Levi wasn't forced to work, they were nevertheless "broken" and pained over the suffering of their Jewish brothers (*Kisvei Abba Mori*, p. 241).

The "Missing" Afikoman

After breaking the matzah in two, the larger piece is set aside to be eaten later as the *afikoman*. The children keep a sharp eye on the *afikoman*, waiting for the opportunity to hide it for their parents to find. Rambam writes (*Hilchos Chametz U'Matzah* 7:3) that the reason behind the custom of children taking the *afikoman* is to encourage their participation in the Seder and to prompt them to ask questions, a central facet of Seder night.

The custom also emerged in order to prompt the children to remain awake. When the children take the *afikoman*, they are motivated to stay awake until the end of the Seder, when their father is required to "ransom" it so that it can be eaten (*Chok Yaakov* 472:2; *Noheig Katzon Yosef*).

The Chasam Sofer's grandson once asked his grandfather about the source of the custom of children "stealing" the *afikoman*. The Chasam Sofer answered that on Seder night we commemorate nearly all the miracles that Hashem performed for us at the Exodus. But there is one miracle that we don't specifically mention: the strange fact that no dog barked at the Jewish people during the plague of the firstborn. This miracle underlines the total tranquillity the Jews experienced that night, in contrast to the chaos the Egyptians faced (*Hegyonei Halachah*).

The Chasam Sofer suggested that this miracle is actually recalled through the stealing of the *afikoman*. The Talmud (*Pesachim* 113a) tells us that a person shouldn't reside in a city without any dogs, as their barks alert property owners of potential robbers. Yet on the night of the slaying of the firstborn, no dog barked, and therefore robbers had open season on theft, without the risk of the owners being alerted by the barking dogs. When children steal the *afikoman*, it reminds us of the night the dogs didn't bark: a night when the thieves could steal without fear (Introduction to *Michtav Sofer*, Vol. 2).

Matzos on Our Shoulders

The Talmud records (*Bechoros* 5b) that although each Jew had 90 donkeys to transport his possessions when he departed Egypt, they chose to carry the matzah themselves, demonstrating their love and devotion for the mitzvah (*Rashi, Shemos* 12:34). When we place the matzos on our shoulders, we are demonstrating to our children our love, attention, and devotion for mitzvos (*Mahari Steif Haggadah*, p. 38).

מַגִּיד

Some recite the following declaration of intent before Maggid:

הִנְנִי מוּכָן וּמְזוּמָן לְקַיֵּם הַמִּצְוָה לְסַפֵּר בִּיצִיאַת מִצְרָיִם. לְשֵׁם יִחוּד קֻדְשָׁא בְּרִיךְ הוּא וּשְׁכִינְתֵּיהּ, עַל יְדֵי הַהוּא טָמִיר וְנֶעְלָם, בְּשֵׁם כָּל יִשְׂרָאֵל. וִיהִי נֹעַם אֲדֹנָי אֱלֹהֵינוּ עָלֵינוּ, וּמַעֲשֵׂה יָדֵינוּ כּוֹנְנָה עָלֵינוּ, וּמַעֲשֵׂה יָדֵינוּ כּוֹנְנֵהוּ:

MAGGID / מַגִּיד

The Mitzvah of Retelling the Story

Rambam writes (*Hilchos Chametz U'Matzah* 7:1), "It is a Torah obligation to recount the miracles and wonders that were performed for our forefathers in Egypt on the fifteenth day [of Nissan] as it says, *Remember the day that I took you out of Egypt* (*Shemos* 13:3)." Rambam further explains (*Sefer HaMitzvos* 157) that we talk about those miracles to thank Him for all the good He has bestowed on the Jewish nation.

The *Sefer HaChinuch* (21) points out that an abundance of mitzvos and *tefillos* mention the Exodus from Egypt. In the words of the *Chinuch*, recalling the Exodus is "a great foundation and mighty pillar" of our faith in Hashem and the Torah. By punishing the Egyptians, Hashem exacted retribution and redeemed the Jewish nation. It became clear to everyone that Hashem is in charge and runs the world.

Some people claim that Hashem created the world and then allowed it to run on its own. The Jewish nation's miraculous Exodus from Egypt clearly refutes such a falsehood. The ten plagues and the splitting of the Red Sea, the open miracles seen by every Egyptian and every Jew, demonstrate Hashem's constant presence in running the world and His ability to change the laws of nature at will. Recalling the events of the Exodus, then, strengthens our faith in Him. This idea is explicit in the *pasuk* regarding the plagues: לְמַעַן תֵּדַע כִּי אֲנִי ה' בְּקֶרֶב הָאָרֶץ, *So that you will know that I am Hashem **in the midst of the land*** (*Shemos* 8:18).

The Exodus from Egypt, then, serves as the bedrock of our belief in Hashem and His constant presence in our daily lives. On

MAGGID

Some recite the following declaration of intent before *Maggid*:

Behold, I am prepared and ready to fulfill the mitzvah of telling of the Exodus from Egypt. For the sake of the unification of the Holy One, Blessed is He, and His presence, through Him Who is hidden and inscrutable — [I pray] in the name of all Israel. May the pleasantness of the Lord, our God, be upon us, and may He establish our handiwork for us; our handiwork may He establish.

---

the night of the Pesach Seder, there is a mitzvah to recount the story of the Exodus, revitalizing that belief.

We also find that the first of the Ten Commandments, "I am Hashem, your God, Who took you out of the land of Egypt," specifically mentions the Exodus. Many commentators question why the first commandment was not "I am Hashem, your God, Who created the world." The *Kuzari* (1:25) explains that the Jewish nation's Exodus from Egypt was witnessed by hundreds of thousands of people, and its tradition has been passed down from generation to generation. It was an event whose existence can't be denied. Hence, this event is a pillar of our nation's belief

> ### ⋽ Selected Laws of Maggid
> - Women are obligated in the mitzvah of telling the story of the Jewish nation's Exodus from Egypt on the night of Pesach (*Shulchan Aruch* 472:14).
> - Specifically, they must be careful to recite [or be present when the others recite] the passage רַבָּן גַּמְלִיאֵל הָיָה אוֹמֵר, *Rabban Gamliel used to say* (see p. 200), until after the second cup is consumed at the end of *Maggid* (*Mishnah Berurah* 473:64). This is an absolutely essential part of the Haggadah, and women who are otherwise occupied in Seder preparations or caring for the children are obligated to recite this section in order to fulfill their mitzvah obligation.
> - Preferably, women should also recite the passages of "*Mah Nishtanah*," "*Avadim Hayinu*," and "*MeTechilah Ovdei Avodah Zarah*," since these passages are mentioned by the Talmud.
>
>   Likewise, it is preferable that women hear or recite the listing of the ten plagues that Hashem brought upon the Egyptians in order to internalize the wondrous miracles Hashem performed for the Jewish people (*Mishnah Berurah* 473:64).
> - Women are obligated to recite the Hallel that is said as part of the Haggadah (*Mishnah Berurah* 479:9).
> - A woman leading the Seder is obligated in the mitzvah of telling the story of the Exodus to her children (*Pri Megadim* 472:16).

in Hashem, and we have an obligation to retell its story every year.

The Haggadah and Its Name

Why is the text we read on the night of the Pesach Seder called the "Haggadah"?

- ☐ The word *haggadah* means "to tell." On the night of Pesach there's a mitzvah to relate the story of our Exodus from Egypt, as it says (*Shemos* 13:8), וְהִגַּדְתָּ לְבִנְךָ בַּיּוֹם הַהוּא, *You shall tell your son on that day* (*Seder HaYom*).

- ☐ The word *haggadah* in Aramaic means "thanks" and "praise." Through reading the Haggadah we thank and praise Hashem for the wondrous miracles and the Divine Providence He showered on us upon our redemption from Egypt (*Avudraham*).

The word *l'haggid* also connotes the idea of conveying a new piece of information of which someone was previously unaware. The mitzvah of discussing the Exodus from Egypt should be done every year in a new and exciting manner, exploring deeper meanings and searching for new insights into the great miracles that Hashem performed for the Jewish nation (*Siach Yitzchak Haggadah*, p. 27; *Malbim, Tehillim* 19:2).

Without a Berachah

Why don't we recite a *berachah* on the mitzvah of recounting the Exodus?

The mitzvah of reciting the Haggadah serves to strengthen our *emunah* in Hashem as we recall the wonders Hashem performed for us, miracles that defied natural law. The mitzvah of strengthening *emunah* takes places in the heart and mind. One only recites blessings on mitzvos fulfilled through actions and not thoughts (*Teshuvos HaRosh* 24:2; *Gevuros Hashem* 62).

How much telling is enough? There is no prescribed and fixed measurement as to how much one must speak about the miracles of our Exodus, as we say, וְכָל הַמַּרְבֶּה לְסַפֵּר בִּיצִיאַת מִצְרַיִם הֲרֵי זֶה מְשֻׁבָּח, *The more one tells about the discussion of the Exodus, the more he is praiseworthy*. Since there is no specific minimum or maximum, a *berachah* is not recited (*Rashba*, quoted in *Avudraham*).

— Think About It —

Maggid —
The Meaning and the Miracles

The night of Pesach is a magical time. Families spanning several generations gather around the beautiful Yom Tov table to relate the story of the Exodus. What a wonderful opportunity to bring to light our *emunah* in Hashem and our appreciation for His deep love for us!

More than simply talking about the technical or esoteric details of the Haggadah, we need to ensure that the underlying themes of the Haggadah are discussed in detail with passion and meaning. Hashem heard the cries of the Jewish people's suffering; He punished the Egyptians measure for measure, performing miracles that demonstrated His control over all aspects of the creation; and He chose us to make us his own nation. These ideas are the foundations of our faith, of *emunah* built on the deep words of the Haggadah.

But the themes of *emunah* and *bitachon* in Hashem should not stop with descriptions of the redemption from Egypt. On this night, with the family gathered together, we should recall those moments when we ourselves have seen the hand of Hashem in our daily lives. *Hashgachah pratis* can be found in the great stories of our lives: how we found our spouse, how we got a job, how we were spared injury by not being in the wrong place at the wrong time.

We can also see Hashem's hand in the small, seemingly insignificant incidents — a chance meeting with an old friend, a phone call, a lost item found — and these personal stories can be used as a springboard to demonstrate how Hashem guides us and cares for us, how He is with us throughout our daily lives.

Rav Yonasan Steif makes this point in his Haggadah. He includes in the mitzvah of telling the story of the Exodus a holy obligation to recount one's own personal recollections of the

The broken matzah is lifted for all to see as the head of the household begins with the following brief explanation of the proceedings.

הָא לַחְמָא עַנְיָא דִי אֲכָלוּ אַבְהָתָנָא בְּאַרְעָא דְמִצְרָיִם. כָּל דִּכְפִין יֵיתֵי וְיֵכוֹל, כָּל דִּצְרִיךְ יֵיתֵי וְיִפְסַח. הָשַׁתָּא הָכָא, לְשָׁנָה הַבָּאָה

---

miracles one merited throughout his life in order to strengthen the *emunah* of all those present (*Mahari Steif Haggadah*, p. 75).

The Targum (to *Shemos* 13:8) translates the word *v'higadeta* as *u'sechavei* (וּתְחַוֵי), meaning "you should bring to life!" Retelling the story of our Exodus vividly and with excitement — making the events come alive — brings home to us the *hashgachah pratis* that Hashem demonstrated through our redemption from Egypt, throughout our nation's long history of survival and growth, and in our everyday lives today.

Lifting the Matzah

The matzos are lifted during the recitation of "*Ha Lachma Anya*." Some have the custom of lifting the Seder plate as well. One reason we do this is because we recall how Hashem took us from the depths of servitude and impurity in Egypt and lifted us up upon our redemption to become the Chosen Nation, the nation of Hashem (*Chaim L'Rosh Haggadah*).

Also, lifting the Seder plate arouses the curiosity of the children and prompts the children to ask additional questions about this night (*Shibbolei HaLeket*).

Hashem's Presence at Every Seder

הָא לַחְמָא עַנְיָא
This is the bread of affliction

Why is the opening stanza of the Haggadah in Aramaic, when the rest of the Haggadah is in Hebrew? Rav Yissacher Dov Rokeach of Belz provides an explanation highlighting the

The broken matzah is lifted for all to see as the head of the household begins with the following brief explanation of the proceedings.

This is the bread of affliction that our fathers ate in the land of Egypt. Whoever is hungry, let him come and eat! Whoever is needy, let him come and celebrate Pesach! Now we are here; next year may we be

---

uniqueness and holiness of the Seder night.

The Talmud states that one should not daven in Aramaic because the ministering angels don't understand this language and are unable to convey such *tefillos* to Hashem (*Shabbos* 12b). Yet, continues the Talmud, one who is, God forbid, unwell may pray in Aramaic because Hashem's presence itself rests above his head, and there's no need for the *malachim* to transmit his *tefillos*.

This is why, explains the Belzer Rebbe, we begin the Haggadah in Aramaic: it is to reflect the night's holiness, when Hashem Himself, in His great glory and honor, is present at each and every person's Pesach Seder!

The *Zohar* (*Bo* 179) relates that on the night of the Pesach Seder, Hashem calls His entire assemblage of heavenly angels to come with Him to hear the Jewish people recall the Exodus from Egypt.

We see, then, that Pesach night is a time of unparalleled closeness to Hashem and a highly auspicious time for *tefillah* (*B'Lailah Shirah Imi*; *Emes L'Yaakov*; *Haggadah shel Pesach Gedolei Yisrael*, p. 13; see also *Haggadah of the Dubner Maggid*).

We Are His and He Is Ours

כָּל דִּצְרִיךְ יֵיתֵי וְיִפְסַח
Whoever is needy, let him come and celebrate Pesach ...

Why does the Torah refer to the Yom Tov as Chag HaMatzos, while the Jewish people generally call it Pesach?

The Kedushas Levi answers this question by quoting the *pasuk* אֲנִי לְדוֹדִי וְדוֹדִי לִי, *I am to my Beloved, and my Beloved is to me* (*Shir HaShirim* 6:3). We, *Klal Yisrael*, praise the glory of Hashem, while Hashem praises the glory of the Jewish nation. This is

בְּאַרְעָא דְיִשְׂרָאֵל. הָשַׁתָּא עַבְדֵי, לְשָׁנָה הַבָּאָה בְּנֵי חוֹרִין.

<small>The Seder plate is removed and the second
of the four cups of wine is poured.</small>

---

why Hashem calls the Yom Tov "Chag HaMatzos" in the Torah, praising the loyalty and trust that the Jewish people placed in Him when they left Egypt in a hurry with only the matzos on their backs.

The Jewish people in turn refer to the Yom Tov as "Pesach," praising Hashem for the miracles He performed in skipping over the Jewish houses while killing the firstborn of Egypt (*Kedushas Levi, Shemos* 12:27).

Pesach and Its Name

How did the Yom Tov of Pesach get its name?

- ☐ The word *pesach* can be divided into the words *peh sach*. *Peh* means "mouth," and the word *sach* means "talk." While the Jews were enslaved in Egypt, they were unable to articulate their *tefillos* to Hashem due to their overwhelming pain and the overbearing workload. The Jews were only able to cry out to Hashem without words. Once Hashem redeemed the Jewish nation, their ability to communicate with Him with words was restored. Hence, this Yom Tov is called Pesach, to convey how our ability to daven and communicate with Hashem was reestablished (*Siddur Arizal*).

- ☐ "*Pesach*" also can mean to jump and skip. On the night of Pesach, Hashem took the Jewish people from the lowest levels of spiritual impurity and brought them close to Him in one moment, skipping over the usual manner of gradual spiritual progression (*Bnei Yissaschar*, Nissan 4:11). What's more, each Pesach a person can attain this unparalleled spiritual freedom and closeness to Hashem, making a spiritual jump, so to speak, that's impossible other times of the year.

- ☐ The word *pesach* can also mean mercy: Hashem had mercy on the Jewish people and redeemed them from the servitude in Egypt (*Hakesav VehaKabbalah*).

in the Land of Israel! Now we are slaves; next year may we be free men!

The Seder plate is removed and the second of the four cups of wine is poured.

Home: A Center of Holiness

הָשַׁתָּא הָכָא, לְשָׁנָה הַבָּאָה בְּאַרְעָא דְיִשְׂרָאֵל

Now we are here; next year may we be in the Land of Israel!

The Chasam Sofer writes that on the night of Pesach our homes are centers of holiness, because on this night we fill them with mitzvos as well as with the wonderful stories of the miracles Hashem performed and continues to perform for us. This strengthens our and our children's belief in Hashem's ever-guiding Hand.

The Talmud (*Megillah* 29a) tells us that when the redemption will come, all the synagogues and Torah study halls throughout the world will be transplanted to Eretz Yisrael. Those who infuse and permeate their homes with *emunah* and *bitachon* in Hashem, and describe the *hashgachah pratis* that He showers upon His people, actively transform their homes into dwellings of holiness. These homes, where mitzvah-filled Pesach Seders take place, will also merit being transported to Eretz Yisrael at the time of redemption.

This explains the words *Now we are here...* If on Pesach, as well as throughout the year, we fill our homes with Torah and *emunah,* those homes that are now in exile can next year be in Eretz Yisrael, transported together with all the synagogues and study halls to our Holy Land (*Derashos Chasam Sofer,* pp. 236, 249).

Thinking of Others

כָּל דִּכְפִין יֵיתֵי וְיֵכוֹל. כָּל דִּצְרִיךְ יֵיתֵי וְיִפְסַח... הָשַׁתָּא הָכָא, לְשָׁנָה הַבָּאָה בְּאַרְעָא דְיִשְׂרָאֵל

Whoever is hungry, let him come and eat! Whoever is needy — let him come and celebrate Pesach... Now we are here; next year may we be in the Land of Israel!

The Midrash tells us that when *Bnei Yisrael* were enslaved in Egypt, they banded together, making a pact in which they agreed to do *chesed* with one another (*Tanna D'Vei Eliyahu*, Ch. 23). The Chofetz Chaim explains that when *Bnei Yisrael* realized there was nothing they could do to save themselves from the servitude in Egypt, and their situation was becoming more dire, they understood that if they would act with kindness to each other, despite their personal pain, Hashem would reflect their *chesed*. He would treat them with kindness and ultimately redeem them. The kindness and love the Jewish people demonstrated toward each other became a catalyst for their early redemption.

It is written, כֹּה אָמַר ה' זָכַרְתִּי לָךְ חֶסֶד נְעוּרַיִךְ אַהֲבַת כְּלוּלוֹתָיִךְ, *So said Hashem: I recall for you the kindness of your youth, the love of your nuptials* (*Yirmiyahu* 2:2). Hashem says that for thousands of years He still recalls the "kindness of your youth" — the good deeds that we performed with each other when in Egypt (*Ahavas Chesed*, Vol. 2, Ch. 5). We recite this *pasuk* each year on Rosh Hashanah in the *Mussaf* prayers to remind Hashem, so to speak, of the *chesed* we did during the darkest days of our slavery and hope that as a result we will merit a favorable judgment.

How powerful and eternal are the acts of *chesed* of the Jewish people! For thousands of years, despite terrible exiles, persecutions, and difficult circumstances, the Jewish people have distinguished themselves as a nation rooted and established on foundations of *chesed* — kindness to each other that still serves as a *zechus* for us today.

In nearly every Jewish community, one can find organizations and *gemachim*, armies of people ready to help another Jew at any time, at any cost. Think of all the Hatzalah organizations whose members are ready to help, without pay, any moment of the day or late at night, in snow or rain, on Shabbos or Yom Tov, dressed in a suit or pajamas, wearing a *kittel* or tefillin. Financial assistance, medical equipment, Tomchei Shabbos, Bikur Cholim, Misaskim — find a Jew with a need, and there's another Jew there to fill it. Read the phone directories in many communities and find the pages and pages of *gemach* listings. *I recall for you the kindness of your youth* — Hashem never forgets these acts of *chesed*. They endure until today, forever invigorating the Jewish nation with life, success, and merit for redemption.

Bringing the Redemption

הָשַׁתָּא הָכָא, לְשָׁנָה הַבָּאָה בְּאַרְעָא דְיִשְׂרָאֵל. הָשַׁתָּא עַבְדֵי, לְשָׁנָה הַבָּאָה בְּנֵי חוֹרִין

Now we are here; next year may we be in the Land of Israel! Now we are slaves; next year may we be free men!

The Chasam Sofer asks how, in the current exile, we can gloriously recall our salvation from Egypt when we are suffering so much.

He answers that the Jews in Egypt were subject to a decree by Hashem to be exiled; they were אָנוּס עַל פִּי הַדִּבּוּר, *constrained by the word of God*, so the Jews in Egypt were not able to change their circumstances. Our redemption after 210 and not 400 years, as was initially decreed, didn't come about because of anything we did (according to some opinions); it happened because in an act of kindness Hashem counted the years of the exile from the birth of Yitzchak and not from when the Jews arrived in Egypt.

By contrast, during the present exile, we are given the ability to redeem ourselves and bring the redemption through charity, as it says, צִיּוֹן בְּמִשְׁפָּט תִּפָּדֶה וְשָׁבֶיהָ בִּצְדָקָה, *Zion will be redeemed through justice, and those who return to her through charity* (*Yeshayahu* 1:27).

With this understanding, it makes sense that we invite guests to the Seder table and say, "Now we are here in the exile." In the merit of the mitzvah of inviting others to eat with us and giving charity, a mitzvah that carries within it the ability to hasten the redemption, we can then say joyfully, "Next year we will be in Jerusalem!" (*Derashos Chasam Sofer*, Pesach 1; *Mahari Steif Haggadah*, p. 50).

The Yom Tov of Pesach is unique in the centrality that *chesed* and caring for others in need plays. Before Pesach begins, we are urged to give *ma'os chitin*, food for those less fortunate than we, a *chesed* that is not stressed before other Yamim Tovim. And, of course, we begin the Seder by inviting those who may not have a place to eat to join us.

Giving *tzedakah* is just one form of *chesed*. We should remember that *chesed* can be performed in a variety of ways, not necessarily involving financial assistance. Call a friend in need of a chat and some encouragement, set up a learning session with someone who can use attention or *chizuk*, bring cookies to a new neighbor, send parents or grandparents a letter or pictures — these are all forms of *chesed*. The Chofetz Chaim writes that one who davens for another Jew in need is also doing *chesed* (*Ahavas Chesed*, Ch. 8).

More, the Torah often repeats the mitzvah to love the convert, reminding us that we, too, were strangers in the land of Egypt. The *Sefer HaChinuch* (mitzvah 431) explains that an extension of this mitzvah is caring for anyone who is a stranger to town, someone new in the office, shul, or grocery store, a guest, an unmarried person in town without family, or a recent *ba'al teshuvah*. We should extend a hand to anyone in need, remembering that we, too, were once strangers in a foreign land. Anyone in need of assistance is considered a "stranger," and helping him fulfills the most oft-repeated mitzvah in the Torah: loving the stranger.

The *Tur* points out (*Siman* 429) that each of the three *mo'adim* corresponds to one of the three patriarchs, Pesach to Avraham, Shavuos to Yitzchak, and Succos to Yaakov. Avraham was the patriarch of *chesed*; Pesach, the Yom Tov of *chesed*, reflects his endless kindness. On Pesach we recall how we felt living in a foreign country among an alien culture. Those searing memories of our difficult beginnings bring us to empathize, understand, and feel compassion for those who feel lonely, misplaced, or uncomfortable in a new setting.

> Erev Pesach is one of the most hectic days of the year. Cleaning, cooking, bathing, last-minute errands, preparing for the Seder — the list of things to do seems endless. Rebbetzin Chaya Pincus always sought for ways to help others in their times of need. Many of her neighbors and friends recall receiving a delicious warm lunch from Rebbetzin Pincus on erev Pesach, the busiest

day of the year. She would say they surely had no time to think about lunch for themselves or their families on such a hectic day!

Rebbetzin Pincus tried to understand people's specific needs and fill them — chesed at its highest level. She taught us that chesed is not a means of satisfying one's personal need to do good, but a means of identifying and satisfying the true needs of others (Nefesh Chayah, page 339).

The mother of Rav Simcha Zissel of Kelm was known for her unwavering selflessness. She often collected charity for the needy people of Kelm, and she would circulate at funerals among the crowds collecting much-needed funds for distribution. When tragedy struck and her own daughter passed away, she collected funds for the poor at the funeral, saying, "Just because I'm in pain and agony, do the poor have to suffer?" (Tenuos HaMussar, Vol. 2, p. 26).

Rebbetzin Batsheva Kanievsky, the wife of Rav Chaim, was a special and holy woman whose heart was open to everyone, whatever their need. On a typical erev Shabbos she would send out homemade food packages, including fish, soup, challah, and kugel, to dozens of families. These included her extended family, close friends, and those in need. In addition to this, for more than 20 years Rebbetzin Kanievsky would send her leftover Shabbos food every motza'ei Shabbos to a poor family that lived nearby.

One motza'ei Shabbos, her grandson came to visit and saw his grandmother cooking a fresh pot of chicken soup. "Savta," he asked, "why are you making your chicken soup tonight right after Shabbos? Don't you usually make it on Thursday?"

"Yes," replied Rebbetzin Kanievsky, "but this week I need extra soup. Every motza'ei Shabbos I send the Shabbos leftovers to a family in need. This Shabbos we had some unexpected guests, and the chicken soup was finished. The poor family is going to be expecting my chicken soup, so I'm making a fresh pot for them" (Rebbetzin Kanievsky, p. 211).

The youngest present asks the reasons for the unusual proceedings of the evening.

מַה נִּשְׁתַּנָּה הַלַּיְלָה הַזֶּה מִכָּל הַלֵּילוֹת?

שֶׁבְּכָל הַלֵּילוֹת אָנוּ אוֹכְלִין חָמֵץ וּמַצָּה, הַלַּיְלָה הַזֶּה כֻּלּוֹ מַצָּה.

שֶׁבְּכָל הַלֵּילוֹת אָנוּ אוֹכְלִין שְׁאָר יְרָקוֹת, הַלַּיְלָה הַזֶּה מָרוֹר.

שֶׁבְּכָל הַלֵּילוֹת אֵין אָנוּ מַטְבִּילִין אֲפִילוּ פַּעַם אֶחָת, הַלַּיְלָה הַזֶּה שְׁתֵּי פְעָמִים.

שֶׁבְּכָל הַלֵּילוֹת אָנוּ אוֹכְלִין בֵּין יוֹשְׁבִין וּבֵין מְסֻבִּין, הַלַּיְלָה הַזֶּה כֻּלָּנוּ מְסֻבִּין.

Six Questions

מַה נִּשְׁתַּנָּה הַלַּיְלָה הַזֶּה מִכָּל הַלֵּילוֹת
Why is this night different from all other nights?

It happened during the darkest days of the Holocaust. A father and his young son were together in a concentration camp. The two had experienced unspeakable torture, starvation, and forced labor. On the night of the Pesach Seder, the father asked his frail young son to recite the four questions of the "Mah Nishtanah."

"Tatty," the young boy said, "this year I don't only have four questions. I have six!"

The boy recited the four questions of the "Mah Nishtanah," and then added, "Tatty, I have two more questions to ask. Will I be alive next year on Pesach so I can recite the 'Mah Nishtanah' again? And will you be alive to answer those questions for me?"

With tears in his eyes, the father replied, "My son, we don't know what the next moment will bring, and certainly we don't know what we face tomorrow or the next year. We don't know what our fate might be. So no, I can't answer those questions. But

The youngest present asks the reasons for the unusual proceedings of the evening.

Why is this night different from all other nights?

1. **On all other nights** we may eat *chametz* and matzah, but on this night — only matzah.
2. **On all other nights** we eat many vegetables, but on this night [we eat] *maror*.
3. **On all other nights** we do not dip even once, but on this night, twice.
4. **On all other nights** we eat either sitting or reclining, but on this night we all recline.

I can tell you with certainty that although we may not be here to make a Pesach Seder next year and recite the 'Mah Nishtanah,' somewhere in the world there will be Jews conducting the Pesach Seder. Hashem will never allow His nation to be eradicated!" (Chashukei Chemed Haggadah, p. 86).

365 Days of Matzah

הַלַּיְלָה הַזֶּה כֻּלּוֹ מַצָּה
But on this night — only matzah

Rav Yisrael Meir Lau, the former chief rabbi of Israel, once met a man who had immigrated to Israel from the Soviet Union. George wanted to receive Israeli citizenship and had to prove his Jewish identity. He brought a witness to substantiate his claim, a religious Jew with a long white beard who knew George and his family from Russia. That fellow told the rav the following story:

"George's mother worked as a nurse in Russia. She smoked several cigarettes a day, but each and every night she would take one cigarette out of the carton and place it in a bag in her closet. She did this every night of the year. Toward Purim time, I would come to George's house and collect a large bag with nearly 365 cigarettes set aside by George's mother, one for each day. With the profit from selling the cigarettes, she bought matzos for Pesach.

The Seder plate is returned. The matzos are kept uncovered as the Haggadah is recited in unison. The Haggadah should be translated, if necessary, and the story of the Exodus should be amplified upon.

עֲבָדִים הָיִינוּ לְפַרְעֹה בְּמִצְרַיִם, וַיּוֹצִיאֵנוּ יהוה אֱלֹהֵינוּ מִשָּׁם בְּיָד חֲזָקָה וּבִזְרוֹעַ נְטוּיָה. וְאִלּוּ לֹא הוֹצִיא הַקָּדוֹשׁ בָּרוּךְ הוּא אֶת אֲבוֹתֵינוּ מִמִּצְרַיִם, הֲרֵי אָנוּ וּבָנֵינוּ וּבְנֵי בָנֵינוּ מְשֻׁעְבָּדִים הָיִינוּ לְפַרְעֹה בְּמִצְרָיִם. וַאֲפִילוּ כֻּלָּנוּ חֲכָמִים, כֻּלָּנוּ נְבוֹנִים, כֻּלָּנוּ זְקֵנִים, כֻּלָּנוּ יוֹדְעִים אֶת הַתּוֹרָה, מִצְוָה עָלֵינוּ לְסַפֵּר בִּיצִיאַת מִצְרָיִם.

"George and his family didn't keep Shabbos or kosher, but his mother was adamant that they should have matzos for Pesach and conduct a Pesach Seder to recall the Exodus from Egypt."

After hearing the story, Rav Lau called George's mother, still residing in Russia, to confirm the events. She told the same remarkable story, and he told her, "Jews throughout the world fulfill the mitzvah of matzah once a year, but you have fulfilled the mitzvah of matzah 365 times a year. Your matzos have undoubtedly brought Hashem much honor and joy" (Yachel Yisrael Haggadah, p. 54).

Four Questions, One Answer

עֲבָדִים הָיִינוּ לְפַרְעֹה בְּמִצְרָיִם
We were slaves to Pharaoh in Egypt

The Chofetz Chaim states that after the children recite the four questions, they should not be put to bed, because their questions have not yet been answered (see *Mishnah Berurah* 472:50).

The recitation of עֲבָדִים הָיִינוּ לְפַרְעֹה בְּמִצְרַיִם, *We were slaves to Pharaoh in Egypt*, begins the response to the four questions. Abarbanel explains that the answer to all four of the children's questions is found in this passage.

The child wonders why on this night he sees signs of slavery intermingled with signs of freedom. The matzah and the *maror* are symbols of slavery and bondage, while reclining and dipping

The Seder plate is returned. The matzos are kept uncovered as the Haggadah is recited in unison. The Haggadah should be translated, if necessary, and the story of the Exodus should be amplified upon.

We were slaves to Pharaoh in Egypt, but HASHEM, our God, took us out from there with a mighty hand and an outstretched arm. Had not the Holy One, Blessed is He, taken our fathers out from Egypt, then we, our children, and our children's children would have remained subservient to Pharaoh in Egypt. Even if we were all men of wisdom, understanding, experience, and knowledge of the Torah, it would still be an obligation upon us to tell about the Exodus from Egypt.

---

vegetables are symbols of freedom and prosperity. We know that children often look for consistency. How can it be, the child asks, that on this night we symbolize such conflicting themes?

The leader of the Seder answers, עֲבָדִים הָיִינוּ לְפַרְעֹה בְּמִצְרָיִם — the Jewish nation was enslaved to Pharaoh in Egypt. This explains why we perform mitzvos that recall the Jewish nation's servitude.

Yet, the leader continues, וַיּוֹצִיאֵנוּ ה' אֱלֹהֵינוּ מִשָּׁם, *Hashem, our God, took us out from there* — Hashem redeemed us from the bonds of servitude, and we became a free nation. To commemorate our salvation, we perform acts that symbolize our freedom.

In just one sentence —עֲבָדִים הָיִינוּ לְפַרְעֹה בְּמִצְרָיִם וַיּוֹצִיאֵנוּ ה' אֱלֹהֵינוּ מִשָּׁם — all four of the child's questions are answered (*Zevach Pesach Haggadah*).

Why Was the Jewish Nation Enslaved?

☐ A small problem in the roots can evolve into a more serious concern in the fruit. Avraham Avinu, the progenitor of the Jewish nation, asked Hashem how he would know he would truly inherit the Land of Israel. This might seem to be a minor but serious deficiency in *bitachon*. Likewise, when Avraham and Sarah descended to Egypt, Avraham told Avimelech that Sarah was his sister so that he would not be killed, and Sarah was taken by Avimelech as a

וְכָל הַמַּרְבֶּה לְסַפֵּר בִּיצִיאַת מִצְרַיִם, הֲרֵי זֶה מְשֻׁבָּח.

- wife. This, too, might be regarded as a small deficiency in Avraham's *bitachon*. In order to repair this deficiency and ensure that the Jewish nation would be totally reliant on Hashem and recognize His abilities to change nature at His will, the Jewish nation was enslaved and through miracles redeemed (*Ramban, Bereishis* 12:10; *Maharal, Gevuros Hashem*).
- ☐ The brothers sold Yosef as a slave, and as a measure-for-measure punishment their children were forced into slavery (*Abarbanel, Bereishis* 15:2).
- ☐ In order to accept the Torah and merit the coveted title of Hashem's nation, the Jewish people were required to attain the traits of humility and subservience. Such traits could only be garnered through a period of servitude (*Shelah, Lech Lecha*).

The Power of a Story

וְכָל הַמַּרְבֶּה לְסַפֵּר בִּיצִיאַת מִצְרַיִם הֲרֵי זֶה מְשֻׁבָּח
The more one tells about the discussion of the Exodus, the more he is praiseworthy

Rav Yerucham Levovitz writes in the name of his Rebbi, the Alter of Slabodka, that Chazal are not merely praising a person who speaks at length about the Exodus. They are actually stating that the more a person speaks about the Exodus, the more he becomes elevated and superior; הֲרֵי זֶה — that is, the person himself — becomes more מְשֻׁבָּח, more worthy of praise, as every moment spent describing God's greatness through the story of our redemption from Egypt brings the person closer to Him.

The tale of our Exodus from Egypt is not merely a history lesson; it is a means of strengthening our *emunah* and *bitachon* in Hashem right now, in the present. The Torah doesn't want us merely to commemorate leaving Egypt; Hashem wants us to relive the past and change ourselves in the present by instilling in ourselves the

The more one tells about the discussion of the Exodus, the more he is praiseworthy.

very same feelings of *emunah*, *bitachon*, and love for Hashem that our ancestors experienced upon leaving Egypt. Therefore, the more one speaks about the Exodus and the miracles that Hashem performed for us, the more he brings himself closer to Hashem (*Da'as Chochmah U'Mussar*, Vol. 1, p. 116; *Lev Eliyahu*, Vol. 1, p. 318).

That's why it's not enough to relate the story in a matter-of-fact, dry manner, focusing on technical insights in the Haggadah. Our miraculous Exodus from Egypt must be told in an exciting, storylike fashion, transporting the listener to the times being described while instilling in him foundational values of *emunah* and *bitachon* in Hashem.

Stories have magic. When related effectively, a story can enter a soul and captivate a heart. Children, especially, can internalize the idea of Hashem's Omnipotence and the *hashgachah pratis* that He shows our nation through a gripping retelling of the story.

Rav Shamshon Refael Hirsch points out that the *pasuk* detailing the requirement to retell the story of the Exodus says, וּלְמַעַן תְּסַפֵּר בְּאָזְנֵי בִנְךָ, *And so that you may relate in the ears of your sons* (*Shemos* 10:2). The seemingly extra word *ears* indicates that the story of the Exodus must be told in a way that each and every individual present understands; it should speak to each person's ears. The story needs to be tailored to each and every listening ear in order to maximize its influence on the listener. The story should transform the past into the present and make what was into what is now. Hashem Who took us out of Egypt with love amid unbelievable miracles is the same Hashem Who continues to watch over us with love and *hashgachah pratis*.

The *pasuk* also tells us that we have a special mitzvah to tell the story to the children, to pass it on to the next generation. A story holds within it the power to leave an indelible impression on the young and permeable minds of children. The Chazon Ish encouraged parents to tell their children stories of great *rabbanim*, *tzaddikim*, and other noble Jewish personages as a means of positively influencing their children's character, development, and outlook. A meaningful story can make an

מַעֲשֶׂה בְּרַבִּי אֱלִיעֶזֶר וְרַבִּי יְהוֹשֻׁעַ וְרַבִּי אֶלְעָזָר בֶּן עֲזַרְיָה וְרַבִּי עֲקִיבָא וְרַבִּי טַרְפוֹן שֶׁהָיוּ מְסֻבִּין בִּבְנֵי בְרַק, וְהָיוּ מְסַפְּרִים בִּיצִיאַת מִצְרַיִם כָּל אוֹתוֹ הַלַּיְלָה. עַד שֶׁבָּאוּ תַלְמִידֵיהֶם וְאָמְרוּ לָהֶם, רַבּוֹתֵינוּ הִגִּיעַ זְמַן קְרִיאַת שְׁמַע שֶׁל שַׁחֲרִית.

אָמַר רַבִּי אֶלְעָזָר בֶּן עֲזַרְיָה, הֲרֵי אֲנִי כְּבֶן שִׁבְעִים שָׁנָה, וְלֹא זָכִיתִי שֶׁתֵּאָמֵר יְצִיאַת מִצְרַיִם בַּלֵּילוֹת, עַד שֶׁדְּרָשָׁהּ בֶּן זוֹמָא, שֶׁנֶּאֱמַר, לְמַעַן תִּזְכֹּר אֶת יוֹם צֵאתְךָ מֵאֶרֶץ מִצְרַיִם כֹּל יְמֵי חַיֶּיךָ.¹ יְמֵי חַיֶּיךָ הַיָּמִים, כֹּל יְמֵי חַיֶּיךָ הַלֵּילוֹת. וַחֲכָמִים אוֹמְרִים, יְמֵי חַיֶּיךָ הָעוֹלָם הַזֶּה, כֹּל יְמֵי חַיֶּיךָ לְהָבִיא לִימוֹת הַמָּשִׁיחַ.

---

everlasting positive impact on a child, guiding him or her on a path of Torah and mitzvos. The dinner table, Shabbos, and bedtime are all opportune times to relate to our children stories of great individuals who can serve as positive examples for them to follow, and this is especially true of Seder night (*Ma'aseh Ish*, Vol. 2, p. 47; *Kovetz Igros* 2:133; *Rav Shlomo Wolbe, Iggeres V'Ksavim* 2:290; *Toldos Yaakov*, foreword by *Rav Chaim Kanievsky*).

On the night of Pesach, the Chasam Sofer didn't delve into the deep mystical explanations of the Haggadah, nor did he deliver penetrating halachic discourses about the night's many mitzvos. He dedicated the Seder to simply explaining to his young sons and daughters what happened in Egypt and how Hashem miraculously punished the Egyptians and redeemed the Jewish nation. He translated each word of the Haggadah and explained the night's overarching themes and concepts, instilling in his family *emunah* and *bitachon* in Hashem (*Derashos Chasam Sofer*, vol. 2, p. 265; *Likutei Chaver ben Chaim*, p. 367).

It happened that Rabbi Eliezer, Rabbi Yehoshua, Rabbi Elazar ben Azaryah, Rabbi Akiva, and Rabbi Tarfon were gathered (at the Seder) in Bnei Brak. They discussed the Exodus from Egypt all that night until their students came and said to them: "Our teachers, the time has come for the reading of the morning *Shema*."

Rabbi Elazar ben Azaryah said: I am like a 70-year-old man, but I could not succeed in having the Exodus from Egypt mentioned every night, until Ben Zoma expounded it, as it is stated: "In order that you may remember the day you left Egypt all the days of your life."[1] The phrase "the days of your life" would have indicated only the days; the addition of the word "all" includes the nights as well. But the Sages declare that "the days of your life" would mean only the present world; the addition of "all" includes the era of the Mashiach.

---

1. *Devarim* 16:3.

Rabbi Michael Ber Weissmandel would recount to the children at the Seder the 10 plagues with such vividness that when he described the plague of wild beasts, one of the children ran to his bedroom in sheer terror (*Ish Chamudos*, p. 409).

This is what is asked of us on Seder night; this is the power of a story.

Each and Every Day

כֹּל יְמֵי חַיֶּיךָ לְהָבִיא לִימוֹת הַמָּשִׁיחַ
The addition of "all" includes the era of the Mashiach

We say in *Shemoneh Esrei*, וּבְנֵה אוֹתָהּ בְּקָרוֹב בְּיָמֵינוּ, *May You rebuild it [Jerusalem] soon in our days*. Rav Naftali of Ropshitz explains that Hashem rebuilds the *Beis HaMikdash* בְּיָמֵינוּ, **with**

בָּרוּךְ הַמָּקוֹם, בָּרוּךְ הוּא. בָּרוּךְ שֶׁנָּתַן תּוֹרָה לְעַמּוֹ יִשְׂרָאֵל, בָּרוּךְ הוּא. כְּנֶגֶד

our days. Every day we dedicate to the fulfillment of mitzvos adds bricks toward the ongoing reconstruction of the Beis HaMikdash.

Similarly, the *pasuk* says, 'בּוֹנֵה יְרוּשָׁלַיִם ה, *The Builder of Jerusalem is Hashem* (*Tehillim* 147:2). The word *boneh* is in the present tense, signaling that Hashem is presently involved in rebuilding the Beis HaMikdash. This is accomplished through "*yameinu*," our days, which are purpose driven, filled with *chesed*, and aimed at drawing close to Hashem; through this we actively participate in the rebuilding of the Beis HaMikdash (*Zera Kodesh, Toldos* and *Ki Seitzei*).

Likewise, we say here in the Haggadah, כֹּל יְמֵי חַיֶּיךָ, *all the days of your life.* Through maximizing each and every day in the service of Hashem, we will merit hastening לְהָבִיא לִימוֹת הַמָּשִׁיחַ, *to bring the era of Mashiach* (*Mekadshei Hashem*, Vol. 2, p. 83).

The renowned founder of Bais Yaakov, Sarah Schenirer, taught her students the value of time and the storehouses of potential growth that each day brings with it. She chose the *pasuk* לִמְנוֹת יָמֵינוּ כֵּן הוֹדַע, *So teach us the number of our days* (*Tehillim* 90:12), as one of the verses etched into the walls of all her Bais Yaakov schools. With these words, we daven to Hashem to help us use each moment as a unique opportunity to come close to Hashem and bring the final redemption (*Eim B'Yisrael*, Vol. 1, p. 179).

— *Think About It* —

Hashem's Constant Presence

בָּרוּךְ הַמָּקוֹם, בָּרוּךְ הוּא
Blessed is the Omnipresent; Blessed is He

Hashem is called "HaMakom" — literally, "the Place" — since His presence is found throughout the entire world, from the faraway galaxies to our very thoughts. We are never alone. There is never a place or a time when Hashem is not with us, cognizant of our thoughts, emotions, and concerns.

Blessed is the Omnipresent; Blessed is He. Blessed is the One Who has given the Torah to His people Israel; Blessed is He. Concerning

Another place where Hashem is referred to as HaMakom is in the *tefillah* with which we bless the Jewish mourner: הַמָּקוֹם יְנַחֵם אֶתְכֶם..., *May the Omnipresent comfort you...* Hashem is specifically referred to as HaMakom because when a close one passes away, a tremendous void is created in the mourner's life. Hashem, Whose presence is everywhere, is the One to fill that void with His presence, love, and care (see *Alei Meroros*, p. 313; *Harerei Kedem*, Vol. 2, p. 215).

The Haggadah refers to Hashem as HaMakom because Pesach was a time when Hashem performed miracles that demonstrated His Omnipresence here in this world. The open miracles of our redemption from Egypt confirmed Hashem's presence and connection to each Jew. He showed that He is HaMakom, the Omnipresent — ever so close.

Teaching the Women

בָּרוּךְ שֶׁנָּתַן תּוֹרָה לְעַמּוֹ יִשְׂרָאֵל
Blessed is the One Who has given the Torah to His people Israel

When Hashem told Moshe to teach the Jewish people the Torah, He commanded, כֹּה תֹאמַר לְבֵית יַעֲקֹב וְתַגֵּיד לִבְנֵי יִשְׂרָאֵל, *So shall you say to the House of Yaakov and relate to the Children of Israel* (*Shemos* 19:3). Rashi comments that כֹּה תֹאמַר לְבֵית יַעֲקֹב, *So shall you say to the House of Yaakov*, refers to the Jewish women, and וְתַגֵּיד לִבְנֵי יִשְׂרָאֵל, *And relate to the Children of Israel*, to the Jewish men. Moshe was instructed first to teach the women the Torah and mitzvos and then to proceed to the men.

Many commentators try to understand why Hashem told Moshe to address the women before the men when women are not even obligated in many areas of Torah study and mitzvos. The Maharsha explains (to *Sotah* 21a) that Hashem commanded the women first because they have the capability of influencing the men and children to adhere to the Torah and mitzvos. They can galvanize their husbands and children to learn Torah and keep mitzvos properly; they are the "*Bais Yaakov*," the very foundation and structure of the Jewish home.

Hence, the women were taught first regarding the Torah because it is they who are capable of directing their families toward a life of Torah and mitzvos.

It's written, וַיִּקְרָא הָאָדָם שֵׁם אִשְׁתּוֹ חַוָּה כִּי הִוא הָיְתָה אֵם כָּל חָי, *The man [Adam] called his wife's name Chavah because she had become the mother of all the living* (*Bereishis* 3:20). Rav Shamshon Refael Hirsch points out that Adam didn't call his wife Chayah, which denotes the giving of physical life. She was called Chavah, which indicates the giving of spiritual life. A mother not only provides her children with their physical needs; she is a central driving force in her children's spiritual lives as well. This is the unique and lofty responsibility of every Jewish mother who has been given the title "*eim kol chai*" (Rav Hirsch, *Bereishis* 3:20; *Collected Writings of Rav Hirsch*, Vol. 8, p. 93).

Many great Torah leaders have attributed much of their success in Torah to their mothers or wives. The Talmud (*Berachos* 17a) tells us that women merit great reward when they send their children to yeshivos and allow their husbands to go learn Torah. After a long day of caring for the children and working, cooking, throwing in a load of laundry, breaking up three fights, serving the kids supper, giving them showers, helping with homework — finally the father comes home. How tough it is to encourage him to go out again and learn a short while later! Yet this is where the woman's reward for *limud haTorah* lies.

Likewise, it is women who establish the atmosphere in the home and are the ones who, with their sensitivity and care, can tap into their children's hearts and direct them onto the path of Torah.

Rav Meir Shapiro, the chief rabbi of Lublin and founder of the *daf yomi* program, is directly responsible for hundreds of thousands of Jews setting aside time each day to learn a daily portion of the Talmud. Where was such a concept born? From where did Rav Shapiro draw his courage, strength, and love for Torah, spurring him to implement such a revolutionary idea in Torah learning?

In a personal letter, Rav Shapiro wrote, "The wise words of my mother have escorted me throughout my life and serve as a candle before my footsteps until this day." Rav Shapiro relates how a certain picture of his mother remained etched into his mind and had a profound impression on his development.

"It was when I was 7 years old," he wrote, "and it was the day after Isru Chag Pesach. I came home in the morning and saw that my mother was clearly worried about something. She was whispering to herself with tears in her eyes, 'A day past is a day that will never return. Who knows, who knows? The Torah is so big! Who knows, who knows?'

"I said, 'Mama, what happened? Is everything all right? Why are you crying and so worried?'

"My mother told me that before Pesach she had arranged for me to learn with a great rebbi from the town of Sochatchov, and here it was, already two days after Pesach, and they had heard no word from him. 'Do you know, my son,' my mother said, with tears pouring down her face, 'each day that passes without Torah study is a day that is lost forever. What will be?'

"My mother's tefillos were answered, and that very day the rebbi arrived. My mother's words, 'Each day that passes without Torah study is lost forever,' constantly resound in my mind. They drove me to create a program where each and every Jew will never have a day that passes without Torah study, and the daf yomi program was born" (HaOhr HaMeir, p. 20; Beis Yisrael, p. 223).

A well-known rabbi once approached Rav Elazar Shach, the rosh yeshivah of Ponevezh, seeking his advice about a dilemma he faced. Throughout the week, the rabbi said, he gave many Torah lectures, and he found himself with one weekly one-hour time slot available. Should he set aside that time for a Torah class for men or for women?

Without hesitation, Rav Shach responded that the shiur should be given to the women. Rav Shach smiled and explained, "When you teach women, the lessons and teachings will permeate the home and effectively be passed on to the rest of the family. Give the shiur to the women and you will accomplish double" (Eishes Lapidos, p. 75).

אַרְבָּעָה בָנִים דִּבְּרָה תוֹרָה. אֶחָד חָכָם, וְאֶחָד רָשָׁע, וְאֶחָד תָּם, וְאֶחָד שֶׁאֵינוֹ יוֹדֵעַ לִשְׁאוֹל.

חָכָם מָה הוּא אוֹמֵר? מָה הָעֵדֹת וְהַחֻקִּים וְהַמִּשְׁפָּטִים אֲשֶׁר צִוָּה יהוה אֱלֹהֵינוּ אֶתְכֶם?¹ וְאַף אַתָּה אֱמָר לוֹ כְּהִלְכוֹת הַפֶּסַח, אֵין מַפְטִירִין אַחַר הַפֶּסַח אֲפִיקוֹמָן.

One Torah for All

בָּרוּךְ הַמָּקוֹם, בָּרוּךְ הוּא.
בָּרוּךְ שֶׁנָּתַן תּוֹרָה לְעַמּוֹ יִשְׂרָאֵל, בָּרוּךְ הוּא.
כְּנֶגֶד אַרְבָּעָה בָנִים דִּבְּרָה תוֹרָה

Blessed is the Omnipresent; Blessed is He.
Blessed is the One Who has given the Torah
to His people Israel; blessed is He.
Concerning four sons does the Torah speak

The Torah is uniquely accessible to all levels of intelligence: only a work authored by Hashem could speak to each and every Jew, men and women alike, no matter their age, their degree of intelligence, or their level of observance. Every Jew can have a unique connection to the Torah.

Go to the library, and you'll find shelves of children's books, sections of young adult fiction, and works aimed at scientists or mathematicians. Not so Hashem's Torah. A second-grade boy or girl today learns the same *Chumash* that Moshe Rabbeinu studied, reads the same words that the greatest Torah luminaries have delved into since the day the Torah was given to us at Har Sinai.

The Torah in its infinite depth, unlike other studies or texts, can be understood on an infinite number of levels, and it is accessible to all. Calculus or nuclear physics can only be understood by the very brightest so it is inherently limited. The Torah is different. Hashem in His infinite and Divine abilities gave us the Torah, and each one of us can understand it according to our intellect and circumstances.

The Haggadah here drives home this point: the Torah has

four sons does the Torah speak: a **wise** one, a **wicked** one, a **simple** one, and **one who is unable to ask.**

The **wise son**—what does he say? "What are the testimonies, decrees, and ordinances which HASHEM, our God, has commanded you?"[1] Therefore explain to him the laws of the *pesach*-offering: that one may not eat dessert after the final taste of the *pesach*-offering.

---
1. *Devarim* 6:20.

---

specific messages for each of the four sons. We praise Hashem for giving us such a Torah, to which each and every Jew — girl, boy, child, teenager, adult, woman, and man — no matter their background or intelligence, can connect (*Ritva; Abarbanel; Haggadah MiBeis Levi,* quoting Rav Chaim Brisker).

Speech and the Essence of a Person

חָכָם מָה הוּא אוֹמֵר?

The wise son — what does he say?

Rav Baruch of Medzhibozh, the grandson of Rav Yisrael Baal Shem Tov, explains that from a person's words and manner of speaking one can ascertain his true essence: we are, in a sense, what and how we speak. As the Haggadah here states, חָכָם מָה הוּא אוֹמֵר, *The wise one — what does he say?* The wise son's words demonstrate his actual essence. The first Rebbe of Slonim called words "the pen of the heart": through words one relays his genuine character and feelings. If our speech is gentle, refined, clean, and measured, it reveals the authentic nature of our essence (*Botzina DiNehora, Imros Tehoros,* p. 49).

Speech: it's our most powerful tool, for good or for bad. The Chofetz Chaim writes, based on the Midrash, that the Jewish nation descended to Egypt and were eventually enslaved and persecuted because of the negative reports Yosef gave to his father concerning his brothers (introduction to *Chofetz Chaim*).

רָשָׁע מָה הוּא אוֹמֵר? מָה הָעֲבֹדָה הַזֹּאת לָכֶם?[1] לָכֶם וְלֹא לוֹ, וּלְפִי שֶׁהוֹצִיא אֶת עַצְמוֹ מִן הַכְּלָל, כָּפַר בְּעִקָּר — וְאַף אַתָּה הַקְהֵה אֶת שִׁנָּיו וֶאֱמֹר לוֹ, בַּעֲבוּר זֶה עָשָׂה יהוה לִי בְּצֵאתִי מִמִּצְרָיִם.[2] לִי וְלֹא לוֹ, אִלּוּ הָיָה שָׁם לֹא הָיָה נִגְאָל.

It's fitting, then, that the Midrash (*Tanchuma, Balak*) recounts that one of the virtues that merited the Jewish nation's release from Egyptian slavery was their restraint in not speaking *lashon hara* among themselves.

The Chofetz Chaim also tells us that one who speaks *lashon hara* transforms his mouth into an unfit receptacle that prevents *tefillos* from being heard by Hashem. Our very lives depend on our *tefillos*, which is why the answer to the question מִי הָאִישׁ הֶחָפֵץ חַיִּים אֹהֵב יָמִים לִרְאוֹת טוֹב, *Who is the man who desires life, who loves days of seeing good?* is נְצֹר לְשׁוֹנְךָ מֵרָע וּשְׂפָתֶיךָ מִדַּבֵּר מִרְמָה, *Guard your tongue from evil and your lips from speaking deceit* (*Tehillim* 34:13).

Guarding our speech and making an effort to learn the laws of *lashon hara* is a tried-and-tested method of bringing salvation and *berachah* into one's home. The Vilna Gaon writes that for each and every second during which one withholds speaking *lashon hara*, he merits a reward so great that no human or angel can describe it (*Iggeres HaGra; Even Sheleimah* 7:1).

Rav Yehudah Zev Segal, the Manchester *rosh hayeshivah*, would tell people that he had personally seen *berachah* and salvation in the homes of those who learned the laws of *lashon hara* from the *sefer Chofetz Chaim* daily.

Labor of Love

רָשָׁע מָה הוּא אוֹמֵר? מָה הָעֲבוֹדָה הַזֹּאת לָכֶם
The wicked son — what does he say?
"Of what purpose is this work to you?"

The evil son views Torah and mitzvah observance as an

The wicked son — what does he say? "Of what purpose is this work to you?"[1] He says, "To you," thereby excluding himself. By excluding himself from the community of believers, he denies the basic principle of Judaism. Therefore, blunt his teeth and tell him: "It is because of this that HASHEM did so for me when I went out of Egypt."[2] "For me," but not for him — had he been there, he would not have been redeemed.

---

1. *Shemos* 12:26. 2. Ibid., 13:8.

---

avodah, a hard, laborious service (*Roke'ach*, quoting *Yerushalmi, Pesachim* 10:4). Rav Levi Yitzchak of Berditchev writes that the word mitzvah comes from the word *tzavsa* which means "together" (*Kedushas Levi, Shemos* 22:12). Hashem commands us to perform mitzvos, not as a means of making us work or merely keeping us busy; it is, rather, a means of bringing us together with Hashem, so to speak, of drawing us closer to Him.

Investing time and effort into a project or helping an individual often brings a person closer to the recipients of the hard work. That's why, in a healthy husband-wife or parent-child relationship, when spouses and parents continuously give to each other and their children, their love for each other and their children increases.

But the evil son views mitzvah observance as a purely physical labor. He sees no resultant closeness to Hashem, and he therefore views the service of God as a burden.

A Perfect Set of Teeth

וְאַף אַתָּה הַקְהֵה אֶת שִׁנָּיו
Therefore, blunt his teeth

Why is the response to the evil son to blunt his teeth?
Rav Shmuel Dovid Walkin explains, based on the Talmud (*Arachin* 15b), that Hashem created the tongue within the mouth

תָּם מַה הוּא אוֹמֵר? מַה זֹּאת? וְאָמַרְתָּ אֵלָיו, בְּחֹזֶק יָד הוֹצִיאָנוּ יהוה מִמִּצְרַיִם מִבֵּית עֲבָדִים.¹

וְשֶׁאֵינוֹ יוֹדֵעַ לִשְׁאוֹל, אַתְּ פְּתַח לוֹ. שֶׁנֶּאֱמַר,

---

and guarded it with two walls, the teeth and the lips. These walls are intended to guard the tongue from speaking words of *lashon hara*, and to prevent a person from espousing ideas that are contrary to the Torah. The evil son clearly can't control his tongue and therefore has no need for his teeth, the natural walls that Hashem provided to control the tongue. Because of this, the evil son's teeth are "blunted" (*Kisvei Abba Mori*, p. 242).

A student of the Chofetz Chaim related that spending time in the home of his rebbi gave him the privilege of witnessing many extraordinary Torah and life lessons.

Once, when the Chofetz Chaim was already elderly and weak, and he was confined to bed, he called me over to him and told me to open his mouth. Naturally, I was hesitant, but when the Chofetz Chaim requested it a second time I couldn't refuse.

> Upon opening the Chofetz Chaim's mouth, I was stunned to see two rows of healthy, strong, perfectly shiny white teeth. This was very unusual in a time of minimal dental care.
>
> The Chofetz Chaim told me to count his teeth. I began counting and, lo and behold, he had exactly 32 teeth! He wasn't missing even one! He took my hand and, with a broad smile, said to me, "I watched over the mouth that Hashem gave me, and, in return, Hashem watched over my mouth for me."
>
> The best dental insurance plan is ensuring that our speech is free from all *lashon hara*.

A student of Rav Yaakov Kamenetsky was once privileged to drive his esteemed rebbi somewhere, and he prepared a list of questions that he wanted to ask. Unbeknownst to Rav Yaakov, the student placed a cassette tape recorder in his pocket.

The simple son — what does he say? "What is this?" Tell him: "With a strong hand did HASHEM take us out of Egypt, from the house of bondage."[1]

As for **the son who is unable to ask**, you must initiate the subject for him, as it is stated:

---

1. *Shemos* 13:14.

As they were driving, the tape recorder made a loud clicking noise, signaling that the tape was full and the recorder had shut. The student was terribly embarrassed, as Rav Yaakov heard the sound of the tape and surely knew that he was being surreptitiously recorded.

"Rebbi, I'm so embarrassed," the flustered student said. "I am so sorry that I was recording our conversation without asking your permission. I treasure the Rebbi's words and advice and just wanted to record them."

Rav Yaakov serenely replied, "There's nothing to be embarrassed about. I have never said anything in my life that I would regret if it were to be recorded and shared with others."

A Mother's Teachings

וְשֶׁאֵינוֹ יוֹדֵעַ לִשְׁאוֹל אַתְּ פְּתַח לוֹ
As for the son who is unable to ask, you must initiate the subject for him

Many Haggadah commentators discuss the use of the feminine pronoun *at*, "you," in this passage. It seems that the mother is urged to open up the heart of the son who has difficulty understanding the themes of Pesach night. Why is the mother the one to speak to this son and clarify his lack of understanding when it's the father who responds to the other three sons?

Rav Aryeh Zev Gurwicz, the former *rosh hayeshivah* of Gateshead, explains that there is a basic difference between the *chinuch* approaches of a father and a mother. A father teaches his child through intellect, study, and understanding, while a mother teaches with her power of love, care, concern, and emotion. Using intellectual tools to teach the child who has difficulty understanding will only result in failure and frustration. Therefore the mother, with her ability to penetrate the heart and soul, is responsible for teaching this particular child. A mother's love, concern, and connection to her son can influence his ability to follow in her ways and be a Torah Jew (*Me'orei She'arim*, p. 275).

The Chasam Sofer gives another reason for the use of the feminine form *at*. The Talmud (*Kiddushin* 49b) tells us that Hashem sent 10 portions of speech down to this world; women took nine-tenths of the portions and men took the remaining one-tenth. Women, then, tend to be naturally more talkative and men quieter and more concise in their speech. A father, naturally reserved, might mistakenly think that on the night of Pesach he should only briefly describe the Jewish nation's redemption from Egypt. He would, however, be wrong.

On this night, it is a mitzvah to recount in great detail the miraculous story of our redemption, as the Haggadah says, וְכָל הַמַּרְבֶּה לְסַפֵּר בִּיצִיאַת מִצְרַיִם הֲרֵי זֶה מְשֻׁבָּח, *The more one tells about the discussion of the Exodus, the more he is praiseworthy*. The Haggadah uses the feminine word *at* to inform all those at the Seder table to use women's natural gift for speech and expand on the topic of Hashem's miracles and our salvation (*Kerem HaTzvi Haggadah*, p. 31).

Rav Yonasan Steif wrote that a father is generally found outside the home, while the mother's continuous presence imbues the child with Torah values from the earliest age. The Haggadah tells us, אַתְּ פְּתַח לוֹ — you, the mother, are charged with opening up the child and introducing him to the Torah and mitzvos. The mother saying "*Modeh Ani*" with the child in the morning, washing his hands, teaching him *berachos*, davening, setting an example, and instilling in the child principles of Judaism opens up the child to the world of Torah and mitzvos (*Mahari Steif Haggadah*, p. 118).

The "son who is unable to ask" is a child who either has difficulty understanding or is young and inexperienced in life. Whichever type of a child he or she may be, a mother can have a lasting impact on the child's *chinuch* despite the child's youth or his intellectual shortcomings.

At the time of the Holocaust, hundreds of Jewish children were given over to Christian monasteries by their parents in the hope that this would save the children's lives from the Nazis. After the war ended, Rav Yosef Shlomo Kahaneman, the Ponevezher rav, went to a large monastery that he had been informed was housing dozens of Jewish children.

Rav Kahaneman, a man of action and fierce determination, walked into the monastery, which doubled as an orphanage, and asked the director to return all the Jewish children whose parents had given to the monastery under duress.

The monastery director regretfully informed him that there were so many orphans from varying denominations it would be impossible to identify which were Jewish.

"I would like to see the children for myself," the Ponevezher Rav insisted.

"I'm sorry, but that won't be possible," the supervisor said. The rabbi would be unable to identify which children were Jewish and which were not, so there was no point in disturbing the children.

"I only need one minute with them," Rav Kahaneman told him. "No more than 60 seconds."

Confident that the rabbi wouldn't be able to accomplish anything in one minute, the supervisor laughed and gave permission.

Rav Kahaneman entered the common area where the children were all gathered and in a loud voice cried out, "Shema Yisrael Hashem Elokeinu Hashem echad!"

The large auditorium was momentarily silent, and then suddenly nearly 200 children came running toward the Ponevezher Rav, crying, "Mama! Mama! Mama!"

Rav Kahaneman turned to the director. "These children are clearly Jewish, and they are coming back with me. They are coming back to the Jewish nation."

Every night before these young children would go to bed, their mothers would sit by their bedsides and recite Krias Shema with them. This is what they remembered and what remained with them from even the youngest ages, even when all their other ties to Yiddishkeit were lost (Tiferes Nashim, p. 40).

וְהִגַּדְתָּ לְבִנְךָ בַּיּוֹם הַהוּא לֵאמֹר, בַּעֲבוּר זֶה עָשָׂה יהוה לִי בְּצֵאתִי מִמִּצְרָיִם.[1]

יָכוֹל מֵרֹאשׁ חֹדֶשׁ, תַּלְמוּד לוֹמַר בַּיּוֹם הַהוּא. אִי בַּיּוֹם הַהוּא, יָכוֹל מִבְּעוֹד יוֹם, תַּלְמוּד לוֹמַר בַּעֲבוּר זֶה. בַּעֲבוּר זֶה לֹא אָמַרְתִּי אֶלָּא בְּשָׁעָה שֶׁיֵּשׁ מַצָּה וּמָרוֹר מֻנָּחִים לְפָנֶיךָ.

Also the Daughters

וְהִגַּדְתָּ לְבִנְךָ בַּיּוֹם הַהוּא
You shall tell your son on that day

The *pasuk* says that you should tell the story of the Exodus from Egypt to your "sons," which might imply that one is not obligated to tell it to his daughters. But many commentators explain that "sons" does not exclude daughters but is a generic term referring to children. According to the majority of opinions, a father has an obligation to tell the story of the Exodus to his daughters as well.

Rav Yechiel Michel Epstein, author of *Aruch HaShulchan*, writes, "It appears to me that even though with regard to many *halachos* there is no obligation to teach girls, on the night of Pesach they need to be told [the story of the Exodus] because the foundations of our belief [in Hashem] are dependent on the Exodus from Egypt" (*Magen Avraham* 471:7; *Kitzur Shulchan Aruch* 119:4).

The girls and women must also absorb the fundamental principles of the Torah and our belief in Hashem. Since this is the goal of retelling the story of the Exodus, the father is obligated to retell the story to both his sons and daughters.

A Living Example

בַּעֲבוּר זֶה לֹא אָמַרְתִּי אֶלָּא בְּשָׁעָה שֶׁיֵּשׁ מַצָּה וּמָרוֹר מֻנָּחִים לְפָנֶיךָ
The pronoun "this" implies something tangible; thus,

You shall tell your son on that day: "It is because of this that HASHEM did so for me when I went out of Egypt."[1]

One might think [that the obligation to discuss the Exodus commences] from the first day of the month of Nissan, but the Torah says: "You shall tell your son on that day." But the expression "on that day" could be understood to mean only during the daytime; therefore the Torah adds: "It is because of this [that HASHEM did so for me when I went out of Egypt]." The pronoun "this" implies something tangible, thus, "You shall tell your son" applies only at the time when matzah and *maror* lie before you — at the Seder.

---

1. *Shemos* 13:8.

"You shall tell your son" applies only at the time when matzah and maror lie before you — at the Seder

Rav Yaakov Rosenthal, a *talmid chacham* and former *dayan* from Eretz Yisrael, explained that the Haggadah here is alluding to the ultimate form of *chinuch*: וְהִגַּדְתָּ לְבִנְךָ, You shall **tell** your sons. If one wants to teach his child, then לֹא אָמַרְתִּי — "speaking" is not enough (the word *amarti* means "I spoke"). Rather, the most effective form of *chinuch* is אֶלָּא בְּשָׁעָה שֶׁיֵּשׁ מַצָּה וּמָרוֹר מֻנָּחִים לְפָנֶיךָ, *at the time when matzah and maror lie before you* — that is, when children see firsthand that their parents are involved in doing mitzvos, they will learn from them and follow their example (*Doresh Tov Haggadah*, p. 167; *Haggadah of Rav Shalom Schwadron* p. 89).

Rav Shamshon Refael Hirsch writes that the initiation of a child into the world of Torah and mitzvos parallels teaching a child to walk. When teaching a child to take his first steps, a parent doesn't simply command the child to start walking or explain to him that walking is accomplished by placing one foot in front of the other. Nothing will come of such instruction. Rather, a child

מִתְּחִלָּה עוֹבְדֵי עֲבוֹדָה זָרָה הָיוּ אֲבוֹתֵינוּ, וְעַכְשָׁו קֵרְבָנוּ הַמָּקוֹם לַעֲבוֹדָתוֹ.

is taught to walk by actual walking. A parent lifts the child to his feet, holds his hands, and begins to walk with him.

The same is true for teaching a child about Torah and mitzvos. Talking about Torah, mitzvos, and good character traits is not enough. A parent must bring his child into the world of mitzvos through mitzvos itself. The Haggadah is teaching us that the mitzvah of telling the story of our miraculous Exodus from Egypt is fulfilled when the matzah and *maror* are right there in front of the child, when the child can perform the mitzvos himself and witnesses his parents' involvement in these mitzvos (*Yesodos HaChinuch*, Vol.1, p. 55).

Sarah Schenirer, the educator par excellence of girls, explained that in order to impress children with Torah values, one shouldn't teach them through abstract concepts that their young and immature minds can't understand. Children need to be taught at the time *when the maror and matzah lie before them* — when there are visual aids and demonstrations for them to see, touch, and experience. By bringing Torah and mitzvos alive, we can truly tap into children's minds and hearts (*Eim B'Yisrael*, Vol. 1, p. 74; *Michtav MeEliyahu*, Vol. 4, p. 154).

On Seder night, how essential is the parents' role in providing a Torah education for your children! It's true that the central responsibility of a teacher is to provide children with knowledge, but it's the central mission of parents to teach their children how to fulfill the mitzvos. Children learn about the joy, spirit, and importance of doing mitzvos by watching how their parents perform the mitzvos and keep the Torah. All the knowledge that teachers impart to their students in school will be lost if parents don't serve as living examples of what their children are learning.

The night of the Pesach Seder is an opportune time for children to watch their parents perform mitzvos with joy and to be influenced forever by this positive exposure (*Yesodos HaChinuch*, Vol.1, p. 122). If a rebbi or *morah* teaches the children that it's not permissible to speak *lashon hara*, but a child hears his parents speaking *lashon hara*, he will very likely ignore what he heard

> Originally our ancestors were idol worshipers, but now the Omnipresent has brought us near to His service, as it is written:

---

from his rebbi or *morah* and follow his parents' real-life example. Children are most influenced by actions, not by words.

In this vein, the Mishnah says, לֹא הַמִּדְרָשׁ הוּא הָעִקָּר אֶלָּא הַמַּעֲשֶׂה, *It is not the teachings that are central but rather the actions* (*Avos* 1:17). Rav Shmuel Binyamin Sofer explains that the message of the Mishnah is that if one wishes to affect others, he has to understand that it's his actions, and not his words, that are truly significant (*Divrei Sofrim*, *Tehillim* 78).

A mother who wants to teach her child *berachos* or the importance of honoring parents can do so effectively by clearly and carefully reciting her *berachos* out loud and treating her parents, in-laws, and husband with respect. Through her example, her children (and all those around her husband included) will be positively influenced.

The days preceding Pesach offer prime opportunities for children to see their parents performing mitzvos with happiness, zeal, and meaning. When a child sees his mother cheerfully cleaning the house until the wee hours of the morning and watches his father taking down the Pesach dishes with loving care, he will treasure these memories, and as he grows up he will enjoy his own Pesach preparations. In a word, this is *chinuch*, and *chinuch* at its best.

The Door Is Always Open

מִתְּחִלָּה עוֹבְדֵי עֲבוֹדָה זָרָה הָיוּ אֲבוֹתֵינוּ,
וְעַכְשָׁו קֵרְבָנוּ הַמָּקוֹם לַעֲבוֹדָתוֹ

> *Originally our ancestors were idol worshipers, but now the Omnipresent has brought us near to His service*

The Talmud relates that there is an obligation the night of Pesach to מַתְחִיל בִּגְנוּת וּמְסַיֵּים בְּשֶׁבַח, *start [the Haggadah discussion] with the disgrace [of the Jewish nation] and conclude with its praise* (*Pesachim* 116a). There are two opinions in the Talmud on what exactly the nature of this "disgrace" is. Rav says that the "disgrace" lies in the mention of our forefathers' (i.e., Terach) worshiping of idols, whereas Shmuel finds it in the allusion to our being slaves to Pharaoh in Egypt (as we said a few passages above, עֲבָדִים הָיִינוּ לְפַרְעֹה בְּמִצְרָיִם, *We were slaves to Pharaoh in Egypt*). We then unanimously conclude with words of praise: וְעַכְשָׁיו קֵרְבָנוּ הַמָּקוֹם לַעֲבוֹדָתוֹ, *But now the Omnipresent has brought us near to His service.*

A vital lesson to learn from this halachah of starting with the disgrace and concluding with the praise is that we can change, and our change is accepted and desired by Hashem. When in Egypt, we were totally devoid of mitzvos. Nevertheless, Hashem redeemed us at this very point and made us His nation.

Rav Moshe Sternbuch writes that the Haggadah teaches us that no matter what one has done in the past or what one's family background may be, he can enjoy closeness to Hashem. Look at Avraham: his father, Terach, worshiped idols, and yet Avraham came incredibly close to Hashem.

One of the *yetzer hara*'s most effective tactics is to convince a person that he can't repair his past, that he can never overcome the effects of his family background, or that past mistakes make him unworthy of serving Hashem. The Haggadah here tells us that this is just not so. Hashem looks at the fruit and not the tree, the present and not the past. Hashem eagerly awaits our return. The door to *teshuvah* is never closed (*Haggadah Ta'am V'Da'as*, p. 55).

Rav Naftali of Ropshitz points out that this is what we say in Kiddush: תְּחִלָּה לְמִקְרָאֵי קֹדֶשׁ, *It is the first of the holy festivals.* Rav Naftali interprets this as saying that one who wishes to start fresh on a life of holiness shouldn't be discouraged by past mistakes. Why? As the Kiddush continues, זֵכֶר לִיצִיאַת מִצְרָיִם, *commemorating the Exodus from Egypt* — he should recall how Hashem took us out of Egypt despite our low spiritual status and made us into His treasured nation (*Zera Kodesh*, *Shemos* 13:3; *Pri Tzaddik*, Pesach 24).

Also, the Maharal says that since Pesach was the birth of the Jewish nation, it's a time of freshness and new beginnings, a time to shed our old limitations and begin anew (*Gevuros Hashem* 39). The Jewish nation emerged from Egypt like a baby emerges from his mother's womb. Despite the nation's spiritual deficiencies, Hashem gave the Jews fresh spiritual wellsprings and strength. We were not just freed from Egypt; we were reborn. So too each year, the night of the Seder, Hashem grants each of us this special ability of refreshing ourselves and making changes (*Sichos HaRav Pincus*, p. 36).

The Torah describes the presence of Hashem as הַשֹּׁכֵן אִתָּם בְּתוֹךְ טֻמְאֹתָם, *dwelling with them [the Jewish people] amid their contamination* (*Vayikra* 16:16). Hashem redeemed us and made us into His nation at a time when we were devoid of any spirituality because His love for us isn't dependent on anything and is therefore eternal. Rav Tzadok HaKohen finds in this the reason for the daily mitzvah to recall the redemption from Egypt. One must constantly recall how Hashem redeemed the Jewish nation and pulled them from the lowest spiritual depths, raising them to great levels of holiness. So too one should never despair of receiving Hashem's help and guidance despite challenges and difficulties. *Yei'ush*, hopelessness, has no place in the hearts of the Jewish people (*Pri Tzaddik*, Pesach).

We can change for the better; we shouldn't hesitate to take steps forward because of past steps taken backward. Despite past wrongdoings, Hashem still loves us and helps those who want to change and improve (see *Toras Avos Haggadah*, p. 55).

Rav Yerucham Levovitz, the famed *mashgiach* of Mir, writes that Avraham became Avraham Avinu *because* he was the son of Terach — because he had to fight, battle, and overcome his family education and heritage. It is as a result of this that he was capable of becoming the leader and father of *Klal Yisrael*.

We too have the ability to overcome our earlier shortcomings. Rav Chaim of Volozhin discusses the mishnah that records, עֲשָׂרָה נִסְיוֹנוֹת נִתְנַסָּה אַבְרָהָם אָבִינוּ, Avraham Avinu was tested with 10 tests (*Avos* 5:3) Why does the Mishnah specifically describe Avraham here as "Avinu," our father?

Rav Chaim explains that Avraham bequeathed his ability to overcome challenges to his children for all generations to come. We are all the children of Avraham Avinu, and ingrained in our DNA is the unique ability to rise above challenges and overcome difficulty. This is why we find throughout the history of the Jewish nation that even unlearned Jews who were ignorant of Torah gave up their lives to sanctify Hashem's Name (*Ruach Chaim*, *Avos* 5:3).

שֶׁנֶּאֱמַר, וַיֹּאמֶר יְהוֹשֻׁעַ אֶל כָּל הָעָם, כֹּה אָמַר יהוה אֱלֹהֵי יִשְׂרָאֵל, בְּעֵבֶר הַנָּהָר יָשְׁבוּ אֲבוֹתֵיכֶם מֵעוֹלָם, תֶּרַח אֲבִי אַבְרָהָם וַאֲבִי נָחוֹר, וַיַּעַבְדוּ אֱלֹהִים אֲחֵרִים. וָאֶקַּח אֶת אֲבִיכֶם אֶת אַבְרָהָם מֵעֵבֶר הַנָּהָר, וָאוֹלֵךְ אוֹתוֹ בְּכָל אֶרֶץ כְּנָעַן, וָאַרְבֶּה אֶת זַרְעוֹ, וָאֶתֵּן לוֹ אֶת יִצְחָק. וָאֶתֵּן לְיִצְחָק אֶת יַעֲקֹב וְאֶת עֵשָׂו, וָאֶתֵּן לְעֵשָׂו אֶת הַר שֵׂעִיר לָרֶשֶׁת אוֹתוֹ, וְיַעֲקֹב וּבָנָיו יָרְדוּ מִצְרָיִם.¹

בָּרוּךְ שׁוֹמֵר הַבְטָחָתוֹ לְיִשְׂרָאֵל, בָּרוּךְ הוּא. שֶׁהַקָּדוֹשׁ בָּרוּךְ הוּא חִשַּׁב אֶת הַקֵּץ, לַעֲשׂוֹת כְּמָה שֶׁאָמַר לְאַבְרָהָם אָבִינוּ בִּבְרִית בֵּין הַבְּתָרִים, שֶׁנֶּאֱמַר, וַיֹּאמֶר לְאַבְרָם, יָדֹעַ תֵּדַע כִּי גֵר יִהְיֶה זַרְעֲךָ בְּאֶרֶץ לֹא לָהֶם,

---

— Think About It —

Hashem's Unconditional Love

וְעַכְשָׁיו קֵרְבָנוּ הַמָּקוֹם לַעֲבוֹדָתוֹ
But now the Omnipresent has brought us near to His service

The Haggadah tells us that the very inception of our nationhood was anything but glorious. We came from a family of idol worshipers, with Terach as the forefather, and we were redeemed from Egypt and became the nation of Hashem at a time of extreme spiritual crisis.

This teaches us that we are so loved and wanted by Hashem that He chose us despite our family history and despite past sins. We should never think our upbringing or past history impedes the love Hashem has for us. מִתְּחִלָּה עוֹבְדֵי עֲבוֹדָה זָרָה הָיוּ אֲבוֹתֵינוּ, *Originally our ancestors were idol worshipers* — although our past was far from Hashem — וְעַכְשָׁיו, *right here, tonight*, קֵרְבָנוּ הַמָּקוֹם לַעֲבוֹדָתוֹ,

Yehoshua said to all the people, "So says HASHEM, God of Israel: Your fathers always lived beyond the Euphrates River, Terach the father of Avraham and Nachor, and they served other gods. Then I took your father Avraham from beyond the river and I led him through all the land of Canaan. I multiplied his offspring and gave him Yitzchak. To Yitzchak I gave Yaakov and Eisav; to Eisav I gave Mount Seir to inherit, but Yaakov and his children went down to Egypt."[1]

Blessed is He Who keeps His pledge to Israel; Blessed is He! For the Holy One, Blessed is He, calculated the end of the bondage in order to do as He said to our father Avraham at the Covenant between the Parts, as it is stated: He said to Avram, "Know with certainty that your offspring will be aliens in a land not their own,

---

1. *Yehoshua* 24:2-4.

Hashem draws us close to him.

Hashem doesn't expect us to be perfect, and He has a special deep love for those who have risen despite challenges and adversity. Pesach is a special and unique time to strengthen our relationship with Hashem and internalize the unconditional love and care He has for us.

A Preamble to Mashiach

וַיֹּאמֶר לְאַבְרָם יָדֹעַ תֵּדַע כִּי גֵר יִהְיֶה זַרְעֲךָ בְּאֶרֶץ לֹא לָהֶם וַעֲבָדוּם וְעִנּוּ אֹתָם אַרְבַּע מֵאוֹת שָׁנָה

He said to Avram, "Know with certainty that your offspring will be aliens in a land not their own, they will serve them, and they will oppress them 400 years

Tishah B'Av 1946. The Holocaust had come to an end just one year earlier; the pain of the loss was still excruciating.

וַעֲבָדוּם וְעִנּוּ אֹתָם, אַרְבַּע מֵאוֹת שָׁנָה. וְגַם אֶת הַגּוֹי אֲשֶׁר יַעֲבֹדוּ דָּן אָנֹכִי, וְאַחֲרֵי כֵן יֵצְאוּ בִּרְכֻשׁ גָּדוֹל.[1]

Rav Yosef Shlomo Kahaneman had lost his wife, children, and hundreds of students in the devastation that had befallen the Jewish people. After reciting the final lamentation of "Eli Tzion," Rav Kahaneman stood up to speak.

"The great author of this lamentation teaches all the generations a great and encouraging lesson," he said. "He compares the many exiles the Jewish nation has undergone to a woman in labor. But the two seem to be totally dissimilar! Of course, the laboring woman feels severe pain, but she understands that in just a short while that pain will be transformed into joy and happiness with the birth of her child. But after the pain of our exiles, the numerous pogroms, the Inquisition, after the terrible Holocaust, what joy are we expecting?

"Despite our wounds," Rav Kahaneman continued, "despite our sorrow, we understand that all the pain that the Jewish people have experienced is truly a preamble to the birth and coming of Mashiach and the Final Redemption. The more intense the pain, the closer we are to Hashem's ultimate salvation" (HaRav MiPonevezh, Vol. 3, p. 152).

The Women's Sacrifice

וַעֲבָדוּם וְעִנּוּ אֹתָם אַרְבַּע מֵאוֹת שָׁנָה
They will serve them, and they will oppress them four hundred years

Hashem told Avraham that his children would be enslaved in Egypt for 400 years, but the slavery lasted only 210 years. The commentators provide several reasons as to why the Jewish nation's term of slavery in Egypt was so drastically reduced, and a number of those explanations are directly connected to the role of women in the story:

☐ The original decree from Hashem was that only the Jewish men were to be enslaved. Yet Pharaoh went and enslaved

they will serve them, and they will oppress them 400 years; but also upon the nation which they shall serve will I execute judgment, and afterward they shall leave with great possessions."[1]

---

1. *Bereishis* 15:13-14.

---

the women as well. Because of this, the time frame for the Jewish nation's enslavement was greatly shortened. The unwarranted women's servitude contributed to the decrease in the length of time the Jewish people needed to complete before they were to be redeemed (*Vayaged Avraham*, quoted in *Otzar Divrei HaMefarshim*, p. 233). This also explains why the Egyptians were punished even though Hashem had decreed that the Jews should be placed into servitude. Hashem only decreed that the men should be forced into labor and not the women. The Egyptians were punished for imposing slavery on the women as well (*Avnei Kodesh, Shemos*).

☐ In the merit of the righteous Jewish women of the generation, the entire Jewish nation's term of slavery was considerably reduced (*Parashas Derachim* 5; *Ein Yaakov*).

☐ The Midrash (*Eliyahu Rabbah* 25) recounts that the Jews merited leaving Egypt early due to the exceptional self-sacrifice of the four Matriarchs, Sarah, Rivkah, Rachel, and Leah. Sarah, who had not yet borne children, gave her maidservant Hagar to her husband, Avraham, in the hopes that a child would be born and the promise of the Jewish nation would be fulfilled. Rivkah left her entire family to marry Yitzchak. Rachel gave her sister Leah the secret code that Yaakov had provided her to spare Leah any embarrassment. Leah, seeing that she had ceased having children, gave her maidservant Zilpah to Yaakov in order to swell the numbers of *Klal Yisrael*. Each of the four mothers' actions was difficult and involved overwhelming sacrifice, and in the merit of these sacrifices Hashem greatly reduced the Jewish nation's enslavement in Egypt years later.

Women's sacrifice for their people and for Torah didn't only happen thousands of years ago.

> Rav Yosef Shlomo Kahaneman worked tirelessly after the Holocaust to establish a place of Torah in Israel, and he founded Ponevezh Yeshivah in Bnei Brak with tremendous self-sacrifice. Many people thought that Rav Kahaneman was delusional in his drive to build a yeshivah in Bnei Brak. Told by someone once that his idea of building a yeshivah was just a dream, Rav Kahaneman responded, "You're correct, it is a dream, except that when you dream, you're sleeping. When I dream, I'm wide awake."
>
> Rav Kahaneman persevered and, despite the challenges and ridicule, went on to build one of the largest and most prestigious Torah institutions in the world. When questioned about where he derived his powerful determination to go against the tides of his time, he explained that his love for the Torah and his ability to sacrifice for it was an inheritance from his mother.
>
> "When I was 3 years old, my widowed mother, my two older brothers, and I lived in terrible poverty. We were so impoverished that there was only one winter coat and one winter hat for all three boys. The bitter Russian winter set in. Snow began to fall heavily, and walking outside without proper winter gear was downright dangerous, even life threatening. Our cheder was a 20-minute walk from home, but with temperatures falling to minus 10 degrees and heavy snowfall, it seemed like we would be staying home for a while.
>
> "My mother understood that each and every day a child needs to learn and grow in Torah whatever the circumstances. What did she do? Early in the morning, while we were still sleeping, she would wake my oldest brother, dress him in the only winter garments we had, and walk with him through the icy Russian winter morning. When they arrived at the yeshivah, she would take off his boots and winter garments and place him near the stove to warm up. She returned back home with the sole set of winter garments, dressed my other brother, walked with him through the freezing temperatures and deep snow, and repeated the process. She then returned a third time for me.
>
> "Six times a day, there and back, my mother trudged through the Russian winters, proudly taking her sons to yeshivah, delighted to sacrifice so they could become Torah scholars. It

was from my mother that I drew the strength and determination to build a yeshivah and sacrifice for Hashem's people!" (L'ha'er, p. 50).

Being Sensitive to Others

וַעֲבָדוּם וְעִנּוּ אֹתָם אַרְבַּע מֵאוֹת שָׁנָה
They will serve them, and they will oppress them 400 years

The Midrash says that one of the reasons the Jewish nation was punished with the long and torturous Egyptian servitude was because the children of Leah belittled their half-brothers who were born to Bilhah and Zilpah, the maidservants (see *Otzar Midrashim* by Y. D. Eisenstein, p. 486). In order to make the Jewish people understand that no one Jew should feel superior to his brothers, Hashem decreed a time period of servitude in which all of the Jewish people equally would be placed under Egyptian servitude, crushing any attitude of supremacy.

We see from this the awful repercussions of insulting others and demonstrating a lack of sensitivity to our fellow Jew.

When Hashem chose Moshe as the leader of the Jewish people and their future redeemer from the terrible Egyptian slavery, Moshe initially refused. Why? Didn't he care about his Jewish brethren's pain and suffering? Rav Chaim Shmulevitz explains (*Sichos Mussar* 5) that Moshe hesitated because Aharon, his older brother, might feel hurt if he, the younger brother, was given the leadership position over the Jewish people. Moshe was willing to relinquish this awesome mission so as not to insult his older brother, Aharon!

We learn from the earlier story of Tamar and Yehudah that it's better to be thrown into a fiery furnace than to shame another Jew publicly (*Sotah* 10b). Even though Tamar had a prophetic vision that great kings, the Sanhedrin, and Mashiach would descend from her, she was willing to sacrifice her life and the life of her future illustrious progeny and be burned to death rather than embarrass Yehudah (*Ohr HaTzafun*, Vol. 1, p. 212).

Here is a much more recent example of such sensitivity to another Jew:

The matzos are covered and the cups lifted as the following paragraph is proclaimed joyously. Upon its conclusion, the cups are put down and the matzos are uncovered.

וְהִיא שֶׁעָמְדָה לַאֲבוֹתֵינוּ וְלָנוּ, שֶׁלֹּא אֶחָד בִּלְבָד עָמַד עָלֵינוּ לְכַלּוֹתֵנוּ. אֶלָּא שֶׁבְּכָל דּוֹר וָדוֹר עוֹמְדִים עָלֵינוּ לְכַלּוֹתֵנוּ, וְהַקָּדוֹשׁ בָּרוּךְ הוּא מַצִּילֵנוּ מִיָּדָם.

As a young boy, Rav Aharon Leib Steinman lived in Brisk, and he was a ben bayis in the home of the Brisker Rav, Rav Yitzchak Zev Soleveitchik. Little Aharon Leib frequented the home of the great Torah luminary, soaking up the Torah and mitzvos that were the mainstay of the Soleveitchik home.

When Rav Steinman turned 7, he suddenly stopped visiting the home of the Brisker Rav. "The Brisker Rav lost a daughter at the age of 7," he explained. "I am now 7, and I'm afraid that when I come to visit him it will remind him of his child who died, and cause him pain. I'm willing to sacrifice spending time in the Rav's home so as not to cause him pain!" (Gadol B'Kirbecha, p. 36).

How do we become more sensitive to others?

The first step is to internalize that there *is* another, someone else with real feelings, emotions, and sensitivities. Once you begin to look at people as they are, and not through the prism of who you are, you can attempt to discover what they're feeling and what may be troubling them.

Say you have a daughter who recently became engaged. If you're sensitive to others, you'll be careful to limit discussions about the wedding plans with a friend who still has a daughter in *shidduchim*.

Another example: Someone is telling you a story, a piece of news, or a *devar Torah*. If you say, "I know this story; I heard this *devar Torah* once already," you will see the speaker's excitement and pride vanish, transformed into feelings of awkwardness and dejection, as if the stage on which he is performing has collapsed beneath him. Isn't it worth hearing a story a second time rather than show such insensitivity to a fellow Jew? (See *Iggeres HaTiyul* by the Maharal's brother, *Chelek HaPeshat*, p. 31.)

The matzos are covered and the cups lifted as the following paragraph is proclaimed joyously. Upon its conclusion, the cups are put down and the matzos are uncovered.

It is this that has stood by our fathers and us. For not only one has risen against us to annihilate us, but in every generation they rise against us to annihilate us. But the Holy One, Blessed is He, rescues us from their hand.

The Midrash teaches, אָמַר לָהֶם הַקָּדוֹשׁ בָּרוּךְ הוּא לְיִשְׂרָאֵל בָּנַי אֲהוּבַי כְּלוּם חָסַרְתָּ דָּבָר שֶׁאֲבַקֵּשׁ מִכֶּם אֲנִי מְבַקֵּשׁ מִכֶּם אֶלָּא שֶׁתִּהְיוּ אוֹהֲבִין זֶה לָזֶה וְתִהְיוּ מְכַבְּדִין זֶה לָזֶה, So says Hashem to the Jewish people: "My beloved children, am I missing anything that I need you to do anything on My behalf? All I ask from you is that you should love each other and respect each other!" (*Tanna D'Vei Eliyahu* 28:15).

The Vital Role of Women

וְהִיא שֶׁעָמְדָה לַאֲבוֹתֵינוּ וְלָנוּ
It is this that has stood by our fathers and us

The word *v'hi* is in the feminine form, a hint to the central role of Jewish women in the survival of our people despite insurmountable challenges. *Bnei Yisrael* were freed from Egypt before the 400-year term of servitude was completed in the merit of righteous Jewish women. Queen Esther played a central role in the revocation of the evil decree passed by Haman when he tried to eradicate the Jewish nation. Yehudis killed Halifornes, a general in the Greek army, which helped the Jewish armies defeat the Greeks during the time of the Chanukah story.

The Midrash (*Yalkut Shimoni, Rus* 4:606) teaches that this is not only true of past redemptions, but also for the future, Final Redemption. It is written, זָכַר חַסְדּוֹ וֶאֱמוּנָתוֹ לְבֵית יִשְׂרָאֵל, *He recalled His kindness and His faithfulness to the House of Israel* (*Tehillim* 98:3). The *pasuk* doesn't say לִבְנֵי יִשְׂרָאֵל, referring to the Jewish men; it says לְבֵית יִשְׂרָאֵל, a reference to the women. As it happened in the past, so it will happen in the future: through Jewish women Hashem will recall, so to speak, His kindness and faithfulness, and through them He will redeem the Jewish nation!

Elsewhere, the Midrash (*Shir HaShirim Rabbah* 4:13) tells us that the Jewish people were given three essential supplies throughout their 40 years of wandering in the wilderness in the merit of three great leaders. Because of Moshe, the Jewish nation was awarded the manna; in the merit of Aharon, they were protected with the Clouds of Glory; and in the *zechus* of Miriam, they were given the well that constantly supplied them with water in the hot, parched wilderness.

Rav Moshe Sternbuch explains, based on the *Chovos HaLevavos* (*Sha'ar HaBechinah* 5), that the more essential something is to human survival, the more accessible Hashem made it in the world. For example, air, the most essential necessity for life, is found in abundance nearly everywhere and is free. Man can survive without a roof over his head but not without food, so food is more accessible and cheaper to find than lodging. Water is even more essential to human survival than lodging and food, and therefore water covers nearly 70 percent of the planet and is inexpensive.

But not in the wilderness. In the wilderness, water is scarce. And in the merit of Miriam, *Bnei Yisrael* miraculously had water, the most fundamental necessity for life. So it is with Jewish women. Righteous Jewish women are vital to the Jewish nation, enveloping their homes with an atmosphere and a spirit that creates closeness to Hashem and His mitzvos (*Ta'am V'Da'as*, Bamidbar 20:2).

Rav Shimshon Pincus points out that the determining factor of a child's Jewishness is his mother. As long as his mother is Jewish, the child will be Jewish. Jewish women are the lifeblood and pulse of the Jewish nation (*Nefesh Chayah*, p. 8).

— Think About It —

A Protected People

וְהִיא שֶׁעָמְדָה לַאֲבוֹתֵינוּ וְלָנוּ
It is this that has stood by our fathers and us

Pesach is a time to strengthen our *emunah* and *bitachon* in Hashem. A brief look at our history clearly demonstrates

Hashem's ever-protecting Hand and how He keeps his promise to His eternal people. Despite the destruction of the two *Batei Mikdash*, the long exile, and endless persecutions, the trauma of the Inquisition, despite hundreds of years of pogroms culminating in the horrors of the Holocaust, despite current intifadas and the global anti-Semitism that we see more clearly every day — despite all this, the Jewish people still live; moreover, they are thriving and growing.

During that first exile in Egypt, we were persecuted and enslaved, but we survived and Hashem brought us out as a purified, priestly nation. That pattern of exile and pain followed by Hashem's redemption has continued throughout our history. The Midrash compares the Jewish nation to a lone sheep surrounded by 70 wolves, symbolic of the 70 nations of the world eager to devour us (*Esther Rabbah* 10:11; *Tanchuma, Toldos* 5). Yet we survive and have grown.

Rabbi Yaakov Emden writes, "When I contemplate the miracle of the survival of the Jewish people, it is in my mind greater than all the miracles and wonders that Hashem performed for our ancestors in Egypt, in the wilderness, and in Eretz Yisrael. The longer the exile endures, the more apparent the miracles and strength of Hashem becomes (*Siddur Beis Yaakov, Sulam Beis Kel*; see *Yoma* 65b). כִּי לֹא יִטֹּשׁ ה' אֶת עַמּוֹ, *For Hashem shall not forsake His people* (*I Shmuel* 12:22) — we are an eternal nation, openly protected, guarded, and enveloped by Hashem.

— Think About It —

Symbol of Salvation

Why do we lift the cup while we say "*V'Hi She'amdah*"?

The passage of "*V'Hi She'amdah*" mentions the continuous protection and salvation that Hashem provides for the Jewish people. David HaMelech wrote (*Tehillim* 116:13): כּוֹס יְשׁוּעוֹת אֶשָּׂא וּבְשֵׁם ה' אֶקְרָא, *I will lift up a cup of salvations and call out in the Name of Hashem*. Reflecting the concept written in the *pasuk*, we lift our cups of wine as we speak of Hashem's salvations (*Roke'ach*).

Also, we lift the cup as we say, וְהִיא שֶׁעָמְדָה לַאֲבוֹתֵינוּ וְלָנוּ, *It is this that has stood by our fathers and us*, because it is the lifting of the cup of wine that has actually stood by us. Chazal prohibited a Jew drinking wine with a non-Jew as a means of preventing assimilation. Wine was commonly regarded as a fraternizing beverage — think of the expression "drinking buddies" — and a barrier restricting a Jew from drinking with non-Jews prevented assimilation, thereby preserving the Jewish nation's existence.

The cup of wine is lifted while we say these words to symbolize that the miracle of our continuous existence happened because we have remained separate and distinct from the non-Jews (*Divrei Chaim; Rav Naftali of Ropshitz; Meshech Chochmah, Shemos* 6:6).

"The World Needs You!"

שֶׁבְּכָל דּוֹר וָדוֹר עוֹמְדִים עָלֵינוּ לְכַלּוֹתֵנוּ
In every generation they rise against us to annihilate us

The Bluzhever Rebbe, Rav Yisrael Spira, his wife Perel, and their only daughter were seized by the Nazis and taken to the gas chambers. Before they were mercilessly brought to their deaths, an SS soldier approached the group and shouted, "Are there any men here younger than 45?"

Not wanting to leave his wife and young daughter at such a dark and terrifying time, Rav Spira remained silent. But Perel wanted to save her husband's life, gathered up her courage and called out, "Here, my husband is under 45."

Rav Spira, determined to remain with his wife and daughter, quickly corrected her and claimed to be over 50. The furious Nazi soldier yelled at the Rebbe, "You want the privilege of dying with your wife and daughter? You don't want to work? Well, you will work, and only then will we kill you!"

The face of the Rebbe was ashen. Words can't describe his pain at the thought of parting from his wife and daughter. But Perel, a true *eishes chayil*, was a pillar of comfort and strength. At this terrible and terrifying moment, she looked at her husband for one last time and said, "Yisrael, go! The world will need you yet! Stay strong and survive. The world will need you!"

After experiencing untold miracles, the Bluzhever Rebbe survived the war and went on to become a leading Torah founder in America, amassing thousands of students and followers and revitalizing Torah Jewry after the war. The world truly did need the Bluzhever Rebbe (Chassidic Tales of the Holocaust, p. 115).

Guardian of the Home

שֶׁבְּכָל דּוֹר וָדוֹר עוֹמְדִים עָלֵינוּ לְכַלּוֹתֵנוּ

In every generation they rise against us to annihilate us

In every generation the Jewish nation faces enemies who seek to destroy it. Sometimes the Jewish nation's foes are clear, as they want physically to wipe us out: Haman, the Crusaders, the Inquisitors, the Cossacks, the Nazis, Hamas. In other generations, the Jewish nation's enemies are not as apparent, as they wage a spiritual war against our people and the qualities, values, and standards we hold dear.

Shortly before her death, Sarah Schenirer, the founder of the Bais Yaakov movement, wrote in her will to her students the following moving passage: "After the destruction of the *Beis HaMikdash*, which the Kohanim were responsible to guard, the responsibility of guarding our homes, our miniature *batei mikdash*, has been entrusted to the Jewish women. They are the Kohanim of today's *batei mikdash*, the homes of the Jewish people" (*Eim B'Yisrael*, Vol. 2, p. 177).

The general atmosphere of the home and what is brought into the home is largely determined by the mother. This is why Rabbi Yose referred to his wife as "*beisi*," my house — because she was the one protecting the very essence of the home itself (*Shabbos* 118b).

A wife is also called "*chomah*," wall (*Yevamos* 62b), since she is the one to build a protective wall around her husband and family, safeguarding her family's spiritual well-being.

In today's morally deprived society, technological advances threaten everything the Jewish family holds sacred, and the mother of the home faces an awesome responsibility. She needs to be vigilant to ensure that her home is a fortress strong enough to withstand the overbearing onslaught of ideas and influences that run contrary to the Torah outlook.

The Jewish Nation Lives

אֶלָּא שֶׁבְּכָל דּוֹר וָדוֹר עוֹמְדִים עָלֵינוּ לְכַלּוֹתֵנוּ, וְהַקָּדוֹשׁ בָּרוּךְ הוּא מַצִּילֵנוּ מִיָּדָם

But in every generation they rise against us to annihilate us. But the Holy One, Blessed is He, rescues us from their hand

The Jewish nation is extraordinary, unique; it is *Am HaNivchar*, the Chosen Nation of Hashem. Our very existence is fundamental proof of this, as our nation still lives despite thousands of years of persecution and anti-Semitism. The great and mighty kingdoms of Greece, Rome, and Persia, history's most powerful empires, are all but forgotten, while the small Jewish nation continues to thrive despite constant threats to its survival.

Dr. Moshe Rothschild was once driving in Rome with Rav Yosef Shlomo Kahaneman, the Ponevezher Rav. During the drive, Rav Kahaneman repeated over and over again, "I'm going to settle the score with him once and for all."

> Dr. Rothschild wondered to whom he was referring to. The answer was soon apparent.
>
> As they neared the Arch of Titus, Rav Kahaneman asked the driver to stop the car. Getting out, he neared the famous monument and said, "Titus, Titus, 2000 ago you wanted to wipe the Jewish people off the face of the earth. Titus, who even knows about you today? Where are the vestiges of all your great feats? Nothing is left of you. Your philosophies, your dynasty, it's all irrelevant!
>
> "Now I'm here from Bnei Brak, where over 500 students are learning Torah in my yeshivah. And the Torah is alive and thriving not only in my yeshivah. In hundreds of yeshivos and kollelim throughout the world, thousands of Jews are learning Torah, keeping mitzvos, and perpetuating the words of Hashem!
>
> "I invite you to go to Eretz Yisrael and see the thousands of Jews praying and learning there daily, awaiting the rebuilding of the Beis HaMikdash you destroyed, beseeching God for its return. We, the Jewish nation, and our Torah are pulsating with life, while you and all that you stand for have been forgotten

for all eternity" (Aleinu L'Shabei'ach, Vol. 3, p. 547; L'Toraso Emunaso, p. 16; see also L'Os U'Le'ad, p. 645).

The Tenacity of a Jew

אֶלָּא שֶׁבְּכָל דּוֹר וָדוֹר עוֹמְדִים עָלֵינוּ לְכַלּוֹתֵנוּ, וְהַקָּדוֹשׁ בָּרוּךְ הוּא מַצִּילֵנוּ מִיָּדָם

But in every generation they rise against us to annihilate us. But the Holy One, Blessed is He, rescues us from their hand

It happened on the eve of Yom Kippur 1944. Kalman Mann and his teenage son, Yitzchak, stood in formation in their forced-labor battalion, starving, weak, and haggard. A well-fed and handsomely clothed German officer announced that although tomorrow was the Day of Atonement, when Jews are obligated to abstain from food and drink, as workers of the Third Reich, they were required to eat so they would be strong enough to work. Any Jew who fasted would be shot to death by a firing squad.

The next day, Yom Kippur, was especially difficult for the Jews, who were forced to work under deplorable conditions while relentless rains pounded down on their frail, shattered bodies. Those who recalled the Yom Kippur tefillos chanted them quietly, their tears mingling with the falling rain. When their meager rations were handed out, all the Jews in Kalman and Yitzchak's work division, even those who hadn't been religious before the war, surreptitiously spilled their coffee on the ground and hid their soaked pieces of bread, to be eaten after dark.

At last, the workday ended and night set in. The starving Jewish workers were eager to break their fast and rest their weary bodies. But the Germans had other plans. The Jews were ordered to gather for roll call at the foot of a mountain. The German commander began to speak.

"We are fully aware that you Jews fasted today, yet we won't shoot anyone. Instead we give you a choice. You may repent and admit that you sinned by disobeying orders and fasting. If you don't want to repent and admit your wrongdoings, you are ordered to climb this mountain and slide down through the wet mud on your stomachs. Those who wish to repent raise your hands."

צֵא וּלְמַד מַה בִּקֵּשׁ לָבָן הָאֲרַמִּי לַעֲשׂוֹת לְיַעֲקֹב אָבִינוּ, שֶׁפַּרְעֹה לֹא גָזַר אֶלָּא עַל

Not one hand was raised. The German officer ordered the Jews, still fasting and exhausted, to run up the mountain and slide down through the mud on their stomachs. When they reached the bottom, they were again given the choice of either "repenting" or repeating the exercise. Again, not one Jew repented, and they were forced to run up the steep mountain and slide down through the mud. This went on until midnight, after which the defiant Jews were given food and allowed to rest from their humiliating and exhausting punishment.

A young German officer walked over to the group of courageous Jews and said, "I don't know who will win this war, but one thing I'm sure of: people like you and a nation like yours will never be defeated!" (Chassidic Tales of the Holocaust, p. 101).

The Remedy Is in the Punishment

וְהַקָּדוֹשׁ בָּרוּךְ הוּא מַצִּילֵנוּ מִיָּדָם
But the Holy One, Blessed is He, rescues us from their hand

Difficult, painful, even agonizing things sometimes happen, and sometimes we don't understand why. If we have *bitachon*, though, we understand that we're incapable of seeing the full picture, and that Hashem, the Mastermind behind the world and our lives, loves us and knows what is best for us.

Moreover, at times Hashem unexpectedly provides our salvation by means of the very hands that sought to destroy us: מַצִּילֵנוּ מִיָּדָם, *He rescues us from their hand*. He saves us through the evil plans set up to hurt us.

Immediately after the Holocaust, many Jews had a spiritual thirst to lay their hands on a volume of Talmud since they had been deprived of precious Torah study for so many long years. The United States Army sponsored a printing of the Talmud, and a festive dedication gathering was to be held in the main party room of the city. The United States Army chaplain stationed

Go and learn what Lavan the Aramean attempted to do to our father Yaakov! For Pharaoh decreed only against the males,

in the displaced persons camp approached Rav Yaakov Galinsky, a superb orator, to deliver words of inspiration and encouragement to the participants of the celebration.

Rav Galinsky asked the chaplain why the affair was to take place in the city hall and not in the local camp dining room. The chaplain responded, "Do you know what happened in the city hall where the celebration of the Talmud dedication is going to take place? Let me tell you. It was in that very hall that Hitler, yemach shemo, publicized his work, Mein Kampf, in which he blatantly proclaimed his plan for total Jewish genocide. It will be in that very same hall where we will celebrate the printing of the Talmud, which confirms the eternity of the Jewish nation!" (Vayevaser Yaakov, p. 199).

Pharaoh sought to kill all the Jewish boys. The result was that Moshe, the savior of *Bnei Yisrael*, was raised in Pharaoh's *very own* royal palace. Haman had a 50-foot gallows built to hang Mordechai the Jew; because of that wicked plan, Haman himself was hung on his *very own* handiwork.

The Midrash tells us, *The wound itself supplies the bandage* (*Shemos Rabbah* 23:3). Hashem sends the remedy within the punishment itself, as it says, עֵת צָרָה הִיא לְיַעֲקֹב וּמִמֶּנָּה יִוָּשֵׁעַ, *It will be a time of trouble for Yaakov, through which he shall be saved* (*Yirmiyahu* 30:7) — from the trouble will come the salvation (*Birkas Peretz, Shemos*).

The Power of Tehillim

צֵא וּלְמַד מַה בִּקֵּשׁ לָבָן הָאֲרַמִּי לַעֲשׂוֹת לְיַעֲקֹב אָבִינוּ

Go and learn what Lavan the Aramean attempted to do to our father Yaakov!

The Midrash says that Yaakov used to recite the entire book of *Tehillim* while living in Lavan's house, and this is one of the reasons that *Tehillim* is called "*tehillos Yisrael*," Yisrael's praises,

הַזְּכָרִים, וְלָבָן בִּקֵּשׁ לַעֲקוֹר אֶת הַכֹּל. שֶׁנֶּאֱמַר:

Yisrael referring to Yaakov, who was given the additional name Yisrael (*Bereishis Rabbah* 68:11).

> The Chofetz Chaim was once brought out the *Tehillim* of his mother. With much emotion, the Chofetz Chaim kissed the old, tear-stained *Tehillim* and said to those present, "Do you know how many tears my mother spilled while saying these words of *Tehillim*? Each day, before I got up in the morning, she would recite *Tehillim* and beseech Hashem that her son, Yisrael Meir, should grow up to be a forthright and good Jew."
>
> What strength there is in a mother's *tefillos*! The Chofetz Chaim's mother davened that her son should be a good Jew, and look what Klal Yisrael merited (*HaMe'oros HaGedolim*, p. 397; *Chofetz Chaim: Chayav U'Po'alav*, Vol. 1, p. 26).

Finding a few minutes a day to say *Tehillim* may not be quite so simple for many women who are juggling countless responsibilities. But placing a *Tehillim* in one's purse, car, or desk, and reciting even just one or two chapters when waiting at the doctor's office, in line at the store, or when things are quiet at home, allows a woman to tap into tremendous wellsprings of *berachah* for herself, her family, and the Jewish people.

> Rav Eliyahu Yitzchak Filmer, the menahel of Yeshivas Chevron, once met Rav Yitzchak Zilberstein. Rav Filmer happily told Rav Zilberstein that he was on his way to get 150 shots.
>
> "A hundred and fifty shots?" Rav Zilberstein asked. "Where do you go to get 150 shots?"
>
> "I'm on my way to the Kosel to recite the book of *Tehillim*," Rav Filmer explained. "All 150 chapters. Each chapter of *Tehillim* has its own unique healing powers, like immunizations and vitamins for the body and soul. Every chapter of *Tehillim* carries with it tremendous berachos that are vital for the physical and spiritual well-being of every Jew" (*Barchi Nafshi*, Vol. 2, p. 97).

Any possible life struggle or difficulty that a person can possibly experience in his lifetime is expressed in *Tehillim*. When David HaMelech wrote *Tehillim*, he composed *tefillos* to address every issue that his people would ever face, whether related to health, sustenance, child-rearing, or any other challenge (*Ma'or*

and Lavan attempted to uproot everything, as it is said:

VaShemesh, *Shemos* 23:25; *Malbim*, introduction to *Tehillim*).

The Shelah (to *Yoma* 28) writes that the chapters of *Tehillim* are a protection for oneself, one's family, and the entire generation, and through them one merits all forms of *berachah* and success.

> Nearly 1,000 years ago, the Crusaders were crisscrossing Europe and devastating Jewish communities in the name of their religion. One town had escaped the wrath of these marauding murderers. In this town lived an old man, totally unlearned and not even able to study Talmud or Mishnah. The old man passed away and was buried by the town's Jewish burial society. Thirty days later, the deceased man appeared to the local rav in a dream, dressed in white and holding a small sefer.
>
> The rav recognized the the elderly man they had buried just a few short weeks before. "What is that small sefer you're holding in your hand?" he asked.
>
> "This small sefer is a sefer Tehillim, and I have come to you to warn the inhabitants of the town to escape from the fast-approaching Crusaders before it's too late. Evil is about to beset the community. All the years I lived here I recited the entire sefer Tehillim each day, and this protected the town all those years. But now that I have passed away, the merit of my Tehillim recitation is no longer there to help you, and the city will be attacked!"
>
> The rav awoke and quickly wrote a letter to the townspeople, warning them of the impending danger. Many of the inhabitants heeded the rav's warning and escaped. Those who disregarded the dream and its warning as a joke were killed when the Crusaders attacked the town soon after (*Minhagos Vermaiza*, p. 281).

Who Was Worse — Lavan or Esau?

וְלָבָן בִּקֵּשׁ לַעֲקוֹר אֶת הַכֹּל

And Lavan attempted to uproot everything

Who was Yaakov's worst enemy? Who most nearly succeeded in destroying him and his family? The Haggadah here suggests

אֲרַמִּי אֹבֵד אָבִי, וַיֵּרֶד מִצְרַיְמָה וַיָּגָר שָׁם בִּמְתֵי מְעָט, וַיְהִי שָׁם לְגוֹי, גָּדוֹל עָצוּם וָרָב.¹

וַיֵּרֶד מִצְרַיְמָה. אָנוּס עַל פִּי הַדִּבּוּר.

וַיָּגָר שָׁם. מְלַמֵּד שֶׁלֹּא יָרַד יַעֲקֹב אָבִינוּ לְהִשְׁתַּקֵּעַ בְּמִצְרַיִם, אֶלָּא לָגוּר שָׁם. שֶׁנֶּאֱמַר, וַיֹּאמְרוּ אֶל פַּרְעֹה, לָגוּר בָּאָרֶץ בָּאנוּ, כִּי אֵין מִרְעֶה לַצֹּאן אֲשֶׁר לַעֲבָדֶיךָ, כִּי כָבֵד הָרָעָב בְּאֶרֶץ כְּנָעַן, וְעַתָּה יֵשְׁבוּ נָא עֲבָדֶיךָ בְּאֶרֶץ גֹּשֶׁן.²

בִּמְתֵי מְעָט. כְּמָה שֶׁנֶּאֱמַר, בְּשִׁבְעִים נֶפֶשׁ יָרְדוּ אֲבֹתֶיךָ מִצְרָיְמָה, וְעַתָּה שָׂמְךָ יהוה אֱלֹהֶיךָ כְּכוֹכְבֵי הַשָּׁמַיִם לָרֹב.³

---

that Lavan was the most destructive, yet we never find in the Torah that Lavan sought to kill Yaakov at all. Lavan did try to fool Yaakov, but surely that's less serious than Esav's intentions to kill Yaakov and his family. Why wasn't Esav chosen as the paragon of evil, the quintessential enemy of Yaakov?

Rav Nissim Telushkin explains that Lavan was more dangerous than Esav. Esav was a clear-cut enemy of Yaakov, and his evil intentions were known to all. Lavan, on the other hand, told Yaakov concerning his children, הַבָּנוֹת בְּנֹתַי וְהַבָּנִים בָּנַי, *The daughters are my daughters, and the sons are my sons* (*Bereishis* 31:43), implying that he would never do anything to hurt them; they were his family too. Lavan attempted to befriend Yaakov and his family, with the intention that his evil ways would gradually permeate their minds and hearts.

Spiritual destruction is far worse than physical destruction. That's why Lavan was chosen as the prime example of one who sought to uproot Yaakov and the Torah virtues he represented (*Al Matzos U'Merorim Haggadah*, p. 62; *Bamidbar Rabbah* 21:5).

An Aramean attempted to destroy my father. Then he descended to Egypt and sojourned there, with few people; and there he became a nation — great, mighty, and numerous.[1]

Then he descended to Egypt — compelled by Divine decree.

He sojourned there — this teaches that our father Yaakov did not descend to Egypt to settle, but only to sojourn temporarily, as it says: They (the sons of Yaakov) said to Pharaoh: "We have come to sojourn in this land because there is no pasture for the flocks of your servants, because the famine is severe in the Land of Canaan. And now, please let your servants dwell in the land of Goshen."[2]

With few people — as it says: With seventy persons, your forefathers descended to Egypt, and now HASHEM, your God, has made you as numerous as the stars of heaven.[3]

---

1. *Devarim* 26:5. 2. *Bereishis* 47:4. 3. *Devarim* 10:22.

One Nation, One Soul

בְּשִׁבְעִים נֶפֶשׁ יָרְדוּ אֲבוֹתֶיךָ מִצְרָיְמָה
With 70 persons your forefathers descended to Egypt

When Yaakov and his family descended to Egypt, they numbered 70 souls. The Torah employs the singular form *nefesh*, "soul," to teach us that though the Jewish people numbered 70 individuals, they were one large cohesive family, living in peace and unity (see *Rashi, Bereishis* 46:27, *Ponevezh Haggadah*, p. 127, and *Ohr Yechezkel, Middos* 112). *Klal Yisrael* is one nation. Whatever our backgrounds or differences, we are all brothers and sisters: we are all the children of Hashem. When there is unity in the home, in the community, and among the Jewish nation at large, it brings special blessings from Hashem.

In the year 1913, the Russian government falsely accused Menachem Mendel Beilis of slaughtering a non-Jewish child in order to use the child's blood for the Pesach matzos. The trial was not only a charge against Mendel Beilis; it was an accusation made against the entire Jewish populace, and its outcome would affect the very survival of Jews throughout the world.

One of the main pieces of incriminating evidence used in the Beilis Trial was the Talmudic passage that states, אַתֶּם קְרוּיִים אָדָם, וְאֵין עוֹבְדֵי כּוֹכָבִים קְרוּיִים אָדָם, "You [the Jewish people] are called "man," and idolaters [non-Jews] are not called "man" (Yevamos 61a). Clearly, said the Russian prosecutors, the Jews had no regard for the life of non-Jews, since according to the Talmud they don't have the status of a man; obviously, then, Jews would kill a non-Jewish child for their needs.

The greatest rabbanim convened to discuss the matter. How could they explain this Talmudic passage that seemed to prove the Jewish people's disregard for non-Jewish life?

Rav Meir Shapiro provided a brilliant understanding of the Talmudic passage that was presented to the Russian judge.

Had a Russian citizen been wrongly convicted of a crime, he said, would it arouse the compassion and concern of the entire Russian population, to the point where they would feel as if they themselves were sitting on the defendant's bench, facing a death sentence? Yet, in the case of Menachem Mendel Beilis, the plight of one Jew raised the concern and support of all Russian Jewry, as well as Jewish communities and rabbanim throughout the world.

The Talmud is telling us, then, that the entire Jewish nation is referred to collectively as "adam," one man. Each Jew cares sincerely for his fellow Jew, no matter who he is or where he can be found. The Jewish people are like one body, where one part of the body feels the pain of another.

On the other hand, would a non-Jewish Russian citizen in Moscow feel the pain of a wrongly convicted fellow Russian living in Vladivostok? Certainly not. Non-Jewish people do not have the status of one person, not because they aren't considered human but because they have no intimate familial connection with their countrymen.

The explanation of Rav Meir Shapiro, the tremendous show of Jewish support, and some obvious falsities in the case *convinced the judge to clear Mendel Beilis of all wrongdoing, and he was set free (HaOhr HaMeir, p. 67; see Apiryon, Tazria).*

We see the tremendous outpouring of concern and prayer in the face of tragedy and challenge: when a child goes missing, when the "three boys" in Eretz Yisrael were kidnapped, during Hurricane Sandy. Suddenly a person's headgear, dress, accent, or level of observance stops being a part of the discussion, and all that matters is that our brothers or our sisters are suffering and need our help. And we see it in our own everyday lives as well: when Chaveirim come to help a stranded passenger, when a Hatzolah volunteer leaves his Shabbos table to assist in a medical emergency, or when a volunteer delivers a hot meal and a smile to a homebound Holocaust survivor.

No matter what *nusach* we daven or what style of clothing we wear, we are one nation, one family, whose care and concern for each other is fundamental to our identity and survival.

Full of Potential

וְעַתָּה שָׂמְךָ ה' אֱלֹהֶיךָ כְּכוֹכְבֵי הַשָּׁמַיִם לָרֹב

And now Hashem, your God, has made you as numerous as the stars of heaven

Rav Yisrael Baal Shem Tov explains the deeper meaning of the comparison between the Jewish nation and the stars.

Look up at the sky: the stars seem minuscule and minute, tiny dots of light. Yet in reality these stars can be many times the size of planet Earth. Although on the outside a Jew may appear ordinary and simple, each Jew is infused with tremendous potential and the ability to become great and unique. Every Jew, no matter how small he or she seems, can be as great as one of those faraway stars (*Baal Shem Tov, Lech Lecha*).

Reaching for the Stars

וְעַתָּה שָׂמְךָ ה' אֱלֹהֶיךָ כְּכוֹכְבֵי הַשָּׁמַיִם לָרֹב

And now Hashem, your God, has made you as numerous as the stars of heaven

It is written, וּמַצְדִּיקֵי הָרַבִּים כַּכּוֹכָבִים לְעוֹלָם וָעֶד, *And those who* teach righteousness to the masses [will shine] like the stars forever and ever (Daniel 12:3). The Talmud says regarding this *pasuk*, *This refers to those who teach children* (Bava Basra 8b). Teaching is compared to the stars, forever shining.

What an awesome responsibility! Doctors provide expert care for the physical health of a patient, but teachers must provide attentive care and dedication for the spiritual welfare of their students. A doctor's checkup promotes physical health; a Torah lesson promotes spiritual growth that has far-reaching effects for generations.

In a letter to teachers of girls' schools, Rav Elazar Menachem Mann Shach impressed on them the far-reaching impact their actions and words could have on their students. A teacher who encourages a student, supports her through difficult times, understands her fears and hopes, will not only help that student, she will mold and shape that student's future and the future of all the student's children and her children's children for generations (*Michtavim U'Ma'amarim*, Vol. 2, 397).

> Rav Shlomo Heiman was the rosh yeshivah of Torah Vodaath in Brooklyn from 1935 to 1945. His shiurim were legendary and are still studied today in yeshivos all over the world.
>
> One winter day, there was a massive snowstorm, and only four dedicated students came to yeshivah. Despite the poor attendance, Rav Shlomo delivered the shiur in his usual emotional style, expending the same amount of energy as when the beis midrash was full. One of the students said to him, "Rebbi, there are only four of us here today. Why did you put so much effort into the shiur as if the room was filled with talmidim?"
>
> "Only speaking to you four?" Rav Heiman replied. "Not at all! I'm speaking to you, to your children, and to your grandchildren. I'm speaking to your students and your students' students and their students!"
>
> The influence a teacher has on a child is eternal, going on for generations: like the stars, lighting up the night sky from generation to generation (*Shemen Rosh*, Vol. 9, p. 8).

What makes a great teacher — and a great parent, for that matter — whose students and children will be open to learning?

The Mishnah says that one should exemplify the ways of Aharon HaKohen, the paradigm of אוֹהֵב אֶת הַבְּרִיּוֹת וּמְקָרְבָן לַתּוֹרָה,

loving people and drawing them close to Torah (*Avos* 1:12). The Tiferes Yisrael explains that in order to "draw people close to the Torah" one has to love them. Students are receptive to the lessons teachers impart only if they feel they are loved and cared for by the teacher.

Rav Chaim Friedlander, the *mashgiach* of Ponevezh, explains that the individual attention and encouragement that teachers shower on their students can unleash their potential, build confidence, and energize the children to want to grow further. Like water to a seed, a teacher's genuine concern for his or her students will allow them to develop and shine (*Mesillos Chaim B'Chinuch*, p. 96; see also *Ma'aseh Ish*, Vol. 1, p. 64, and *HaChazon Ish B'Dorosav*, p. 258).

> Rav Shlomo Zalman Auerbach's nephew was getting married. The young man was also a student of Rav Shach, and right before the start of the wedding, a disagreement erupted. Here were two great Torah giants. Who should be honored with conducting the wedding ceremony?
>
> Arguments about kibbudim at a wedding are not unheard of, but this was a very unusual case, since each rav wanted the honor to be given to the other. Rav Shach said that the honor belonged to Rav Shlomo Zalman, as the uncle of the chassan. But Rav Shlomo Zalman said to Rav Shach, "I'm just an uncle, but you, Rav Shach, as the rebbi and rosh yeshivah of the chassan, you are the father!"
>
> Without a rebuttal, Rav Shach went up to the chuppah to be mesader kiddushin (Kazeh Ra'ah V'Chanech, p. 313).

> Rav Yosef Elias, dean of the Bais Yaakov Rabbi Samson Raphael Hirsch girls' school, asked Rav Yaakov Kamenetsky if he was obligated to attend the wedding of every student, both present and past. Rav Yaakov responded, "A rebbi is a father. Have you ever seen a father who didn't attend his daughter's wedding?"
>
> This is the kind of deep-rooted care, concern, and devotion that a rebbi and morah must have for each and every one of their students (Reb Yaakov, p. 73).

וַיְהִי שָׁם לְגוֹי. מְלַמֵּד שֶׁהָיוּ יִשְׂרָאֵל מְצֻיָּנִים שָׁם.

A student of Rav Shmuel Berenbaum, the rosh yeshivah of the Mirrer Yeshivah in Brooklyn, had to attend a vort in a town far from the yeshivah on a freezing cold night. Heavy snow was falling, and the roads were nearly impassable. Imagine the young man's surprise when the elderly Rav Shmuel walked into the party!

"Rebbe, you didn't have to take the trouble to come all the way here in such terrible weather!"

Rav Shmuel said, "Doesn't a father come to the simchah of his child?" (Kisrah shel Torah, p. 117).

The Merit of Being Modest

מְלַמֵּד שֶׁהָיוּ יִשְׂרָאֵל מְצֻיָּנִים שָׁם
This teaches that the Israelites were distinctive there

The word *metzuyanim* comes from the word *tziyun*, which connotes an easily identifiable marker (*Maharal, Gevuros Hashem* 54). The Jewish people were distinct and recognizable because of their unpretentious and modest dress, a style that contrasted greatly with that of the Egyptians. Spiritually, the Jewish people in Egypt were at a very low level, yet they understood that if they donned the clothing of the Egyptians they would become enmeshed in Egyptian society to the point of no return (*Chasam Sofer, Toldos*).

The Midrash says that this is one of the reasons for the Jews' redemption: that they didn't change their mode of dress while in Egypt (*Lekach Tov, Shemos* 6:6). They lived in a foreign land, among foreign people, for hundreds of years, but they never adopted Egyptian society's style of dress. They held on to their tradition of modest clothing befitting a Jew.

The clothes we wear define who we truly are and who we aspire to be: "clothes make the man," says the old adage. The *Kav HaYashar* (82) says that just as the redemption from Egypt came in the merit of the modesty of the Jewish women, so, too, the final redemption will come about in the merit of the Jewish women's modesty. The *Kav HaYashar* therefore implores women to dress

> **There he became a nation** — this teaches that the Israelites were distinctive there.

---

modestly, since they have the power to hasten the redemption for which we have been waiting for so long.

Some people mistakenly assume that women were given the mitzvah of *tznius* because they are inferior and therefore need to cover themselves. Rebbetzin Zahava Braunstein saw a serious flaw in this way of thinking. In fact, she would say, the exact opposite is true!

Take a look at a *Sefer Torah*, one of the holiest objects in Judaism. One might think that because of that holiness and the Jewish people's love for mitzvos, *Sifrei Torah* would be on public display in Jewish homes and shuls, demonstrating the Jews' passion for this sanctified mitzvah. Instead the *Sefer Torah* is encased in the privacy of a special *aron kodesh* and is only removed on certain specific days and only if there is a quorum of 10 men. Even when the *Sefer Torah* is removed from the *aron kodesh*, it's sheathed in a special mantle and only opened once the reader and the one reciting the *berachah* are ready to begin. Moreover, in the brief moments between *aliyah*s, the *Sefer Torah* is again covered.

The holier something is in the eyes of Hashem, the more privacy it is accorded. The same is true with Jewish women. So rather than demonstrating a woman's inferiority, appropriate and *tzniusdik* dress indicates the Jewish woman's holiness and her unique role.

Rav Shimshon Pincus explains that the more valuable an item is, the more protection it requires. Banks ensure that their cash and valuables are locked up securely and transported by armed guards in armored trucks. Jewish women play an extremely valuable, treasured, and absolutely necessary role in the Jewish nation's vitality and existence: halachah dictates that the Jewishness of a child is determined by the mother, and not the father. Since Jewish women are indispensable to the very existence and continuity of the Jewish nation, they require the special protection and care provided through modest dress and behavior (*Nefesh Chayah*, p. 50).

What defines a woman as a *tzaddeikes*, a righteous person? It's not how much *chesed* she does, or her work with the school board, or her participation in shul functions. These are all certainly noble and highly praiseworthy mitzvos, but the defining factor of her righteousness is *tznius*.

The Talmud teaches, אֵין מְזַוְּגִין לוֹ לְאָדָם אִשָּׁה אֶלָּא לְפִי מַעֲשָׂיו, *Hashem only pairs a man to a woman according to his deeds* (Sotah 2a). Rashi explains, צְנוּעָה לַצַּדִּיק, *A modest girl for a righteous man*.

Rashi didn't write, *A tzaddeikes for a tzaddik*. He wrote, *A tzenuah for a tzaddik*, because the righteousness of a Jewish woman is defined by her *tzniusdik* dress and behavior (*Nefesh Chayah*, p. 13; see also *Maharal, Gevuros Hashem* 60).

> Rav Avraham Yosef Wolf, founding dean of the Bais Yaakov Seminar in Bnei Brak, went to the Chazon Ish with a question especially relevant to him as dean of a large girls' school. The Talmud (Kiddushin 30b) says that Hashem created within every person a yetzer hara, but He gave us the Torah as a means of controlling this evil inclination.
>
> "This is all well and good for the men who are obligated to learn Torah. They can use the Torah as a tool to counter the evil inclination," Rav Wolf said. "But what about women and girls? They don't have an obligation to study Torah. How can they fight the yetzer hara?"
>
> The Chazon Ish answered that women can overcome their yetzer hara by being scrupulous with the laws of tznius. Tznius is the "Torah" of women that affords them protection from the evil inclination (Ma'aseh Ish, Vol. 3, p. 169; Iggeres HaGra, Aram Tzoba edition).

Rav Aharon Leib Steinman takes this idea further. He writes that the *yetzer hara* wages its fiercest battle against men studying Torah, since Torah learning is anathema to the evil inclination. Similarly, for women, the *yetzer hara* battles most fiercely to prevent them from safeguarding their *tznius*. A woman can say *Tehillim*, perform acts of *chesed*, and host *tzedakah* parlor meetings; disrupting such deeds is not the main concern of the *yetzer hara*. What the evil inclination wants most is to prevent women from being modest (*Yemalei Pi Tehillasecha, Inyanei HaTzibbur*, p. 262).

> Teachers and principals from the Bais Yaakov school system in Israel met to discuss how to most effectively teach the lessons

of tznius to the girls in their schools. After formulating lesson plans, several of the more senior teachers scheduled a meeting with the gadol hador, Rav Elazar Menacham Mann Shach.

At the appointed time, the select group of teachers arrived at the home of Rav Shach in Bnei Brak. Walking up the steps to his apartment, they hesitated. "Are we really going to disturb the preeminent Torah leader with our outlines and lessons of how we're going to teach tznius?" the women questioned one another.

Rav Shach, hearing the commotion and sensing the hesitancy of the women, stepped outside and said, "Come inside, dear teachers. Why are you hesitant? You're teaching our daughters about tznius. The entire future of the Jewish nation is dependent on what you are doing!" (Orchos HaBayis, p. 155).

One of the descriptions of the "woman of valor" in "*Eishes Chayil*" is הָיְתָה כָּאֳנִיּוֹת סוֹחֵר מִמֶּרְחָק תָּבִיא לַחְמָהּ, *She is like a merchant's ship; from afar she brings her sustenance* (*Mishlei* 31:14). The Shinover Rav, Rav Yechezkel Shraga Halberstam, points out that this seems to be a contradiction between the comparison of the woman to a "merchant ship," out in public for all to see, and the famous praise of modest women, כָּל כְּבוּדָּה בַת מֶלֶךְ פְּנִימָה, *All the honor of the King's daughter is from within* (*Tehillim* 45:14).

The Shinover Rav explains that a ship at sea raises a flag, clearly identifying it so that other vessels won't attack. When the *pasuk* compares the *eishes chayil* to a merchant ship, it's suggesting that the Jewish woman who dresses modestly raises a flag stating, "I am the daughter of Hashem."

The *mashgiach* of the Mir Yeshivah, Rav Yerucham Levovitz, says that the greatness of a person is measured by his ability to rise over his current challenges and the difficulties presented by his contemporary society (see *Da'as Torah, Shelach*, p. 147). We tend to think that great people lived hundreds and thousands of years ago. And it's true — there were great Jews who faced the incredible challenges of their times with courage and sacrifice. But today's environment makes *tznius* more challenging than ever, and those who stand up to the challenge, those who go against the tide and dress with *tznius*, achieve greatness in their own time! The merit that women bring to the world by surmounting the challenges of *tznius* has never been greater than it is today.

גָּדוֹל עָצוּם. כְּמָה שֶׁנֶּאֱמַר, וּבְנֵי יִשְׂרָאֵל פָּרוּ וַיִּשְׁרְצוּ וַיִּרְבּוּ וַיַּעַצְמוּ בִּמְאֹד מְאֹד, וַתִּמָּלֵא הָאָרֶץ אֹתָם.[1]

When describing the clothing of the Jewish woman, Shlomo HaMelech wrote, עוֹז וְהָדָר לְבוּשָׁהּ, *Strength and beauty are her clothing* (*Mishlei* 31:25). The Jewish woman can and should dress with taste and beauty, yet she should also dress with the "*oz,*" the strength, to go against the tide of fashion and dress in a way that is truly modest. Working on this difficult area brings a woman an exceptional closeness to Hashem. It also brings *berachah* to her family — and brings to her, as well, the true beauty and *chein* for which the Jewish woman is acclaimed.

It's not easy. But Rav Yitzchak Meir Alter, the first Rebbe of Gur, reminds us of the promise in the *berachah* that we recite each morning: אוֹזֵר יִשְׂרָאֵל בִּגְבוּרָה, *He girds Israel with strength.* These words are a promise of special heavenly strength to overcome the colossal challenges that seek to undermine the principles of our Torah and what Hashem wants from us (*Chiddushei HaRim al HaTorah,* p. 333).

Hashem's Guiding Hand

וּבְנֵי יִשְׂרָאֵל פָּרוּ וַיִּשְׁרְצוּ וַיִּרְבּוּ וַיַּעַצְמוּ מְאֹד

And the Children of Israel were fruitful, increased greatly, multiplied, and became very, very mighty

Rav Yechezkel Levenstein explains that we see from here that even in the darkest times, when it appears that Hashem's presence has all but faded, there are still clear signs of His guiding hand; Hashem is always with us even during the most difficult and painful times, as it says, עִמּוֹ אָנֹכִי בְצָרָה, *I [Hashem] am with him in distress* (*Tehillim* 91:15). Bnei Yisrael endured terrible persecutions and hardships during their time of slavery in Egypt; it was a time of *hester panim* from Hashem. Yet there were clear signs of Hashem's presence throughout the Egyptian exile. One of these is the way the Jewish people miraculously multiplied, having six babies at one time (*Ohr Yechezkel, Emunah* 100).

Great, mighty — as it says: And the Children of Israel were fruitful, increased greatly, multiplied, and became very, very mighty; and the land was filled with them.[1]

---

1. *Shemos* 1:7.

Rav Eliezer Zusha Portugal, the first Skulener Rebbi, lived in Communist Romania. The Rebbe would encourage Jewish men to do what they could to avoid the Romanian Army draft, knowing that keeping the Torah in such a setting was nearly impossible. The Romanian government discovered the Rebbe's antidraft activities and promptly arrested him, accusing him of traitorous activity against his country. The police confiscated the Rebbe's glasses and head covering and imprisoned him in a dark, frigid cellar, in solitary confinement.

Weak, with little contact with the outside world, the Rebbe constantly heard from his Romanian guards that he would remain there forever, and he began to think that his time in this world was coming to an end.

One morning, the Rebbe got up, as usual, to daven Shacharis as best he could under such circumstances. He covered his head with part of his shirt and began to daven slowly and loudly. He said each word with passionate concentration, thinking this could be one of his last tefillos.

The Rebbe came to "Baruch She'amar," the first tefillah of Pesukei D'Zimrah, a tefillah filled with praise to Hashem. He recited the words of praise with love and tremendous intensity. But when he got to the words בָּרוּךְ גּוֹזֵר, Blessed is He Who decrees, the Rebbe stopped. The word gozeir means "decree," a judgment upon a human being. Why would we praise Hashem for a decree against us, for bringing us something painful and distressing? All the years the Rebbe had said these words, how had he never raised this question?

Then the Rebbe, alone, sickly, and imprisoned, suffering from a severe decree for reasons he would never know, finally understood. בָּרוּךְ גּוֹזֵר, Blessed is He Who decrees; וּמְקַיֵּם, and Who fulfills. The word mekayeim can also mean "sustains." Even when Hashem decrees that a person must face a difficult challenge, He doesn't abandon him. Rather, He "sustains" the

וָרָב. כְּמָה שֶּׁנֶּאֱמַר, רְבָבָה כְּצֶמַח הַשָּׂדֶה נְתַתִּיךְ, וַתִּרְבִּי וַתִּגְדְּלִי וַתָּבֹאִי בַּעֲדִי עֲדָיִים, שָׁדַיִם נָכֹנוּ

person, granting him the necessary strength to overcome and endure the difficulties.

Suddenly, the Rebbe viewed his predicament in a new light. He realized that Hashem was right there with him in the dark and freezing cold cellar, supporting him and giving him strength. The Rebbe was revitalized.

A few days later the Rebbe was released, and he went on to establish the Skulener dynasty in the United States, becoming one of the leading Torah figures involved in rebuilding Judaism after the Holocaust (Ein Od Milvado, Vol. 1, p. 47).

It is written, מַשְׁגִּיחַ מִן הַחַלֹּנוֹת מֵצִיץ מִן הַחֲרַכִּים, [Hashem] watches over us through windows and peers at us through lattices (Shir HaShirim 2:9). What's the difference between a window and a lattice?

Rav Yechiel Michel Epstein explains that when two people stand on opposite sides of a window, they can see each other, while a lattice is similar to a peephole in a door, where the one on the inside can look and see who is outside, but the one on the outside can't see who's inside.

Hashem is *always* watching over us and providing us with His loving protection and shelter. When the Jewish people follow Hashem's will, Hashem watches over us through a window; He looks out over us and we can see Him, because His *hashgachah* is clear. But when we don't fulfill the will of Hashem, He *continues* to watch over us, yet it is from behind a lattice: we can't see Him, but He can see us (*Derashos Kol Ben Levi* 11; *Lev Eliyahu*, Vol. 1, p. 269; *Atarah L'Melech*, p. 137).

The Number Six

וּבְנֵי יִשְׂרָאֵל פָּרוּ וַיִּשְׁרְצוּ וַיִּרְבּוּ וַיַּעַצְמוּ בִּמְאֹד מְאֹד
And the Children of Israel were fruitful, increased greatly, multiplied, and became very, very mighty

Rashi explains that the Jewish women miraculously gave birth to

> **Numerous** — as it says: I made you as numerous as the plants of the field; you grew and developed, and became charming, beautiful of figure;

six babies at one time. Rav Naftali Tzvi Yehudah Berlin, the Netziv, writes that when multiple babies are born they are often weak, unhealthy, and frail. Yet the babies born to the Jewish women in Egypt were וַיַּעַצְמוּ בִּמְאֹד מְאֹד, *very, very mighty* — strong, healthy, and resilient — despite the fact that several were born at once (*Haamek Davar*; *Rav Shamshon Refael Hirsch, Shemos* 1:7; see also *Da'as Zekeinim MiBa'alei HaTosafos* and *Rabbeinu Bachya*).

Why did Hashem perform the miracle that the Jewish women in Egypt gave birth specifically to six babies at one time? What is unique about the number six?

The Maharal explains, based on the Midrash (*Shemos Rabbah* 1:28), that Pharaoh originally worked the Jews seven days a week, without respite. Moshe went to Pharaoh and explained that the Jews would work more diligently if they had one day off each week. Pharaoh agreed and allowed Moshe to choose the day to rest from their labors. Moshe, of course, chose Shabbos as the Jewish people's day of rest.

It says, וְכַאֲשֶׁר יְעַנּוּ אֹתוֹ כֵּן יִרְבֶּה וְכֵן יִפְרֹץ, *But as much as they would afflict it [the Jewish nation], so it would increase and so it would spread out* (*Shemos* 1:12). The Jewish people multiplied in relation to the amount of work the Egyptians forced them to do. With one day off per week the Jews were forced to work six days a week, and as a parallel to those six days of backbreaking labor, the Jewish women miraculously gave birth specifically to six children at a time (*Maharal, Gevuros Hashem* 12; see also *Gur Aryeh, Shemos* 1:7).

The Lesson of the Esrog

רְבָבָה כְּצֶמַח הַשָּׂדֶה נְתַתִּיךְ
I made you as numerous as the plants of the field

The Egyptian stargazers reported that the savior of the Jewish nation would be a boy. Upon hearing this news, Pharaoh decreed that all newborn baby boys be thrown into the river. How did the Egyptians know when a Jewish mother gave birth? Pharaoh ordered Egyptian families to move into the Jewish neighborhoods. When a Jewish baby would cry, the Egyptian baby next door would begin crying as well, alerting the Egyptians to the presence of a Jewish baby. Immediately the Jewish baby would be grabbed from his mother and thrown into the river (*Midrash Lekach Tov* 1:21).

When the Jewish women went into labor, they understood that the slightest cry of pain would alert the Egyptians, who would immediately take their babies. The Jewish women stifled their cries, not allowing even a single moan escape their lips, despite the excruciating pain of childbirth. Immediately after a baby boy was born, he was whisked down into the cellar of the house so his cries wouldn't alert the suspicious Egyptians.

Yet the malicious Egyptians' evil knew no bounds. They would take their young babies into the homes of the Jews and pinch them so they would cry, causing the Jewish baby in the cellar to begin crying as well. The baby was found and, in front of his pleading and hysterical parents, snatched and thrown into the river (Talmud, *Sotah* 12a; *Midrash Rabbah, Shemos* 1:20).

Afraid of giving birth within the city, many Jewish women opted to give birth in the fields, away from the prying eyes and ears of the Egyptian murderers. The Midrash recounts that when they were ready to give birth, the Jewish women would go alone to the fields and under a tree deliver six babies.

The new Jewish mothers had to return to the city, but they were afraid to take their newborns back with them, since the Egyptians would find and kill them. Forced to leave their innocent newborns alone, these new mothers demonstrated their trust in Hashem and said, "Hashem, I did my part and now please do Yours." When the Talmud states, בִּשְׂכַר נָשִׁים צִדְקָנִיּוֹת שֶׁהָיוּ בְּאוֹתוֹ הַדּוֹר נִגְאֲלוּ יִשְׂרָאֵל מִמִּצְרַיִם, *In the merit of the righteous women who were in that generation, Israel was redeemed from Egypt* (*Sotah* 11b), it's speaking of these heroic women who left their newborns under His protection (*Midrash Rabbah, Shemos* 23:8).

The Midrash tells us that immediately after the mothers left their babies in the field and returned to the city, Hashem Himself came and cut each baby's umbilical cord, washed him, cleaned him, and provided him with two rocks, one that flowed with honey for the baby to drink and one that flowed with oil to clean him (see *Sotah* 11b and *Midrash Rabbah*, *Shemos* 1:12, where it describes how an angel then cared for the newborn boys).

The Egyptians' savage hunt for Jewish baby boys was relentless. When they realized that Jewish women were giving birth in the fields, they searched for them there, seeking to find each and every baby and murder him. But the women's faith in Hashem was well placed: Hashem performed a miracle and the babies were swallowed into the ground, impervious to the Egyptians' swords and spears.

The evil and desperate Egyptians still didn't give up, despite witnessing open miracles with their very own eyes. They brought in heavy oxen and plowed the ground where the babies had been swallowed, hoping to kill them. Again Hashem protected the Jewish babies, even from within the depths of the ground, and they remained unharmed. After the Egyptians left, the Jewish baby boys miraculously popped out of the ground like blades of grass: רְבָבָה כְּצֶמַח הַשָּׂדֶה, *as numerous as the plants of the field*. Eventually these children returned to their homes, miraculously recognizing their parents despite their separation from birth (*Sotah* 11b; *Midrash Rabbah*, *Shemos* 1:12).

These children, who had lived and experienced firsthand the Hand of Hashem, grew up, and they were the ones who at *Krias Yam Suf* pointed and said, זֶה אֵלִי, *This is my God*. When children are raised with *emunah* and *bitachon* in Hashem, it becomes part and parcel of their life; as they develop and mature, they recognize Hashem's ways and trust in Him fully, regardless of the challenges life may bring.

> *A well-known Torah scholar had built a home on strong foundations of emunah and bitachon in Hashem. The night of the Pesach Seder he told his children the story of the Exodus from Egypt in great detail, trying to bring the story to life, to captivate the imaginations of the young children at the table.*
>
> *After describing the miracle of the splitting of the Yam Suf, all the children were clearly enraptured and drawn to their father's fascinating stories of Hashem's great miracles. All, that is, except one child, a 5-year-old boy, who seemed unimpressed by his father's retelling of the miraculous events.*
>
> *"Have you heard the story before, my son?" the father asked the child. "Is that why it doesn't seem miraculous to you?"*

וּשְׂעָרֵךְ צִמֵּחַ, וְאַתְּ עֵרֹם וְעֶרְיָה; וָאֶעֱבֹר עָלַיִךְ וָאֶרְאֵךְ מִתְבּוֹסֶסֶת בְּדָמָיִךְ, וָאֹמַר לָךְ, בְּדָמַיִךְ חֲיִי, וָאֹמַר לָךְ, בְּדָמַיִךְ חֲיִי.[1]

> The boy responded, "Abba, I just don't understand what's the big deal here. So Hashem split the sea. Didn't He create the water? Didn't He create dry land? If He can do that, why is it so amazing that He can make dry land run through the water as well?"
>
> The father beamed: with Hashem's help, he had succeeded in instilling in his young son pure unadulterated emunah in Hashem!

According to Tosafos, the tree referred to here was an *esrog* tree. Why did the righteous Jewish women specifically choose the shade of an *esrog* tree to give birth?

Rav Zalman Sorotzkin sees in this story an insight into what the Torah considers the defining trait of a righteous Jewish woman. The Torah tells us that it was in the merit of the righteous Jewish women in Egypt that *Bnei Yisrael* were redeemed, but this was before mitzvos were given to *Bnei Yisrael*. So how do we define a righteous Jewish woman?

By her *emunah* and *bitachon*, by her faith in Hashem. Pharaoh decreed that all newborn boys be thrown into the river, but the Jewish women didn't stop trusting that Hashem would take care of their children.

These courageous Jewish women took inspiration from the *esrog* tree. The Talmud (Tosafos, *Shabbos* 88a) tells us that the *esrog* tree is unique among all trees because its fruit blossoms *before* its leaves. The leaves of other trees grow first, in order to protect the young, delicate fruit when it blossoms. Not so the *esrog* tree. It doesn't wait for the protection of the leaves to bear fruit, but trusts in the protection of Hashem and produces its fruit immediately.

The Jewish women in Egypt did the same, bearing their children when there seemed to be no protection, trusting that Hashem would guard and nurture their babies. This is the faith that defines a righteous woman: the faith that Hashem rewarded, both by protecting the babies and finally releasing all the Jewish people from slavery (*HaDe'ah V'Hadibbur*, p. 212).

your hair grown long; but you were naked and bare. And I passed over you and saw you downtrodden in your blood and I said to you: "Through your blood shall you live!" And I said to you: "Through your blood shall you live!"[1]

1. *Yechezkel* 16:7,6.

Hashem's Protection

וָאֹמַר לָךְ בְּדָמַיִךְ חֲיִי וָאֹמַר לָךְ בְּדָמַיִךְ חֲיִי

And I said to you: "Through your blood shall you live!"
And I said to you: "Through your blood shall you live!"

The Jewish people were commanded to slaughter a sheep, the deity of the Egyptian people, and place its blood on their doorposts. Rabbeinu Bachya (to *Shemos* 12:13) explains that there was nothing special about the sheep's blood itself; it was the Jewish people's *emunah* and *bitachon* that merited them Hashem's protection. The Jews had faith that Hashem would protect them even though they publicly slaughtered the Egyptian deity and smeared its blood on their doorposts.

The Midrash says that it was because of this *emunah* that they merited to be redeemed (*Yalkut Shimoni, Beshalach* 240), and so too, says Rav Tzadok HaKohen, will the final redemption come in the merit of those who put their trust in Hashem (*Pri Tzaddik, Kedushas Shabbos* 7).

Two Mitzvos

בְּדָמַיִךְ חֲיִי...בְּדָמַיִךְ חֲיִי

"Through your blood shall you live!"...
"Through your blood shall you live!"

Rashi comments (*Shemos* 12:6) that the repetition of the phrase בְּדָמַיִךְ חֲיִי, *Through your blood shall you live*, refers to the blood of circumcision and the blood of the *pesach* sacrifice. *Bnei Yisrael* merited חֲיִי, *to live*, because of the merit of these two mitzvos, *bris milah* and the *pesach* sacrifice.

The Magen Avraham (187:3) points out that in Bircas HaMazon, even women say the words עַל בְּרִיתְךָ, *for Your covenant*, even though they do not have a *bris milah*. He explains, citing the Gemara (*Avodah Zarah* 27a) that women are considered to be already circumcised.

The Beauty of Silence

וָאֹמַר לָךְ בְּדָמַיִךְ חֲיִי וָאֹמַר לָךְ בְּדָמַיִךְ חֲיִי
And I said to you: "Through your blood shall you live!"
And I said to you: "Through your blood shall you live!"

Generally, the word *b'damayich* means "through your blood," but the Chozeh of Lublin sees a second meaning in the word: "through your silence." When someone remains silent, when he doesn't answer despite being insulted, when he gives up his rights to something in order to keep the peace, he merits חֲיִי, *life* (*Divrei Emes, Likutei Nevi'im*). Rav Menachem Mendel of Kotzk, the Kotzker Rebbe, would say, "Silence is the most beautiful sound."

> There is a tradition that on Simchas Torah the purchase of Kol HaNe'arim, when all the children are called up to the Torah and gather under a tallis, is a segulah for someone who is childless. The story is told about a shul in Israel where Kol HaNe'arim was purchased by a congregant who didn't have children. When the time came for the aliyah, the purchaser was nowhere to be found. The men decided to wait a short while, but when 20 minutes passed and the man still didn't show up, they resold the aliyah to another congregant, someone who also had no children.
>
> The second man was called up for Kol HaNe'arim and was about to begin reciting the berachah. Before he could utter the first word of the blessing, the first man ran into shul breathless, apologizing for his delay; he had run home to attend to an emergency. Now he was back, and he desperately wanted his aliyah. But what to do about the second purchaser? Who would get this significant aliyah?
>
> The first purchaser was adamant and unrelenting: he had bought it first, it was his absolute right to get the aliyah, and he wasn't willing to give it up. The second purchaser could have made as strong a claim, and he too desperately wanted the merit

of the aliyah, but he didn't want to start a conflict, especially not in a shul, so he remained quiet and let the first purchaser have the aliyah.

One year later the second purchaser, the one who had remained quiet, was blessed with a child (Aleinu L'Shabei'ach, Vol. 6, p. 488).

Sometimes a person gives in through silence; occasionally one does so through speech. Two sisters who became our mothers were rewarded when each gave up what was rightfully hers for the other. The Midrash (*Eichah Pesichta* 24) describes how the *Avos*, Avraham, Yitzchak, Yaakov, and Moshe all came before Hashem during the destruction of the *Beis HaMikdash*, begging Him to save the Jewish people in the *zechus* of their deeds. As much as they had sacrificed, as great as their accomplishments were, though, it wasn't enough to attain mercy for the Jewish nation.

Then Rachel Imeinu came before Hashem and reminded Him, so to speak, of how she had yielded her rightful husband to her sister, Leah: "Hashem, I gave my sister, Leah, the secret signs that Yaakov and I had prearranged to ensure our marriage so that Leah would not be shamed. I sacrificed everything; I was not jealous — I gave up my rights to avoid causing Leah pain. Certainly You, Hashem, should not be jealous when the Jewish people serve idols of sticks and stones."

Immediately, the mercy of Hashem was aroused, and He said, מִנְעִי קוֹלֵךְ מִבֶּכִי וְעֵינַיִךְ מִדִּמְעָה כִּי יֵשׁ שָׂכָר לִפְעֻלָּתֵךְ נְאֻם ה'... וְיֵשׁ תִּקְוָה לְאַחֲרִיתֵךְ נְאֻם ה' וְשָׁבוּ בָנִים לִגְבוּלָם, *Restrain your voice from weeping and your eyes from tears, for there is reward for your accomplishment — the word of Hashem — ...There is hope for your future — the word of Hashem — and your children will return to their border* (*Yirmiyahu* 31:15-16). By telling Leah the signs, and by silently allowing her sister to marry Yaakov, Rachel merited the salvation of hers — and Leah's — children.

The other sister who spoke and therefore gave up what was rightfully hers was, of course, Leah herself. When Leah was expecting her seventh son, she realized that now her sister Rachel would not even have as many sons as their maidservants, Bilhah and Zilpah. Leah therefore prayed that her unborn baby boy should be a girl, and Dinah was born (see *Rashi*, *Bereishis* 30:21).

Rav Chaim Kamiel points out that when somebody sacrifices

וַיָּרֵעוּ אֹתָנוּ הַמִּצְרִים, וַיְעַנּוּנוּ, וַיִּתְּנוּ עָלֵינוּ עֲבֹדָה קָשָׁה.[1]

וַיָּרֵעוּ אֹתָנוּ הַמִּצְרִים. כְּמָה שֶׁנֶּאֱמַר, הָבָה נִתְחַכְּמָה לוֹ, פֶּן יִרְבֶּה, וְהָיָה כִּי תִקְרֶאנָה מִלְחָמָה, וְנוֹסַף גַּם הוּא עַל שֹׂנְאֵינוּ, וְנִלְחַם בָּנוּ, וְעָלָה מִן הָאָרֶץ.[2]

---

for another, not only does he not lose, he actually gains. Leah sacrificed an additional tribe so that her sister Rachel wouldn't feel pained. In the end, Leah was paid back double. Dinah gave birth to Osnas, who married Yosef; they had two boys, Efraim and Menasheh, who were counted as *two* tribes in *Bnei Yisrael* (*Rabboseinu SheBedarom*, p. 101).

The Crucial Role of the Jewish Mother

הָבָה נִתְחַכְּמָה לוֹ פֶּן יִרְבֶּה
Let us deal with them wisely lest they multiply

To prevent the rapid growth of the Jewish population, Pharaoh ordered the head midwives, Shifrah and Puah, to kill all Jewish newborn baby boys as soon as they were born.

Who were Shifrah and Puah? The Talmud (*Sotah* 11b) tells us that they were Yocheved and Miriam. Yocheved was called Shifrah because מְשַׁפֶּרֶת אֶת הַוָּלָד, she made the babies "beautiful" and healthy by caring for the baby after it was born. Miriam was called Puah because she would make sounds such as "*pu pu*" in order to calm the crying babies.

Rav Shmuel Rozovsky, the *rosh hayeshivah* of Ponevezh, looks more closely at these brave women and their names. Yocheved and Miriam would play a crucial role in the story of their son and brother Moshe, leader of the Jewish people.

Why would the Torah introduce them first, not by their real names, but by terms that signified their roles as midwives? If the Torah wanted to begin by letting us know the qualities of

> The Egyptians did evil to us and afflicted us; and imposed hard labor upon us.[1]
>
> **The Egyptians did evil to us** — as it says: Let us deal with them wisely lest they multiply and, if we happen to be at war, they may join our enemies and fight against us and then leave the country.[2]

---

1. *Devarim* 26:6. 2. *Shemos* 1:10.

---

these women, wouldn't it have been more appropriate to mention that they were both prophetesses? Or that they were the wife and daughter of the *gadol hador*? Even if the focus was to be the astounding courage of these two women who were willing to give up their lives by defying Pharaoh's direct orders to kill the Jewish babies, why introduce them by names that signify such seemingly small and insignificant acts? Why not proudly proclaim they were Yocheved and Miriam?

Rav Rozovsky concludes that the highest acclaim one could give Yocheved and Miriam is to point out that they did what Jewish mothers throughout generations have done: they cared for their children and lovingly ensured that all their needs were met. The ultimate greatness of a woman is not the fact that she is an author, lawyer, rebbetzin, acclaimed speaker, *chesed* organizer, or even, as in the case of Yocheved and Miriam, a prophetess. In the eyes of the Torah, the Jewish woman receives the highest praise for taking care of her family. Thus, Yocheved and Miriam are first introduced to us as Shifrah and Puah, those who cared so tenderly for the children of Israel (*Zichron Shmuel*, p. 587).

Rav Yerucham Levovitz writes that true greatness is taking something that the world views as small and meaningless and infusing it with importance and significance. Yocheved and Miriam cared for, soothed, and coddled newborn babies, seemingly insignificant acts. Yet, the Torah teaches us that these were defining acts of greatness, and they were called Shifrah and Puah to mark these actions (*Da'as Torah*, *Shemos*, p. 6).

A similar idea emerges from the story of the prophetess Devorah. After successfully defeating the armies of Sisera, Devorah composed *Shiras Devorah*, a song of victory praising

וַיְעַנּוּנוּ. כְּמָה שֶׁנֶּאֱמַר, וַיָּשִׂימוּ עָלָיו שָׂרֵי מִסִּים, לְמַעַן עַנֹּתוֹ בְּסִבְלֹתָם, וַיִּבֶן עָרֵי מִסְכְּנוֹת לְפַרְעֹה, אֶת פִּתֹם וְאֶת רַעַמְסֵס.¹
וַיִּתְּנוּ עָלֵינוּ עֲבֹדָה קָשָׁה. כְּמָה שֶׁנֶּאֱמַר, וַיַּעֲבִדוּ מִצְרַיִם אֶת בְּנֵי יִשְׂרָאֵל בְּפָרֶךְ.²

Hashem and the miraculous unfolding of the Jewish nation's military triumph. Describing her role in the Jewish nation's success, Devorah says, עַד שַׁקַּמְתִּי דְּבוֹרָה שַׁקַּמְתִּי אֵם בְּיִשְׂרָאֵל, *Until I, Devorah, arose; I arose as a mother in Israel* (Shoftim 5:7). Devorah's role as both prophetess and judge of the Jewish nation was less central than her role as "*eim b'Yisrael*," a mother of the Jewish people (*Tevuos Shemesh Haggadah*, p. 138).

Endless loads of laundry, preparing meal after meal and between-meal treats, driving car pools, helping with homework, shopping for clothing — are all the tasks that go into building and running a home considered mitzvos? The Avudraham answers with an emphatic yes, and backs up his answer with the following discussion.

The halachah states that women are exempt from performing positive mitzvos that are time-bound. The Avudraham explains that this is because women have to take care of their husbands, their children, and their homes, and keeping time-bound mitzvos might make it impossible to accomplish this effectively. A woman is thus exempt from such mitzvos as tefillin, shofar, succah, and tzitzis because caring for her family takes precedence and is deemed a greater mitzvah (*L'ha'er*, p. 25).

One might think that this in some way diminished a woman's status, but one would be wrong. We know that if someone who is on his way to fulfill the great mitzvah of circumcising his son or sacrificing the *korban pesach* hears that there is a Jewish corpse requiring burial, and no one but he can do this, he must change his plans and make burying the forlorn Jewish corpse his top priority, since this mitzvah takes precedence. In other words, an exemption from a mitzvah, even a crucial one like bris milah or *korban pesach*, is only granted when another, more critical mitzvah comes up. When one is exempted from a mitzvah, it's

> **And they afflicted us** — as it says: They set taskmasters over them in order to oppress them with their burdens; and they built Pithom and Raamses as treasure cities for Pharaoh.¹
>
> **They imposed hard labor upon us** — as it says: The Egyptians subjugated the Children of Israel with hard labor.²
>
> ---
> 1. *Shemos* 1:11. 2. Ibid., 1:13.

because there is an even greater and more pressing mitzvah that requires attention.

This explains women's exemption from time-bound mitzvos: the more pressing — and precious — mitzvos of maintaining a home affords them their exemption from time-bound obligations.

Building the Home

וַיַּעֲבִדוּ מִצְרַיִם אֶת בְּנֵי יִשְׂרָאֵל בְּפָרֶךְ
The Egyptians subjugated the Children of Israel with hard labor

In addition to physically subjugating and torturing the Jews, the Egyptians wanted to destroy them spiritually by breaking up the strong fibers that comprise the Jewish home. The method they used was simple, but effective: forbid Jewish men from returning home at night. The alleged reason was to save the time spent on travel between work and home, but the Egyptians' true intention was to destroy the Jewish home and thus put an end to the nation's growth.

But the Jewish women would not allow that to happen. The Talmud (*Sotah* 11b) describes Jewish women cooking warm food for their husbands and, after working all day at their own backbreaking labor, walking to the distant fields to encourage them with soft words of inspiration and *bitachon*. The women would tell their husbands, "Do not despair. We will surely not be slaves to these lowly people forever; Hashem has promised us that He will have mercy on us" (*Yalkut Me'am Lo'ez, Parashas Shemos,* page 10).

The women encouraged and assisted the men through the worst of times. With their extraordinary trust in Hashem and His ways, they influenced their husbands to share that trust, to see the light despite the darkness. No wonder, then, that it was a woman who was entrusted with the secret redemption codes throughout the servitude period.

The Midrash (*Shemos Rabbah* 5:13) says that *Bnei Yisrael* believed Moshe to be the redeemer when he proclaimed the secret code of פָּקֹד יִפְקֹד, *[God] will surely remember you* (*Bereishis* 50:25). Hashem gave Avraham this code, and from Avraham it was passed to Yitzchak, who bequeathed it to Yaakov, who passed it to Yosef. Prior to his death, Yosef passed the secret redemption code to his brothers. Finally, right before the death of the last brother, which coincided with the onset of the enslavement, the code was entrusted to Serach, the daughter of Asher. When Moshe came to Egypt with the secret code of פָּקֹד יִפְקֹד, signaling the time for redemption, the Jewish elders immediately went to Serach to confirm the veracity of the code. After Serach confirmed the code, וַיַּאֲמֵן הָעָם..., *And the people believed [Moshe]...* (*Shemos* 4:31).

Times of Jewish oppression and servitude are immensely challenging and confusing. That's why the secret redemption codes were entrusted to Serach, a woman: even during the hardest times the codes would be guarded, protected, and given over at the appropriate time with full *emunah* and *bitachon* in Hashem (*Imrei Yatziv*, p. 375).

The *pasuk* calls Devorah, the prophetess, *the wife of Lapidos* (*Shoftim* 4:4). Chazal tell us (*Megillah* 14a; *Tanna D'Vei Eliyahu* 9:1) that Devorah merited becoming a prophetess and the presiding judge over the Jewish nation due to a small but highly influential act. Devorah's husband was a simple, unlearned man. Devorah said to him, "Come, I will make wicks for the Menorah for you to bring to the Mishkan in order for you to merit a portion in the next world."

Lapidos took the wicks and made them thicker so that there would be extra light in the Mishkan. That's why her husband was called "Lapidos," which means "torch."

Hashem told Devorah that as a reward she and her husband would merit tremendous *berachah*. This is the woman that Shlomo HaMelech refers to when he writes, חַכְמוֹת נָשִׁים בָּנְתָה בֵיתָהּ,

The wisdom of the woman built the home (Mishlei 14:1). A wife has an enormous influence over her husband, and through her love, concern, and encouragement, she has the ability to mold her husband and family into greatness.

> Rav Isser Zalman Meltzer was the rosh yeshivah in Slutsk, the father-in-law of Rav Aharon Kotler, and a tremendous Torah scholar. His wife, Rebbetzin Baila Hinda, once asked him why he didn't compile his sichos and chiddushim and publish a sefer. He had given hundreds of shiurim over the years; surely it would be worthwhile to publish his Torah so that many others could benefit from it.
>
> "I don't have enough original insights to fill an entire sefer," Rav Isser Zalman responded.
>
> Rebbetzin Baila Hinda did not relent. "Even if you don't have enough material to fill an entire sefer, surely you have enough original Torah thoughts to put together a small pamphlet."
>
> Rav Isser Zalman thought about it and agreed that, yes, he did have enough chiddushim of his own to at least fill a small pamphlet.
>
> Rebbetzin Baila Hinda herself prepared the selected Torah novella for printing, transcribing them in her own handwriting. After that, Rebbetzin Baila Hinda Meltzer encouraged her husband to continue putting out his chiddushim. Eventually these small pamphlets were transformed into the monumental seven-volume Even HaEzel.
>
> Through the brilliance and dedicated Torah study of Rav Isser Zalman and the encouragement, support, and devotion of his wife, Rebbetzin Baila Hinda, the world merited a set of sefarim that is one of the foundational study guides to the teachings of the Rambam (HaMashgiach Rav Meir, p. 358; see also the introduction to Even HaEzel, Vol. 3).

The Nature of the Labor

וַיַּעֲבִדוּ מִצְרַיִם אֶת בְּנֵי יִשְׂרָאֵל בְּפָרֶךְ
The Egyptians subjugated the Children of Israel with hard labor

Through a particularly malicious decree designed to break the spirit of the Jewish slaves, the Egyptians forced men to perform jobs intended for women and women to do jobs intended for men (*Sotah* 11b). Rav Yosef Chaim from Baghdad points out that making women do the heavy labor of men — carrying heavy bricks, plowing fields, digging wells, cutting trees, constructing buildings — is clearly torture. But how hard was it for men to perform labors associated with women? Wouldn't slavery be easier for them if they had to cook, bake, and sew?

Rav Yosef Chaim sees an answer in an attribute found more in women than in men: patience. The Egyptians forced the Jewish men to perform labors that required a great deal of patience, such as picking out minuscule thorns from dirt, something not inherent in their nature. The Maharal explains that any job that is in total opposition to one's nature is considered taxing; hence the Egyptians forced the men and women to switch jobs (*Ben Yehoyada*, *Sotah* 11a; *Gevuros Hashem* 15).

Moreover, Rav Shmuel of Sochatchov explains in the name of his father, the Avnei Nezer, that labor that has no purpose other than to expend the energies, time, and hopes of the laborer is considered "*parech*," backbreaking. Man was created to achieve, produce, construct, and effect positive change on this world. When the Jewish men were charged with performing labor more suited to women, and the Jewish women were charged with performing jobs appropriate for men, it became clear that the point of the work wasn't constructive and effective building; here was only purposeless, meaningless labor. That's slavery: working toward nothing (*Shem MiShmuel*, *Shemos* תרע"ג.)

— Think About It —

Breaking Free

וַיַּעֲבִדוּ מִצְרַיִם אֶת בְּנֵי יִשְׂרָאֵל בְּפָרֶךְ
The Egyptians subjugated the Children of Israel with hard labor

The Midrash describes the slavery in Egypt as relentless and all encompassing (*Shemos Rabbah* 18:9; see *Malbim*, *Shemos* 1:14). Day and night were blurred as the Jews were forced to work without respite, week after week, month after month, year after year. After hours of backbreaking labor, the Jewish slaves had to wait on the Egyptian slave-owners at parties that lasted until the wee hours of the morning, when the arduous work of slavery began once again.

The *Mesillas Yesharim* (Ch. 2) explains that Pharaoh specifically ordered the labor to be relentless, not giving the Jews a moment of respite, to prevent them from having time to think even for an instant about themselves, their lives, and possible ways to end their acute suffering.

The *Mesillas Yesharim* takes this description of our ancestors' slavery further — and brings it home to us. He says that this strategy of keeping slaves too busy to think is exactly what the *yetzer hara* tries to do to us: to prevent us from thinking and questioning the objectives of our existence. Why am I here in this world? What are my ultimate goals and responsibilities? What is my relationship with Hashem? These are the deep questions we should be focused on, but the *yetzer hara* does all it can to keep us from asking them and from acting on the answers.

The *sefarim* say that the word *olam*, "world," comes from the word *helem*, "hidden." Our true purpose here on this world can often be hidden and masked by all the distractions of life (*Arizal, Pri Eitz Chaim, Sha'ar Shofar* 5; *Sfas Emes, Acharei Mos* 632).

The Jews in Egypt couldn't think about the deeper meaning of their lives because of the relentless slavery that broke their backs — and their spirits. With no time to think about the meaning of their lives, their lives lost all meaning. In our own time, the *yetzer hara*'s strategy seems totally different, but it actually has the same objective. Instead of endless hours of work, we face the rush and the roar of everyday life, the stresses that prevent us from being *misbonen*, from thinking about our responsibilities and relationship with Hashem.

A case in point: the technology revolution. Putting aside the question of the often problematic content of technology, the fact that the entire world is at our fingertips, that we can contact anyone anywhere on earth, that we are constantly being bombarded with news updates, that we can order any item with the push of a button, and that all this is available in our homes, in our cars, at work, even in shul — all the technology that we view as a gift has robbed many of us of the ability to think about what

וַנִּצְעַק אֶל יהוה אֱלֹהֵי אֲבֹתֵינוּ, וַיִּשְׁמַע יהוה אֶת קֹלֵנוּ, וַיַּרְא אֶת עָנְיֵנוּ, וְאֶת עֲמָלֵנוּ, וְאֶת לַחֲצֵנוּ.[1]

is truly important: ourselves and the greater meaning of our lives. Technology and the media may connect us more as a society, but to ourselves, our families, and all that truly matters, it has caused a great disconnect. E-mails, text messages, ever-ringing cell phones, social media — all the technology that we think we control actually controls us. This is today's slavery: the *yetzer hara* has created an environment in which people are subservient and addicted to the world's distractions.

Even those areas of our lives that are supposed to lead us closer to Hashem and His Torah can sometimes be poisoned by the *yetzer hara's* machinations. Be honest now: Can we enjoy Shabbos and Yom Tov only if we have certain publications, dips, artisanal *challos*, fine wines, and clothing to match? Is it about Shabbos — or is it about us? Of course, *oneg Shabbos* includes the pleasures of this world, but only as a means, never as an end. And if preparing these pleasures means we have no time to think about the main message of Shabbos, something has gone terribly wrong – and the *yetzer hara* rejoices.

In the context of Pesach, whose preparations are the most labor-intensive of all, we should remember that all the technical details of preparing for Yom Tov must not come at the expense of the most important factor: our emotions and thoughts, those which bring us closer to Hashem and grant us true happiness.

A suggestion: The next time you are in the car and the radio is playing or you are talking on the phone, take two minutes, shut everything off, and use these few precious moments of quiet to talk to Hashem. Use this time to take a spiritual measurement of your life, how your home is being run, how your children are being raised.

Only our spirituality and our relationship with Hashem make us different from the other seven billion people on this planet. The only thing that will bring us true, long-lasting happiness in this world and that will accompany us into the next is our spiritual accomplishments and closeness to Hashem. If we can rescue a

> We cried out to Hashem, the God of our fathers; and Hashem heard our cry and saw our affliction, our burden, and our oppression.[1]

---

1. Devarim 26:7.

---

few moments each day from the *yetzer hara*'s tenacious grasp and connect with ourselves and with Hashem, we will feel the spiritual elevation for which our *neshamos* yearn.

David HaMelech wrote, וַאֲנִי קִרְבַת אֱלֹהִים לִי טוֹב, *But as for me, nearness to Hashem is my good* (*Tehillim* 73:28). By lifting ourselves above the routine of our day and the ever-distracting environment around us, we will have the ability to hear the music of our *neshamos* and to connect to Hashem, His Torah, Shabbos, and Yom Tov, and attain true happiness.

Hashem, Maker of Shidduchim

וַנִּצְעַק אֶל ה' אֱלֹהֵי אֲבוֹתֵינוּ
We cried out to Hashem, the God of our fathers

Shidduchim. Too often, it's a time of stress and worry, when parents erroneously assume that their success — or, God forbid, their failure — at finding the right *shidduch* for a child depends on their connection to *shadchanim*, a large network of friends, money, or a prestigious family lineage. Girls without connections, money, or family prestige worry about their chances of finding a suitable marriage partner. Such thinking directly contradicts Torah values and beliefs.

The Talmud says, *We find in the Torah, Nevi'im, and Kesuvim that the match between a man and a woman is from Hashem* (*Yevamos* 63a). The Midrash (*Midrash Rabbah, Bereishis* 68:4) tells the story of a noblewoman who approached Rabbi Yose bar Chalafta and asked him how many days it had taken Hashem to create the world. Rabbi Yose responded that Hashem created the world in six days.

וַנִּצְעַק אֶל יהוה אֱלֹהֵי אֲבֹתֵינוּ. כְּמָה שֶׁנֶּאֱמַר, וַיְהִי בַיָּמִים הָרַבִּים הָהֵם, וַיָּמָת מֶלֶךְ מִצְרַיִם, וַיֵּאָנְחוּ בְנֵי יִשְׂרָאֵל מִן הָעֲבֹדָה,

"If so," the noblewoman said, "what has Hashem been doing since then?"

"Hashem is making *shidduchim*," Rabbi Yosei replied. "He matches this man to this woman."

If that's the case, why do we need the *shadchanim*, friends, and networks of people to make connections and phone calls and set up meetings? Those who work at *shidduchim* are messengers of Hashem. We need the UPS man to deliver our package, but we never mistake him for the source of the goods.

The Midrash (*Midrash Rabbah, Bereishis* 68:2) tells us that when Yaakov Avinu was looking for his match, he was concerned because his possessions had been taken by Elifaz, and he had nothing to present to his future wife. Yaakov recited *Tehillim* 121, which begins, שִׁיר לַמַּעֲלוֹת אֶשָּׂא עֵינַי אֶל הֶהָרִים מֵאַיִן יָבֹא עֶזְרִי, *A song to the ascents. I raise my eyes upon the mountains; from where will my help come?* Yaakov was calling out to Hashem: *From where will come* עֶזְרִי, *my help?* — a reference to one's wife (see *Bereishis* 2:18, where Hashem calls a wife an "*ezer*," a helper).

Then Yaakov strengthened his *emunah* and *bitachon* in Hashem and resolutely declared, עֶזְרִי מֵעִם ה' עֹשֵׂה שָׁמַיִם וָאָרֶץ, *My help is from Hashem, Maker of heaven and earth*. Yaakov understood that only Hashem would find him his "help" — his match — and the fact that he was poor, a stranger in exile, would not matter: *My help is from Hashem, Who made everything!*

(Rav Menachem Azariah MiPano writes in his *sefer Asarah Ma'amaros* (*Chikur Hadin* 4:17) that reciting *Tehillim* 121 at the end of *Shemoneh Esrei* is a source of *berachah*, particularly for *shidduchim*.)

We should realize that Hashem, and only Hashem, orchestrates and arranges *shidduchim*, and we should cry out to Him for guidance and help. Of course, phone calls need to be made, *shadchanim* contacted, and other steps have to be taken to find one's match. But these steps are just the *hishtadlus* that Hashem requires each of us to make, not the source of the salvation

We cried out to Hashem, the God of our fathers — as it says: It happened in the course of those many days that the king of Egypt died; and the Children of Israel groaned because of the servitude

itself. The Mabit writes that the essential point of *tefillah* is to bring us to the realization that only Hashem can provide us with our needs — including finding us a spouse (*Beis Elokim, Sha'ar HaTefillah*).

Rav Elazar Menachem Shach told the following story, highlighting the supreme role Hashem plays in *shidduchim*.

> *Rav Yosef Dov Soloveitchik, the Beis HaLevi and the first Brisker Rav, was one of the most intelligent, diligent, and sought-after students in the Volozhin Yeshivah. Rav Itzele of Volozhin, the rosh yeshivah and Rav Yosef Dov's uncle, was seeking a marriage partner par excellence for his nephew. Rav Itzele wanted to find his nephew a wife with good middos from a prestigious family, wealthy enough to support his nephew, who would learn Torah without hindrance. Many girls were suggested, but not one fit all of Rav Itzele's specifications.*
>
> *One day a man from the neighboring town approached Rav Yosef Dov himself and suggested a marriage partner. Who was the girl he suggested for the best boy in yeshivah? From which wealthy and prestigious family did she come?*
>
> *As it happened, the girl was none other than the daughter of the town baker. No wealth, no yichus, but Rav Yosef Dov inquired about the girl's character, and he discovered that she was a God-fearing woman with wonderful character traits. He met her briefly, and they became engaged.*
>
> *When Rav Itzele found out about his nephew's engagement to a girl from such a simple background, he lifted his eyes toward Heaven and said, "Mazel tov! Hashem, You beat me, You beat me."*

"We see," Rav Shach concluded, "that Hashem is the Mastermind behind *shidduchim* despite the attempts of others, as it says (*Mishlei* 19:21), רַבּוֹת מַחֲשָׁבוֹת בְּלֶב אִישׁ, *Many are the designs that are in the heart of man*, but וַעֲצַת ה' הִיא תָקוּם, *the counsel of Hashem, only it will prevail!* (*Kinyan Torah Haggadah*, p. 286).

וַיִּזְעָקוּ, וַתַּעַל שַׁוְעָתָם אֶל הָאֱלֹהִים מִן הָעֲבֹדָה.[1]

A Mother's Tears

וַיִּזְעָקוּ, וַתַּעַל שַׁוְעָתָם אֶל הָאֱלֹהִים
And they cried; their cry because of the servitude rose up to God

We usually daven with words, but sometimes, when we cry out to Hashem without enunciating words, Hashem hears our pain and answers our prayers. When we cry, we are saying, "Hashem, I'm in such pain and so confused that I can't even find words to speak. Please hear the cry of my soul calling out to You for help and salvation."

The Jews in Egypt had suffered for so long and under such desperate conditions that they were unable to enunciate their *tefillos*. But their cries, the sobs emanating from the depths of their hearts, were heard by Hashem and hastened the redemption (*Yalkut Tehillim* 865; *Ramban, Shemos* 2:25).

The Talmud (*Yoma* 53b) describes the *tefillah* said by the Kohen Gadol when he exited the *Kodesh HaKodashim* on Yom Kippur after successfully completing the *avodas haketores*, the service of the incense offering. He davened for the success of the Jewish nation and included a special prayer: לֹא תִכָּנֵס לְפָנֶיךָ תְּפִלַּת עוֹבְרֵי דְרָכִים, *May You not heed the prayers of travelers*. This referred to travelers who came to Yerushalayim for Succos and needed to make their way home. They might daven that the rain shouldn't begin right away in order to make their journey easier. But the land needs rain, so the Kohen Gadol would ask Hashem not to listen to these *tefillos* of the travelers.

Rav Yechezkel of Kuzmir pointed out the exceptional message of this extraordinary prayer. Picture the scene. A Jew is returning home from his *aliyah l'regel* to Yerushalayim on Succos. Suddenly, a few drops of rain fall on his face. He would surely know that he shouldn't daven for the rain to stop: his fields will need the rain as much as anyone's! But perhaps a small, faint sigh escapes his lips as he thinks about how difficult it will be for him to get home. The Rebbe of Kuzmir says that even this slight, faint cry of the traveler is so treasured by Hashem that on the holiest day of the

> and they cried; their cry because of the servitude rose up to God.[1]
>
> 1. *Shemos* 2:23.

year, after completing the holiest *avodah*, the Kohen Gadol himself must ask Hashem, for the sake of all the Jewish people, not to listen to the traveler. How awesome and powerful are the sighs and cries of the Jewish people (*Mareh Yechezkel, Tefillah* 19)!

What gives the cries of a Jew such power?

Rav Levi Yitzchak of Berditchev notes that when a baby is crying, the greatest geniuses and most brilliant professors can't figure out what the baby wants. Only the baby's mother or father, only one who loves him and understands his needs, can truly comprehend the meaning of his cries.

We are all the children of Hashem: בָּנִים אַתֶּם לַה' אֱלֹקֵיכֶם, *You are children of Hashem, your God* (*Devarim* 14:1), and even when we merely cry out to Hashem without words He understands our troubles and needs (*Yalkut Kedushas Levi*, p. 217).

> *One Rosh Hashanah in Yeshivas Kfar Chassidim, the venerable and holy mashgiach, Rav Eliyahu Lopian, was getting ready to walk up to the aron kodesh to give a few words of inspiration prior to the blowing of the shofar. It was one of the holiest and most spiritually charged moments of the year.*
>
> *There was special need for tefillos that year. The child of one of the rabbanim was sick; the doctors held out no hope for his recovery. The child's mother, Rebbetzin Rina, sat at her son's bedside constantly. At these moments, such as prior to tekias shofar, she saw her precious son literally hovering between life and death.*
>
> *Realizing the severity of the moment, Rebbetzin Rina ran down to the beis midrash. The room was packed with men davening and getting ready to hear the mashgiach speak before tekias shofar. The mashgiach stood on the platform of the aron kodesh, about to begin, when Rebbetzin Rina ran into the beis midrash, went over to the aron kodesh, opened the doors of the ark, and with heart-piercing cries called out to Hashem that her son should be saved.*
>
> *The entire yeshivah, including the mashgiach, stood*

וַיִּשְׁמַע יהוה אֶת קֹלֵנוּ. כְּמָה שֶׁנֶּאֱמַר, וַיִּשְׁמַע אֱלֹהִים אֶת נַאֲקָתָם, וַיִּזְכֹּר אֱלֹהִים אֶת בְּרִיתוֹ אֶת אַבְרָהָם, אֶת יִצְחָק, וְאֶת יַעֲקֹב.[1]

וַיַּרְא אֶת עָנְיֵנוּ. זוֹ פְּרִישׁוּת דֶּרֶךְ אֶרֶץ, כְּמָה שֶׁנֶּאֱמַר וַיַּרְא אֱלֹהִים אֶת בְּנֵי יִשְׂרָאֵל, וַיֵּדַע אֱלֹהִים.[2]

---

immobile, listening to the heartrending and pure cries of a mother pleading on behalf of her son. Moments later, she closed the aron kodesh doors and left the beis midrash. Rav Elya, without hesitation, banged on the table near him and announced, "Tekios!" signaling that the shofar blowing should begin at once. After the cries heard from Rebbetzin Rina, he knew there was no further need for words of inspiration (Doresh Tov Haggadah, p. 233).

The Merit of Praying for Others

וַיִּשְׁמַע אֱלֹהִים אֶת נַאֲקָתָם וַיִּזְכֹּר אֱלֹהִים אֶת בְּרִיתוֹ
God heard their groaning, and God recalled His covenant

In a similar *pasuk*, we find that Hashem told Moshe, וְגַם אֲנִי שָׁמַעְתִּי אֶת נַאֲקַת בְּנֵי יִשְׂרָאֵל אֲשֶׁר מִצְרַיִם מַעֲבִדִים אֹתָם, *And I, too, have heard the groan of the Children of Israel whom Egypt enslaves* (*Shemos* 6:5). The Chasam Sofer asks about the words וְגַם אֲנִי, when Hashem says, "I, too, have heard the cries of the Jews." Who was Hashem referring to who also heard the cries of the Jewish people?

The Chasam Sofer answers that when the Jews were enslaved under brutal conditions in Egypt and would cry out to Hashem, they didn't just cry out because of their own pain; one Jew would hear the cries of a fellow Jew and pray on behalf of his friend, ignoring his own sorrow. When Hashem heard how each Jew heard the cries of his friend and prayed for his friend's welfare despite his own personal pain, Hashem said, in the merit of this, וְגַם אֲנִי שָׁמַעְתִּי, *And I, too, have heard the groan* — I hear the cries

HASHEM heard our cry — as it says: God heard their groaning, and God recalled His covenant with Avraham, with Yitzchak, and with Yaakov.[1]

And He saw our affliction — that is the disruption of family life, as it says: God saw the Children of Israel and God knew.[2]

---

1. *Shemos* 2:24. 2. Ibid. 2:25.

---

of those who hear the cries of their brethren, and I will redeem you in this merit.

> Rav Baruch Mordechai Ezrachi, the rosh hayeshivah of Ateres Yisrael, told the story of a couple who didn't have children for many long years. The husband and wife would pour out their hearts to Hashem in tefillah, to no avail. Finally, the husband decided to ask a rebbi of his for a berachah. After hearing his story, the rebbi told him that he, too, had a son who remained childless for many years, despite the many tefillos that had been recited.
>
> The rebbi thought for a moment and then reminded the man of the Talmud's statement that one who davens for his friend and is need of that same thing will be answered first (*Bava Kamma* 92a).
>
> "I'll call my son and tell him to pray for you, and you will begin davening for him," the rebbi suggested.
>
> The "deal" went through, and from that day forward both husbands davened that the other should merit children. Within the year both couples were blessed with new babies — and what's more, the babies were born on the very same day (*Ish L'Rei'eihu, Lech Lecha*, p. 96).

A Lesson in Humility

וַיַּרְא אֶת עָנְיֵנוּ, זוֹ פְּרִישׁוּת דֶּרֶךְ אֶרֶץ
*And He saw our affliction —
that is the disruption of family life*

Many Haggadah commentators explain that this passage refers to the story in the Talmud (*Sotah* 12b) about how Amram, the preeminent leader of the Jewish nation, divorced his wife Yocheved after Pharaoh decreed that all Jewish boys be thrown into the river. Amram reasoned that it's better to divorce one's wife and not have more children than to doom every boy born to death. The Jewish people followed their leader and divorced as well.

Amram's 6-year-old daughter, Miriam, went to her father and said, "Your decree is harsher than Pharaoh's. For Pharaoh's decree affects only the Jewish boys, whereas yours destroys both boys and girls. Pharaoh's decree is only against their life in this world, while yours is against their life in this world and the next."

Amram agreed and immediately remarried his wife, Yocheved. All the Jews followed him again and remarried their wives. From Amram and Yocheved's remarriage Moshe Rabbeinu was born, so his older sister Miriam made possible the birth of the leader of the Jewish people who would lead them out of Egypt!

Amram was the most important Jewish figure at the time, but when his 6-year-old daughter pointed out his mistake, he was humble enough to admit his error, despite the fact that the entire Jewish nation would be aware of his change of mind. No wonder, then, that immediately after he remarried Yocheved they merited giving birth to Moshe, whom the Torah depicts as being the most humble of all people.

Furthermore, Amram was the *gadol hador* and had myriad responsibilities that took up much of his time. Nevertheless, he had the time and patience to listen to his daughter and to take her words seriously. Amram understood that parents, no matter what their stature, can learn from their children, no what matter their age. The Mishnah says, אֵיזֶהוּ חָכָם הַלּוֹמֵד מִכָּל אָדָם, *Who is wise? One who learns from all people* (*Avos* 4:1). The commentators explain that the wise man learns from everyone, even those who are younger and less learned or intelligent than he, as he understands that every individual has something unique to teach him.

Compassion and Redemption

וַיַּרְא אֱלֹהִים אֶת בְּנֵי יִשְׂרָאֵל וַיֵּדַע אֱלֹהִים
God saw the Children of Israel and God knew

What exactly did Hashem see that influenced Him to bring the redemption at last?

Rav Mordechai HaKohen, author of the *Sifsei Kohen*, quotes a midrash (see *Torah Sheleimah*, *Shemos* 3:25) describing how the Jewish people had mercy on each other despite their own agonizing labors. Every day a quota of 400 bricks had to be completed by each Jewish slave. If one Jew finished his quota, and he saw that his friend was still struggling to meet his, he would assist him in completing his workload. Giving up on the break he so desperately needed, with each additional brick another ache in a shoulder, another pain in the back, the Jew would push away all thoughts of rest and say, "Come, let me help you."

When Hashem saw how the Jewish people had such mercy on each other, He said, "These people deserve to be redeemed, for whoever has mercy on another is deserving of mercy from Heaven."

Rav Chaim Friedlander, the *mashgiach* of Ponevezh, teaches us a tremendously valuable lesson in the art of helping others. The Torah says, וַיֵּצֵא אֶל אֶחָיו וַיַּרְא בְּסִבְלֹתָם, *Moshe went out to see the pain of his brothers* (*Shemos* 2:11). The Midrash (*Midrash Rabbah, Shemos* 1:27) relates that when Moshe would see his fellow Jews staggering under the burden of their excruciating workload, he would cry out to Hashem and help his brethren as much as he could. Rav Friedlander explains that according to many opinions in Chazal there were three million enslaved Jewish men in Egypt. How does one man go about helping so many in such great need? Many ordinary people, faced with the pain of three million of their brothers, would undoubtedly simply cry out in despair and say there's nothing to be done. But not Moshe Rabbeinu. Undiscouraged, he went out to help his brothers.

Such determination is inspiring, but how could one man physically help three million Jews fill their quotas? And if he did manage to help each one just a little, what good would that really do? The answer is: the good it could do was immeasurable. Moshe's demonstration of care and concern encouraged and comforted the Jewish people. Just seeing Moshe's sincere compassion and caring, knowing that this man who had grown up in Pharaoh's palace, who wasn't a slave himself, could feel their pain, was enough to lighten their load, encourage them, and help them persevere despite the mounting difficulties (*Sifsei Chaim, Middos*, Vol. 1, p. 383).

Empathy and caring seem to be family traits in Moshe Rabbeinu's family. The Midrash says (*Yalkut Shimoni, Shemos* 165; see also *Rashi, Shir HaShirim* 2:13) that when Miriam was born, the Egyptian servitude had just begun. Amram and Yocheved named her Miriam (מִרְיָם), recalling the bitter slave labor the Jews were forced into, as it says, וַיְמָרֲרוּ אֶת חַיֵּיהֶם, *They embittered their lives* (*Shemos* 1:14). Their choice of name is remarkable since Amram and Yocheved were from the tribe of Levi, whose members were not forced to work. Nevertheless, they felt the pain of their fellow Jews and named their daughter Miriam as a token of their shared pain (see also *Shelah, Shemos* 6:14).

We might not always have the capability or the means to help another in need. We learn from Moshe Rabbeinu not to throw up our hands in despair. Show the person that you care; demonstrate to him even in the smallest way that you are thinking about him and that you truly want to help. Everyone can lend a listening and sympathetic ear. As the adage goes, "A problem shared is a problem halved." Chazal tell us that when one is in pain, merely having someone to share his concerns with lightens his load (*Sotah* 42b). Through demonstrating our concern and showing our love, we can encourage those in pain and fulfill a remarkable act of *chesed*.

> *Anyone who has lived in Israel is familiar with Ezer Mizion, an organization that provides health services to the sick, meals to those in need, and numerous other chesed projects to hundreds of thousands throughout the country. The organization was founded by Rabbi Chananyah Chollak and his wife, Rebbetzin Leah.*
>
> *The rebbetzin was well known for her chesed, her attention to detail, and for feeling the pain of others no matter who they were.*
>
> *Toward the end of her life, Rebbetzin Chollak was very sick, and thousands who had benefited from her chesed prayed for her recovery. One day the rebbetzin's daughter came into her room and in an attempt to encourage her mother told her that more than 3,000 women had collectively decided to accept Shabbos upon themselves 15 minutes early in the merit of her recovery.*
>
> *"Do you know who arranged this?" the rebbetzin asked.*
>
> *"Certainly," her daughter said. "I know her personally."*

"Then please tell her thank you so much, but ask that this should stop immediately."

"Stop?" her bewildered daughter asked. "Why should it stop? It's an incredible zechus for you and your recovery!"

Gently, the rebbetzin explained, "There are so, so many sick people in need of a recovery and salvation. Some of the others who need a refuah sheleimah may hear about these 3,000 women who will accept Shabbos early in the merit of my recovery, and they will know that for them not one person has taken an extra mitzvah upon herself. Think of the ill will, sorrow, hopelessness, and pain this may cause so many others to feel! So I'm asking you to cease these goodwill gestures."

The rebbetzin's daughter suggested that the 3,000 women accepting Shabbos early do so in the merit of all those in need of a recovery. Rebbetzin Chollak readily agreed, and as a result of the rebbetzin's sensitivity to other people's pain, every Jew in need of a recovery was granted an enormous zechus (On the Second Floor Behind the Door: Stories from the Life of Leah Chollak, the Mother of Ezer Mizion, p. 211).

The Shechinah Feels Our Pain

וַיַּרְא אֱלֹהִים אֶת בְּנֵי יִשְׂרָאֵל וַיֵּדַע אֱלֹהִים
God saw the Children of Israel and God knew

Rashi writes (to *Shemos* 3:25) that the words וַיֵּדַע אֱלֹהִים, *And God knew*, mean that Hashem empathized with the painful plight of His people. But Hashem doesn't only feel the pain of the Jewish nation as a whole; He empathizes with the suffering, challenges, and difficulties of each and every Jew. The *Tanna D'Vei Eliyahu* (18:1) says that Hashem feels the pain of the Jewish nation and the pain of each Jew on an individual level.

Along these lines, the Talmud says, בְּשָׁעָה שֶׁאָדָם מִצְטַעֵר שְׁכִינָה מַה לָּשׁוֹן אוֹמֶרֶת קַלַּנִי מֵרֹאשִׁי קַלַּנִי מִזְּרוֹעִי, *When a man is in pain, what does the Shechinah say? "Pain to My Head! Pain to My Hand!"* (*Sanhedrin* 46a). Rav Zusha explains that this is a reference to the tefillin of Hashem, which is worn on the head and arm, so to speak. The Talmud tells us that within the tefillin of Hashem are parashiyos, verses, including the phrase מִי כְּעַמְּךָ יִשְׂרָאֵל, *Who is like you, the nation of Yisrael?*

וְאֶת עֲמָלֵנוּ. אֵלוּ הַבָּנִים, כְּמָה שֶׁנֶּאֱמַר, כָּל

When a Jew is in pain, Hashem is a partner in this pain, feeling it, so to speak, in the tefillin in which His love and connection to the Jewish people is inscribed. During difficult, challenging times one may feel that Hashem is distant, but the opposite is true. It is specifically at this time that Hashem is ever so close, as it says (*Tehillim* 91:15), עִמּוֹ אָנֹכִי בְצָרָה, *I [Hashem] am with him in distress* (*Imrei Pinchas, Sha'ar Toras HaAdam*).

Rav Shmuel Birnbaum develops this idea, saying that the love Hashem has for each Jew far exceeds even the love a parent has for a child. When a child is in great agony due to an infection in his leg, his parents are distressed by their child's throbbing discomfort, but at the same time their own legs don't feel the pain their child is experiencing. Yet, as we see, when a Jew suffers pain, emotional or physical, Hashem Himself experiences the pain, so to speak: קַלַּנִי מֵרֹאשִׁי קַלַּנִי מִזְּרוֹעִי, *Pain to My Head! Pain to My Hand!* (*Kisrah shel Torah*, p. 128).

Worthy of the Kohen Gadol

וְאֶת עֲמָלֵנוּ, אֵלּוּ הַבָּנִים
Our burden — this refers to the children

Rav Moshe Aharon Stern, a well-known expert in child-rearing, was once approached by a mother whose newborn baby would wake up several times a night, making it hard for her to function by day. After weeks of sleep deprivation, she was afraid that the initial joy she had felt in taking care of her baby was quickly dissipating.

Rav Stern told her that Rav Aryeh Levin, the tzaddik of Jerusalem, would tell his married daughters that before they begin to care for their children each day, they should say, "I am hereby preparing myself to fulfill the mitzvah of raising children." Rav Stern explained that if a mother views caring for her children as an act of chesed that can be performed by no other, if she knows that it is an act that brings pure nachas to Hashem, it becomes easier and more fulfilling for her to handle the difficulties inherent in raising a child.

Our burden — refers to the children, as it says:

The woman took Rav Stern's advice, changed her viewpoint, and became a happier and more loving mother (HaMashgiach D'Kaminetz, p. 257).

The Haggadah relates the word *amaleinu* to raising children. Rav Shlomo Zalman Auerbach suggests that it might have been more understandable to define *amaleinu*, which literally means "our toil," as a reference to the intense slave labor the Jews were forced to perform in Egypt. How does it connect to children?

Rav Shlomo Zalman explains that the word *amaleinu* describes a toil that is desirable and rewarding; for example, the word *amal* is used to describe the labor of Torah learning, a kind of toil that is spiritual and gratifying, and very unlike the labor of slavery. The Haggadah uses the word *amal* and not, for example, the word *tirchah* to remind us that the effort and work that goes into raising children is also a toil that is both desirable and rewarding (see *Arzei HaLevanon Haggadah*, Vol. 2, p. 147).

Sefer Vayikra describes the laws of the *korbanos*, the offerings brought by Aharon and his descendants. The Chasam Sofer points out that generally the Torah says that Moshe should "speak" to בְּנֵי אַהֲרֹן, *the children of Aharon*. Only once does the Torah say, צַו אֶת אַהֲרֹן, *Command Aharon* (*Vayikra* 6:2) — that Moshe should command Aharon directly, and this is when he describes how to remove the ashes from the Altar.

This mitzvah had to do with the cleanup, a routine and even menial portion of the work of the Mishkan. This special command was directed to Aharon himself to suggest that although one mitzvah may look more honorable than another to us, in the eyes of Hashem they are all equal (*Chasam Sofer*, *Vayikra* 6:2). The job of cleaning the ashes from the Altar might seem like routine drudgery, but it was an honor for Aharon to personally clean the Mishkan.

The responsibility for running and maintaining a home often falls on women, and all the jobs that keep a home thriving — the cooking and cleaning, the shopping, the sweeping, the washing — are mitzvos and an honor worthy of the Kohen Gadol himself!

הַבֵּן הַיִּלּוֹד הַיְאֹרָה תַּשְׁלִיכֻהוּ, וְכָל הַבַּת תְּחַיּוּן.¹

Bringing Ourselves Closer to Hashem

כָּל הַבֵּן הַיִּלּוֹד הַיְאֹרָה תַּשְׁלִיכֻהוּ וְכָל הַבַּת תְּחַיּוּן
Every son that is born you shall cast into the river, but every daughter you shall let live

Pharaoh passed a decree declaring that all Jewish boys were to be thrown into the river. When she could no longer hide her newborn baby Moshe, his mother, Yocheved, placed him in a small box that she floated down the Nile. His sister Miriam *stood from afar in order to know what would be with him [Moshe]* (*Shemos* 2:4). Rav Yekusiel Yehudah Halberstam, the Klausenberger Rebbe, wondered why Miriam would have stood "from afar." Wouldn't she be able to watch her brother more closely by standing nearer to the river?

The Klausenberger added question to question when he cited an explanation for this verse from the Talmud (*Sotah* 11a). In a puzzling statement, the Gemara suggests that the description of Miriam "standing from afar" actually refers to Hashem. What can this mean?

The Klausenberger Rebbe provides an explanation that answers all the questions. Miriam didn't approach the river but rather stood from afar because the riverside is not a place of *tznius*. Miriam's demonstrating and care for the laws and principles of *tznius* brought Hashem closer to her, which explains what the Talmud means when it says that this *pasuk* refers to Hashem. One who is careful with the laws of *tznius* merits bringing Hashem into their lives (*Imrei Yatziv*, Ch. 16).

Rebbetzin Zahava Braunstein would speak of the popularity of *segulos*. Girls recite *Shir HaShirim* 40 days in a row for the merit of finding a *shidduch*. Women make *shlissel challah* the Shabbos after Pesach, recite *Tefillas HaShelah* on *erev* Rosh Chodesh Sivan, or wear a red "*bendel*" from Kever Rochel. While she did not disparage any *minhag* or *segulah*, she pointed out that the Torah tells us of the ultimate *segulah*: וְהָיָה מַחֲנֶיךָ קָדוֹשׁ — *so your camp shall be holy* (*Devarim* 23:15). How to keep it holy? Dressing and acting with modesty. And if we do so? כִּי

Every son that is born you shall cast into the river, but every daughter you shall let live.[1]

1. *Shemos* 1:22.

ה' אֱלֹהֶיךָ מִתְהַלֵּךְ בְּקֶרֶב מַחֲנֶיךָ לְהַצִּילְךָ, *For Hashem, your God, walks within your camp to rescue you* (ibid.). Using the "*segulah*" of modesty we will be protected, and He will rest His presence on our homes, our families, and ourselves.

A Mother's Faith

כָּל הַבֵּן הַיִּלּוֹד הַיְאֹרָה תַּשְׁלִיכֻהוּ וְכָל הַבַּת תְּחַיּוּן
Every son that is born you shall cast into the river, but every daughter you shall let live

As we have noted, after giving birth to Moshe, Yocheved concealed him at home for three months, as the Egyptians did not know that she had given birth early. Once nine months had passed since the beginning of her pregnancy, Yocheved knew that it would be a matter of days before the Egyptians came to see if she had given birth to a boy, and Moshe would be found and thrown mercilessly into the river. Yocheved put her 3-month-old baby into a small waterproof box, and Miriam placed it in the river.

Rav David HaNagid, the grandson of Rambam, writes that when Yocheved handed over her precious newborn baby to be placed into the river, she said, "My child, I have deposited you into the hands of the One Who never rejects deposits" — a reference to Hashem (*Midrash David HaNagid on the Haggadah*, p. 81). We can hardly imagine the pain this mother felt when placing her tiny child in a fragile box to be put in the merciless waters of the Nile. But Yocheved's *bitachon* in Hashem gave her the strength to face the challenge.

In our own time, we have seen fathers and mothers demonstrate the same kind of *emunah* when facing the most devastating challenges.

Nachshon Wachsman was a 19-year-old Israeli soldier who had been kidnapped and held hostage by Hamas militants. For six

וְאֶת לַחֲצֵנוּ. זוֹ הַדְּחַק, כְּמָה שֶׁנֶּאֱמַר, וְגַם רָאִיתִי אֶת הַלַּחַץ אֲשֶׁר מִצְרַיִם לֹחֲצִים אֹתָם.[1]

וַיּוֹצִאֵנוּ יהוה מִמִּצְרַיִם בְּיָד חֲזָקָה, וּבִזְרֹעַ נְטוּיָה, וּבְמֹרָא גָּדֹל, וּבְאֹתוֹת וּבְמֹפְתִים.[2]

---

days the Jewish world was united in tears and tefillos, pleading with Hashem to bring him home.

Then came the shattering news: Nachshon had been murdered during a failed mission to rescue him.

The Jewish world was in mourning. The bullet that killed the young man shattered hopes throughout the world. But it didn't destroy the emunah of his family.

During the six nightmarish days of Nachshon's kidnapping, his parents, Yehuda and Esther Wachsman, spoke numerous times to the media about the need to strengthen our emunah in Hashem, strong in their belief that only Hashem could save their child. Nachshon's parents beseeched Jews around the world to intensify their tefillos and mitzvah observance.

At the funeral, Yehuda Wachsman, with staunch emunah in Hashem, said, "If people are wondering what happened to all the tefillos that were prayed in the merit of Nachshon's release and how Hashem could say no, I will tell them, 'A father has the right to say no.'"

Nachshon's mother, Esther said at the funeral, "The single thing that supported us throughout this ordeal was our emunah in Hashem. When a person has fulfilled his purpose here on this world, he is taken away. With emunah we understand that these 19 years were the years that were set for our son Nachshon, and he fulfilled the purpose and goals that he was sent to this world to accomplish. Only emunah gives us strength to move on and look ahead."

When Esther Wachsman was in New York, she visited Rav Avraham Pam, the former rosh yeshivah of Torah Vodaath. He spent more than half an hour praising her immense bitachon and emunah in Hashem. He told her that she and her husband had made a tremendous kiddush Hashem and called her an

Our oppression — refers to the pressure expressed in the words: I have also seen how the Egyptians are oppressing them.[1]

HASHEM **took us out of Egypt with a mighty hand and with an outstretched arm, with great awe, with signs and with wonders.**[2]

---

1. *Shemos* 3:9. 2. *Devarim* 26:8.

---

exemplary role model of a true "gibbores" — an immeasurably strong woman (*Ahuv al Kulam*, p. 111).

Moshe Rabbeinu was rescued — his task on earth, to lead his people out of bondage and give them the Torah, was still ahead of him; Nachshon Wachsman had, apparently, completed his task on earth. The *emunah* and *bitachon* of the Jewish mothers remain an inspiration for all time.

The Jewish Girls

כָּל הַבֵּן הַיִּלּוֹד הַיְאֹרָה תַּשְׁלִיכֻהוּ וְכָל הַבַּת תְּחַיּוּן

Every son that is born you shall cast into the river, but every daughter you shall let live

Pharaoh decreed that Jewish baby boys should be thrown into the Nile. The obvious implication is that Jewish girls would not be killed. If so, why does the Torah go out of its way and explicitly say, וְכָל הַבַּת תְּחַיּוּן, *But every daughter you shall let live*?

Rav Mordechai Gifter, the *rosh yeshivah* of Telz, explains that Pharaoh had sinister motives in leaving the Jewish baby girls alive. The Jewish women at that time, Chazal tell us, miraculously gave birth to six babies at once. Though babies born in multiple births are often frail and weak, these Jewish babies were healthy and strong. Pharaoh's wicked plan was to kill all the Jewish boys, leaving the Jewish baby girls alive so they could be taken by the Egyptian men as wives and then likewise give birth to a large number of strong and robust children. The aim was to strengthen and increase the Egyptian nation (*Pirkei Mo'ed*, p. 76).

וַיּוֹצִאֵנוּ יהוה מִמִּצְרַיִם. לֹא עַל יְדֵי מַלְאָךְ, וְלֹא עַל יְדֵי שָׂרָף, וְלֹא עַל יְדֵי שָׁלִיחַ, אֶלָּא הַקָּדוֹשׁ בָּרוּךְ הוּא בִּכְבוֹדוֹ וּבְעַצְמוֹ. שֶׁנֶּאֱמַר, וְעָבַרְתִּי בְאֶרֶץ מִצְרַיִם בַּלַּיְלָה הַזֶּה, וְהִכֵּיתִי כָל בְּכוֹר בְּאֶרֶץ מִצְרַיִם מֵאָדָם וְעַד בְּהֵמָה, וּבְכָל אֱלֹהֵי מִצְרַיִם אֶעֱשֶׂה שְׁפָטִים, אֲנִי יהוה.¹

וְעָבַרְתִּי בְאֶרֶץ מִצְרַיִם בַּלַּיְלָה הַזֶּה — אֲנִי וְלֹא מַלְאָךְ. וְהִכֵּיתִי כָל בְּכוֹר בְּאֶרֶץ מִצְרַיִם — אֲנִי וְלֹא שָׂרָף. וּבְכָל אֱלֹהֵי מִצְרַיִם אֶעֱשֶׂה שְׁפָטִים — אֲנִי וְלֹא הַשָּׁלִיחַ. אֲנִי יהוה — אֲנִי הוּא, וְלֹא אַחֵר.

בְּיָד חֲזָקָה. זוֹ הַדֶּבֶר, כְּמָה שֶׁנֶּאֱמַר, הִנֵּה יַד יהוה הוֹיָה בְּמִקְנְךָ אֲשֶׁר בַּשָּׂדֶה, בַּסּוּסִים בַּחֲמֹרִים בַּגְּמַלִּים בַּבָּקָר וּבַצֹּאן, דֶּבֶר כָּבֵד מְאֹד.²

Like a Mother Cares for Her Child

אֲנִי וְלֹא מַלְאָךְ
I and no angel

Hashem Himself took us out of Egypt and not through any intermediary. Why?

Rav Moshe Shternbuch, citing the teachings of Rav Yitzchak Blazer, the outstanding disciple of Rav Yisrael Salanter, suggests an answer based on the verse אִם רָחַץ ה' אֵת צֹאַת בְּנוֹת צִיּוֹן, *When Hashem will have washed the dirt of the daughters of Zion* (*Yeshayahu* 4:4). When a child is soiled and dirty, people find him repulsive and refuse to clean him. Only his mother, with her boundless love for her child, will care for him no matter how filthy he may be.

When the Jews left Egypt, they were at the 49th level of impurity, soiled and unclean with sin. But Hashem loves us like a mother loves a child, so only He was willing to clean us and

HASHEM took us out of Egypt — not through an angel, not through a seraph, not through a messenger, but the Holy One, Blessed is He, in His glory, Himself, as it says: I will pass through the land of Egypt on that night; I will slay all the firstborn in the land of Egypt from man to beast; and upon all the gods of Egypt will I execute judgments; I, HASHEM.[1]

"I will pass through the land of Egypt on that night" — I and no angel; "I will slay all the firstborn in the land of Egypt" — I and no seraph; "And upon all the gods of Egypt will I execute judgments" — I and no messenger; "I, HASHEM" — it is I and no other.

With a mighty hand — refers to the pestilence, as it says: Behold, the hand of HASHEM shall strike your cattle which are in the field, the horses, the donkeys, the camels, the herds, and the flocks — a very severe pestilence.[2]

---

1. *Shemos* 12:12. 2. Ibid. 9:3.

---

redeem us from Egypt (*Ta'am V'Da'as Haggadah*, p. 68).

This helps explain the statement that appears in the *Zohar*, that when Hashem comes to redeem the Jewish people from exile, He appears as a mother figure. Rav Chaim Volozhin explains that both a father and a mother have mercy on their children and love them dearly. But when a child is dirty, a father will often call the mother to clean the child. Hence, when Hashem comes to redeem and cleanse His children from their sins and wrongdoings, He appears in the form of a mother figure (*Kol Tzofayich*, Vol. 3, p. 45).

The Maharal gives another reason why it was Hashem Himself Who took the Jewish people out of Egypt. He explains that upon the redemption of the Jewish nation from Egypt Hashem designated us to be His people and His servants, so it was appropriate that Hashem Himself would take us out of Egypt to be His special nation (*Gevuros Hashem* 55).

וּבִזְרֹעַ נְטוּיָה. זוֹ הַחֶרֶב, כְּמָה שֶׁנֶּאֱמַר, וְחַרְבּוֹ שְׁלוּפָה בְּיָדוֹ, נְטוּיָה עַל יְרוּשָׁלָיִם.[1]

וּבְמֹרָא גָּדֹל. זוֹ גִּלּוּי שְׁכִינָה, כְּמָה שֶׁנֶּאֱמַר, אוֹ הֲנִסָּה אֱלֹהִים לָבוֹא לָקַחַת לוֹ גוֹי מִקֶּרֶב גּוֹי, בְּמַסֹּת, בְּאֹתֹת, וּבְמוֹפְתִים, וּבְמִלְחָמָה, וּבְיָד חֲזָקָה, וּבִזְרוֹעַ נְטוּיָה, וּבְמוֹרָאִים גְּדֹלִים, כְּכֹל אֲשֶׁר עָשָׂה לָכֶם יהוה אֱלֹהֵיכֶם בְּמִצְרַיִם לְעֵינֶיךָ.[2]

וּבְאֹתוֹת. זֶה הַמַּטֶּה, כְּמָה שֶׁנֶּאֱמַר, וְאֶת הַמַּטֶּה הַזֶּה תִּקַּח בְּיָדֶךָ, אֲשֶׁר תַּעֲשֶׂה בּוֹ אֶת הָאֹתֹת.[3]

וּבְמוֹפְתִים. זֶה הַדָּם, כְּמָה שֶׁנֶּאֱמַר, וְנָתַתִּי מוֹפְתִים בַּשָּׁמַיִם וּבָאָרֶץ:[4]

As each of the words דָּם, blood, אֵשׁ, fire, and עָשָׁן, smoke, is said, a bit of wine is removed from the cup, with the finger or by pouring.

דָּם וָאֵשׁ וְתִימְרוֹת עָשָׁן.

דָּבָר אַחֵר בְּיָד חֲזָקָה, שְׁתַּיִם. וּבִזְרֹעַ נְטוּיָה, שְׁתַּיִם. וּבְמֹרָא גָּדֹל, שְׁתַּיִם. וּבְאֹתוֹת, שְׁתַּיִם. וּבְמוֹפְתִים, שְׁתַּיִם: אֵלּוּ עֶשֶׂר מַכּוֹת שֶׁהֵבִיא הַקָּדוֹשׁ בָּרוּךְ הוּא עַל הַמִּצְרִים בְּמִצְרַיִם, וְאֵלּוּ הֵן:

— Think About It —

Hashgachah Pratis and the Ten Plagues

אֵלּוּ עֶשֶׂר מַכּוֹת שֶׁהֵבִיא הַקָּדוֹשׁ בָּרוּךְ הוּא עַל הַמִּצְרִים בְּמִצְרַיִם

These are the Ten Plagues which the Holy One, Blessed is He, brought upon the Egyptians in Egypt

The Ten Plagues instilled within the Jews the knowledge

With an outstretched arm — refers to the sword, as it says: His drawn sword in His hand, outstretched over Jerusalem.[1]

With great awe — alludes to the revelation of the *Shechinah*, as it says: Has God ever attempted to take unto Himself a nation from the midst of another nation by trials, miraculous signs, and wonders, by war and with a mighty hand, and outstretched arm, and by awesome revelations, as all that HASHEM your God did for you in Egypt, before your eyes?[2]

With signs — refers to the miracles performed with the staff as it says: Take this staff in your hand, that you may perform the miraculous signs with it.[3]

With wonders — alludes to the blood, as it says: I will show wonders in the heavens and on the earth:[4]

As each of the words דָּם, *blood*, אֵשׁ, *fire*, and עָשָׁן, *smoke*, is said, a bit of wine is removed from the cup, with the finger or by pouring.

Blood, fire, and columns of smoke.

Another explanation of the preceding verse: [Each phrase represents two plagues,] hence: **mighty hand** — two; **outstretched arm** — two; **great awe** — two; **signs** — two; **wonders** — two. These are the Ten Plagues which the Holy One, Blessed is He, brought upon the Egyptians in Egypt, namely:

---

1. *I Divrei HaYamim* 21:16. 2. *Devarim* 4:34. 3. *Shemos* 4:17. 4. *Yoel* 3:3.

---

of Hashem's *hashgachah pratis*, the individual attention and protection Hashem gives each one of His people. For instance, during the first plague of blood, the Egyptians had no drinking water and were dying from thirst. If an Egyptian chanced upon a Jew drinking a cup of water, he would stick his straw into the cup. When Hashem miraculously ensured that the Jew continued to drink water while the Egyptian drank blood, His *hasghachah pratis* became evident, down to the smallest drop of water.

In telling about the plagues, the Torah says, לְמַעַן תֵּדַע כִּי אֲנִי ה' בְּקֶרֶב הָאָרֶץ, *So that you will know that I am Hashem in the midst of the land* (*Shemos* 8:18). This lesson of Hashem's Divine protection is central to the Seder we celebrate every year.

Rav Tzadok HaKohen says, "Just as one is obligated to believe in Hashem, one is obligated to believe that Hashem has a personal connection with him…and that Hashem receives pleasure when he does His will" (*Tzidkas HaTzaddik* 154).

Hashem's Justice

אֵלּוּ עֶשֶׂר מַכּוֹת שֶׁהֵבִיא הַקָּדוֹשׁ בָּרוּךְ הוּא עַל הַמִּצְרִים בְּמִצְרַיִם
These are the Ten Plagues which the Holy One, Blessed is He, brought upon the Egyptians in Egypt

The Midrash (*Midrash Rabbah, Shemos* 9:10 and *Bamidbar* 10:2) explains that the Ten Plagues with which Hashem punished the Egyptians were meted out measure for measure for all the evil the Egyptians had brought upon the Jewish people. We find that when Yisro saw the clear demonstration of Hashem's exact retribution, it influenced him to convert to Judaism (*Shemos* 18:11). The principle that Hashem rewards and punishes in direct accordance to one's actions is central to our belief in Hashem; only He has the ability to repay a person for his exact actions, down to the smallest detail.

The Ten Plagues were appropriate punishments for the Egyptians, but they also delivered a message to the whole world, for all generations: Hashem's awesome might and His ability to change nature at His will (*Rashi, Vayeira* 7:3; *Ramban, Shemos* 10:1). The plagues demonstrated to the world how Hashem is intricately involved in all aspects of creation and in every individual's life, down to the smallest detail. This is known as *hashgachah pratis*.

Today, one of the words people frequently use is *random* — I met a random person, a random taxi happened along, I got a random letter. The Ten Plagues taught the world that there is no "random": Hashem is intricately involved in every area of our lives, and there is no such concept as mere chance or coincidence.

The Hebrew word for coincidence is *mikreh*. The *sefarim* explain that the word מִקְרֶה is actually comprised of the words רַק מֵ'ה, *only from Hashem*. Every "random" event that takes place in the world and in our lives is a direct, personal message from Hashem.

> A student of Rav Yisrael Salanter once purchased a lottery ticket and then sold it to a friend. The next day, the winner was announced, and that ticket turned out to be the winning ticket.
>
> The student who had sold the winning ticket met his rebbi, Rav Yisrael, who told him, "It's not the lottery number or the ticket that merits winning but rather the person!"
>
> Clearly, it was Divinely ordained that the friend, and not the original buyer of the ticket, should get the winnings (Kedosh Yisrael, p. 69).

> Rav Yosef Yozel Horowitz, the Alter of Novardok, would teach his students that if you see someone running to catch a train and he arrives just as the train pulls out of the station, you shouldn't think he was late for this train. You should realize that he was early for the next train: everything that happens to a person is with hashgachah pratis (HaMe'oros HaGedolim, p. 267).

> In the first weeks of World War II, the German air force strafed Polish cities mercilessly. Rav Elchanan Wasserman, the prized student of the Chofetz Chaim, escaped to the city of Mir with a group of students. Upon arrival, many of the students were terrified of what would happen to them, but Rav Elchanan was serene.
>
> "Rebbi," a student asked Rav Elchanan, "how can you be so calm at a terrifying time like this?"

Rav Elchanan explained, "I received a tradition from my rebbi, the Chofetz Chaim, that every bullet has its address. Whatever Hashem has decreed will happen to a person will happen to him regardless of where he is, so there is no reason to be frightened."

The students were immediately calmed (Ohr Elchanan, Vol. 2, p. 242; Me'or Einei Yisrael, Vol. 2, p. 274).

Vital Appreciation

אֵלּוּ עֶשֶׂר מַכּוֹת שֶׁהֵבִיא הַקָּדוֹשׁ בָּרוּךְ הוּא
עַל הַמִּצְרִים בְּמִצְרָיִם

These are the Ten Plagues which the Holy One, Blessed is He, brought upon the Egyptians in Egypt

The Midrash (*Midrash Rabbah, Shemos* 9:10; *Tanchuma, Va'eira* 14) tells us that Aharon rather than Moshe struck the water and the ground, actions that brought about the first three plagues of blood, frogs, and lice, because Moshe had *hakaras hatov*, appreciation, for the benefit that the water and ground had afforded him. When Moshe was a baby, he was placed in the water, and that protected him until Bisya, the daughter of Pharaoh, discovered and rescued him. Later, when Moshe killed the Egyptian who was beating up a Jew, the ground quickly covered up the corpse, protecting Moshe from any incriminating evidence.

Rav Eliyahu Dessler explains that the trait of *hakaras hatov* is so vital because it allows one to recognize and thank Hashem for all that He does for him. In Moshe's case, he even demonstrated *hakaras hatov* to inanimate objects. The water and ground wouldn't have been hurt if Moshe had hit them and didn't appreciate that Moshe didn't; but *hakaras hatov* is as much about the one who recognizes and appreciates the favor as it is about the one whom we are thanking. Our ability to recognize good and appreciate it is central to our relationships to others, and especially to the way we relate to Hashem (*Michtav MeEliyahu*, Vol. 1, pp. 50–51, and Vol. 3, pp. 98–101).

Rav Yerucham Levovitz explains that one of the central themes of Seder night and the Haggadah is to show gratitude to Hashem for all the good He gave us both in the past and the present. Rav Mattisyahu Salomon explains that the Torah's messages of *hakaras hatov* are brought specifically in the parashah of the Ten Plagues, whose purpose was to demonstrate Hashem's existence and *hashgachah pratis*. This is because it is through working on our *hakaras hatov* that we strengthen our *emunah* in Hashem (*Matnas Chaim Haggadah*, p. 18).

There is a well-known custom to feed the birds prior to Shabbos *Parashas Beshalach*, also known as *Shabbos Shirah*. Rav Yaakov Yitzchak Horowitz, the Chozeh of Lublin, explains that the custom evolved when Moshe told *Bnei Yisrael* to gather a double portion of manna on Friday, since no manna would descend on Shabbos.

The parashah goes on to relate that on Friday night Dasan and Aviram went out and placed manna throughout the camp in an attempt to undermine Moshe's authority; the Jews would wake up and see that Moshe was wrong and the manna had come on Shabbos, after all! But in the morning, there was no manna to be found: the birds had eaten all of it, protecting the honor of Hashem and proving Moshe's words true. In appreciation of what the birds did thousands of years ago, we have the custom to feed them at this time as a demonstration of our gratitude and thankfulness (*Ta'amei HaMinhagim* page 531).

> *Mazel tov! A daughter was born to a couple within a year of their marriage. The new father approached Rav Shach to ask if they should make a celebratory kiddush. Rav Shach responded, "Had this baby girl been born after eight years of marriage, wouldn't you make a festive celebration thanking Hashem? Hashem has saved you the pain of waiting eight years for a child — don't you think there is an even greater reason to thank Hashem and celebrate?" (Kinyan Torah Haggadah, p. 199).*

Rav Nosson Tzvi Finkel, the rosh yeshivah of the Mir, suffered from debilitating Parkinson's disease, but he didn't allow his condition to stand in the way of his building one of the largest Torah institutions in the world.

Rav Nosson Tzvi was supposed to officiate at the wedding of one of his students. A few days before the wedding, a member

As each of the plagues is mentioned, a bit of wine is removed from the cup. The same is done by each word of Rabbi Yehudah's mnemonic.

דָּם. צְפַרְדֵּעַ. כִּנִּים. עָרוֹב. דֶּבֶר. שְׁחִין. בָּרָד. אַרְבֶּה. חֹשֶׁךְ. מַכַּת בְּכוֹרוֹת.

of the rosh yeshivah's family phoned the chassan and told him that the rosh yeshivah wouldn't be able to come to the wedding because of his extreme weakness. The chassan fully understood, and another rosh yeshivah was given the honor of officiating.

On the day of his wedding the chassan attended Rav Nosson Tzvi's class for selected students and then left for his wedding. Hours later, in the middle of the wedding, the chassan was surprised to see that none other than the rosh yeshivah, Rav Nosson Tzvi, entered the hall!

The joyous chassan ran over to the rosh yeshivah and thanked him for coming, but asked him why he had troubled himself to come when he was so weak.

"You're right," said Rav Nosson Tzvi. "I am extremely weak. But when I saw how you sacrificed and came to my shiur today, on the day of your wedding, despite the extreme difficulty of finding time on such a busy day, I wanted to reciprocate and show my appreciation for your sacrifice by coming to your wedding despite the extreme difficulty involved" (B'Chol Nafshecha, p. 164).

Hakaras Hatov in Honoring Parents

דָּם. צְפַרְדֵּעַ. כִּנִּים.

Blood. Frogs. Lice.

One of the lessons we learn from the Ten Plagues is the importance of showing gratitude to those who have done good for us, and especially to recognize that we owe so much to HaKadosh Baruch Hu Who is constantly doing good for us. Moshe Rabbeinu wouldn't strike the Nile to bring the plague of blood because it was a source of salvation for him when he was a baby.

Hakaras hatov is central to our relationship with Hashem. It's

> As each of the plagues is mentioned, a bit of wine is removed from the cup. The same is done by each word of Rabbi Yehudah's mnemonic.

1. Blood 2. Frogs 3. Lice 4. Wild Beasts 5. Pestilence 6. Boils 7. Hail 8. Locusts 9. Darkness 10. Plague of the Firstborn.

---

also the root of the mitzvah to honor one's father and mother, the mitzvah of *kibbud av va'eim*, according to the *Sefer HaChinuch* (mitzvah 33). We need to appreciate all that our parents have done for us — including bringing us into the world — and to thank them. Furthermore, through our appreciation of our parents, we will come to appreciate and thank Hashem for all the overwhelming good He provides with every breath we take.

The Torah says that the reward for those who properly honor their parents is the blessing of long life (*Shemos* 20:12). Rav Saadiah Gaon explains that as parents age, their children become their prime caretakers, and this can take up much of the child's time and energy. The Torah guarantees that the time spent caring for their parents is not lost; on the contrary, it's an investment and a merit for long life (*Rabbeinu Bachya, Shemos* 20:12).

One might erroneously think that we are obligated to honor our parents because of all the material gifts they give us: food,

---

◆§ Ten Drops of Wine

As we name each plague, we dip a finger into the wine and remove a drop. Why do we do this?

- The cup of wine symbolizes our joy at the redemption from Egypt. The punishment and destruction of the Egyptian nation was central to the Exodus, but we know that one should not rejoice over the downfall of his enemies (see *Mishlei* 24:17). Therefore we remove a small amount of wine from the cup to lessen our joy just a little (*Abarbanel*).
- Although Hashem decreed that the Jewish nation were to be enslaved, the Egyptians went beyond this and prevented the Jews from learning Torah and practicing mitzvos as well. The Egyptians were therefore punished for the disruption of the Jewish nation's spiritual life. The Torah is compared to wine (*Ta'anis* 7a). When reciting the Ten Plagues, we remove a small amount of wine to remind us that the Egyptians were punished because they prohibited the Jewish nation from learning and keeping the Torah, which is compared to wine (*Chodesh HaAviv Haggadah*).

money, shelter, clothing. If that's the case, then if parents no longer can or will provide financial support, the obligation to respect them is diminished, right?

The Ksav Sofer proves from the Torah just how mistaken such a way of thinking is. After the Jewish nation left Egypt and arrived in the desert, all their physical needs were provided miraculously by Hashem. Food came from the manna, clothing never wore out and grew with the person, and protection from the elements came from the Clouds of Glory. Yet Chazal tell us that at this very point, even prior to the giving of the Torah, Hashem commanded the Jewish nation the mitzvah to honor their parents (*Sanhedrin* 56b). We see that honoring and respecting parents is an absolute obligation, irrespective of the parents' ability to provide material assistance for their children (*Ksav Sofer, Devarim* 5:16; *Meshech Chochmah, Kedoshim*).

Although, as the *Chinuch* explains, *hakaras hatov* is at the root of *kibbud av va'eim*, it's not the only reason for this central mitzvah. There might be times when a child may justly feel that his parents don't deserve respect and honor; they might not have treated him well, they might be difficult to deal with, or they may never have provided his physical or emotional needs. But still he is obligated to honor them.

The reason is in the command itself. The Torah says, כַּבֵּד אֶת אָבִיךָ וְאֶת אִמֶּךָ כַּאֲשֶׁר צִוְּךָ ה' אֱלֹהֶיךָ, *Honor your father and your mother, as Hashem, your God, commanded you* (*Devarim* 5:16). Rav Chaim Palagi asks why the Torah added the words כַּאֲשֶׁר צִוְּךָ ה' אֱלֹהֶיךָ, *as Hashem, your God, commanded you*; isn't it clear that the command comes from Hashem?

Rav Palagi answers that the Torah is teaching us that the mitzvah of honoring parents is not conditional on how someone was treated by his parents. The reason one is commanded to honor one's parents is simply because Hashem commanded us and not for any other reason or reward (*Tochachas Chaim, Toldos*).

> *The Chazon Ish would tell students that before returning home from yeshivah for the Yamim Tovim, they were obligated to learn the halachos of kibbud av va'eim. The Chazon Ish would also tell people that when they were seeking a wife, they should look for one who dresses modestly and who honors her parents: two defining characteristics in a potential shidduch (Ana Avda).*

Anger: The Antithesis of Sound Judgment

צְפַרְדֵּעַ
Frogs

The Midrash tells us (*Tanchuma, Va'eira* 14; *Eliyahu Rabbah* 8) that initially one large frog emerged from the river, and when the Egyptians began to strike it, hundreds of frogs emerged from it, until eventually the entire Egypt was filled with millions of frogs. Once the Egyptians saw that hitting the large frog only made matters worse, why did they continue to strike it?

Rav Yaakov Yisrael Kanievsky, the Steipler Gaon, answers that when people are angry, all logic and levelheadedness go out the window. Anger is the antithesis of sound judgment and the ability to reason rationally (*Birchas Peretz*).

> Rav Yaakov Yitzchak Horowitz, the Chozeh of Lublin, was extremely scrupulous to ensure that the three matzos he used for Seder night satisfied all the various halachic stringencies. On the night of Pesach, the Rebbe was in shul, and a poor man knocked on the door of the Horowitz home, begging the rebbetzin for matzos. The rebbetzin unknowingly gave the poor man the three special matzos that the Rebbe had baked, using all possible halachic stringencies.
>
> When he came home and went to put the matzos on the table, he couldn't find the ones he had prepared. His wife told him that she had inadvertently given them to a poor man who had no matzos. The Rebbe calmly took three regular matzos and said, "Using matzos made with all the various stringencies is only a rabbinic law. Yet becoming angry is a transgression of a Torah law!" (*HaChozeh MiLublin*, p. 220).

Turn to Hashem

כִּנִּים
Lice

Strangely, it doesn't say that the plague of lice had ended before the next plague of wild beasts began. Rav Shalom Schwadron explains that in reality the plague of lice was not yet removed, since Pharaoh never asked Moshe to daven for it to stop, as he had for the earlier plagues. Rav Shalom explains that without *tefillah* nothing good can happen, so the lice continued to plague the Egyptians until the end of the plague of wild beasts. At that point Pharaoh again pleaded with Moshe to daven, and both plagues ended (*Lev Shalom, Va'eira*, p. 89).

When Hashem charged Moshe Rabbeinu with the task of leading the Jewish nation out of Egypt, Moshe said that he was incapable of taking on such a mission because of his speech impediment. Hashem responded that He would help him through this difficulty and Moshe should not worry about his orating skills. Moshe continued to argue until Hashem told him that he would appoint Aharon, his brother, as the speaker; Moshe would tell Aharon what to say, and Aharon would say it.

This brings up an obvious question: why didn't Hashem simply heal Moshe's speech impediment? The Ramban (*Shemos* 4:10) answers that Moshe was not healed because he never asked that his impediment be cured! Only once we open ourselves up to *tefillah* can we receive *berachos*.

How fortunate we are that we can turn to Hashem at any moment, at any time of day or night, with any request. Try to speak to the president of the United States: it's nearly impossible, and even if it could happen, it would take months or years to arrange such a meeting, and only for some affair that affects the whole country. The president — or, for that matter, the governor of the state, or the mayor of the city — has no time or interest in your personal affairs. But we can turn to Hashem at any moment of the day, wherever we are, with any problem, concern, or worry, no matter how small, knowing that the Creator of the world will listen to our every *tefillah*.

The Chazon Ish explains that if one wants to strengthen his *emunah* in Hashem, he should turn to Hashem for help and guidance for any need that arises, no matter how simple. If someone needs new shoes but doesn't have enough money, he should turn to Hashem and say, "Hashem, I need new shoes. Please help me find a way to pay for them." One who constantly turns to Hashem and converses with Him will undoubtedly strengthen his *emunah* in Hashem (*Ma'aseh Ish*, Vol.1, p. 280).

The story is told of Rav Dovid Biderman of Lelov, who was traveling and stopped off at a friend's home to spend the night. Rav Dovid's friend was delighted to have the Rebbe as his guest and asked his wife to prepare a special meal.

She wanted to make something delicious, but their grinding poverty didn't allow them even basic ingredients such as sugar, spices, and oil. She prepared fresh porridge from the little flour and water she had in the house. Rav Dovid ate the porridge, thanked his host, and departed the next morning.

Upon returning home, Rav Dovid told his wife that he had tasted a porridge dish that was truly extraordinary: it was so tasty that it tasted like Gan Eden! Rebbetzin Biderman knew that her husband never spoke about the physical taste of food, and she understood that the dish this woman had prepared must have had some special spiritual properties.

Rebbetzin Biderman traveled to her husband's friend and asked his wife how she had prepared the porridge dish. The woman replied, "We are so poor that when I was preparing the porridge I had nothing to sweeten it, no sugar or spices. But I wanted to prepare something special for the Rebbe. I took the flour and the water and davened to Hashem: 'Please, Hashem, You know that if we had spices and ingredients to make this porridge sweet and delicious for our guest, the righteous tzaddik, we would surely use them. But there is nothing in the house to use. You, Hashem, You have Gan Eden. Please put some of the taste of Gan Eden into this dish so that we can benefit the tzaddik.'

"My tefillos were accepted, and Rav Dovid of Lelov tasted Gan Eden in his porridge."

We can daven for even the smallest things. Are you preparing the kugel and chicken for Shabbos, putting up the cholent, or making a cake for a friend's *simchah*? You can daven to Hashem that the food should taste good and come out beautiful. Nothing is too small or insignificant for us to ask Hashem (*Mekudeshes At*, p. 182).

Rav Pinchas Koritzer, a student of the Baal Shem Tov, was once overheard davening to Hashem that "the helper should return." His students were curious about their Rebbi's strange tefillah and asked him about it.

THE EISHES CHAYIL HAGGADAH

"The cleaning woman who helps my wife left, and the rebbetzin truly needs her assistance. I'm davening that the cleaning lady should return to work!" (Birkas Avraham, Lech Lecha).

Hashem Controls Nature

בָּרָד
Hail

The plague of hail demonstrated to the Jewish people for all generations Hashem's total control over the laws of nature. Fire and ice can't coexist naturally; one always prevails over the other. Yet when striking the Egyptian people, fire and ice harmoniously joined together in fulfilling the will of Hashem.

Even in our times we can see Hashem's control over the laws of nature. Rav Yechezkel Abramsky, *av beis din* of London, told of his experiences in Siberia, which bear this out.

> Growing up, I was a weak child who would catch a cold from the smallest temperature changes. After being arrested by the Russian authorities, I was sentenced to hard labor in Siberia. I was wearing just a thin shirt when I arrived there, and we were ordered each morning to remove our shoes and run in the snow, in temperatures that reached minus 40 degrees! People died daily during this exercise, running through deadly ice, wind, and cold. I, who was always weak, who caught cold so easily, how would I survive?
>
> Shivering, I lifted my eyes up to the heavens and spoke to Hashem: "Hashem, it says in Your Torah, הַכֹּל בִּידֵי שָׁמַיִם חוּץ מִצִּנִּים פַּחִים, All matters [of misfortune] are in the Hands of Heaven except for sickness brought about by exposure to cold and heat (Kesubos 30a). Illness caused by one's own negligence is one's own responsibility. But, Hashem, the evil Russians have given me no clothing to protect me from the cold; they even took away the little clothing I came with! If so, the responsibility that man was given to clothe himself properly and avoid catching a cold no longer applies. I can't take care of myself and therefore it's Your responsibility to protect me, Hashem!"
>
> So there, in one of the coldest, iciest, and windiest places in

the world, Hashem protected me, and I, who was always infirm, never got sick even once while in Siberia *(Melech B'Yofyav*, p. 209).

— Think About It —
The Fast of the Firstborn

מַכַּת בְּכוֹרוֹת
Plague of the Firstborn

The halachah mandates that all firstborn male children fast on *erev Pesach* to remember the miracle of Hashem taking the lives of all the firstborn Egyptians while the firstborn Jews were spared, despite being at the lowest point of sin themselves.

The Midrash (*Pesikta Rabbah* 2:198) says that Bisyah, the oldest child of Pharaoh, wasn't killed during the plague of the firstborn because she saved and raised Moshe Rabbeinu. This seems to imply that other firstborn Egyptian women were killed during the plague of the firstborn. If so, Jewish firstborn women should have to fast on *erev Pesach* as well.

This is, in fact, the opinion of some authorities (*Shulchan Aruch, Orach Chaim* 470:1), but the more general opinion is that firstborn women are not required to fast. Several reasons are given. First, there are conflicting midrashim touching on whether the Egyptian women were included in the death of the firstborn plague, as the Midrash implies that only the Egyptian firstborn males were struck (*Midrash Rabbah, Shemos* 15:13).

Second, even if the plague affected the Egyptian firstborn women, the commemoration that the Jewish people hold by fasting on *erev Pesach* only includes those who have the halachic status of a firstborn, and that excludes women.

In addition, the Jewish nation was redeemed in the merit of the righteous women, and hence there was never even a thought that they should be killed along with the firstborn Egyptians (*Mishnah Berurah* 470:4; *Yalkut Shimoni Haggadah*, p. 7; See *Yechaveh Da'as* 3:25).

The Ten Plagues
Measure for Measure

Here follows a list indicating how each plague was appropriate punishment for the cruelty of the Egyptians, based on several midrashim:

דָם / Blood

- The Egyptians decreed that all Jewish boys be thrown into the river, so the punishment began there.
- In addition, they did not permit the Jewish women to use the river for ritual immersion. Hashem therefore punished them measure for measure, turning the Nile and all the waters in Egypt into blood.
- Furthermore, the Torah is compared to water. The Egyptians prevented the Jews from learning Torah, so their water was rendered unusable.
- Also, Pharaoh claimed that he was the god of the Nile; Hashem therefore struck the waters first, demonstrating that Pharaoh had no control over the waters and that Hashem is the God of all of creation.

צְפַרְדֵּעַ / Frogs

- The Egyptians forced the Jews to catch bugs, insects, and other pests, a demeaning and cruel labor, so measure for measure Hashem brought an infestation of frogs.
- Moreover, the Egyptians would wake the Jews in the middle of the night and force them out to work. In retribution, Hashem brought upon them the plague of frogs, and the Egyptians were unable to sleep because of the frogs' incessant croaking.
- Jewish women delivering babies were forced to stifle their cries for fear that the Egyptians would hear them and kill their babies. In return, Hashem sent the plague of frogs, whose croaks were deafening to the Egyptians' ears.
- The Jewish women screamed and cried out when the merciless Egyptians took their babies and threw them into the river. As a result, the frogs' croaks mimicked human cries and screams, reminding the Egyptians of the cries and screams of the Jewish people.

כִּנִּים / Lice

- ☐ The Egyptians didn't allow the Jews to wash themselves in the bathhouses, and as a result many of them suffered from lice.
- ☐ The Egyptians forced the Jews to sweep the streets and marketplaces to keep them clean, so, measure for measure, Hashem sent upon them the plague of lice, which made them feel unclean.

עָרוֹב / Wild Beasts

- ☐ The Jews were forced to hunt wild and exotic animals for the Egyptians' entertainment.
- ☐ The Egyptians also humiliated the Jews by forcing them to carry the Egyptian children on their shoulders. As a result, Hashem sent the plague of wild beasts, which tore apart many Egyptians and snatched away their children.

דֶּבֶר / Pestilence

- ☐ The Jews were forced to tend the Egyptians' flocks in remote pastures so the men wouldn't be able to return home at night to their wives.
- ☐ The Egyptians treated their animals with greater respect than they did the Jews. In order not to tire out their oxen, they forced the Jews to pull the hoes used to plow the fields, a backbreaking and extremely demeaning task. Measure for measure, Hashem sent the plague of pestilence.

שְׁחִין / Boils

- ☐ The Jews were beaten by the Egyptian taskmasters until their bodies were full of bruises and lesions.
- ☐ Also, the Egyptians did everything in their control to prevent the Jewish men from returning home to their wives and family at night. Measure for measure, the Egyptians were unable to come close to their family members due to the painful and unsightly boils.
- ☐ In addition, the Jews were forced to work under the blazing hot Egyptian sun until their skin blistered. As a direct result, Hashem sent the plague of boils.

רַבִּי יְהוּדָה הָיָה נוֹתֵן בָּהֶם סִמָּנִים:
דְּצַ"ךְ. עֲדַ"שׁ. בְּאַחַ"ב.

The cups are refilled. The wine that was removed is not used.

רַבִּי יוֹסֵי הַגְּלִילִי אוֹמֵר: מִנַּיִן אַתָּה אוֹמֵר שֶׁלָּקוּ הַמִּצְרִים בְּמִצְרַיִם עֶשֶׂר מַכּוֹת, וְעַל הַיָּם לָקוּ חֲמִשִּׁים מַכּוֹת? בְּמִצְרַיִם

בָּרָד / Hail

- ☐ The Jews were forced to guard the Egyptian fields, trees, and gardens. As a result, Hashem sent the hail, which destroyed the trees and gardens of the Egyptian people.
- ☐ The Egyptians demeaned the Jews by forcing them to sleep out in the open fields and forests together with the animals. As a measure-for-measure punishment, Hashem sent the hail, forcing the Egyptians to bring their animals indoors and sleep next to them.

אַרְבֶּה / Locusts

- ☐ The Jews were required to work in distant fields in order to prevent the Jewish nation from increasing, since the men were unable to return home at night. Measure for measure, Hashem sent a plague affecting the Egyptian fields and their yield.
- ☐ The Egyptians starved the Jews, feeding them only barely edible bread. Measure for measure, Hashem sent the plague of locusts, which consumed their wheat and grain, resulting in starvation.

חֹשֶׁךְ / Darkness

- ☐ When the Egyptians made a feast, they would force a Jew to bend down and put a candle on his head to provide light. If the Jew moved, they would cut off his head. In retribution, Hashem brought darkness.
- ☐ The Jews were forced to hide their newborn babies in dark cellars, so measure for measure, Hashem brought the darkness.

Rabbi Yehudah abbreviated them by their Hebrew initials:

D'TZACH, ADASH, B'ACHAV.

The cups are refilled. The wine that was removed is not used.

Rabbi Yose the Galilean said: How does one derive that the Egyptians were struck with 10 plagues in Egypt, but with 50 plagues at the sea? — Concerning the plagues in Egypt

- ☐ The Egyptians forced the Jews to work day and night, not distinguishing between the two; as a result, Hashem sent the plague of darkness.

מַכַּת בְּכוֹרוֹת / Plague of the Firstborn

- ☐ The Egyptians wanted to destroy the Jewish nation, who is described with the words בְּנִי בְכוֹרִי יִשְׂרָאֵל, *My firstborn son is Yisrael*! (*Shemos* 4:22). Measure for measure, the firstborn Egyptians were killed.

The Lesson of the Plagues

שֶׁלָּקוּ הַמִּצְרִים בְּמִצְרַיִם עֶשֶׂר מַכּוֹת
That the Egyptians were struck with ten plagues in Egypt?

Why was it necessary for Hashem to punish the Egyptians with ten different plagues? Could He not have afflicted them with one gigantic, destructive epidemic?

The Ten Plagues demonstrated to the Egyptians and the world the Oneness of Hashem and His total control over all aspects of creation. The Egyptians believed that Pharaoh was the god of the Nile and that other gods ruled over other facets of creation. The Ten Plagues came to prove Hashem's absolute control over the entire world and all its creations.

Blood demonstrated Hashem's complete control over the water, while the plague of Frogs confirmed Hashem's control over the creatures of the sea. The Lice demonstrated Hashem's control of the ground. The plague of Wild Beasts and Pestilence

מַה הוּא אוֹמֵר, וַיֹּאמְרוּ הַחַרְטֻמִּם אֶל פַּרְעֹה, אֶצְבַּע אֱלֹהִים הִוא.¹ וְעַל הַיָּם מָה הוּא אוֹמֵר, וַיַּרְא יִשְׂרָאֵל אֶת הַיָּד הַגְּדֹלָה אֲשֶׁר עָשָׂה יהוה בְּמִצְרַיִם, וַיִּירְאוּ הָעָם אֶת יהוה, וַיַּאֲמִינוּ בַּיהוה וּבְמֹשֶׁה עַבְדּוֹ.² כַּמָּה לָקוּ

---

established Hashem's dominance over the animal kingdom. The Locusts proved Hashem's authority over the bird kingdom and the winds. The plague of Boils confirmed that Hashem controls the health of a person. The deadly Hail demonstrated Hashem's dominion over the rain and weather, while the plague of Darkness proved Hashem's control over the celestial beings. Finally, the Plague of the Firstborn demonstrated Hashem's control over human life (*Chayei Olam*, Vol. 1, Ch. 15; see also *Maharal, Gevuros Hashem* 34).

Had the purpose of *yetzias Mitzrayim* been only to redeem us, Hashem could have instantaneously wiped out the evil Egyptians and taken us out of Egypt. This was clearly not the case. Hashem sent 10 nature-defying plagues upon Egypt followed by the miracles at the splitting of the Yam Suf to demonstrate His Omnipotence, as it says, בַּעֲבוּר תֵּדַע כִּי אֵין כָּמֹנִי בְּכָל הָאָרֶץ, *So that you may know there is none like Me in all the earth* (*Shemos* 9:14).

The thunderous display of awe-inspiring, Godly miracles happened not so much to free us from the Egyptians but to serve as a beacon of light and understanding for all generations, to let us know without a doubt that Hashem is with us and that He controls all aspects of our lives.

Why So Many Plagues?

מִנַּיִן אַתָּה אוֹמֵר שֶׁלָּקוּ הַמִּצְרִים בְּמִצְרַיִם עֶשֶׂר מַכּוֹת
How does one derive that the Egyptians were struck with ten plagues in Egypt?

If Hashem decreed that the Jewish nation should be enslaved, why were the Egyptians punished so severely?

Hashem decreed that the Jews were to be enslaved. The

the Torah states: The magicians said to Pharaoh, "It is the finger of God."[1] However, of those at the sea, the Torah relates: Israel saw the great "hand" which HASHEM laid upon the Egyptians, the people feared HASHEM, and they believed in HASHEM and in His servant Moshe.[2] How many

---

1. *Shemos* 8:15. 2. Ibid. 14:31.

Egyptians not only enslaved them but embittered their lives with forced labor and an attempt to wipe out the Jewish nation, killing their children and keeping the men apart from the women (*Ramban, Bereishis* 15:14)

When Moshe came to Pharaoh demanding the Jewish people's freedom, Pharaoh refused. This clearly exposed that he was not enslaving the Jewish people in order to fulfill the will of Hashem but rather as a means of torturing and enslaving them for personal, venomous reasons (*Kedushas Levi, Shemos* 10:1).

Also, the decree was only for the Jewish nation to be physically enslaved. The Egyptians went beyond this and enslaved the Jews spiritually as well, not permitting them to practice mitzvos and to learn Torah. This is what eventually caused the Jews to sink to the 49th level of spiritual impurity (*Noda BiYehudah, Derashos HaTzlach* 44; *Kedushas Levi, Klalei HaNissim* 1).

In addition, the decree of servitude was only supposed to affect the men. Pharaoh went ahead and enslaved the women and children as well (*Avnei Kodesh, Shemos*).

Where Is Moshe in the Haggadah?

וַיִּירְאוּ הָעָם אֶת ה' וַיַּאֲמִינוּ בַּה' וּבְמשֶׁה עַבְדּוֹ

The people feared Hashem, and they believed in Hashem and in His servant Moshe

Moshe Rabbeinu, the leader of the Jewish people and the one to lead them out of Egypt, is mentioned only once throughout the Haggadah, and only in passing: in this passage that informs us that וַיַּאֲמִינוּ בַּה' וּבְמשֶׁה עַבְדּוֹ, *They believed in Hashem and in His servant Moshe*. The commentators supply several explanations

בְּאֶצְבַּע? עֶשֶׂר מַכּוֹת. אֱמוֹר מֵעַתָּה, בְּמִצְרַיִם לָקוּ עֶשֶׂר מַכּוֹת, וְעַל הַיָּם לָקוּ חֲמִשִּׁים מַכּוֹת.

רַבִּי אֱלִיעֶזֶר אוֹמֵר. מִנַּיִן שֶׁכָּל מַכָּה וּמַכָּה שֶׁהֵבִיא הַקָּדוֹשׁ בָּרוּךְ הוּא עַל הַמִּצְרִים בְּמִצְרַיִם הָיְתָה שֶׁל אַרְבַּע מַכּוֹת? שֶׁנֶּאֱמַר, יְשַׁלַּח בָּם חֲרוֹן אַפּוֹ — עֶבְרָה, וָזַעַם, וְצָרָה, מִשְׁלַחַת מַלְאֲכֵי רָעִים.[1] עֶבְרָה, אַחַת. וָזַעַם, שְׁתַּיִם. וְצָרָה, שָׁלֹשׁ. מִשְׁלַחַת מַלְאֲכֵי רָעִים, אַרְבַּע. אֱמוֹר מֵעַתָּה, בְּמִצְרַיִם לָקוּ אַרְבָּעִים מַכּוֹת, וְעַל הַיָּם לָקוּ מָאתַיִם מַכּוֹת.

רַבִּי עֲקִיבָא אוֹמֵר. מִנַּיִן שֶׁכָּל מַכָּה וּמַכָּה שֶׁהֵבִיא הַקָּדוֹשׁ בָּרוּךְ הוּא עַל הַמִּצְרִים בְּמִצְרַיִם הָיְתָה שֶׁל חָמֵשׁ מַכּוֹת? שֶׁנֶּאֱמַר, יְשַׁלַּח בָּם חֲרוֹן אַפּוֹ, עֶבְרָה, וָזַעַם, וְצָרָה, מִשְׁלַחַת מַלְאֲכֵי רָעִים. חֲרוֹן אַפּוֹ, אַחַת. עֶבְרָה, שְׁתַּיִם. וָזַעַם, שָׁלֹשׁ. וְצָרָה, אַרְבַּע. מִשְׁלַחַת מַלְאֲכֵי רָעִים, חָמֵשׁ. אֱמוֹר מֵעַתָּה, בְּמִצְרַיִם לָקוּ חֲמִשִּׁים מַכּוֹת, וְעַל הַיָּם לָקוּ חֲמִשִּׁים וּמָאתַיִם מַכּוֹת.

כַּמָּה מַעֲלוֹת טוֹבוֹת לַמָּקוֹם עָלֵינוּ.

---

for his absence in our retelling of the story of the Exodus.

The night of the Seder is dedicated purely to strengthening our trust and belief in Hashem and His absolute Oneness. Hence, even Moshe is mentioned only once and in reference to him being an *eved Hashem*, a servant of God, so we shouldn't think that he played any role other than that of dedicated emissary of Hashem (*Vilna Gaon*).

Another reason: Moshe Rabbeinu was the most humble of

plagues did they receive with the finger? Ten! Then conclude that if they suffered 10 plagues in Egypt [where they were struck with a finger], they must have been made to suffer 50 plagues at the sea [where they were struck with a whole hand].

Rabbi Eliezer said: How does one derive that every plague that the Holy One, Blessed is He, inflicted upon the Egyptians in Egypt was equal to four plagues? — for it is written: He sent upon them His fierce anger: wrath, fury, and trouble, a band of emissaries of evil.[1] [Since each plague in Egypt consisted of] 1) wrath, 2) fury, 3) trouble, and 4) a band of emissaries of evil, therefore conclude that in Egypt they were struck by 40 plagues and at the sea by 200!

Rabbi Akiva said: How does one derive that each plague that the Holy One, Blessed is He, inflicted upon the Egyptians in Egypt was equal to five plagues? — for it says: He sent upon them His fierce anger, wrath, fury, trouble, and a band of emissaries of evil. [Since each plague in Egypt consisted of] 1) fierce anger, 2) wrath, 3) fury, 4) trouble, and 5) a band of emissaries of evil, therefore conclude that in Egypt they were struck by 50 plagues and at the sea by 250!

The Omnipresent has bestowed so many favors upon us!

---
1. *Tehillim* 78:49.

---

all people, and Moshe would not have wanted his name to be placed in the Haggadah. It is therefore omitted (*Chofetz Chaim al HaTorah*, p. 199).

	אִלּוּ הוֹצִיאָנוּ מִמִּצְרַיִם
דַּיֵּנוּ.	וְלֹא עָשָׂה בָהֶם שְׁפָטִים
	אִלּוּ עָשָׂה בָהֶם שְׁפָטִים
דַּיֵּנוּ.	וְלֹא עָשָׂה בֵאלֹהֵיהֶם
	אִלּוּ עָשָׂה בֵאלֹהֵיהֶם
דַּיֵּנוּ.	וְלֹא הָרַג אֶת בְּכוֹרֵיהֶם
	אִלּוּ הָרַג אֶת בְּכוֹרֵיהֶם
דַּיֵּנוּ.	וְלֹא נָתַן לָנוּ אֶת מָמוֹנָם
	אִלּוּ נָתַן לָנוּ אֶת מָמוֹנָם
דַּיֵּנוּ.	וְלֹא קָרַע לָנוּ אֶת הַיָּם
	אִלּוּ קָרַע לָנוּ אֶת הַיָּם
דַּיֵּנוּ.	וְלֹא הֶעֱבִירָנוּ בְתוֹכוֹ בֶּחָרָבָה

Clothing for the Children

וְלֹא נָתַן לָנוּ אֶת מָמוֹנָם דַּיֵּנוּ
But not given us their wealth, it would have sufficed us

Prior to the Exodus from Egypt, Hashem commanded Moshe Rabbeinu to tell *Bnei Yisrael*, וְשָׁאֲלָה אִשָּׁה מִשְּׁכֶנְתָּהּ וּמִגָּרַת בֵּיתָהּ כְּלֵי כֶסֶף וּכְלֵי זָהָב וּשְׂמָלֹת וְשַׂמְתֶּם עַל בְּנֵיכֶם וְעַל בְּנֹתֵיכֶם וְנִצַּלְתֶּם אֶת מִצְרָיִם, *Each woman shall request from her [Egyptian] neighbor and for the one who lives in her house silver vessels, gold vessels, and garments, and you shall put them on your sons and daughters, and you shall empty out Egypt* (Shemos 3:22).

Rav Yekusiel Yehudah Halberstam, the Klausenberger Rebbe, asks why the Jewish women were told to take the Egyptians' clothing for their sons and daughters and not for themselves.

The Midrash tells us that in the merit of the Jewish nation not changing their mode of dress they merited redemption (*Midrash Rabbah, Bamidbar* 13:20). The Rebbe explains that Egypt has a particularly hot climate throughout most of the year. The clothing of the Egyptians was most assuredly short and revealing, certainly

Had He brought us out of Egypt,
but not executed judgments against the Egyptians,
>it would have sufficed us.

Had He executed judgments against them,
but not upon their gods,
>it would have sufficed us.

Had He executed [judgments] against their gods,
but not slain their firstborn,
>it would have sufficed us.

Had He slain their firstborn,
but not given us their wealth,
>it would have sufficed us.

Had He given us their wealth,
but not split the sea for us,
>it would have sufficed us.

Had He split the sea for us,
but not led us through it on dry land,
>it would have sufficed us.

---

not the kind of dress Jewish women would wear. The Jewish women didn't take the Egyptian clothing for themselves, since the Egyptian women's fashions were too short and immodest. They gave the clothing to their children, who were smaller and shorter, and therefore the Egyptian clothing fit them (*Imrei Yatziv*, p. 448).

Deserving of Salvation

אִלּוּ קָרַע לָנוּ אֶת הַיָּם וְלֹא הֶעֱבִירָנוּ בְּתוֹכוֹ בֶּחָרָבָה דַּיֵּנוּ

Had He split the sea for us, but not led us through it on dry land, it would have sufficed us

After a year of seeing Hashem's miracles, after a night of watching Him wreak vengeance upon the Egyptian firstborn, *Bnei*

אִלּוּ הֶעֱבִירָנוּ בְתוֹכוֹ בֶּחָרָבָה
וְלֹא שִׁקַּע צָרֵינוּ בְּתוֹכוֹ דַּיֵּנוּ.
אִלּוּ שִׁקַּע צָרֵינוּ בְּתוֹכוֹ
וְלֹא סִפֵּק צָרְכֵּנוּ בַּמִּדְבָּר אַרְבָּעִים שָׁנָה דַּיֵּנוּ.

Yisrael arrive at the Yam Suf and find themselves surrounded by danger on all sides. In front of them — the treacherous sea; on both sides — the dark and ominous desert; and behind them — the furious Egyptian Army, out for blood. *Bnei Yisrael* cry out to Hashem to save them. Hashem responds, מַה תִּצְעַק אֵלָי דַּבֵּר אֶל בְּנֵי יִשְׂרָאֵל וְיִסָּעוּ, *Why do you cry out to Me? Speak to Bnei Yisrael and tell them to travel forward* (Shemos 14:15).

The Ohr HaChaim asks the obvious question: Haven't we been told to daven to Hashem at all times, and certainly at a time of enormous need and great national desperation? At such a time, when *Bnei Yisrael* clearly had nowhere else to turn, should they not have looked to HaKadosh Baruch Hu for salvation?

The Ohr HaChaim answers by citing the *Zohar* that tells us that at the moment the Jewish people were cornered, a heavenly tribunal passed judgment, declaring that they were undeserving of Divine assistance since their sins were too numerous to merit their being saved from the Egyptians. Hashem therefore told Moshe, מַה תִּצְעַק אֵלָי, *Why do you cry out to Me?* I can no longer help! The heavenly tribunal has found *Bnei Yisrael* to be at such an impure level that nothing can be done to save them.

"Yet there is *one* merit that can still save them," Hashem continues. "When all else fails, דַּבֵּר אֶל בְּנֵי יִשְׂרָאֵל וְיִסָּעוּ, *Speak to Bnei Yisrael and tell them to travel into the sea*. In the merit of their *emunah* and *bitachon* in Me and My words, in the *zechus* of their following Me even when I send them into the churning waters of the Yam Suf — for that they will deserve My love and protection."

When all else fails, *emunah* and *bitachon* in Hashem is the sole merit that can bring about heavenly salvation and *berachah* (see also *Chasam Sofer, Toras Moshe,* Shemos 14:15; *Rav Shamshon Refael Hirsch* and *Meshech Chochmah* on Shemos 14:15; *Ruach Chaim, Avos* 2:4).

Had He led us through it on dry land,
but not drowned our oppressors in it,
it would have sufficed us.
Had He drowned our oppressors in it,
but not provided for our needs in the desert
for 40 years, it would have sufficed us.

The Women's Song

אִלּוּ קָרַע לָנוּ אֶת הַיָּם
Had He split the sea for us

After *Bnei Yisrael* miraculously crossed the Yam Suf and the waters came crashing down on the Egyptians, they broke into song and praise to Hashem, singing "*Az Yashir.*" Then, after the men had recited their song of thanks, the women, led by Miriam, took their drums and recited a short song of praise: שִׁירוּ לַה' כִּי גָאֹה גָּאָה סוּס וְרֹכְבוֹ רָמָה בַיָּם, *Sing to Hashem, for He is exalted above the arrogant, having hurled horse with its rider into the sea* (Shemos 15:21).

Why did Miriam choose to sing this specific stanza from the lengthy song that the men had sung? What significance does this particular passage have to Jewish women?

One of the central reasons the Jews deserved to be redeemed from Egypt was that they agreed to accept the Torah at Sinai. But what of the women, who are not obligated in many of the mitzvos, nor in the study of Torah? Why did they deserve redemption?

The Talmud (*Berachos* 17a) tells us that women are worthy of a reward in the next world because they send their children to yeshivos and eagerly greet their husbands when they return from their Torah study. Women who encourage, support, and enable their husbands and children to study Torah merit great reward.

Rav Yeshayahu Cheshin explains that this is exactly why Miriam chose to sing the passage of סוּס וְרֹכְבוֹ רָמָה בַיָּם, *He hurled horse with its rider into the sea.* Why did the horses of the Egyptian army deserve to be thrown into the ocean? What was their sin?

One who supports evil is given the status of the one who performs the evil act itself, so the Egyptian horses were punished

אִלּוּ סִפֵּק צָרְכֵּנוּ בַּמִּדְבָּר אַרְבָּעִים שָׁנָה
וְלֹא הֶאֱכִילָנוּ אֶת הַמָּן דַּיֵּנוּ.
אִלּוּ הֶאֱכִילָנוּ אֶת הַמָּן
וְלֹא נָתַן לָנוּ אֶת הַשַּׁבָּת דַּיֵּנוּ.
אִלּוּ נָתַן לָנוּ אֶת הַשַּׁבָּת
וְלֹא קֵרְבָנוּ לִפְנֵי הַר סִינַי דַּיֵּנוּ.

---

because they supported the evil Egyptian riders. From this passage, we learn that the opposite is also true: the Jewish women, who supported and encouraged their families' Torah study, merited redemption (*Divrei Yeshayahu* 9).

Chesed in the Desert

אִלּוּ סִפֵּק צָרְכֵּנוּ בַּמִּדְבָּר אַרְבָּעִים שָׁנָה
Had He provided for our needs in the desert for 40 years

The Torah (*Devarim* 2:7) describes how for 40 years in the desert all of the Jews' physical needs were miraculously provided by Hashem. Food was supplied in the form of the manna. Clothing never wore out, and it grew along with the person, always remaining clean and crisp. The Clouds of Glory provided shelter and protection (*Shibbolei HaLeket*). It sounds ideal, but it elicits a question: if everyone's needs were fulfilled in the desert, how were the Jewish people capable of fulfilling the mitzvah of *chesed* and *tzedekah*, something so fundamental to the Jewish nation's identity?

The *Sefer HaChinuch* (mitzvah 479) explains that the mitzvah of *chesed* and *tzedakah* is fulfilled through helping one's friend with whatever he needs. At times, a friend may not require financial assistance as much as emotional support. Acknowledgment, a comforting word, encouragement, and a warm smile are all essential components of *mitzvas chesed*.

The Talmud tells us, טוֹב הַמַּלְבִּין שִׁנַּיִם לַחֲבֵירוֹ יוֹתֵר מִמַּשְׁקֵהוּ חָלָב, *Better is the one who shows the white of his teeth to his friend than the one who gives him milk to drink* (*Kesubos* 111b). Sometimes a

Had He provided for our needs in the desert
for 40 years, but not fed us the manna,
    it would have sufficed us.
Had He fed us the manna,
but not given us the Shabbos,
    it would have sufficed us.
Had He given us the Shabbos,
but not brought us close to Har Sinai,
    it would have sufficed us.

---

person needs a smile more than a cup of refreshing milk. Milk is cooling, nourishing, full of protein, but a smile can change a person's entire perspective on a problem.

The Talmud also tells us that someone who gives charity to the poor is granted six blessings, while someone who gives charity and also blesses the poor person is granted 11 blessings (*Bava Basra* 9b). The Maharal explains that the benefit of food or money given to one in need only lasts a short while. On the other hand, a blessing, warm words of encouragement, or a smile can make a difference that will last forever, and therefore one is rewarded with additional blessings (*Nesivos Olam, Nesiv Tzedakah* 4).

Along these lines, it is written, אָנֹכִי ה' אֱלֹקֶיךָ... הַרְחֶב פִּיךָ וַאֲמַלְאֵהוּ, *I am Hashem, your God... Open your mouth wide and I will fill it* (*Tehillim* 81:11). How does one widen his mouth? When we smile, our mouths widen. Hashem is telling us that if we widen our mouths through smiling at others, He will fill us with *berachah* (*MeHashem Yatza HaDavar*).

Even in the desert, with all their physical needs provided by Hashem, there was still opportunity for the Jews to perform acts of *chesed* by helping those needing encouragement, attention, and a simple smile. Likewise, Rav Moshe Feinstein explains that *chesed* performed in the desert involved making peace between man and his friend, as well as between spouses (*Dibros Moshe, Bava Basra* 12:49).

Rav Aryeh Levin would remark, "Do you know why people come to pour out their hearts to me? Not because I am a *tzaddik*; there are greater *tzaddikim* than I. Not because I am a

אִלּוּ קֵרְבָנוּ לִפְנֵי הַר סִינַי וְלֹא נָתַן לָנוּ אֶת הַתּוֹרָה דַּיֵּנוּ.

talmid chacham; there are superior *talmidei chachamim* than I. People turn to me because they feel that I am not only listening to them but that I make an extreme effort to understand them. I try to tap into their hearts and feel their pain, and the petitioners acutely feel how much I feel for them" (*Tzaddik Yesod Olam*, p. 75; see also the *Steipler Gaon, Pninei Rabbeinu Kehillos Yaakov*, p. 20).

The Merit of Humility

אִלּוּ קֵרְבָנוּ לִפְנֵי הַר סִינַי
Had He brought us close to Har Sinai

The Talmud (*Sotah* 5a) tells us that Hashem chose to give His Torah to His people on Har Sinai because of its humility. Har Sinai was a small, lowly mountain, and Hashem wanted to teach the Jewish people that the Torah can only be accepted by those who are humble and modest.

In that case, the Rebbe of Kotzk asks, why wasn't the Torah given in a valley? Wouldn't that more dramatically give the message that the Torah must be accepted with humility?

The Rebbe answered that being humble doesn't mean seeing yourself as bad or stupid or worthless; that's what we call today suffering from "low self-esteem." True humility comes from having an accurate picture of what you can achieve, knowing where your strengths lie, but remaining humble in the knowledge that these strengths are gifts from Hashem, given to us in order to fulfill our missions on earth. A person can only be humble and modest if he recognizes his true value and self-worth — only someone who is a mountain and has authentic stature can demonstrate genuine modesty and humility (*Emes VeEmunah; Ruach Chaim, Avos* 4:1).

When asked if he knew he was the *gadol hador* of the generation, the Chazon Ish replied that yes, he knew that he was the leader of the generation. But, he added, if someone else had had his

> Had He brought us close to Har Sinai,
> but not given us the Torah,
> it would have sufficed us.

---

abilities and opportunities, he would surely have surpassed him in his accomplishments (*Ma'aseh Ish*, Vol. 2, p. 178).

> *Sarah Schenirer was visiting one of her Bais Yaakov schools. After learning with the pupils and testing their knowledge, she joined the girls and teachers in dancing and singing the song "V'Taher Libeinu" (And You should purify our hearts). The students then sat in a circle, and Sarah Schenirer asked them, "Tell me, young ones, what is the most important trait that will help a person have a pure heart in her service of Hashem?"*
>
> *The answers varied. One student responded that fear of Heaven would create a pure heart. Another suggested that acting with kindness or respect is crucial for perfecting a pure heart. All the girls in the class responded to Sarah Schenirer's question, except one young girl who remained quiet.*
>
> *Finally, Sarah Schenirer asked the girl what she thought the most important trait was to give one a pure heart. The little girl answered shyly, "I don't know, Frau Schenirer."*
>
> *Sarah Schenirer smiled and told the girl, "You are absolutely correct. One who can say, 'I don't know,' one who is humble, who can subject herself to the will of Hashem — that, my talmidos, is precisely the person who will gain a pure heart!"* (*Eim B'Yisrael*, Vol. 2, p. 51).

Rav Chaim Yosef Dovid Azulai, known as the Chida, noted that in the generation of Rav Yosef Karo, the author of the Beis Yosef and Shulchan Aruch, there lived three outstanding Torah scholars, all of whom were capable of authoring such significant works. But Heaven decreed that Rav Yosef Karo receive the privilege of authoring these essential and monumental books of Jewish law, simply because he was the most humble and modest of them all (*Shem HaGedolim, Ma'areches HaSefarim* 2:59).

אִלּוּ נָתַן לָנוּ אֶת הַתּוֹרָה
וְלֹא הִכְנִיסָנוּ לְאֶרֶץ יִשְׂרָאֵל דַּיֵּנוּ.
אִלּוּ הִכְנִיסָנוּ לְאֶרֶץ יִשְׂרָאֵל
וְלֹא בָנָה לָנוּ אֶת בֵּית הַבְּחִירָה דַּיֵּנוּ.

עַל אַחַת כַּמָּה וְכַמָּה טוֹבָה כְפוּלָה וּמְכֻפֶּלֶת לַמָּקוֹם עָלֵינוּ. שֶׁהוֹצִיאָנוּ מִמִּצְרַיִם, וְעָשָׂה בָהֶם שְׁפָטִים, וְעָשָׂה בֵאלֹהֵיהֶם, וְהָרַג אֶת בְּכוֹרֵיהֶם, וְנָתַן לָנוּ אֶת מָמוֹנָם, וְקָרַע לָנוּ אֶת הַיָּם, וְהֶעֱבִירָנוּ בְתוֹכוֹ בֶּחָרָבָה, וְשִׁקַּע צָרֵינוּ בְּתוֹכוֹ, וְסִפֵּק צָרְכֵּנוּ בַּמִּדְבָּר אַרְבָּעִים שָׁנָה, וְהֶאֱכִילָנוּ אֶת הַמָּן, וְנָתַן לָנוּ אֶת הַשַּׁבָּת, וְקֵרְבָנוּ לִפְנֵי הַר סִינַי, וְנָתַן לָנוּ אֶת הַתּוֹרָה, וְהִכְנִיסָנוּ לְאֶרֶץ יִשְׂרָאֵל, וּבָנָה לָנוּ אֶת בֵּית הַבְּחִירָה, לְכַפֵּר עַל כָּל עֲוֹנוֹתֵינוּ.

רַבָּן גַּמְלִיאֵל הָיָה אוֹמֵר. כָּל שֶׁלֹּא אָמַר שְׁלֹשָׁה דְּבָרִים אֵלּוּ בַּפֶּסַח, לֹא יָצָא יְדֵי חוֹבָתוֹ, וְאֵלּוּ הֵן,

פֶּסַח. מַצָּה. וּמָרוֹר.

פֶּסַח שֶׁהָיוּ אֲבוֹתֵינוּ אוֹכְלִים בִּזְמַן שֶׁבֵּית הַמִּקְדָּשׁ הָיָה קַיָּם, עַל שׁוּם מָה?

To Each His Own

פֶּסַח שֶׁהָיוּ אֲבוֹתֵינוּ אוֹכְלִים בִּזְמַן שֶׁבֵּית הַמִּקְדָּשׁ הָיָה קַיָּם עַל שׁוּם מָה

Pesach — Why did our fathers eat a pesach offering during the period when the Beis HaMikdash still stood?

Immediately prior to taking them out of Egypt, Hashem

Had He given us the Torah,
but not brought us into the Land of Israel,
it would have sufficed us.
Had He brought us into the Land of Israel,
but not built the *Beis HaMikdash* for us,
it would have sufficed us.

Thus, how much more so should we be grateful to the Omnipresent for all the numerous favors He showered upon us: He brought us out of Egypt; executed judgments against the Egyptians; executed [judgments] against their gods; slew their firstborn; gave us their wealth; split the sea for us; led us through it on dry land; drowned our oppressors in it; provided for our needs in the desert for 40 years; fed us the manna; gave us the Shabbos; brought us close to Har Sinai; gave us the Torah; brought us to the Land of Israel; and built us the *Beis HaMikdash*, to atone for all our sins.

Rabban Gamliel used to say: Whoever has not explained the following three things on Pesach has not fulfilled his duty; namely,

> **Pesach** — the *pesach* offering;
> **Matzah** — the unleavened bread;
> **Maror** — the bitter herbs.

Pesach — Why did our fathers eat a *pesach* offering during the period when the *Beis HaMikdash* still stood? Because the Holy One,

---

commanded the Jewish people to eat the sacrificial *pesach* lamb. Hashem told them they should be careful not to break any bones when eating the sacrifice: וְעֶצֶם לֹא תִשְׁבְּרוּ בוֹ , *And you shall not break a bone in it* (*Shemos* 12:46). The *Sefer HaChinuch* (mitzvah 16) explains that when they were redeemed from Egypt, the Jewish nation became the *Am Segulah*, the treasured nation of

עַל שׁוּם שֶׁפֶּסַח הַקָּדוֹשׁ בָּרוּךְ הוּא עַל בָּתֵּי אֲבוֹתֵינוּ בְּמִצְרַיִם. שֶׁנֶּאֱמַר, וַאֲמַרְתֶּם,

Hashem (see *Shemos* 19:5). We were now a מַמְלֶכֶת כֹּהֲנִים וְגוֹי קָדוֹשׁ, *a kingdom of ministers and holy nation* (ibid. v. 6). One who is of such exalted lineage must behave, eat, and interact in a manner befitting royalty.

Someone who eats quickly, gluttonously, without dignity, can come to break the bones of the meat he is consuming. Therefore, at this time of our princely coronation, so to speak, we were especially commanded to eat and behave like princes and princesses, like the children of Hashem, the King of kings — like the *Am Segulah*, His Chosen Nation.

Although usually we are supposed to distance ourselves from all forms of haughtiness, there is one aspect of pride that we are allowed — no, that we are commanded — to feel: pride in our status as a holy people. Pride in our royal standing as the children of Hashem — that kind of pride is permitted and encouraged (*Ya'aros Devash*, Vol. 1, *drush* 15; *Tzidkas HaTzaddik* 247; *Malbim, Tehillim* 34:3).

Our sense of pride in being part of the Chosen Nation is applicable on the individual level as well. Rav Levi Yitzchak of Berditchev writes that one who says that his *tefillos* and mitzvos make no difference to Hashem is not a humble person; rather, he is leaning toward heresy, because he is denying a fundamental Jewish principle. Even as we feel humility, we simultaneously take pride in the fact that the mitzvos we perform here on this world and the small challenges that we overcome bring Hashem tremendous joy and *nachas* (*Kedushas Levi, Kedushah Shelishis* on Purim; see *Rav Tzadok HaKohen, Machashavos Charutz* 9).

Pesach is a time to recognize the true *nachas* we bring to Hashem. The Talmud teaches, כָּל אֶחָד וְאֶחָד חַיָּיב לוֹמַר בִּשְׁבִילִי נִבְרָא הָעוֹלָם, *A person is obligated to say, "The world was created for me"* (*Sanhedrin* 37a). I, as an individual, with all of my strengths and weaknesses, all my virtues and faults, am so special and beloved by Hashem that it was worth it for Him to create the entire world, with all its galaxies, billions of stars, and miraculous complexities, just for me! Clearly there is something unique about me that is so

Blessed is He, passed over the houses of our fathers in Egypt, as it is written: You shall say:

dear to Hashem that He wanted to create this entire world just for me. I am not just one of seven billion people in the world. I am the only child of Hashem. I was brought into this world to accomplish something that only I, with my unique personality, intelligence, and emotions can achieve, and no one else in the entire world can do what I can do (*Pri Tzaddik, Parashas Shekalim*).

The Birkas Avraham of Slonim points out that the word *bishvili*, "for me," in the Talmud's statement *The world was created for me* comes from the word *shvil*, "path." Every Jew has his own specific pathway in life that he must follow to fulfill the specific goals he is here to accomplish. I, and only I, can fulfill these goals, and no matter how small or insignificant these goals may seem to be, when I complete a task that Hashem created me for, it brings tremendous benefit and joy to Hashem (*Inyanei Bein HaMetzarim*; *Pri Tzaddik, Parashas Shekalim*).

> Rav Naftali Amsterdam, one of the foremost students of Rav Yisrael Salanter, once said to his venerated rebbi, "If I would have had the mind of the Sha'agas Aryeh, the heart of the Yesod V'Shoresh HaAvodah, and your middos, Rebbi, then I would be capable of serving Hashem properly."
>
> "Naftali," Rav Yisrael responded, "with your mind, your heart, and your middos you will be able to serve Hashem as well!"
>
> Hashem gave each of us the precise and exact tools that we need to serve Him in our unique ways, with our unique abilities and nature (*Alei Shur*, Vol. 1, pp. 36–38).

Against the Odds

עַל שׁוּם שֶׁפֶּסַח הַקָּדוֹשׁ בָּרוּךְ הוּא עַל בָּתֵּי אֲבוֹתֵינוּ בְּמִצְרַיִם

Because the Holy One, Blessed is He, passed over the houses of our fathers in Egypt

Rav Yonasan Steif states that in this *pasuk* is an indication that Hashem passed over the homes of the Jewish people and spared the Jewish firstborn in the merit of the righteous Jewish

זֶבַח פֶּסַח הוּא לַיהוה, אֲשֶׁר פָּסַח עַל בָּתֵּי בְנֵי יִשְׂרָאֵל בְּמִצְרַיִם בְּנָגְפּוֹ אֶת מִצְרַיִם, וְאֶת בָּתֵּינוּ הִצִּיל, וַיִּקֹּד הָעָם וַיִּשְׁתַּחֲווּ.[1]

---

women. It says, פָּסַח הַקָּדוֹשׁ בָּרוּךְ הוּא, *The Holy One, Blessed is He, passed over* the homes of the Jewish people when killing the Egyptian firstborns, עַל בָּתֵּי אֲבוֹתֵינוּ בְּמִצְרַיִם, **because** of the homes of the Jewish people in Egypt. The "home" is a reference to the Jewish woman, as we find that Rabbi Yose referred to his wife as his "home" (*Shabbos* 118b). Hashem's protection of the Jewish homes came about *because* of the Jewish "homes": the women (*Mahari Steif Haggadah*, p. 326).

The Jewish women in Egypt faced insurmountable challenges in tending to their families. Their husbands were away for weeks and months at a time, and they themselves were forced to work at backbreaking tasks while raising large families. They could have refused to have more children; they could have refused to go out to the fields to help and encourage their husbands. Instead they chose to bear children and raise them, and they did what they could to strengthen their husbands. The Jews were taken out of Egypt in the merit of their steadfast *emunah* and *bitachon* in Hashem. What's more, Jewish history is full of stories of strong women demonstrating incredible faith under the worst of circumstances.

> Yocheved Scheinberg was 4 months old when the Nazis swept into Holland and assembled all the Jews to be sent to their deaths. Her parents and siblings were among those transported and sent to the gas chambers. Baby Yocheved was placed in a faraway hamlet in northern Holland, in the custody of a non-Jewish family.
>
> The war years passed. Yocheved always assumed she was a non-Jew, like those around her. When she turned 7, she found out that she was Jewish, and her entire family had been killed by the Nazis. She went to live with her Jewish relatives in Amsterdam and found her way back to living a Jewish life.
>
> Yocheved's extended family told her what they knew about her parents and grandparents, but she was always curious about the origins of her name. In her genealogical research she found

"It is a *pesach* offering for HASHEM, Who passed over the houses of the Children of Israel in Egypt when He struck the Egyptians and spared our houses"; and the people bowed down and prostrated themselves.[1]

---

1. Shemos 12:27.

---

no trace of the name Yocheved in her family. Yocheved expanded her research and began writing about the history of Jewish Holland before and after the Holocaust. The research took her to a local library, where she spent hours poring over newspapers from prewar Holland. Flipping through a newspaper printed two months after the outbreak of the war, she was startled to see the names Ita and Hans Scheinberg — the names of of her parents! It was a letter to the editor of the local Jewish newspaper:

"Over the last few months we have heard voices of despair and hopelessness. People have lost their wish to live, and many have even taken their own lives. At this time we are expecting a baby. People have questioned us, even berated us for bringing a child into this dark and hopeless world. 'Why bring into this world another child who is going to perish like the rest of us?' they ask.

"To these people and to the Jews of Holland we want to cite the story in the Talmud about Pharaoh's decree that all Jewish boys be thrown into the Nile. Amram and Yocheved decided to separate: why would they bring children into the dark world of Egyptian slavery and persecution? But their daughter Miriam told her father that Pharaoh only decreed death to the boys, while his decision to separate from his wife doomed the girls as well. Amram and Yocheved accepted their daughter's words and remarried, and from this remarriage Moshe Rabbeinu was born. Therefore, we have decided that if the child born to us will be a boy, we will name him Amram, and if the child born to us will be a girl we will name her Yocheved."

Yocheved Scheinberg's parents had trusted in Hashem, as Yocheved and Amram had trusted Him, and they merited a baby girl named Yocheved, the only surviving member of their immediate family. They placed their trust in Hashem like

The middle matzah is lifted and displayed while the following paragraph is recited.

מַצָּה זוּ שֶׁאָנוּ אוֹכְלִים, עַל שׁוּם מָה? עַל שׁוּם שֶׁלֹּא הִסְפִּיק בְּצֵקָם שֶׁל אֲבוֹתֵינוּ

the righteous Jewish women in Egypt, and Hashem ensured that their memory lives on through their daughter, Yocheved (Emunah Sheleimah, Vol. 4, p. 454).

Rav Aryeh Levin, known affectionately as the "Tzaddik of Jerusalem," insisted that his wife's bitachon was deeper and stronger even than his. During World War I, food was scarce in Jerusalem. Rav Aryeh had brought home nothing to eat for days, and the children cried from hunger.

At the time a wealthy man whom Rav Aryeh had once helped would lend money to people in need. At his wife's urging, Rav Aryeh took a few sefarim to be used as a security deposit and asked the wealthy man for a loan.

The man refused.

Why would somebody who had loaned money to so many others refuse to lend to Rav Aryeh Levin? The wealthy man explained that he knew that others would bear a grudge against him if he said no, but he was certain that Rav Aryeh would never bear a grudge, and therefore with apologies he had to refuse to give him any money.

Rav Aryeh returned home, hopeless and disheartened. Rav Aryeh's wife, hearing the story, said to her discouraged husband, "Aryeh, where is your bitachon in Hashem! Let's think it over. This man refused to lend you money — not because he has none, he's rich! And not because he never lends money — we know he has extended many loans! Could it be that he doesn't trust you? Impossible! He must remember how last month you ran to his house in the middle of the night to return a gold coin he accidentally left in our house.

"There is no natural way to understand his decision not to lend you money. Clearly, then, Hashem is sending us a message.

The middle matzah is lifted and displayed while the following paragraph is recited.

Matzah — Why do we eat this unleavened bread? Because the dough of our fathers

---

The money should not come from this man. Hashem wants us to strengthen our bitachon, as the pasuk says, הַשְׁלֵךְ עַל ה' יְהָבְךָ וְהוּא יְכַלְכְּלֶךָ, Cast upon Hashem your burden and He will sustain you (Tehillim 55:23)."

Rav Aryeh accepted his wife's encouraging words and was comforted. A little while later, there was a knock on the door. It was the postman with a letter from America — and inside the envelope was a $10 bill! The attached letter explained that the money was an inheritance from the estate of a recently deceased man whom Rav Aryeh had befriended many years earlier. Ten dollars was a large sum in those days and would buy a lot of food. More than that, the money was part of the message that Rav Aryeh's wife had understood: strengthen your bitachon and help will come (Mekudeshes At, p. 168).

Above the Angels

מַצָּה זוּ שֶׁאָנוּ אוֹכְלִים עַל שׁוּם מָה
Matzah — Why do we eat this unleavened bread?

One can only fulfill the requirement of eating matzah on Pesach with ingredients that can potentially turn into *chametz* if left long enough to rise. The Chasam Sofer asks, If on Pesach we are prohibited from eating *chametz*, wouldn't it make more sense for matzah to be made of ingredients that *cannot* turn into *chametz*?

The *sefarim* say that *chametz* symbolizes the *yetzer hara*, the evil inclination within each person, while they view matzah as symbolic of the *yetzer tov*, the good inclination. This means that if matzah must be made from ingredients that can potentially become *chametz*, we are saying that there is a place for the *yetzer hara* within us. What can this mean?

The Chasam Sofer points out that angels have no *yetzer hara*. Their service of Hashem is therefore performed without difficulty

לְהַחֲמִיץ, עַד שֶׁנִּגְלָה עֲלֵיהֶם מֶלֶךְ מַלְכֵי הַמְּלָכִים הַקָּדוֹשׁ בָּרוּךְ הוּא וּגְאָלָם. שֶׁנֶּאֱמַר, וַיֹּאפוּ אֶת הַבָּצֵק אֲשֶׁר הוֹצִיאוּ מִמִּצְרַיִם עֻגֹת מַצּוֹת כִּי לֹא חָמֵץ, כִּי גֹרְשׁוּ מִמִּצְרַיִם, וְלֹא יָכְלוּ לְהִתְמַהְמֵהַּ, וְגַם צֵדָה לֹא עָשׂוּ לָהֶם.[1]

---

or challenges. Human beings, on the other hand, have been given both a *yetzer hara* and a *yetzer tov*, and then are told to fulfill the will of Hashem by overcoming their *yetzer hara*. Someone who struggles but overcomes difficulties becomes stronger and reaches a higher place than one who has not been challenged at all. By overcoming our *yetzer hara* and performing the will of Hashem, we demonstrate dedication to Hashem that far supersedes the service of the ministering angels, who face no resistance.

The matzah, which symbolizes our inclination toward the service of Hashem, is only made possible by the use of *chametzdik* ingredients — by the presence of the *yetzer hara*, whose existence serves to strengthen our service of Hashem (*Toras Moshe Haggadah*; see *Tzavas HaRivash*, p. 20; *Kedushas Levi, Bereishis* 49:140).

As any athlete or gym teacher can tell you, to build strength one needs to lift weights that cause the muscles to strain and resist. Resistance and struggle expand the muscles, and the more someone wants to develop and build muscles, the heavier the weights must be. Our spiritual muscles similarly require resistance and challenge in order to grow.

> After the death of her husband, Rav Shlomo Heiman, the rosh yeshivah of Torah Vodaath, at the young age of 52, Rebbetzin Chaya Feige Heiman wrote a letter to a student of Rav Heiman's. In this letter she expresses her loneliness, pain, and sadness at the loss of her husband.
>
> At the end of the letter, she writes, "The ways of Hashem are proper and just. We just cannot understand them. A person has to know with clarity that if Hashem were to say to him, 'Here is the world and you run it,' our only reply would be, 'Hashem, only You can run this world. Please take it back and

did not have time to become leavened before the King of kings, the Holy One, Blessed is He, revealed Himself to them and redeemed them, as it is written: They baked the dough which they had brought out of Egypt into unleavened bread, for it had not fermented, because they were driven out of Egypt and could not delay, nor had they prepared provisions for the way.[1]

---

1. *Shemos* 12:39.

---

run it according to Your will'" (*Chiddushei Rav Shlomo*, Vol.1, Introduction).

The Blessing in the Dough

וְגַם צֵדָה לֹא עָשׂוּ לָהֶם
Nor had they prepared provisions for the way

Before any journey, one question always arises, What about food? Are there kosher restaurants and products along the way? Do we pack potato chips, peanut butter, rice cakes, other snacks for the kids? Before we plan the highway routes, before we make sure the passports and tickets are in order, we make our food list, part of the basic planning for any trip.

When *Bnei Yisrael* left Egypt, they departed with just a small amount of dough on their backs, enough to last perhaps a few meals. The Jewish people didn't even ask Moshe how they would manage to survive traveling into the desert with their families and barely anything to eat. With deep faith in Hashem, they marched out of Egypt into the barren desert with only the matzah dough on their backs (see *Rashi, Shemos* 12:39).

When we place our trust in Hashem, we can see blessings that even defy nature: בָּרוּךְ הַגֶּבֶר אֲשֶׁר יִבְטַח בַּה' וְהָיָה ה' מִבְטַחוֹ, *Blessed is the man who trusts in Hashem, and Hashem will be his trust* (*Yirmiyahu* 17:7). Chazal tell us that because of the *bitachon* *Bnei Yisrael* showed, the very matzah dough they carried was

The maror is lifted and displayed while the following paragraph is recited.

מָרוֹר זֶה שֶׁאָנוּ אוֹכְלִים, עַל שׁוּם מָה? עַל שׁוּם שֶׁמֵּרְרוּ הַמִּצְרִים אֶת חַיֵּי אֲבוֹתֵינוּ בְּמִצְרָיִם. שֶׁנֶּאֱמַר, וַיְמָרְרוּ אֶת חַיֵּיהֶם, בַּעֲבֹדָה קָשָׁה, בְּחֹמֶר וּבִלְבֵנִים, וּבְכָל עֲבֹדָה בַּשָּׂדֶה, אֵת כָּל עֲבֹדָתָם אֲשֶׁר עָבְדוּ בָהֶם בְּפָרֶךְ.[1]

---

blessed, sufficing for all their meals for a full month until the manna began to fall (*Be'er Yosef*, Vol. 2, p. 346).

Part of the Redemption

מָרוֹר זֶה שֶׁאָנוּ אוֹכְלִים עַל שׁוּם מָה
Maror — why do we eat this bitter herb?

The Jews were commanded to slaughter the *pesach* offering immediately before they left the land of bitter slavery. This offering, then, is connected with the Jewish nation's redemption. The *maror*, on the other hand, reminds us of the bitter labor and servitude the Jewish nation experienced in Egypt. If so, why does the Haggadah mention the *pesach* offering, the end of the bitter slavery, before the *maror*, reminder of that slavery? Shouldn't slavery come before redemption?

The Noda BiYehudah finds an answer in the fact that though the Jewish people were supposed to be in Egypt 400 years, Hashem redeemed them much sooner, after only 210 years, because of the severe intensity of the forced labor. Hashem had decreed that the Jews were to be slaves, but the Egyptians forced them to do *avodas parech*, backbreaking and grueling labor. This bitter slavery, represented by the *maror*, ultimately gave the Jews their early release from Egypt.

Therefore, explains the Noda BiYehudah, the *pesach*, matzah, and *maror* is not out of order, as the *maror* is part and parcel of the redemption (*Tzelach, Pesachim* 116b).

The maror *is lifted and displayed while the following paragraph is recited.*

Maror — Why do we eat this bitter herb? Because the Egyptians embittered the lives of our fathers in Egypt, as it says: They embittered their lives with hard labor, with mortar and bricks, and with all manner of labor in the field: Whatever service they made them perform was with hard labor.[1]

---

1. *Shemos* 1:14.

The Good in the Bad

מָרוֹר זֶה שֶׁאָנוּ אוֹכְלִים עַל שׁוּם מָה
Maror — Why do we eat this bitter herb?

The Talmud (*Pesachim* 39a) tells us that one should use "*chasah*" (lettuce, as understood by many) for *maror* since the word חסה can be broken down to mean חס ה', *Hashem had mercy*. It seems strange to use the *maror*, which recalls our bitter and arduous slavery, to remind us of Hashem's mercy. The Noda BiYehudah's explanation suggests that even in the most bitter of experiences, Hashem's mercy can be found.

> When the Soviet Union conquered Lithuania, yeshivos were prohibited from remaining open, and many students went underground to continue their Torah studies, including Rav Yaakov Galinsky. One night the students returned from one of their hidden Torah-study sessions, and the Soviets were waiting for them. Some of Rav Yaakov's friends managed to escape, but he and several others were caught and transported that very week to Siberia.
>
> "How jealous we were of our friends who had managed to escape," Rav Yaakov recalled. "But the very next day the Germans invaded Russia, and my friends and I who had been sent to Siberia were ultimately saved, while those who remained in Lithuania were mercilessly killed by the Germans" (V'Higadeta Haggadah, p. 247).

בְּכָל דּוֹר וָדוֹר חַיָּב אָדָם לִרְאוֹת אֶת עַצְמוֹ כְּאִלּוּ הוּא יָצָא מִמִּצְרַיִם. שֶׁנֶּאֱמַר, וְהִגַּדְתָּ לְבִנְךָ בַּיּוֹם הַהוּא לֵאמֹר, בַּעֲבוּר זֶה עָשָׂה יהוה לִי, בְּצֵאתִי מִמִּצְרָיִם.[1] לֹא אֶת אֲבוֹתֵינוּ בִּלְבַד גָּאַל הַקָּדוֹשׁ בָּרוּךְ הוּא, אֶלָּא אַף אוֹתָנוּ גָּאַל עִמָּהֶם. שֶׁנֶּאֱמַר, וְאוֹתָנוּ הוֹצִיא מִשָּׁם, לְמַעַן הָבִיא אֹתָנוּ לָתֶת לָנוּ אֶת הָאָרֶץ אֲשֶׁר נִשְׁבַּע לַאֲבוֹתֵינוּ.[2]

We may perceive some life experiences as bitter, but the *maror* may in reality be part of the redemption and salvation.

Sometimes, it can take years until we see the mercy in the "*maror.*"

> *Tuesday November 18, 2014. Two Palestinian terrorists enter Kehillas Bnei Torah in Har Nof, brutally murdering four and injuring many others, one of whom subsequently died. Rabbi Yaakov Tavin should have been there, since he davened every day with this particular minyan.*
>
> *Except for Tuesdays. On Tuesdays, Rabbi Tavin davened earlier so he could help his wife with their son, who has Down syndrome. Mrs. Tavin recalls that when their child was born, she traveled to Bnei Brak to meet with Rebbetzin Kanievsky for encouragement. The rebbetzin looked at the newborn child, Binyomin Dovid, and said, "You don't know what shemirah (protection) you have in your home."*
>
> *"At the time, I thought she meant perhaps that other things would be easier because this would be difficult," Mrs. Tavin recalls. "But now, nearly 13 years later, I truly understand. Binyomin Dovid was the only reason my husband was not in his minyan that morning. And the shemirah went further: my husband's post-davening chavrusa was also not there that morning because he knew my husband wouldn't be there and he davened elsewhere."*

The word *Divine* means "related to Hashem." The same word also means to perceive something. At times it may be difficult

In every generation it is one's duty to regard himself as though he personally had gone out of Egypt, as it says: You shall tell your son on that day: "It was because of this that HASHEM did for 'me' when I went out of Egypt."¹ It was not only our fathers whom the Holy One, Blessed is He, redeemed from slavery; we, too, were redeemed with them, as it says: He brought "us" out from there so that He might take us to the land which He had promised to our fathers.²

1. *Shemos* 13:8. 2. *Devarim* 6:23.

---

to perceive the good when something that seems to be bad has occurred. But our view is limited, and Hashem in His infinite love for us guides us, protects us, and knows what is truly good for us — and sometimes He even lets us get a glimpse of His Divine plan.

— Think About It —

Reliving the Experience

בְּכָל דּוֹר וָדוֹר חַיָּב אָדָם לִרְאוֹת אֶת עַצְמוֹ כְּאִלּוּ הוּא יָצָא מִמִּצְרָיִם

In every generation it is one's duty to regard himself as if he personally had gone out of Egypt

The Haggadah tells us that we are obligated to feel as if we ourselves left Egypt.

So there we are sitting at the Seder table, in our cozy 21st-century homes. The lights are on, the air conditioning is humming quietly, the food is staying warm on the electric- or gas-stove top. How can we really make ourselves feel as if we were redeemed from ancient Egypt as we sit comfortably in our modern homes, without the faintest trace of a reminder of the servitude we suffered and the redemption we enjoyed so many thousands of years ago? How are we to approach this mitzvah?

One way we can bring ourselves closer to actually feeling the

The matzos are covered and the cup is lifted and held until it is to be drunk. According to some customs, however, the cup is put down after the following paragraph, in which case the matzos should once more be uncovered. If this custom is followed, the matzos are to be covered and the cup raised again upon reaching the blessing אֲשֶׁר גְּאָלָנוּ, *Who has redeemed us* (p. 224).

לְפִיכָךְ אֲנַחְנוּ חַיָּבִים לְהוֹדוֹת, לְהַלֵּל, לְשַׁבֵּחַ, לְפָאֵר, לְרוֹמֵם, לְהַדֵּר, לְבָרֵךְ, לְעַלֵּה, וּלְקַלֵּס, לְמִי שֶׁעָשָׂה לַאֲבוֹתֵינוּ וְלָנוּ אֶת כָּל הַנִּסִּים הָאֵלּוּ, הוֹצִיאָנוּ מֵעַבְדוּת לְחֵרוּת, מִיָּגוֹן לְשִׂמְחָה, וּמֵאֵבֶל לְיוֹם טוֹב, וּמֵאֲפֵלָה לְאוֹר גָּדוֹל, וּמִשִּׁעְבּוּד לִגְאֻלָּה. וְנֹאמַר לְפָנָיו שִׁירָה חֲדָשָׁה, הַלְלוּיָהּ.

הַלְלוּיָהּ הַלְלוּ עַבְדֵי יהוה, הַלְלוּ אֶת שֵׁם יהוה. יְהִי שֵׁם יהוה מְבֹרָךְ, מֵעַתָּה וְעַד עוֹלָם. מִמִּזְרַח שֶׁמֶשׁ עַד מְבוֹאוֹ,

---

experience is through words. *Haggadah* means "to tell," and through a detailed retelling of the story of our Exodus from Egypt and the miracles Hashem performed on our behalf we can in some way relive it, transporting ourselves to that time and feeling as if we ourselves were redeemed.

Because of this, we're told that on this night, כָּל הַמַּרְבֶּה לְסַפֵּר בִּיצִיאַת מִצְרַיִם הֲרֵי זֶה מְשֻׁבָּח, *The more one tells about the discussion of the Exodus, the more he is praiseworthy*, since the detailed and vivid narrative depicting the Exodus allows us to relive these past experiences (*Pnei Dovid*).

A person must feel that he himself has left Egypt. The root of the word *Mitzrayim* is *metzer*, "boundary" (see *Alshich, Shemos* 12:41, and *Ohr HaChaim, Bereishis* 46:4). Everyone has his own unique boundaries and limits, his own struggles, whether he's wrestling with external challenges such as financial difficulties or internal ones like anger. Life brings with it challenges, unexpected twists, concerns, and worries. On Pesach we strengthen our

The matzos are covered and the cup is lifted and held until it is to be drunk. According to some customs, however, the cup is put down after the following paragraph, in which case the matzos should once more be uncovered. If this custom is followed, the matzos are to be covered and the cup raised again upon reaching the blessing אֲשֶׁר גְּאָלָנוּ, *Who has redeemed us* (p. 224).

Therefore it is our duty to thank, praise, pay tribute, glorify, exalt, honor, bless, extol, and acclaim Him Who performed all these miracles for our fathers and for us. He brought us forth from slavery to freedom, from grief to joy, from mourning to festivity, from darkness to great light, and from servitude to redemption. Let us, therefore, recite a new song before Him! Halleluyah!

Halleluyah! Praise, you servants of HASHEM, praise the Name of HASHEM. Blessed is the Name of HASHEM from now and forever. From the rising of the sun to its setting,

---

emunah and *bitachon* in Hashem and His Godly abilities to care for us and help us rise over our "*metzarim.*"

When they left Egypt, the Jews went from the depths of pain, suffering, and servitude and became the nation of Hashem, a people for whom every need was miraculously provided. When we remember how the Egyptians were punished measure for measure, when we retell the story of slaves becoming free, when we remind ourselves of Hashem's *hashgachah pratis* and how He embraced us with His fatherly love, we feel that Divine protection in our own lives.

If we truly see ourselves as having been redeemed from Egypt, we can suppress worries about the future, like the Jews did when they followed Hashem out of Egypt. With the perfect faith our forefathers showed when they followed Him into the desert, we can enjoy His loving protection (*Rav Yerucham Levovitz, Da'as Chochmah U'Mussar* 1:41).

מְהֻלָּל שֵׁם יהוה. רָם עַל כָּל גּוֹיִם יהוה, עַל הַשָּׁמַיִם כְּבוֹדוֹ. מִי כַּיהוה אֱלֹהֵינוּ, הַמַּגְבִּיהִי לָשָׁבֶת. הַמַּשְׁפִּילִי לִרְאוֹת, בַּשָּׁמַיִם וּבָאָרֶץ. מְקִימִי מֵעָפָר דָּל, מֵאַשְׁפֹּת יָרִים אֶבְיוֹן.

A Direct Line to Hashem

**רָם עַל כָּל גּוֹיִם ה׳ עַל הַשָּׁמַיִם כְּבוֹדוֹ
מִי כַּה׳ אֱלֹקֵינוּ הַמַּגְבִּיהִי לָשָׁבֶת**

High above all nations is Hashem, above the heavens is His glory. Who is like Hashem, our God, Who is enthroned on high?

The Alshich explains that non-Jews believe God's presence is found high up in the heavens and not in this world: עַל הַשָּׁמַיִם כְּבוֹדוֹ, *Above the heavens is His glory.* Commentators explain that idolatry first developed because many people believed that Hashem was too great and too Godly to have a connection with simple human beings of flesh and blood. These individuals mistakenly assumed that although they could not have a connection to God, they could serve His servants such as the sun, moon, and stars. Over time such practices spiraled out of control, losing its original intent, and people began thinking that the sun, moon, and other creations contain Divine powers themselves.

The Ran explains that the first generation of idol worshipers, and those who followed in their ways, made an immense mistake. Hashem is great and Hashem is Godly, but it is specifically *because* of His limitless powers that He has a direct connection to each and every living being in this world. Hashem is not just the God of the solar system, celestial bodies, and galaxies. He is the God of every Dovid, Avraham, Yaakov, Sarah, Rochel, and Dinah on this world as well. Hashem is personally involved in our individual lives, down to the smallest detail.

This is why the Jewish people, unlike the non-Jews, praise Hashem, מִי כַּה׳ אֱלֹקֵינוּ הַמַּגְבִּיהִי לָשָׁבֶת, *Who is like Hashem, our God, Who is enthroned on high.* Hashem is Almighty and powerful,

HASHEM's Name is praised. High above all nations is HASHEM, above the heavens is His glory. Who is like HASHEM, our God, Who is enthroned on high, yet lowers Himself to look upon heaven and earth? He raises the destitute from the dust; from the trash heaps He lifts the needy —

מְקִימִי מֵעָפָר דָּל, מֵאַשְׁפֹּת יָרִים אֶבְיוֹן yet, *He raises the destitute from the dust; from the trash heaps He lifts the needy.* Hashem Himself in all His glory and honor goes down to lift up those in need (*Alshich, Tehillim* 113; *Ya'aros Devash, Tochachas Mussar, drush* 3; *Nefesh HaChaim* 3:9; *Yismach Yisrael*, Pesach; *Chafetz Chaim, Shem Olam, Sha'ar Shemiras HaShabbos* 3; *Michtav MeEliyahu*, Vol. 3, p. 165).

We are often told to try to follow in the ways of Hashem. A truly great person is not one who is inaccessible; a great leader is not cut off and far away from his people. One who is great tries to emulate Hashem by reaching down to his people, connecting to them and lifting them up, understanding the basic needs and concerns of his flock.

> *There was great excitement in the city. Sarah Schenirer was coming to visit! Throngs of her students crowded the train station to greet the woman who had started the Bais Yaakov movement.*
>
> *Everyone wanted to get close to their beloved teacher, to hear her wisdom or simply revel in her presence, but to the disappointment of the crowd, a carriage had been ordered to take Sarah Schenirer to the city center where she would be staying. She was hurried into the carriage, and the door slammed behind her.*
>
> *Two of the more daring girls jumped on the back of the slow-moving carriage, hoping to be close to her and catch her words. A teacher who saw this reckless behavior shouted at the girls to get down. When Sarah Schenirer realized what was happening, she asked that the carriage be stopped and quietly told the teacher, "We should never distance children who want to come close to us, and we should never suppress children who want to grow higher. We either need to go down to them or bring them*

לְהוֹשִׁיבִי עִם נְדִיבִים, עִם נְדִיבֵי עַמּוֹ. מוֹשִׁיבִי עֲקֶרֶת הַבַּיִת, אֵם הַבָּנִים שְׂמֵחָה; הַלְלוּיָהּ.[1]

> up to us. In this case, since I can't bring all the girls up into the carriage with me, I will go down to them."
>
> She stepped out of the carriage, placed her hands in the hands of the two girls, and walked with them and the throng of girls toward the city (Eim B'Yisrael, Vol. 2, p. 30).

Sometimes a great person "comes down" even to the level of the youngest and least learned.

> On Simchas Torah, Rav Isser Zalman Meltzer, the Slutsker rosh yeshivah, would gather the young children and make a special hakafah just for them. For an hour the great rosh yeshivah danced with the children, giving them their own special time and attention. As they danced, Rav Isser Zalman sang with them: "Kamatz alef — ah!" and all the children would joyfully repeat the words after him, Hebrew letter after letter (L'Chanech B'Simchah, p. 114).

> Rav Yosef Shlomo Kahaneman, the Ponevezher rav, also "came down" to help the most helpless: he was once observed lining up mattresses and lying down on each one for a few moments. When asked what he was doing, he replied, "These mattresses are going to be used for the children's orphanage and I am checking which are the most comfortable for the children to sleep on" (Ma'aseh Ish, Vol. 7, p. 90).

We've read many stories about *gedolim*, great men who lived long ago or are still alive today, and stories about "regular" people who were great in their own way. The following story differs from the others in one way: I witnessed this story myself.

> The legendary Rav Avraham Blumenkrantz was the chazzan for the tefillos of the Yamim Nora'im. Every year his pure voice stormed the heavens and inspired his congregation.
>
> Toward the end of his life, Rav Blumenkrantz suffered unbearable pain in his legs because of poor circulation, and he had to wear large casts. Merely taking a few steps or even

to seat them with nobles, with nobles of His people. He transforms the barren wife into a glad mother of children. Halleluyah![1]

---

1. *Tehillim* 113.

---

standing for a few moments was painful for the rav, and leading the lengthy Rosh Hashanah and Yom Kippur tefillos caused excruciating agony. But he was determined, and despite his suffering he led the congregation in his beautiful, spirited, and heartrending tefillos.

It happened on Yom Kippur, during the chazzan's repetition of the Mussaf service, at the point where the congregation bows down to the ground. Rav Blumenkrantz was weak from fasting and in pain from standing for so long, and getting down onto the floor and then back up again was torture. But at this moment, on the holiest day of the year, at the climax of the Mussaf tefillah, despite his pain, Rav Blumenkrantz with his holy countenance and immense concentration looked like the Kohen Gadol himself preparing to perform the avodah in the Beis HaMikdash.

Incredibly, I had the zechus to help the rav. I took his hand and I helped him go down onto the floor. His pain was so intense, I almost felt it myself. After I helped him get up again, for a few moments Rav Blumenkrantz still held my hand as he caught his breath and composed himself to continue the davening. At that moment, he looked at me with his warm eyes and squeezed my hand in appreciation for helping him. Despite his pain, despite the holiness of the day and the moment, he wanted to show his appreciation for my small act of chesed. This was true greatness!

No Such Thing as Despair

מוֹשִׁיבִי עֲקֶרֶת הַבַּיִת, אֵם הַבָּנִים שְׂמֵחָה; הַלְלוּיָהּ

He transforms the barren wife into a glad mother of children. Halleluyah!

Hashem's abilities have no limit. We saw it in the miracles of the Ten Plagues and the Exodus from Egypt, and we can see it in our everyday lives, every time a child is born.

בְּצֵאת יִשְׂרָאֵל מִמִּצְרָיִם, בֵּית יַעֲקֹב מֵעַם לֹעֵז.

Every birth is a miracle, but in the case of Sarah Imeinu, we are told, Hashem actually changed nature so she could bear a child.

The Torah says, וַתְּהִי שָׂרַי עֲקָרָה אֵין לָהּ וָלָד, *Sarai was barren; she had no child* (*Bereishis* 11:30). The Talmud tells us that it was physically impossible for Sarah to ever have children because she had no womb (*Yevamos* 64b). But Hashem controls nature, and despite her total physical inability to have children, Sarah bore a son, Yitzchak (*Oznayim LaTorah, Bereishis* 11:30).

Not only Sarah but also Rivkah and Rachel were barren, because Hashem yearns for the *tefillos* of His righteous ones (*Yevamos* 64a). Hashem wanted the founding of the Jewish nation to be a showcase for all generations of the strength of *tefillah*, a power so great and powerful that it can alter the laws of nature. The concept of hopelessness doesn't exist in Judaism, since nothing is beyond Hashem's capabilities (*Sfas Emes, Bereishis* 18:1; *Rav Tzadok HaKohen, Divrei Sofrim*).

> The Maharil Diskin and the Chazon Ish would tell sick people about whom the doctors had given up hope, "Hashem gave doctors the right to make people feel better, but not the right to make them feel despair" (*HaSaraf MiBrisk,* p. 468; *Ma'aseh Ish,* Vol. 1, p. 198; see also *Tzaddik Yesod Olam,* p. 141).

The Blessings in the Home

עֲקֶרֶת הַבַּיִת
The barren wife

The Midrash writes that as long as Sarah was alive, Hashem's presence dwelled above her home, her doors were open wide to guests, her bread was blessed, and the light from the Shabbos candles burned from *erev Shabbos* to *erev Shabbos* (*Midrash Rabbah, Bereishis* 60:16). When Sarah died, these four blessings ceased and only returned once Yitzchak brought Rivkah, his *kallah,* into their home.

Rav Hirsch learns from this midrash that the presence and

When Yisrael went forth from Egypt, Yaakov's household from a people of alien

---

blessings of Hashem and the atmosphere of tranquillity and *chesed* in the home are all products of the woman residing within it (*Collected Writings of Rav Hirsch*, Vol. 8, p. 102).

This is why Rabbi Yose would refer to his wife as his "home" — since a wife sets the atmosphere of Torah and mitzvos in the home (*Shabbos* 118b).

> Rav Aryeh Levin was once traveling in a taxi, and the driver asked him where his home was located. Rav Aryeh paused and then said, "From the day my wife died, I do not have a home. A street I have, but not a home" (*HaMashgiach D'Kaminetz*, p. 223).

All the Women

בְּצֵאת יִשְׂרָאֵל מִמִּצְרָיִם, בֵּית יַעֲקֹב מֵעַם לוֹעֵז
When Yisrael went forth from Egypt, Yaakov's household from a people of alien tongue

We say, *When Yisrael went forth from Egypt*, and then we say, *[When] Yaakov's household [departed] from a people of alien tongue*. Why does the verse repeat what seems to be the same message?

The Roke'ach explains, based on the Talmud (*Sotah* 11b), that בֵּית יַעֲקֹב, literally, "the House of Yaakov," refers to the righteous Jewish women in whose merit the Jewish nation was redeemed. *Bnei Yisrael* were deemed worthy of leaving Egypt because of *Beis Yaakov*, the righteous Jewish women.

Rav Yechiel Michel Epstein points out that *When Yisrael went forth from Egypt* refers to the Jewish men; it says *Yisrael* and not *Beis Yisrael*. This implies that only a portion of the men were redeemed since those who sinned died in Egypt. Ultimately, only a fraction of the Jewish men merited leaving Egypt.

The women, on the other hand, were all righteous and all of them merited redemption. Therefore it says *Beis Yaakov* — that is, the entire House of Yaakov — referring to all the Jewish women who were redeemed (*Leil Shimurim Haggadah*).

הָיְתָה יְהוּדָה לְקָדְשׁוֹ, יִשְׂרָאֵל מַמְשְׁלוֹתָיו. הַיָּם רָאָה וַיָּנֹס, הַיַּרְדֵּן יִסֹּב לְאָחוֹר. הֶהָרִים רָקְדוּ כְאֵילִים, גְּבָעוֹת כִּבְנֵי צֹאן. מַה לְּךָ הַיָּם כִּי תָנוּס, הַיַּרְדֵּן תִּסֹּב לְאָחוֹר. הֶהָרִים תִּרְקְדוּ כְאֵילִים, גְּבָעוֹת כִּבְנֵי צֹאן. מִלִּפְנֵי אָדוֹן חוּלִי אָרֶץ, מִלִּפְנֵי אֱלוֹהַּ יַעֲקֹב. הַהֹפְכִי הַצּוּר אֲגַם מָיִם, חַלָּמִישׁ לְמַעְיְנוֹ מָיִם.[1]

An Inheritance of Sacrifice

הָיְתָה יְהוּדָה לְקָדְשׁוֹ יִשְׂרָאֵל מַמְשְׁלוֹתָיו
Yehudah became His sanctuary,
Yisrael His dominion

Yehudah refers to Nachshon ben Aminadav, the leader of the tribe of Yehudah, who was the first of *Bnei Yisrael* to jump into the Yam Suf and thus sanctify the Name of Hashem.

Strangely, the word *hayesah* is a feminine verb. Why would the *pasuk* use a feminine form to describe a man's actions?

Rav Yaakov Loberbaum of Lisa explains that Nachshon's willingness to sanctify Hashem's Name was a direct inheritance from his grandmother Tamar. Tamar was willing to sacrifice her life and die a fiery death in order not to embarrass Yehudah. Such an act of sacrifice created a tremendous *kiddush Hashem*. This spirit of sacrifice and the public sanctification of Hashem's Name were bequeathed to Tamar's descendants, most specifically to Nachshon.

The feminine term *hayesah* hints at the connection between the grandmother's willingness to sacrifice herself when necessary and the grandson's self-sacrifice (*Ma'aseh Nissim Haggadah*).

Hallel in Two Parts

Why is Hallel divided into two parts, with the first part recited before the meal and the second part recited after the meal?

tongue, Yehudah became His sanctuary, Yisrael His dominion. The sea saw and fled; the Yarden turned backward. The mountains skipped like rams, and the hills like young lambs. What ails you, O sea, that you flee? O Yarden, that you turn backward? O mountains, that you skip like rams? O hills, like young lambs? Before HASHEM's presence: tremble, O earth, before the presence of the God of Yaakov, Who turns the rock into a pond of water, the flint into a flowing fountain.[1]

---

1. *Tehillim* 114.

- ☐ In order that we will drink the second cup of wine while praising Hashem, as the other three cups are all drunk amid praise to Hashem (*Kol Bo*).

- ☐ The first two chapters of Hallel recited prior to the meal mention the Exodus from Egypt, the theme of the Haggadah, and of the eating of the matzah and *maror*. After the meal, the remainder of Hallel is recited in order to focus on our future redemption (*Abarbanel*; *Levush*).

- ☐ By placing the meal in the middle of Hallel, we demonstrate that even eating and drinking are vehicles of holiness that can be used to serve and praise Hashem (*Imrei Shefer*). In other religions, those wanting to preach and practice holiness separate themselves from society and all its physical aspects. It's easy to be holy when one is cut off from all physical temptations. Our challenge as Jews is to take the physical and mundane and elevate it. We don't run away from marriage, food, and society. We attempt to transform them into holiness and channel them for Hashem's service (*Nefesh Chayah*, p. 55).

- ☐ Dividing Hallel into two parts is unusual, and this will motivate the children to ask questions, a focus of this night (*Seder HaYom*).

THE EISHES CHAYIL HAGGADAH

According to all customs the cup is lifted and the matzos covered during the recitation of this blessing. (On Motza'ei Shabbos the phrase in parentheses substitutes for the preceding phrase.)

בָּרוּךְ אַתָּה יהוה אֱלֹהֵינוּ מֶלֶךְ הָעוֹלָם, אֲשֶׁר גְּאָלָנוּ וְגָאַל אֶת אֲבוֹתֵינוּ מִמִּצְרַיִם, וְהִגִּיעָנוּ הַלַּיְלָה הַזֶּה לֶאֱכָל בּוֹ מַצָּה וּמָרוֹר. כֵּן יהוה אֱלֹהֵינוּ וֵאלֹהֵי אֲבוֹתֵינוּ, יַגִּיעֵנוּ לְמוֹעֲדִים וְלִרְגָלִים אֲחֵרִים הַבָּאִים לִקְרָאתֵנוּ לְשָׁלוֹם, שְׂמֵחִים בְּבִנְיַן עִירֶךָ וְשָׂשִׂים בַּעֲבוֹדָתֶךָ, וְנֹאכַל שָׁם מִן הַזְּבָחִים וּמִן הַפְּסָחִים (מִן הַפְּסָחִים וּמִן הַזְּבָחִים) אֲשֶׁר יַגִּיעַ דָּמָם עַל קִיר מִזְבַּחֲךָ לְרָצוֹן. וְנוֹדֶה לְךָ שִׁיר חָדָשׁ עַל גְּאֻלָּתֵנוּ וְעַל פְּדוּת נַפְשֵׁנוּ. בָּרוּךְ אַתָּה יהוה, גָּאַל יִשְׂרָאֵל.

Some have the custom to recite the following declaration of intent.

הִנְנִי מוּכָן וּמְזוּמָּן לְקַיֵּם מִצְוַת כּוֹס שֵׁנִי מֵאַרְבַּע כּוֹסוֹת. לְשֵׁם יִחוּד קֻדְשָׁא בְּרִיךְ הוּא וּשְׁכִינְתֵּיהּ, עַל יְדֵי הַהוּא טָמִיר וְנֶעְלָם, בְּשֵׁם כָּל יִשְׂרָאֵל. וִיהִי נֹעַם אֲדֹנָי אֱלֹהֵינוּ עָלֵינוּ, וּמַעֲשֵׂה יָדֵינוּ כּוֹנְנָה עָלֵינוּ, וּמַעֲשֵׂה יָדֵינוּ כּוֹנְנֵהוּ.

Beyond Gratitude

כֵּן ה' אֱלֹהֵינוּ וֵאלֹהֵי אֲבוֹתֵינוּ יַגִּיעֵנוּ לְמוֹעֲדִים וְלִרְגָלִים אֲחֵרִים הַבָּאִים לִקְרָאתֵנוּ לְשָׁלוֹם

So, Hashem, our God and God of our fathers, bring us also to future holidays and festivals in peace

Leah named her son Yehudah, from the word *hoda'ah*, "to thank," in order to express her gratitude to Hashem. Immediately afterward Leah stopped having children (*Bereishis* 29:35). The Chozeh of Lublin explains that when one thanks Hashem for the good he received, he should not stop there but should immediately ask Hashem for additional *berachah*. Leah thanked Hashem, but she didn't daven further, and this resulted in her

According to all customs the cup is lifted and the matzos covered during the recitation of this blessing. (On Motza'ei Shabbos the phrase in parentheses substitutes for the preceding phrase.)

Blessed are You, HASHEM, our God, King of the universe, Who redeemed us and redeemed our ancestors from Egypt and enabled us to reach this night that we may eat on it matzah and *maror*. So, HASHEM, our God and God of our fathers, bring us also to future holidays and festivals in peace, gladdened in the rebuilding of Your city and joyful at Your service. There we shall eat of the offerings and *pesach* sacrifices (of the *pesach* sacrifices and offerings) whose blood will gain the sides of Your Altar for gracious acceptance. We shall then sing a new song of praise to You for our redemption and for the liberation of our souls. Blessed are You, HASHEM, Who has redeemed Israel.

Some have the custom to recite the following declaration of intent.

Behold, I am prepared and ready to fulfill the mitzvah of the second of the Four Cups. For the sake of the unification of the Holy One, Blessed is He, and His Presence, through Him Who is hidden and inscrutable — [I pray] in the name of all Israel. May the pleasantness of the Lord, our God, be upon us, and may He establish our handiwork for us; our handiwork may He establish.

---

stopping, for the time being, to give birth to additional offspring.

The Klausenberger Rebbe uses this idea to explain the *berachah* that we say right before we drink the second cup of wine. We thank Hashem for redeeming us from Egypt, but we don't stop there. We immediately ask Hashem to allow us to experience the coming Yamim Tovim in the *Beis HaMikdash* (Responsa *Divrei Yatziv*, Vol. 7, 25:1, quoting *the Chozeh of Lublin*; see likewise *Tur, Bereishis* 29:35).

בָּרוּךְ אַתָּה יהוה אֱלֹהֵינוּ מֶלֶךְ הָעוֹלָם, בּוֹרֵא פְּרִי הַגָּפֶן.

The second cup is drunk while leaning on the left side — preferably the entire cup, but at least most of it.

רחצה

The hands are washed for matzah and the following blessing is recited. It is preferable to bring water and a basin to the head of the household at the Seder table. Preferably one should not talk unnecessarily until after the *Korech* sandwich has been eaten.

בָּרוּךְ אַתָּה יהוה אֱלֹהֵינוּ מֶלֶךְ הָעוֹלָם, אֲשֶׁר קִדְּשָׁנוּ בְּמִצְוֹתָיו, וְצִוָּנוּ עַל נְטִילַת יָדָיִם.

מוציא / מצה

Some recite the following before the blessing *hamotzi*.

הִנְנִי מוּכָן וּמְזוּמָּן לְקַיֵּם מִצְוַת אֲכִילַת מַצָּה. לְשֵׁם יִחוּד קֻדְשָׁא בְּרִיךְ הוּא וּשְׁכִינְתֵּיהּ, עַל יְדֵי הַהוּא טָמִיר וְנֶעְלָם, בְּשֵׁם כָּל יִשְׂרָאֵל. וִיהִי נֹעַם אֲדֹנָי אֱלֹהֵינוּ עָלֵינוּ, וּמַעֲשֵׂה יָדֵינוּ כּוֹנְנָה עָלֵינוּ, וּמַעֲשֵׂה יָדֵינוּ כּוֹנְנֵהוּ.

MOTZI / MATZAH / מוציא מצה

— Think About It —

The Bread of Faith

Science teaches us that when we bite into food, we benefit from certain nutrients. When we bite into the matzah, we are granted spiritual nourishment, as this simple food, symbolic of *Yetziyas Mitzrayim*, reminds us of our unbreakable bond with Hashem. Different *mefarshim* have derived a broad range of messages from the thin cracker that is so central to our Pesach Seder:

☐ The *Zohar* refers to matzah as מִיכְלָא דִּמְהֵימְנוּתָא, *the bread*

Blessed are You, HASHEM, our God, King of the universe, Who creates the fruit of the vine.

The second cup is drunk while leaning on the left side — preferably the entire cup, but at least most of it.

RACHTZAH

The hands are washed for matzah and the following blessing is recited. It is preferable to bring water and a basin to the head of the household at the Seder table. Preferably one should not talk unnecessarily until after the Korech sandwich has been eaten.

Blessed are You, HASHEM, our God, King of the universe, Who has sanctified us with His commandments, and has commanded us concerning the washing of the hands.

MOTZI / MATZAH

Some recite the following before the blessing hamotzi.

Behold, I am prepared and ready to fulfill the mitzvah of eating matzah. For the sake of the unification of the Holy One, Blessed is He, and His Presence, through Him Who is hidden and inscrutable — [I pray] in the name of all Israel. May the pleasantness of the Lord, our God, be upon us, and may He establish our handiwork for us; our handiwork may He establish.

---

of faith. The Meshech Chochmah (*Shemos* 12:19) explains that when the Jewish nation left Egypt the only food they took with them was matzah. Millions of Jews — men, women, and children — marched into the fearsome desert with only matzah on their backs, asking no questions, confident that Hashem would provide for them. Hashem recalls our trust in Him fondly, as the *pasuk* says, כֹּה אָמַר ה' זָכַרְתִּי לָךְ חֶסֶד נְעוּרַיִךְ אַהֲבַת כְּלוּלֹתָיִךְ לֶכְתֵּךְ אַחֲרַי בַּמִּדְבָּר בְּאֶרֶץ לֹא זְרוּעָה, *So said Hashem: "I recall for you the kindness of your youth, the love of your nuptials, your following Me into the wilderness, into an unsown land"* (*Yirmiyahu* 2:2). When we eat the matzah, we recall the Jewish nation's heroic faith in Hashem's ability to care for them, even as we strengthen our faith in Hashem and His ability to care for our every need, under any circumstance.

The following two blessings are recited over matzah; the first is recited over matzah as food, and the second for the special mitzvah of eating matzah on the night of Passover. [The latter blessing is to be made with the intention that it also apply to the "sandwich" and the *afikoman*.] The head of the household raises all the matzos on the Seder plate and recites the following blessing:

בָּרוּךְ אַתָּה יהוה אֱלֹהֵינוּ מֶלֶךְ הָעוֹלָם,
הַמּוֹצִיא לֶחֶם מִן הָאָרֶץ.

☐ The *Bnei Yissaschar* (*Nissan, Ma'amar* 4) also cites the *Zohar*'s description of the matzah as מֵיכְלָא דִמְהֵימְנוּתָא, *the bread of faith*. He explains that there is an inherent difference in the way matzah is prepared and the way bread is made. When preparing bread, the baker adds water to flour, kneads the dough, and then waits while the bread ferments and rises on its own. The baker is not the sole active preparer; the bread itself takes part in the bread-making process, so to speak.

On the other hand, matzah is not left to rise. The baker mixes the water and dough and quickly shapes it, pats it down, and speedily places it into the oven, making sure it has no time to rise or ferment. When it comes to preparing the matzah, the baker is the sole active participant in the process. The *Bnei Yissaschar* explains that when we eat the matzah, which unlike bread has only one active participant in its preparation, we strengthen our *emunah* in the Omnipotence of Hashem, reminding ourselves symbolically that He and only He is the One Who determines our successes and destiny.

☐ Matzah represents humility, while bread and *chametz* represent arrogance and haughtiness (see *Sefer HaChinuch*, mitzvah 117; *Kli Yakar, Shemos* 13:14; *Toldos Yaakov Yosef, Bo; Degel Machaneh Ephraim, Acharei Mos; Drashos Chasam Sofer*, Pesach 1). Matzah hides nothing; it shows the world

---

►§ Motzi / Matzah

- The Chasam Sofer writes (Responsa *Chasam Sofer, Choshen Mishpat* 196) that one should fulfill the mitzvah of eating the matzah with intense joy, concentration, and care, since it is currently the only mitzvah we have involving eating that is Torah mandated (as we no longer have the mitzvos to offer *korbanos, terumos*, or *ma'asros*).

The following two blessings are recited over matzah; the first is recited over matzah as food, and the second for the special mitzvah of eating matzah on the night of Passover. [The latter blessing is to be made with the intention that it also apply to the "sandwich" and the *afikoman*.] The head of the household raises all the matzos on the Seder plate and recites the following blessing:

Blessed are You, HASHEM, our God, King of the universe, Who brings forth bread from the earth.

---

its true properties, that of a thin cracker. Bread, on the other hand, puffs itself up with air, attempting to give itself an appearance greater than its actual weight, like one who is arrogant and inflates his abilities. Moreover, one who is haughty believes that his skills, his strengths, and his intelligence bring him success, as he proudly proclaims, כֹּחִי וְעֹצֶם יָדִי עָשָׂה לִי אֶת הַחַיִל הַזֶּה, *My strength and the might of my hand made me all this wealth* (*Devarim* 8:17). The Talmud (*Sotah* 4b) compares such a person to one who serves idolatry, as he, too, ascribes success and power to someone other than Hashem.

Thus matzah is called מֵיכְלָא דִּמְהֵימְנוּתָא, *the bread of faith*. Matzah represents the person who ascribes and understands that his success comes only from the goodness of Hashem. If a person strengthens his *emunah* in Hashem, if he understands that Hashem provides him with whatever is best for him, there will be no need to be egocentric or narcissistic, no need to impress others with his superiority.

One who has *emunah* in Hashem isn't jealous and doesn't get angry. He's happy when others succeed, and most of all he is serene, knowing that he has a loving Father Who knows what is truly best for him and loves him with a strength that is beyond human comprehension.

Complimenting One's Wife

הַמּוֹצִיא לֶחֶם מִן הָאָרֶץ
Who brings forth bread from the earth

Rav Eliyahu Lopian was once a guest at the home of his rebbi, Rav

The bottom matzah is put down and the following blessing is recited while the top (whole) matzah and the middle (broken) piece are still raised.

בָּרוּךְ אַתָּה יהוה אֱלֹהֵינוּ מֶלֶךְ הָעוֹלָם, אֲשֶׁר קִדְּשָׁנוּ בְּמִצְוֹתָיו, וְצִוָּנוּ עַל אֲכִילַת מַצָּה.

Each participant is required to eat an amount of matzah equal in volume to an egg. Since it is usually impossible to provide a sufficient amount of matzah from the two matzos for all members of the household, other matzos should be available at the head of the table from which to complete the required amounts. However, each participant should receive a piece from each of the top two matzos. The matzos are to be eaten while reclining on the left side and without delay; they need not be dipped in salt.

The head of the household takes a half-egg volume of *maror*, dips it into *charoses*, and gives each participant a like amount.

Some recite the following before *maror*:

הִנְנִי מוּכָן וּמְזֻמָּן לְקַיֵּם מִצְוַת אֲכִילַת מָרוֹר. לְשֵׁם יִחוּד קֻדְשָׁא בְּרִיךְ הוּא וּשְׁכִינְתֵּיהּ, עַל יְדֵי הַהוּא טָמִיר וְנֶעְלָם, בְּשֵׁם כָּל יִשְׂרָאֵל. וִיהִי נֹעַם אֲדֹנָי אֱלֹהֵינוּ עָלֵינוּ, וּמַעֲשֵׂה יָדֵינוּ כּוֹנְנָה עָלֵינוּ, וּמַעֲשֵׂה יָדֵינוּ כּוֹנְנֵהוּ.

The following blessing is recited with the intention that it also apply to the *maror* of the "sandwich." The *maror* is eaten without reclining, and without delay.

בָּרוּךְ אַתָּה יהוה אֱלֹהֵינוּ מֶלֶךְ הָעוֹלָם, אֲשֶׁר קִדְּשָׁנוּ בְּמִצְוֹתָיו, וְצִוָּנוּ עַל אֲכִילַת מָרוֹר.

Simcha Zissel Ziv, the Alter of Kelm. The Alter recited Kiddush, everyone washed their hands, and then the Alter recited the berachah of hamotzi on the freshly baked challos the rebbetzin had prepared that day.

After tasting the challah, the Alter turned to his wife and said, "I made the berachah of hamotzi on the challah because I thought it was bread, but I think I made the wrong berachah.

The bottom matzah is put down and the following blessing is recited while the top (whole) matzah and the middle (broken) piece are still raised.

Blessed are You, HASHEM, our God, King of the universe, Who has sanctified us with His commandments, and has commanded us concerning the eating of the matzah.

Each participant is required to eat an amount of matzah equal in volume to an egg. Since it is usually impossible to provide a sufficient amount of matzah from the two matzos for all members of the household, other matzos should be available at the head of the table from which to complete the required amounts. However, each participant should receive a piece from each of the top two matzos. The matzos are to be eaten while reclining on the left side and without delay; they need not be dipped in salt.

 MAROR

The head of the household takes a half-egg volume of *maror*, dips it into *charoses*, and gives each participant a like amount.

Some recite the following before *maror*:

Behold, I am prepared and ready to fulfill the mitzvah of eating *maror*. For the sake of the unification of the Holy One, Blessed is He, and His Presence, through Him Who is hidden and inscrutable — [I pray] in the name of all Israel. May the pleasantness of the Lord, our God, be upon us, and may He establish our handiwork for us; our handiwork may He establish.

The following blessing is recited with the intention that it also apply to the *maror* of the "sandwich." The *maror* is eaten without reclining, and without delay.

Blessed are You, HASHEM, our God, King of the universe, Who has sanctified us with His commandments, and has commanded us concerning the eating of *maror*.

◆§ The Charoses
- The *charoses* should be thick since it reminds us of the mortar the Jewish nation was forced to build with in Egypt.
- Red wine is traditionally added to the *charoses*, recalling the blood of the hundreds of Jewish children slaughtered daily in Egypt so Pharaoh could bathe in their blood. The color also reminds us of the plague of Blood.

כּוֹרֵךְ

The bottom (thus far unbroken) matzah is now taken. From it, with the addition of other matzos, each participant receives a half-egg volume of matzah with an equal-volume portion of *maror* (dipped into *charoses* which is shaken off). The following paragraph is recited and the "sandwich" is eaten while reclining.

זֵכֶר לְמִקְדָּשׁ כְּהִלֵּל. כֵּן עָשָׂה הִלֵּל בִּזְמַן שֶׁבֵּית הַמִּקְדָּשׁ הָיָה קַיָּם. הָיָה כּוֹרֵךְ (פֶּסַח) מַצָּה וּמָרוֹר וְאוֹכֵל בְּיַחַד. לְקַיֵּם מַה שֶּׁנֶּאֱמַר, עַל מַצּוֹת וּמְרֹרִים יֹאכְלֻהוּ.¹

שֻׁלְחָן עוֹרֵךְ

The meal should be eaten in a combination of joy and solemnity, for the meal, too, is part of the Seder service. While it is desirable that *zemiros* and discussion of the laws and events of Pesach be part of the meal, extraneous conversation should be avoided. It should be remembered that the *afikoman* must be eaten while there is still some appetite for it. In fact, if one is so sated that he must literally force himself to eat it, he is not credited with the performance of the mitzvah of *afikoman*. Therefore, it is unwise to eat more than a moderate amount during the meal.

Many have the custom to eat an egg dipped in salt water before the meal begins.

The challah is so delicious it tastes like cake, which requires the berachah of mezonos!"

The rebbetzin beamed, and Rav Eliyahu learned an important lesson in appreciating the worth of one's wife, not taking her for granted, and letting her see how much you appreciate her (Bayis U'Menuchah, p. 156).

SHULCHAN ORECH / שֻׁלְחָן עוֹרֵךְ

Concern for Others

Rav Yaakov Kamenetsky would read and explain the Haggadah in a clear and understandable manner, only pausing for questions

KORECH

The bottom (thus far unbroken) matzah is now taken. From it, with the addition of other matzos, each participant receives a half-egg volume of matzah with an equal-volume portion of *maror* (dipped into *charoses* which is shaken off). The following paragraph is recited and the "sandwich" is eaten while reclining.

In remembrance of the *Beis HaMikdash* [we do] as Hillel [did]. So did Hillel do at the time that the *Beis HaMikdash* was still standing: He would combine (the *pesach* offering,) matzah and *maror* in a sandwich and eat them together, to fulfill what it says [in the Torah]: They shall eat it with matzos and bitter herbs.[1]

SHULCHAN ORECH

The meal should be eaten in a combination of joy and solemnity, for the meal, too, is part of the Seder service. While it is desirable that *zemiros* and discussion of the laws and events of Pesach be part of the meal, extraneous conversation should be avoided. It should be remembered that the *afikoman* must be eaten while there is still some appetite for it. In fact, if one is so sated that he must literally force himself to eat it, he is not credited with the performance of the mitzvah of *afikoman*. Therefore, it is unwise to eat more than a moderate amount during the meal.

Many have the custom to eat an egg dipped in salt water before the meal begins.

---

1. Bamidbar 9:11.

---

or to share an occasional insight. Rav Yaakov would cover the text of the Haggadah fairly quickly since the Kamenetsky family always had guests who were undoubtedly hungry, and Rav Yaakov didn't want them to have to wait for their *seudah*.

In addition, Rav Yaakov reasoned that if *Maggid* would be too drawn out, the meal would have to be shortened so the *afikoman* could be eaten before *chatzos* (around midnight). Rav Yaakov felt that rushing the meal would show a lack of care and concern for the hard work his wife had put into preparing the Yom Tov meal (*V'Hayu Mesaprim*, Vol. 2, p. 656; see *Rav Avraham Pam, Mareh Kohen Haggadah*).

From the *afikoman* matzah (and from additional matzos to make up the required amount) a half-egg volume portion — according to some, a full egg's volume portion — is given to each participant. It should be eaten before midnight, while reclining, without delay, and uninterruptedly. Nothing may be eaten or drunk after the *afikoman* (with the exception of water and the like) except for the last two Seder cups of wine.

Some recite the following before eating the *afikoman*:

הִנְנִי מוּכָן וּמְזוּמָן לְקַיֵּם מִצְוַת אֲכִילַת אֲפִיקוֹמָן. לְשֵׁם יִחוּד קֻדְשָׁא בְּרִיךְ הוּא וּשְׁכִינְתֵּיהּ, עַל יְדֵי הַהוּא טָמִיר וְנֶעֱלָם, בְּשֵׁם כָּל יִשְׂרָאֵל. וִיהִי נֹעַם אֲדֹנָי אֱלֹהֵינוּ עָלֵינוּ, וּמַעֲשֵׂה יָדֵינוּ כּוֹנְנָה עָלֵינוּ, וּמַעֲשֵׂה יָדֵינוּ כּוֹנְנֵהוּ:

The third cup is poured and *Bircas HaMazon* (Grace After Meals) is recited. According to some customs, the Cup of Eliyahu is poured at this point.

The Significance of the Egg

During the meal, some people eat an egg dipped into salt water. Why?

- ☐ An egg is the food of mourners, because its round shape reminds us of the cycle of life and death. Eating an egg recalls the destruction of the *Beis HaMikdash* and the fact that presently we are not able to bring the *pesach* offering. On a similar note, the Pesach Seder and the evening of Tishah B'Av, the day we mourn for the *Mikdash*, always come out on the same night of the week (*Rema, Orach Chaim* 476:2).

- ☐ The egg is a remembrance of the *chagigah* offering that was brought in addition to the *pesach* offering (*Mishnah Berurah* 476:11).

- ☐ The longer an egg is cooked, the harder it becomes. Eating an egg recalls the stubborn defiance of the Jewish people: the more the Egyptians enslaved them and increased their labor, the more the Jewish people flourished, as it is written (*Shemos* 1:12), וְכַאֲשֶׁר יְעַנּוּ אֹתוֹ כֵּן יִרְבֶּה וְכֵן יִפְרֹץ, *But as much as*

⁘TZAFUN⁘

From the *afikoman* matzah (and from additional matzos to make up the required amount) a half-egg volume portion — according to some, a full egg's volume portion — is given to each participant. It should be eaten before midnight, while reclining, without delay, and uninterruptedly. Nothing may be eaten or drunk after the *afikoman* (with the exception of water and the like) except for the last two Seder cups of wine.

Some recite the following before eating the *afikoman*:

Behold, I am prepared and ready to fulfill the mitzvah of eating the *afikoman*. For the sake of the unification of the Holy One, Blessed is He, and His Presence, through Him Who is hidden and inscrutable — [I pray] in the name of all Israel. May the pleasantness of the Lord, our God, be upon us, and may He establish our handiwork for us; our handiwork may He establish.

⁘BARECH⁘

The third cup is poured and *Bircas HaMazon* (Grace After Meals) is recited. According to some customs, the Cup of Eliyahu is poured at this point.

---

they would afflict it [the Jewish nation], so it would increase and so it would spread out (Rav Meir Shapiro, *Ohr HaMeir Haggadah*, p. 64).

☐ Chickens and birds give birth to their young in two stages. First, the egg is laid; second, the egg matures and a chick emerges. When the Jewish people left Egypt, they experienced their birth as a nation in two stages. First they gained their freedom from slavery. But the final stage of birth as the nation of Hashem only happened when they accepted the Torah at Har Sinai (*Toras Emes, Pesach Leil Rishon*).

BARECH / ברך

— *Think About It* —

The Significance of Bircas HaMazon

The Midrash (*Tanchuma, Lech Lecha* 12) tells us that when Avraham invited guests, he would feed them a large meal. Before

שִׁיר הַמַּעֲלוֹת בְּשׁוּב יהוה אֶת שִׁיבַת צִיּוֹן, הָיִינוּ כְּחֹלְמִים. אָז יִמָּלֵא שְׂחוֹק פִּינוּ, וּלְשׁוֹנֵנוּ רִנָּה; אָז יֹאמְרוּ בַגּוֹיִם: הִגְדִּיל יהוה לַעֲשׂוֹת עִם אֵלֶּה. הִגְדִּיל יהוה לַעֲשׂוֹת עִמָּנוּ, הָיִינוּ שְׂמֵחִים. שׁוּבָה יהוה אֶת שְׁבִיתֵנוּ, כַּאֲפִיקִים בַּנֶּגֶב. הַזֹּרְעִים בְּדִמְעָה, בְּרִנָּה יִקְצֹרוּ. הָלוֹךְ יֵלֵךְ וּבָכֹה נֹשֵׂא מֶשֶׁךְ הַזָּרַע; בֹּא יָבֹא בְרִנָּה, נֹשֵׂא אֲלֻמֹּתָיו.[1]

they left, the guests would thank him for the wonderful food and hospitality. Avraham would respond that it was not he who deserved thanks, but Hashem, the One Who provided the food. Avraham would then teach his guests about Hashem and how He supplies mankind with all its needs, whereupon many became believers in God.

The Kotzker Rebbe added that we see from here that thanking Hashem for the food He provides us carries with it the ability to transform a person into an observant Jew (*Siach Sarfei Kodesh, Inyanei Shonim*, p. 15).

Bircas HaMazon is not merely a polite means of thanking Hashem. When we *bentch*, we are recognizing and internalizing that our entire existence is in the hands of Hashem (*Rav Shamshon Refael Hirsch, Devarim* 8:10).

Unlike the text of the *tefillah*, which is rabbinic, Bircas HaMazon is a Torah-mandated obligation. In that case, Bircas HaMazon requires even more concentration and attentiveness than *tefillah* (*Ta'amei HaMinhagim*, p. 174). In addition, those who are careful with the mitzvah of *bentching* merit great blessings:

- One should try to recite Bircas HaMazon from a *bentcher* since this stimulates deeper concentration, and one who does so merits God-fearing children and heavenly protection (*Bach, Orach Chaim* 185; *Maharal Diskin*).
- One who is careful in saying Bircas HaMazon will have a comfortable livelihood (*Sefer HaChinuch*, mitzvah 430).

A song of Ascents. When HASHEM brings back the exiles to Zion, we will have been like dreamers. Then our mouth will be filled with laughter, and our tongue with glad song. Then will it be said among the nations: HASHEM has done great things for these. HASHEM has done great things for us, and we rejoiced. Restore our captives, HASHEM, like streams in the dry land. Those who sow in tears shall reap in joy. Though the farmer bears the measure of seed to the field in tears, he shall come home with joy, bearing his sheaves.[1]

1. Tehillim 126.

- ☐ One who recites Bircas HaMazon carefully and with concentration merits a long life (*Kol Chaim*).
- ☐ One who recites Bircas HaMazon out loud and with joy merits *parnassah* (*Chida*).

A young man whose family had suffered several tragedies approached Rav Shach for guidance, asking him what he could do as a merit for the success of his family. Rav Shach told the young man, "Accept upon yourself one small thing, but make sure that you do it consistently."

"What one thing should I do?" the young man asked the venerable rosh yeshivah.

"Recite Bircas HaMazon from a bentcher!" (*Kinyan Torah Haggadah*, p. 124; see also *Michtavim U'Ma'amarim*, Vol. 3, 151).

The Chief Rabbi

הַזֹּרְעִים בְּדִמְעָה בְּרִנָּה יִקְצֹרוּ
Those who sow in tears shall reap in joy

Rav Aryeh Levin's son was asked to run for the position of chief rabbi of Jerusalem. He flatly refused, stating that he would not run against the other candidate, Rav Betzalel Zolty, because of a story his father, Rav Aryeh, had told him.

Some recite the following before Bircas HaMazon:

הִנְנִי מוּכָן וּמְזוּמָּן לְקַיֵּם מִצְוַת עֲשֵׂה שֶׁל בִּרְכַּת הַמָּזוֹן, כַּכָּתוּב, וְאָכַלְתָּ וְשָׂבָעְתָּ, וּבֵרַכְתָּ אֶת ה׳ אֱלֹהֶיךָ עַל הָאָרֶץ הַטֹּבָה אֲשֶׁר נָתַן לָךְ.

If three or more males, aged 13 or older, participated in the meal, the leader is required to formally invite the others to join him in the recitation of Grace After Meals. Following is the *Zimun*, or formal invitation.

The leader begins:

רַבּוֹתַי נְבָרֵךְ.

The group responds:

יְהִי שֵׁם יהוה מְבֹרָךְ מֵעַתָּה וְעַד עוֹלָם.

The leader continues:

יְהִי שֵׁם יהוה מְבֹרָךְ מֵעַתָּה וְעַד עוֹלָם.

If 10 men join in the *Zimun*, אֱלֹהֵינוּ, *our God* (in parentheses), is included.

בִּרְשׁוּת מָרָנָן וְרַבָּנָן וְרַבּוֹתַי, נְבָרֵךְ [אֱלֹהֵינוּ] שֶׁאָכַלְנוּ מִשֶּׁלּוֹ.

The group responds:

בָּרוּךְ [אֱלֹהֵינוּ] שֶׁאָכַלְנוּ מִשֶּׁלּוֹ וּבְטוּבוֹ חָיִינוּ.

The leader continues:

בָּרוּךְ [אֱלֹהֵינוּ] שֶׁאָכַלְנוּ מִשֶּׁלּוֹ וּבְטוּבוֹ חָיִינוּ.

The following line is recited if 10 men join in the Zimun.

בָּרוּךְ הוּא וּבָרוּךְ שְׁמוֹ.

בָּרוּךְ אַתָּה יהוה אֱלֹהֵינוּ מֶלֶךְ הָעוֹלָם, הַזָּן אֶת הָעוֹלָם כֻּלּוֹ, בְּטוּבוֹ, בְּחֵן בְּחֶסֶד

"My father told us that years ago he was walking home late at night when he saw a widow mending socks by the light of a small wax candle. Rav Aryeh knocked on her door and asked why she was working in the middle of the night. With tears in her eyes, the woman responded that she had lost her husband, and she mended socks deep into the night in order to pay for her son's rebbi. The woman was the mother of Rav Betzalel Zolty."

Rav Aryeh's son said to those urging him to enter the Chief Rabbinate of Jerusalem race, "Can I compete against a child who has been brought up on the path of Torah with his mother's tears?" (*V'Hi Tis'hallal*, p. 56).

Some recite the following before Bircas HaMazon:

Behold, I am prepared and ready to fulfill the mitzvah of Grace After Meals, as it is stated: "And you shall eat and you shall be satisfied and you shall bless HASHEM, your God, for the good land that He gave you."

If three or more males, aged 13 or older, participated in the meal, the leader is required to formally invite the others to join him in the recitation of Grace After Meals. Following is the Zimun, or formal invitation.

The leader begins:
Gentlemen, let us bless.

The group responds:
Blessed is the Name of HASHEM from this moment and forever!

The leader continues:
Blessed is the Name of HASHEM from this moment and forever!

If 10 men join in the Zimun, אֱלֹהֵינוּ*, our God (in parentheses), is included.*

With the permission of the distinguished people present, let us bless [our God] for we have eaten from what is His.

The group responds:
Blessed is He [our God] of Whose we have eaten and through Whose goodness we live.

The leader continues:
Blessed is He [our God] of Whose we have eaten and through Whose goodness we live.

The following line is recited if 10 men join in the Zimun.
Blessed is He and Blessed is His Name.

Blessed are You, HASHEM, our God, King of the universe, Who nourishes the entire world; in His goodness, with grace, with lovingkindness,

---

"Gift Wrapped" Just for Us

בְּטוּבוֹ בְּחֵן בְּחֶסֶד וּבְרַחֲמִים
In His goodness, with grace, with lovingkindness, and with mercy

We say that Hashem sustains us and nourishes us with *chein*, favor. What exactly does that mean?

[239] **THE EISHES CHAYIL HAGGADAH**

וּבְרַחֲמִים, הוּא נֹתֵן לֶחֶם לְכָל בָּשָׂר, כִּי לְעוֹלָם חַסְדּוֹ. וּבְטוּבוֹ הַגָּדוֹל, תָּמִיד לֹא חָסַר לָנוּ, וְאַל יֶחְסַר לָנוּ מָזוֹן לְעוֹלָם וָעֶד. בַּעֲבוּר שְׁמוֹ הַגָּדוֹל, כִּי הוּא אֵל זָן וּמְפַרְנֵס לַכֹּל, וּמֵטִיב לַכֹּל, וּמֵכִין מָזוֹן לְכָל בְּרִיּוֹתָיו אֲשֶׁר בָּרָא. בָּרוּךְ אַתָּה יהוה, הַזָּן אֶת הַכֹּל.

נוֹדֶה לְךָ יהוה אֱלֹהֵינוּ, עַל שֶׁהִנְחַלְתָּ לַאֲבוֹתֵינוּ אֶרֶץ חֶמְדָּה טוֹבָה וּרְחָבָה, וְעַל שֶׁהוֹצֵאתָנוּ יהוה אֱלֹהֵינוּ מֵאֶרֶץ מִצְרַיִם,

---

Rav Yechezkel Sarna points us to the sweet and juicy orange, which is both delicious and nutritious. Clearly we would still enjoy the orange even if it came wrapped in an ugly black peel. But Hashem not only provides us with delicious and nutritious foods, He sends them to us with *chein* — "gift wrapped" in an aesthetic and appealing fashion to increase our enjoyment.

Moreover, Hashem designed the orange with small individual segments to make it convenient and easy to eat. Food is much more than nourishing, and even more than delicious; it's nice to look at and convenient to eat: it's full of *chein* (*Achar HeAsof Zichron L'Rav Sarna*, p. 133; *Melech B'Yofyav*, page 262 and *Ma'aseh Rav Haggadah*, p. 182 quoting *Rav Yechezkel Abramsky*).

Count Your Blessings

נוֹדֶה לְךָ ה' אֱלֹהֵינוּ
We thank You, Hashem, our God

We thank Hashem for all He gives us. Sometimes that very act of thanking Hashem helps us realize just *how much* He has given us, and that can help us when things seem difficult.

A man suffering from bouts of depression once came to Rav Nosson Tzvi Finkel, the rosh yeshivah of Mir, for help. He told Rav Nosson Tzvi how sad and alone he felt.

Rav Nosson Tzvi suggested that the man purchase a small

and with mercy. He gives nourishment to all flesh, for His lovingkindness is eternal. And through His great goodness, nourishment was never lacking to us, and may it never be lacking to us forever. For the sake of His Great Name, because He is God Who nourishes and sustains all, and benefits all, and He prepares food for all of His creatures which He has created. Blessed are You, HASHEM, Who nourishes all.

We thank You, HASHEM, our God, because You have given to our forefathers as a heritage a desirable, good, and spacious land; because You removed us, HASHEM, our God, from the land of

---

notebook, and each time he experienced the Hand of Hashem in his life, he should write it down. When the times of loneliness would occur, he could take out his notebook and remind himself of how Hashem was truly with him, keeping him company at all times (B'Chol Nafshecha, p. 336).

A similar story is told about a man whose daughter had recently become engaged. The grateful father asked his rav how he could thank Hashem for all the good He had bestowed on him and his family. The rav suggested he start a journal and write down all the times he experienced the guiding Hand of Hashem in his everyday life.

The man followed his rav's advice and began making entries into his journal. On the day of his daughter's wedding, he showed her the journal he had begun the day of her engagement. Tears filled the kallah's eyes, and she went to her closet and pulled out a large box with more than 150 notebooks.

"Abba," the kallah told her father, "for years I have been writing down each and every time I felt the Hand of Hashem as a means of strengthening my emunah and bitachon. These are the boxes of journals that I have accumulated throughout the years!" (L'Chanech B'Simchah, p. 245).

וּפְדִיתָנוּ מִבֵּית עֲבָדִים, וְעַל בְּרִיתְךָ שֶׁחָתַמְתָּ בִּבְשָׂרֵנוּ, וְעַל תּוֹרָתְךָ שֶׁלִּמַּדְתָּנוּ, וְעַל חֻקֶּיךָ שֶׁהוֹדַעְתָּנוּ, וְעַל חַיִּים חֵן וָחֶסֶד שֶׁחוֹנַנְתָּנוּ, וְעַל אֲכִילַת מָזוֹן שָׁאַתָּה זָן וּמְפַרְנֵס אוֹתָנוּ תָּמִיד, בְּכָל יוֹם וּבְכָל עֵת וּבְכָל שָׁעָה.

וְעַל הַכֹּל יהוה אֱלֹהֵינוּ, אֲנַחְנוּ מוֹדִים לָךְ וּמְבָרְכִים אוֹתָךְ, יִתְבָּרַךְ שִׁמְךָ בְּפִי כָּל חַי תָּמִיד לְעוֹלָם וָעֶד. כַּכָּתוּב, וְאָכַלְתָּ וְשָׂבָעְתָּ, וּבֵרַכְתָּ אֶת יהוה אֱלֹהֶיךָ, עַל הָאָרֶץ הַטֹּבָה אֲשֶׁר נָתַן לָךְ.¹ בָּרוּךְ אַתָּה יהוה, עַל הָאָרֶץ וְעַל הַמָּזוֹן.

The Strength of a Jewish Mother

וְעַל בְּרִיתְךָ
For Your covenant

Pharaoh commanded that every baby boy be thrown into the Nile. The Nazis went further, much further.

On May 7, 1942, the Germans announced that Jews could no longer have children, and if a Jewish baby was born, the child would be shot, along with his mother. But, like Yocheved in Egypt, many Jewish women continued to bear children despite the dangers.

> One such mother, Mrs. Bloch, gave birth to her first child after five years of marriage. In order to drown out the sounds of the newborn baby's cries, the Bloch family moved to a building that housed a factory, in the hopes the baby boy's cries wouldn't be heard above the clamor of the machinery.
>
> Rav Ephraim Oshry, one of the few Lithuanian rabbis who survived the war and published his searing responsa from that terrible time, described the bris of this child:

Egypt and You redeemed us from the house of bondage; for Your covenant which You sealed in our flesh; for Your Torah that You taught us and for Your statutes that You made known to us; for life, grace, and lovingkindness which You granted us; and for the provision of food with which You nourish and sustain us constantly, in every day, in every season, and in every hour.

For all, HASHEM, our God, we thank You and bless You. May Your Name be blessed continuously by the mouth of all the living, continuously for all eternity. As it is written: "And you shall eat and you shall be satisfied, and you shall bless HASHEM, your God, for the good land which He gave you."[1] Blessed are You, HASHEM, for the land and for the food.

---

1. *Devarim* 8:10.

"The mohel arrived and was about to perform the bris, when we heard the sound of car doors slamming and Gestapo members entering the building. Indescribable fear and terror swept through the room. The mohel's hands began to shake. We had no idea how to save the poor mother and her newborn baby, about to be discovered — and shot.

"While we stood immobile, frightened to the bone, only one person showed her strength: Mrs. Bloch, the mother of the baby boy. With authority and poise, she turned toward the mohel and cried out, 'Quickly, the Nazis are coming to kill us. Circumcise the child so that my baby will die a Jew!'

"Miracles of miracles, the Nazis entered the building only to inspect the factory and did not enter the room where the baby was circumcised and entered into the covenant of Hashem" (*Ani Ma'amin*, p. 105).

רַחֵם (נָא) יהוה אֱלֹהֵינוּ עַל יִשְׂרָאֵל עַמֶּךָ, וְעַל יְרוּשָׁלַיִם עִירֶךָ, וְעַל צִיּוֹן מִשְׁכַּן כְּבוֹדֶךָ, וְעַל מַלְכוּת בֵּית דָּוִד מְשִׁיחֶךָ, וְעַל הַבַּיִת הַגָּדוֹל וְהַקָּדוֹשׁ שֶׁנִּקְרָא שִׁמְךָ עָלָיו. אֱלֹהֵינוּ אָבִינוּ, רְעֵנוּ זוּנֵנוּ פַּרְנְסֵנוּ וְכַלְכְּלֵנוּ וְהַרְוִיחֵנוּ, וְהַרְוַח לָנוּ יהוה אֱלֹהֵינוּ מְהֵרָה מִכָּל צָרוֹתֵינוּ. וְנָא אַל תַּצְרִיכֵנוּ, יהוה אֱלֹהֵינוּ, לֹא לִידֵי מַתְּנַת בָּשָׂר וָדָם, וְלֹא לִידֵי הַלְוָאָתָם, כִּי אִם לְיָדְךָ הַמְּלֵאָה הַפְּתוּחָה הַקְּדוֹשָׁה וְהָרְחָבָה, שֶׁלֹּא נֵבוֹשׁ וְלֹא נִכָּלֵם לְעוֹלָם וָעֶד.

On Shabbos add the following paragraph.

רְצֵה וְהַחֲלִיצֵנוּ יהוה אֱלֹהֵינוּ בְּמִצְוֹתֶיךָ, וּבְמִצְוַת יוֹם הַשְּׁבִיעִי הַשַּׁבָּת הַגָּדוֹל וְהַקָּדוֹשׁ הַזֶּה, כִּי יוֹם זֶה גָּדוֹל וְקָדוֹשׁ הוּא לְפָנֶיךָ, לִשְׁבָּת בּוֹ וְלָנוּחַ בּוֹ בְּאַהֲבָה כְּמִצְוַת רְצוֹנֶךָ, וּבִרְצוֹנְךָ הָנִיחַ לָנוּ יהוה אֱלֹהֵינוּ, שֶׁלֹּא תְהֵא צָרָה וְיָגוֹן וַאֲנָחָה בְּיוֹם מְנוּחָתֵנוּ, וְהַרְאֵנוּ יהוה אֱלֹהֵינוּ בְּנֶחָמַת צִיּוֹן עִירֶךָ, וּבְבִנְיַן יְרוּשָׁלַיִם עִיר קָדְשֶׁךָ, כִּי אַתָּה הוּא בַּעַל הַיְשׁוּעוֹת וּבַעַל הַנֶּחָמוֹת.

The Source of Blessing

הַשַּׁבָּת הַגָּדוֹל וְהַקָּדוֹשׁ הַזֶּה,
כִּי יוֹם זֶה גָּדוֹל וְקָדוֹשׁ הוּא לְפָנֶיךָ
This great and holy Sabbath.
For this day is great and holy before You

Shabbos is the source of all *berachah*, and all the days of the week receive their "nourishment" from Shabbos. That's why one

Have mercy (we beg You) HASHEM, our God, on Your people Israel, on Your city Jerusalem, on Zion the resting place of Your Glory, on the monarchy of the house of David, Your anointed, and on the great and holy House upon which Your Name is called. Our God, our Father — tend us, nourish us, sustain us, support us, relieve us; HASHEM, our God, grant us speedy relief from all our troubles. Please, HASHEM, our God, make us not needful of the gifts of human hands nor of their loans, but only of Your Hand that is full, open, holy, and generous, that we not feel inner shame nor be humiliated for ever and ever.

On Shabbos add the following paragraph.

May it please You to strengthen us, HASHEM, our God — through Your commandments, and through the commandment of the seventh day, this great and holy Shabbos. For this day is great and holy before You to rest on it and be content on it in love, as ordained by Your will. May it be Your will, HASHEM, our God, that there be no distress, grief, or lament on this day of our contentment. And show us, HASHEM, our God, the consolation of Zion, Your city, and the rebuilding of Jerusalem, city of Your holiness, for You are the Master of salvations and Master of consolations.

---

who guards and honors the Shabbos properly will be blessed with a week full of *berachah* and success.

> *A story is told about a young boy who ran into the street without looking and was struck and seriously injured by a truck driving by. The young boy was immediately rushed to the emergency room in critical condition. Police investigators cleared the truck driver of any wrongdoing, since the child had dashed in front of the truck and the driver couldn't avoid hitting him. Despite this, the driver felt he was responsible for the boy's terrible injuries.*

אֱלֹהֵינוּ וֵאלֹהֵי אֲבוֹתֵינוּ, יַעֲלֶה, וְיָבֹא, וְיַגִּיעַ, וְיֵרָאֶה, וְיֵרָצֶה, וְיִשָּׁמַע, וְיִפָּקֵד, וְיִזָּכֵר זִכְרוֹנֵנוּ וּפִקְדוֹנֵנוּ, וְזִכְרוֹן אֲבוֹתֵינוּ, וְזִכְרוֹן מָשִׁיחַ בֶּן דָּוִד עַבְדֶּךָ, וְזִכְרוֹן יְרוּשָׁלַיִם עִיר קָדְשֶׁךָ, וְזִכְרוֹן כָּל עַמְּךָ בֵּית יִשְׂרָאֵל לְפָנֶיךָ, לִפְלֵיטָה לְטוֹבָה לְחֵן וּלְחֶסֶד וּלְרַחֲמִים, לְחַיִּים וּלְשָׁלוֹם, בְּיוֹם חַג הַמַּצּוֹת הַזֶּה. זָכְרֵנוּ יהוה אֱלֹהֵינוּ בּוֹ לְטוֹבָה, וּפָקְדֵנוּ בוֹ לִבְרָכָה, וְהוֹשִׁיעֵנוּ בוֹ לְחַיִּים (טוֹבִים). וּבִדְבַר יְשׁוּעָה וְרַחֲמִים, חוּס וְחָנֵּנוּ וְרַחֵם עָלֵינוּ וְהוֹשִׁיעֵנוּ, כִּי אֵלֶיךָ עֵינֵינוּ, כִּי אֵל (מֶלֶךְ) חַנּוּן וְרַחוּם אָתָּה.

וּבְנֵה יְרוּשָׁלַיִם עִיר הַקֹּדֶשׁ בִּמְהֵרָה בְיָמֵינוּ. בָּרוּךְ אַתָּה יהוה, בּוֹנֵה (בְרַחֲמָיו) יְרוּשָׁלָיִם. אָמֵן.

בָּרוּךְ אַתָּה יהוה אֱלֹהֵינוּ מֶלֶךְ הָעוֹלָם, הָאֵל אָבִינוּ מַלְכֵּנוּ אַדִּירֵנוּ בּוֹרְאֵנוּ גּוֹאֲלֵנוּ יוֹצְרֵנוּ קְדוֹשֵׁנוּ קְדוֹשׁ יַעֲקֹב, רוֹעֵנוּ רוֹעֵה יִשְׂרָאֵל, הַמֶּלֶךְ הַטּוֹב וְהַמֵּטִיב לַכֹּל, שֶׁבְּכָל יוֹם

The driver visited the boy in the hospital and asked his mother how he could compensate her for what he had done to her son. Assuming the boy's mother would ask for money, the truck driver was surprised to hear a totally different request: "Accept upon yourself to keep Shabbos, and in this merit our son will get better. All Jews are responsible for one another, and when one Jew keeps Shabbos, it brings berachah to the entire Jewish nation."

With tears in his eyes, the truck driver pledged to accept upon himself the laws of Shabbos. A few months later this

Our God and God of our fathers, may there rise, come, reach, be noted, be favored, be heard, be considered, and be remembered before You — the remembrance and consideration of ourselves; the remembrance of our fathers; the remembrance of Mashiach, son of David, Your servant; the remembrance of Jerusalem, Your holy city; and the remembrance of Your entire people, the House of Israel — for deliverance, for well-being, for grace, for lovingkindness, and for mercy, for life and for peace on this day of the Festival of Matzos. Remember us on it, HASHEM, our God, for goodness; consider us on it for blessing; and help us on it for (good) life. In the matter of salvation and mercy, have pity, show grace, and be merciful upon us and help us, for our eyes are turned to You; for You are the Almighty (King), the gracious, and compassionate.

Rebuild Jerusalem, the Holy City, soon in our days. Blessed are You, HASHEM, Who rebuilds Jerusalem (in His mercy). Amen.

Blessed are You, HASHEM, our God, King of the universe, the Almighty, our Father, our King, our Sovereign, our Creator, our Redeemer, our Maker, our Holy One, Holy One of Yaakov, our Shepherd, the Shepherd of Israel, the good and beneficent King. For every single day He

---

truck driver married a frum girl — and the young boy injured in the accident had recovered enough to dance joyously at the wedding (Melachim Omanayich, p. 8).

וָיוֹם הוּא הֵטִיב, הוּא מֵטִיב, הוּא יֵיטִיב לָנוּ. הוּא גְמָלָנוּ הוּא גוֹמְלֵנוּ הוּא יִגְמְלֵנוּ לָעַד, לְחֵן וּלְחֶסֶד וּלְרַחֲמִים וּלְרֶוַח הַצָּלָה וְהַצְלָחָה, בְּרָכָה וִישׁוּעָה נֶחָמָה פַּרְנָסָה וְכַלְכָּלָה וְרַחֲמִים וְחַיִּים וְשָׁלוֹם וְכָל טוֹב, וּמִכָּל טוּב לְעוֹלָם אַל יְחַסְּרֵנוּ.

הָרַחֲמָן הוּא יִמְלוֹךְ עָלֵינוּ לְעוֹלָם וָעֶד. הָרַחֲמָן הוּא יִתְבָּרַךְ בַּשָּׁמַיִם וּבָאָרֶץ. הָרַחֲמָן הוּא יִשְׁתַּבַּח לְדוֹר דּוֹרִים, וְיִתְפָּאַר בָּנוּ לָעַד וּלְנֵצַח נְצָחִים, וְיִתְהַדַּר בָּנוּ לָעַד וּלְעוֹלְמֵי עוֹלָמִים. הָרַחֲמָן הוּא יְפַרְנְסֵנוּ בְּכָבוֹד. הָרַחֲמָן הוּא יִשְׁבּוֹר עֻלֵּנוּ מֵעַל צַוָּארֵנוּ, וְהוּא יוֹלִיכֵנוּ קוֹמְמִיּוּת לְאַרְצֵנוּ. הָרַחֲמָן הוּא יִשְׁלַח לָנוּ בְּרָכָה מְרֻבָּה בַּבַּיִת הַזֶּה, וְעַל שֻׁלְחָן זֶה שֶׁאָכַלְנוּ עָלָיו. הָרַחֲמָן הוּא יִשְׁלַח לָנוּ אֶת אֵלִיָּהוּ הַנָּבִיא זָכוּר לַטּוֹב, וִיבַשֶּׂר לָנוּ בְּשׂוֹרוֹת טוֹבוֹת יְשׁוּעוֹת וְנֶחָמוֹת.

The Talmud (*Berachos* 46a) gives a rather lengthy text of the blessing that a guest inserts here for the host. It is quoted with minor variations in *Shulchan Aruch* (*Orach Chaim* 201) and many authorities are at a loss to explain why the prescribed text has fallen into disuse in favor of the briefer version commonly used. The text found in *Shulchan Aruch* is:

יְהִי רָצוֹן שֶׁלֹּא יֵבוֹשׁ וְלֹא יִכָּלֵם בַּעַל הַבַּיִת הַזֶּה, לֹא בָּעוֹלָם הַזֶּה, וְלֹא בָּעוֹלָם הַבָּא, וְיַצְלִיחַ בְּכָל נְכָסָיו, וְיִהְיוּ נְכָסָיו מֻצְלָחִים וּקְרוֹבִים לָעִיר, וְאַל יִשְׁלוֹט שָׂטָן בְּמַעֲשֵׂה יָדָיו, וְאַל יִזְדַּקֵּק לְפָנָיו שׁוּם דְּבַר חֵטְא וְהִרְהוּר עָוֹן, מֵעַתָּה וְעַד עוֹלָם.

did good, does good, and will do good to us. He was bountiful with us, is bountiful with us, and will forever be bountiful with us — with grace and with lovingkindness and with mercy, with relief, salvation, success, blessing, help, consolation, sustenance, support, mercy, life, peace, and all good; and of all good things may He never deprive us.

The compassionate One! May He reign over us forever. The compassionate One! May He be blessed in heaven and on earth. The compassionate One! May He be praised throughout all generations, may He be glorified through us forever to the ultimate ends, and be honored through us to the inscrutable everlasting. The compassionate One! May He sustain us in honor. The compassionate One! May He break the yoke of oppression from our necks and guide us erect to our Land. The compassionate One! May He send us abundant blessing to this house and upon this table at which we have eaten. The compassionate One! May He send us Eliyahu HaNavi — may he be remembered for good — to proclaim to us good tidings, salvations, and consolations.

The Talmud (*Berachos* 46a) gives a rather lengthy text of the blessing that a guest inserts here for the host. It is quoted with minor variations in *Shulchan Aruch (Orach Chaim* 201) and many authorities are at a loss to explain why the prescribed text has fallen into disuse in favor of the briefer version commonly used. The text found in *Shulchan Aruch* is:

May it be God's will that his host not be shamed nor humiliated in this world or in the World to Come. May he be successful in all his dealings. May his dealings be successful and conveniently close at hand. May no evil impediment reign over his handiwork, and may no semblance of sin or iniquitous thought attach itself to him from this time and forever.

הָרַחֲמָן הוּא יְבָרֵךְ

Guests recite the following.
Children at their parents' table add words in parentheses.

אֶת [אָבִי מוֹרִי] בַּעַל הַבַּיִת הַזֶּה,
וְאֶת [אִמִּי מוֹרָתִי] בַּעֲלַת הַבַּיִת הַזֶּה,

Those eating at their own table recite the following,
adding the appropriate parenthesized phrases:

אוֹתִי [וְאֶת אִשְׁתִּי / וְאֶת בַּעֲלִי. וְאֶת זַרְעִי] וְאֶת כָּל אֲשֶׁר לִי.

All guests recite the following:

אוֹתָם וְאֶת בֵּיתָם וְאֶת זַרְעָם וְאֶת כָּל אֲשֶׁר לָהֶם.

All continue here:

אוֹתָנוּ וְאֶת כָּל אֲשֶׁר לָנוּ, כְּמוֹ שֶׁנִּתְבָּרְכוּ אֲבוֹתֵינוּ אַבְרָהָם יִצְחָק וְיַעֲקֹב בַּכֹּל מִכֹּל כֹּל, כֵּן יְבָרֵךְ אוֹתָנוּ כֻּלָּנוּ יַחַד בִּבְרָכָה שְׁלֵמָה, וְנֹאמַר, אָמֵן.

Honoring Parents Through Bentching

הָרַחֲמָן הוּא יְבָרֵךְ אֶת (אָבִי מוֹרִי) בַּעַל הַבַּיִת הַזֶּה, וְאֶת (אִמִּי מוֹרָתִי) בַּעֲלַת הַבַּיִת הַזֶּה

The compassionate One! May He bless
(my father, my teacher) the master of this house,
and (my mother, my teacher) lady of this house

When she was 18 years old, Rebbetzin Shoshana Aliza (later Rebbetzin Zilberstein) left the Jerusalem home of her parents, Rav and Rebbetzin Elyashiv, to teach in Holon. Every day the young woman would bring a sandwich to school, wash her hands, take a few small bites, and then recite Bircas HaMazon. One of the principals asked Shoshana why she bothered

The compassionate One! May He bless

Guests recite the following.
Children at their parents' table add words in parentheses.

(my father, my teacher)
the master of this house,
and (my mother, my teacher)
lady of this house,

Those eating at their own table recite the following, adding the appropriate parenthesized phrases:

me (my wife/husband and family)
and all that is mine,

All guests recite the following:

them, their house, their family,
and all that is theirs,

All continue here:

ours and all that is ours — just as our forefathers Avraham, Yitzchak, and Yaakov were blessed in everything, from everything, with everything. So may He bless all of us together, with a perfect blessing. And let us say: Amen!

---

washing and reciting the lengthy Bircas HaMazon when she merely took a few bites of bread. Wouldn't it be easier to eat some crackers instead of washing for a small portion of bread and then saying a lengthy Bircas HaMazon?

"That's not the point," Shoshana explained with a smile. "Reciting Bircas HaMazon gives a person the opportunity to give a blessing to her father and mother by reciting the special 'HaRachaman' included in bentching. My parents live in Yerushalayim. Since I live here in Holon, I don't have as many opportunities to fulfill the mitzvah of honoring my parents as I would like. That's why I wash on a small sandwich each day — so I'll have the privilege of blessing my parents in the Bircas HaMazon and fulfilling the mitzvah of honoring my father and mother" (Shoshanas HaAmakim, p. 13).

בַּמָּרוֹם יְלַמְּדוּ עֲלֵיהֶם וְעָלֵינוּ זְכוּת, שֶׁתְּהֵא לְמִשְׁמֶרֶת שָׁלוֹם. וְנִשָּׂא בְרָכָה מֵאֵת יהוה, וּצְדָקָה מֵאֱלֹהֵי יִשְׁעֵנוּ, וְנִמְצָא חֵן וְשֵׂכֶל טוֹב בְּעֵינֵי אֱלֹהִים וְאָדָם.[1]

Judging Favorably

בַּמָּרוֹם יְלַמְּדוּ עֲלֵיהֶם וְעָלֵינוּ זְכוּת שֶׁתְּהֵא לְמִשְׁמֶרֶת שָׁלוֹם
On high, may merit be pleaded upon them and upon us, for a safeguard of peace

We ask Hashem here to judge us favorably, to be *melamed zechus* and search for our merits even when we have done wrong. The Talmud tells us that Hashem mirrors our actions, so to speak (*Shabbos* 127b). If we give others the benefit of the doubt, trying to understand their actions through the prism of their lives and the difficulties they may be going through, Hashem will reflect our actions and do the same for us.

We may see a friend or coworker or family member doing something we think is wrong. The Mishnah tells us how to react: הֱוֵי דָן אֶת כָּל הָאָדָם לְכַף זְכוּת, *Judge every person in a favorable way* (*Avos* 1:6). The Sfas Emes points out that the word *kol*, "every," seems extraneous. Had it said הֱוֵי דָן אֶת הָאָדָם, *Judge every person*, wouldn't it have meant the same thing?

The Sfas Emes explains that we can never accurately judge a person because we don't know everything about him; we don't know the *kol*, the "all," about a person that might explain or even justify his actions. His family background, his financial troubles, his health concerns, all that we don't know about a person might help us better understand what he did or said. We should always judge others favorably because we don't know his *kol*; we don't know all the things in his life that might be making him act or speak the way he does (see also *Chofetz Chaim, Ahavas Yisrael*, Ch. 5).

> Rav Levi Yitzchak of Berditchev was known to all as the defender of the Jewish people, and the stories of how he found the good in every Jew have become legend.
>
> An elderly man from Berditchev who had lived his whole

O n high, may merit be pleaded upon them and upon us, for a safeguard of peace. May we receive a blessing from HASHEM and just kindness from the God of our salvation, and find favor and good understanding in the eyes of God and man.[1]

---

1. Cf. *Mishlei* 3:4.

---

life as a religious Jew suddenly left the path of Judaism. When the townspeople informed Rav Levi Yitzchak of what had happened, he replied, "See, even the lowest Jewish person has within him sparks of holiness. This man was able to fight his yetzer hara for 70 years!" (Ohev V'Ahuv, p. 157).

A butcher once came to Rav Chaim Ozer Grodzensky to show him a cow's lung that he wasn't sure was kosher. Sure enough, Rav Chaim Ozer ruled that the animal was a treifeh and couldn't be eaten. The butcher, realizing the tremendous financial setback he had just suffered, began yelling at Rav Chaim Ozer, accusing him of not knowing the halachos properly!

Members of Rav Chaim Ozer's family wanted to throw the impudent butcher out of the home for showing disrespect to someone whom many considered the gadol hador. Rav Chaim Ozer stopped them. "Leave him," he said. "We cannot judge the butcher for his disrespectful response at this time, not when he is upset about his financial loss" (Rabban shel Yisrael, p. 30).

Hashem created everything for a beneficial reason. Rav Aryeh Levin once asked what positive aspect there could possibly be to twisted thinking. The answer, explained Rav Aryeh, is linked to the idea of judging favorably.

"Sometimes we have to use crooked thinking as a means of judging people favorably. When there is no logical or rational reason to give a person the benefit of the doubt, crooked thinking allows us to think of the most wild and unexpected reasons as to why someone acted in a certain manner. If you can't think of a good reason to judge a person favorably, that's the time to look for wild rationales and improbable excuses" (*Tzaddik Yesod Olam*; *HaRav MiPonevezh*).

THE EISHES CHAYIL HAGGADAH

On Shabbos add the following sentence:

הָרַחֲמָן הוּא יַנְחִילֵנוּ יוֹם שֶׁכֻּלּוֹ שַׁבָּת וּמְנוּחָה לְחַיֵּי הָעוֹלָמִים.

The words in parentheses are added on the two Seder nights in some communities.

הָרַחֲמָן הוּא יַנְחִילֵנוּ יוֹם שֶׁכֻּלּוֹ טוֹב (יוֹם שֶׁכֻּלּוֹ אָרוּךְ, יוֹם שֶׁצַּדִּיקִים יוֹשְׁבִים וְעַטְרוֹתֵיהֶם בְּרָאשֵׁיהֶם וְנֶהֱנִים מִזִּיו הַשְּׁכִינָה, וִיהִי חֶלְקֵנוּ עִמָּהֶם).

הָרַחֲמָן הוּא יְזַכֵּנוּ לִימוֹת הַמָּשִׁיחַ וּלְחַיֵּי הָעוֹלָם הַבָּא. מִגְדּוֹל יְשׁוּעוֹת מַלְכּוֹ וְעֹשֶׂה חֶסֶד לִמְשִׁיחוֹ לְדָוִד וּלְזַרְעוֹ עַד עוֹלָם.[1] עֹשֶׂה שָׁלוֹם בִּמְרוֹמָיו, הוּא יַעֲשֶׂה שָׁלוֹם עָלֵינוּ וְעַל כָּל יִשְׂרָאֵל. וְאִמְרוּ, אָמֵן.

יְראוּ אֶת יהוה קְדֹשָׁיו, כִּי אֵין מַחְסוֹר לִירֵאָיו. כְּפִירִים רָשׁוּ וְרָעֵבוּ, וְדֹרְשֵׁי יהוה לֹא יַחְסְרוּ כָל טוֹב. הוֹדוּ לַיהוה כִּי טוֹב, כִּי לְעוֹלָם חַסְדּוֹ.[2] פּוֹתֵחַ אֶת יָדֶךָ, וּמַשְׂבִּיעַ לְכָל חַי רָצוֹן.[3] בָּרוּךְ הַגֶּבֶר אֲשֶׁר יִבְטַח בַּיהוה, וְהָיָה יהוה מִבְטַחוֹ.[4] נַעַר הָיִיתִי גַם

Absolute Trust

בָּרוּךְ הַגֶּבֶר אֲשֶׁר יִבְטַח בַּה' וְהָיָה ה' מִבְטַחוֹ
Blessed is the man who trusts in Hashem, and Hashem will be his trust

When asked to describe true *bitachon*, faith in Hashem, the Vilna Gaon, cited the *pasuk* כְּגָמֻל עֲלֵי אִמּוֹ כַּגָּמֻל עָלַי נַפְשִׁי, *I was like a nursing child at his mother's side, like the nursing child is my*

> On Shabbos add the following sentence:
>
> The compassionate One! May He cause us to inherit the day which will be completely a Shabbos and rest day for eternal life.

The words in parentheses are added on the two Seder nights in some communities.

The compassionate One! May He cause us to inherit that day which is altogether good (that everlasting day, the day when the just will sit with crowns on their heads, enjoying the reflection of God's majesty — and may our portion be with them!).

The compassionate One! May He make us worthy of the days of Mashiach and the life of the World to Come. He Who is a tower of salvations to His king and shows lovingkindness for His anointed, to David and his descendants forever.[1] He Who makes peace in His heavenly heights, may He make harmony for us and for all Israel. Say: Amen!

Fear HASHEM, His holy ones, for those who fear Him feel no deprivation. Young lions may feel want and hunger, but those who seek HASHEM will not lack any good. Give thanks to God for He is good; His lovingkindness is eternal.[2] You open up Your hand and satisfy the desire of every living thing.[3] Blessed is the man who trusts in HASHEM, and HASHEM will be his trust.[4] I was a youth and also have aged, and I have not seen a righteous man

---

1. *II Shmuel* 22:51. 2. *Tehillim* 34:10-11. 3. Ibid. 145:16. 4. *Yirmiyah* 17:7.

---

soul" (*Tehillim* 131:2). A nursing baby is totally content and serene, with no worries or fears with regard to where his next meal will come from. This is the level of *bitachon* one should strive to attain: complete reliance on Hashem, faith that makes

זָקַנְתִּי, וְלֹא רָאִיתִי צַדִּיק נֶעֱזָב, וְזַרְעוֹ מְבַקֶּשׁ לָחֶם.[1] יהוה עֹז לְעַמּוֹ יִתֵּן, יהוה יְבָרֵךְ אֶת עַמּוֹ בַשָּׁלוֹם.[2]

Upon completion of Bircas HaMazon the blessing over wine is recited and the third cup is drunk while reclining on the left side. It is preferable to drink the entire cup, but at the very least, most of the cup should be drained.

Some recite the following before the third cup:

הִנְנִי מוּכָן וּמְזוּמָּן לְקַיֵּם מִצְוַת כּוֹס שְׁלִישִׁי שֶׁל אַרְבַּע כּוֹסוֹת. לְשֵׁם יִחוּד קֻדְשָׁא בְּרִיךְ הוּא וּשְׁכִינְתֵּיהּ, עַל יְדֵי הַהוּא טָמִיר וְנֶעְלָם, בְּשֵׁם כָּל יִשְׂרָאֵל. וִיהִי נֹעַם אֲדֹנָי אֱלֹהֵינוּ עָלֵינוּ, וּמַעֲשֵׂה יָדֵינוּ כּוֹנְנָה עָלֵינוּ, וּמַעֲשֵׂה יָדֵינוּ כּוֹנְנֵהוּ.

בָּרוּךְ אַתָּה יהוה אֱלֹהֵינוּ מֶלֶךְ הָעוֹלָם, בּוֹרֵא פְּרִי הַגָּפֶן.

The fourth cup is poured. According to most customs, the Cup of Eliyahu is poured at this point.

---

one totally serene and unworried about the future (*Divrei Eliyahu, Tehillim* 131; see also *Malbim, Tehillim* 131).

David HaMelech's comparison of a person's level of trust in Hashem to that of a nursing baby can help us better understand our relationship with Hashem and what it means to have true *bitachon*.

A baby depends totally on his mother; he relies only on her to change him, clean him, feed him, and take care of all his necessities. Our reliance on Hashem is also absolute; one who has complete *bitachon* knows he is totally dependent on Hashem to supply him with all his needs (*She'arim BiTefillah*, p. 97).

The *Chovos HaLevavos* (Introduction to *Sha'ar HaBitachon*) says that the more we trust in Hashem, the more Hashem watches over us and provides for us. This is similar to a baby nursing from his mother. The more a child nurses, the more milk is produced;

forsaken, with his children begging for bread.[1] HASHEM will give might to His nation; HASHEM will bless His nation with peace.[2]

Upon completion of Bircas HaMazon the blessing over wine is recited and the third cup is drunk while reclining on the left side. It is preferable to drink the entire cup, but at the very least, most of the cup should be drained.

Some recite the following before the third cup:

Behold, I am prepared and ready to fulfill the mitzvah of the third of the Four Cups. For the sake of the unification of the Holy One, Blessed is He, and His Presence, through Him Who is hidden and inscrutable — [I pray] in the name of all Israel. May the pleasantness of the Lord, our God, be upon us, and may He establish our handiwork for us; our handiwork may He establish.

Blessed are You, HASHEM, our God, King of the universe, Who creates the fruit of the vine.

The fourth cup is poured. According to most customs, the Cup of Eliyahu is poured at this point.

---

1. *Tehillim* 37:25. 2. Ibid. 29:11.

---

the less a baby nurses, the less milk is produced.

Rav Pinchas HaLevi Horowitz, the author of the *Haflaah*, uses this idea to explain the seemingly redundant phrases in the *pasuk* בָּרוּךְ הַגֶּבֶר אֲשֶׁר יִבְטַח בַּה׳, *Blessed is the man who trusts in Hashem*, which is immediately followed by וְהָיָה ה׳ מִבְטַחוֹ, *and Hashem will be his trust*. The *Haflah* explains that the *pasuk* is telling us that Hashem's protection over us comes directly from our level of *bitachon* in Him. The more we trust in Hashem, the more Hashem protects us and provides for us. *Blessed is the man who trusts in Hashem*; and according to the person's level of *bitachon*, then *Hashem will be his trust* (*Haflaah, Shemos* 16:6; *Metzudas Tzion, Yirmiyahu* 17:7).

[257] **THE EISHES CHAYIL HAGGADAH**

The door is opened in accordance with the verse, "It is a guarded night." Then the following paragraph is recited.

שְׁפֹךְ חֲמָתְךָ אֶל הַגּוֹיִם אֲשֶׁר לֹא יְדָעוּךָ וְעַל מַמְלָכוֹת אֲשֶׁר בְּשִׁמְךָ לֹא קָרָאוּ. כִּי

A Night of Protection

שְׁפוֹךְ חֲמָתְךָ אֶל הַגּוֹיִם
Pour Your wrath upon the nations

Before we say "*Shefoch Chamascha*," we open the door to our homes. One reason we do this is to express our belief and our longing for an end to the exile and persecution by the nations and for the coming of Mashiach; the night we celebrate our redemption is an auspicious time for his coming (*Mateh Moshe* 655).

Another reason we open the door at the end of the Seder: we are demonstrating our absolute belief that tonight is *Leil Shimurim*, a night of protection, and we are not afraid of anyone. This demonstration of belief and trust in Hashem serves as a *zechus* to hasten the coming of Mashiach (*Rema, Orach Chaim* 480:1).

When *Bnei Yisrael* crossed the Yam Suf and saw the Egyptian corpses strewn on the beach, they broke out into song and sang "*Az Yashir*." Then, led by Miriam, the women played music on their drums and musical instruments. Where did the Jewish women get musical instruments?

Rashi tells us (*Shemos* 16:20) that these righteous women had steadfast *emunah* on leaving Egypt. They were so certain that Hashem would perform wondrous miracles for the Jews that they brought musical instruments with them so they would be ready to celebrate and thank Hashem. This kind of *emunah* brings *berachah* to us as a nation and as individuals. We recall this extraordinary faith each morning when we say the *berachah* of "*Ahavah Rabbah*" before *Krias Shema*, and we plead with Hashem to grant us mercy and success in keeping the Torah in the merit of אֲבוֹתֵינוּ שֶׁבָּטְחוּ בְךָ, *our forefathers who trusted in You [when leaving Egypt]*.

> The door is opened in accordance with the verse, *"It is a guarded night."* Then the following paragraph is recited.

Pour Your wrath upon the nations that do not recognize You and upon the kingdoms that do not invoke Your Name. For they have

---

It is written, ה' צִלְּךָ, *Hashem is your shadow* (*Tehillim* 121:5). The *sefarim* explain that Hashem "shadows us," so to speak; that is, He acts toward us and moves in tandem with us according to our actions (*Kedushas Levi, Shemos* 15:1, quoting *the Baal Shem Tov; Midrash Shmuel, Avos* 3:1). When we turn to Hashem for guidance and help, Hashem turns toward us.

Rav Moshe Greenwald quotes the Kedushas Levi, who writes that in the word *bitachon* is the word *tach* (טח), to stick. When we have *bitachon*, it creates a "sticking agent" between us and Hashem: we are stuck to Hashem and He is firmly attached to us. The more *bitachon* we have in Hashem, the stronger this sticking agent is, and the more Hashem is attached to us (*Arugos HaBosem, Beshalach*).

Hence, *Hashem is your shadow;* we have the ability to bring about *berachah* through turning toward Hashem, beseeching Him for constant guidance, and strengthening our *emunah* in Him. When opening the door for "*Shefoch Chamascha,*" we should internalize our faith in Hashem and no other. This itself will bring the hastening of the redemption and a heavenly showering of *berachah* (*Ohr Yisrael* 24; *Chovos HaLevavos*, Introduction to Sha'ar HaBitachon; *Nefesh HaChaim* 1:7).

The Cup of Eliyahu

שְׁפוֹךְ חֲמָתְךָ אֶל הַגּוֹיִם
Pour Your wrath upon the nations

It's customary to pour a cup of wine in honor of Eliyahu HaNavi at this point in the Seder. One reason is that by pouring the Cup of Eliyahu we show that just as Hashem redeemed us from the Egyptian exile, we believe that He will redeem us from the present exile as well, and Eliyahu HaNavi will herald the coming of Mashiach (*Mishnah Berurah, Orach Chaim* 480:10).

אָכַל אֶת יַעֲקֹב וְאֶת נָוֵהוּ הֵשַׁמּוּ. שְׁפָךְ עֲלֵיהֶם זַעְמֶךָ וַחֲרוֹן אַפְּךָ יַשִּׂיגֵם. תִּרְדֹּף בְּאַף וְתַשְׁמִידֵם מִתַּחַת שְׁמֵי יהוה.

≈הלל≈

The door is closed and the recitation of the Haggadah is continued.

לֹא לָנוּ יהוה, לֹא לָנוּ, כִּי לְשִׁמְךָ תֵּן כָּבוֹד, עַל חַסְדְּךָ עַל אֲמִתֶּךָ. לָמָּה יֹאמְרוּ הַגּוֹיִם, אַיֵּה נָא אֱלֹהֵיהֶם. וֵאלֹהֵינוּ בַשָּׁמַיִם,

---

Also, there's a disagreement in the Talmud as to how many cups of wine one is obligated to drink on Seder night. The majority opinion holds that four cups need to be consumed, paralleling the four expressions of redemption used by the Torah: וְהוֹצֵאתִי, וְהִצַּלְתִּי וְגָאַלְתִּי וְלָקַחְתִּי, *I shall take you out… I shall rescue you… I shall redeem you… I shall take you to Me…* (Shemos 6:6–7).

The other opinion maintains that one is obligated to drink five cups of wine on the night of Pesach, symbolic of the four terms of redemption, plus a fifth expression, וְהֵבֵאתִי, *I shall bring you*, which refers to Hashem bringing the Jewish people into Eretz Yisrael. We are waiting for Eliyahu to arrive and settle this question; hence we pour a fifth cup and call it the Cup of Eliyahu (*Kol Eliyahu, Va'eira*).

The Nations' All-Consuming Hatred

שְׁפֹךְ חֲמָתְךָ אֶל הַגּוֹיִם אֲשֶׁר לֹא יְדָעוּךָ וְעַל מַמְלָכוֹת אֲשֶׁר בְּשִׁמְךָ לֹא קָרָאוּ. כִּי אָכַל אֶת יַעֲקֹב וְאֶת נָוֵהוּ הֵשַׁמּוּ.

Pour Your wrath upon the nations that do not recognize You and upon the kingdoms that do not invoke Your Name. For they have devoured Yaakov and destroyed His habitation

Rav Yisrael Meir Lau asks why we begin "*Shefoch Chamascha*" with the words גּוֹיִם and מַמְלָכוֹת, *nations* and *kingdoms*, in the plural form, and then end by using the singular form כִּי אָכַל אֶת

devoured Yaakov and destroyed His habitation. Pour Your anger upon them and let Your fiery wrath overtake them. Pursue them with wrath and annihilate them from beneath the heavens of HASHEM.

 HALLEL

The door is closed and the recitation of the Haggadah is continued.

Not for our sake, O Lord, not for our sake, but for Your Name's sake give glory, for the sake of Your kindness and Your truth! Why should the nations say, "Where is their God now?" Our God is in the heavens;

יַעֲקֹב, *And he devoured Yaakov.*

Rav Lau, a child survivor of the Holocaust, explains that even though the nations of the world have major cultural, social, economic, political, and religious differences, when it comes to their hatred of the Jews, they are collectively undivided (*Haggadah al Matzos U'Merorim*, p. 155; see also *Kisvei Abba Mori*, p. 246).

Rav Tzvi Hirsch Ferber points out that the Haggadah uses the word *achal*, "devour," to describe the absolute desire of the nations of the world to consume and destroy the Jewish people. The desire of the non-Jewish nations to swallow, consume, and destroy the Jews seems to be as natural to them, as ingrained and necessary, as eating.

HALLEL / הלל

Crying for Hashem

לָמָּה יֹאמְרוּ הַגּוֹיִם, אַיֵּה נָא אֱלֹהֵיהֶם

Why should the nations say, "Where is their God now?"

Rav Yekusiel Yehudah Halberstam, the Klausenberger Rebbe, was forced by the Nazis to perform horrendous and inhumane

כֹּל אֲשֶׁר חָפֵץ עָשָׂה. עֲצַבֵּיהֶם כֶּסֶף וְזָהָב, מַעֲשֵׂה יְדֵי אָדָם. פֶּה לָהֶם וְלֹא יְדַבֵּרוּ, עֵינַיִם לָהֶם וְלֹא יִרְאוּ. אָזְנַיִם לָהֶם וְלֹא יִשְׁמָעוּ, אַף לָהֶם וְלֹא יְרִיחוּן. יְדֵיהֶם וְלֹא יְמִישׁוּן, רַגְלֵיהֶם וְלֹא יְהַלֵּכוּ, לֹא יֶהְגּוּ בִּגְרוֹנָם. כְּמוֹהֶם יִהְיוּ עֹשֵׂיהֶם, כֹּל אֲשֶׁר בֹּטֵחַ בָּהֶם. יִשְׂרָאֵל בְּטַח בַּיהוה, עֶזְרָם וּמָגִנָּם הוּא. בֵּית אַהֲרֹן בִּטְחוּ בַיהוה, עֶזְרָם וּמָגִנָּם הוּא. יִרְאֵי יהוה בִּטְחוּ בַיהוה, עֶזְרָם וּמָגִנָּם הוּא.

יהוה זְכָרָנוּ יְבָרֵךְ; יְבָרֵךְ אֶת בֵּית יִשְׂרָאֵל, יְבָרֵךְ אֶת בֵּית אַהֲרֹן. יְבָרֵךְ יִרְאֵי יהוה, הַקְּטַנִּים עִם הַגְּדֹלִים. יֹסֵף יהוה עֲלֵיכֶם, עֲלֵיכֶם וְעַל בְּנֵיכֶם. בְּרוּכִים אַתֶּם לַיהוה, עֹשֵׂה שָׁמַיִם וָאָרֶץ. הַשָּׁמַיִם שָׁמַיִם לַיהוה, וְהָאָרֶץ נָתַן לִבְנֵי אָדָם. לֹא הַמֵּתִים יְהַלְלוּ יָהּ, וְלֹא כָּל יֹרְדֵי דוּמָה. וַאֲנַחְנוּ נְבָרֵךְ יָהּ, מֵעַתָּה וְעַד עוֹלָם; הַלְלוּיָהּ.[1]

---

labor. After the Warsaw Ghetto uprising was crushed by the Germans, most of a once-grand city lay in ruins. The Jewish population was nearly extinct. Yet beneath the collapsed buildings were valuables that the greedy Germans wanted. They gathered a unit of Jewish workers, including the Rebbe, to spend 12 hours a day in brutal heat or freezing cold lifting massive slabs of concrete, piling up dead bodies, and collecting valuables for the German beasts.

The Rebbe had lost his wife, 11 children, and countless students. As he slaved, with tears in his eyes he whispered quietly to himself, לָמָּה יֹאמְרוּ הַגּוֹיִם, אַיֵּה נָא אֱלֹהֵיהֶם, Why should

whatever He pleases, He does! Their idols are silver and gold, the handiwork of man. They have a mouth, but cannot speak; they have eyes, but cannot see; they have ears, but cannot hear; they have a nose, but cannot smell; their hands — they cannot feel; their feet — they cannot walk; nor can they utter a sound with their throat. Those who make them should become like them, whoever trusts in them! O Israel! Trust in HASHEM; He is their help and their shield! House of Aharon! Trust in HASHEM! He is their help and their shield! You who fear HASHEM — trust in HASHEM, He is their help and their shield!

HASHEM Who has remembered us will bless — He will bless the House of Israel; He will bless the House of Aharon; He will bless those who fear HASHEM, the small as well as the great. May HASHEM increase upon you, upon you, and your children! You are blessed of HASHEM, Maker of heaven and earth. As for the heaven — the heaven is HASHEM's, but the earth He has given to mankind. Neither the dead can praise HASHEM, nor any who descend into silence; but we will bless God henceforth and forever. Halleluyah![1]

---

1. *Tehillim* 115.

---

the nations say, "Where is their God now?" — the pasuk in which King David expresses his concern and sadness over the desecration of Hashem's honor.

The Rebbe's own pain and suffering didn't concern him: he cried for Hashem and the wounding of His honor (*Lapid Eish, Vol. 1, p. 182*).

אָהַבְתִּי כִּי יִשְׁמַע יהוה, אֶת קוֹלִי תַּחֲנוּנָי. כִּי הִטָּה אָזְנוֹ לִי, וּבְיָמַי אֶקְרָא. אֲפָפוּנִי חֶבְלֵי מָוֶת, וּמְצָרֵי שְׁאוֹל מְצָאוּנִי; צָרָה וְיָגוֹן אֶמְצָא. וּבְשֵׁם יהוה אֶקְרָא: אָנָּה יהוה מַלְּטָה נַפְשִׁי. חַנּוּן יהוה וְצַדִּיק, וֵאלֹהֵינוּ מְרַחֵם. שֹׁמֵר פְּתָאיִם יהוה, דַּלּוֹתִי וְלִי יְהוֹשִׁיעַ. שׁוּבִי נַפְשִׁי לִמְנוּחָיְכִי, כִּי יהוה גָּמַל עָלָיְכִי. כִּי חִלַּצְתָּ נַפְשִׁי מִמָּוֶת; אֶת עֵינִי מִן דִּמְעָה, אֶת רַגְלִי מִדֶּחִי. אֶתְהַלֵּךְ לִפְנֵי יהוה, בְּאַרְצוֹת הַחַיִּים. הֶאֱמַנְתִּי כִּי אֲדַבֵּר, אֲנִי עָנִיתִי מְאֹד. אֲנִי אָמַרְתִּי בְחָפְזִי, כָּל הָאָדָם כֹּזֵב.

מָה אָשִׁיב לַיהוה, כָּל תַּגְמוּלוֹהִי עָלָי. כּוֹס יְשׁוּעוֹת אֶשָּׂא, וּבְשֵׁם יהוה אֶקְרָא. נְדָרַי לַיהוה אֲשַׁלֵּם, נֶגְדָה נָּא לְכָל עַמּוֹ. יָקָר בְּעֵינֵי יהוה, הַמָּוְתָה לַחֲסִידָיו. אָנָּה יהוה כִּי

"With the Help of Hashem"

הֶאֱמַנְתִּי כִּי אֲדַבֵּר
I kept faith although I say

Rav Mordechai of Lechovitch explains that our faith in Hashem comes through speech: הֶאֱמַנְתִּי, *I believe [in Hashem]*; כִּי אֲדַבֵּר, *because I speak about Him.* When we discuss the miracles He performs, talk about our history, speak of our miraculous survival despite adversity, and discuss the wonders we are witness to in our daily lives, we become bigger believers in Hashem.

Pesach is, of course, the night when our speech most strongly strengthens our faith. It is a magical night when we share with the next generation the foundational principles of *emunah* as we tell the story of our enslavement and redemption and the miracles Hashem performed for our people. We should bring this lesson

I love [Him], for HASHEM hears my voice, my supplications. For He has inclined His ear to me, all my days I will call upon Him. The ropes of death encompassed me; the confines of the grave have found me; trouble and sorrow have I found. Then I called upon the Name of HASHEM: "Please, HASHEM, save my soul." Gracious is HASHEM and righteous, our God is merciful. The Lord protects the simple; I was brought low but He saved me. Return to your rest, my soul, for HASHEM has been kind to you. You delivered my soul from death, my eyes from tears, and my feet from stumbling. I shall walk before the Lord in the lands of the living. I kept faith although I say: "I suffer exceedingly." I said in my haste: "All mankind is deceitful."

How can I repay HASHEM for all His kindness to me? I will raise the cup of salvations and invoke the Name of HASHEM. My vows to HASHEM I will pay in the presence of His entire people. Precious in the eyes of HASHEM is the death of His devout ones. Please, HASHEM — for

---

home by sharing our own personal experiences and telling how we have seen and felt the Hand of Hashem protecting us (*Toras Avos*, p. 149).

The Shelah (*Sha'ar HaOsiyos* 1, *Emes VeEmunah* 46–53) suggests another way of strengthening our *emunah* by speech: say *im yirtzeh Hashem*, "if it is the will of Hashem," before setting out to perform a task. By consistently saying *b'ezras Hashem* or *im yirtzeh Hashem*, we remind ourselves that every event, decision, and action requires Hashem's assistance. Incorporating a prayer to Hashem in all that we do brings special Divine help and helps us form a moment-to-moment relationship with Hashem as we realize just how much our life depends on Him.

אֲנִי עַבְדֶּךָ; אֲנִי עַבְדְּךָ בֶּן אֲמָתֶךָ, פִּתַּחְתָּ לְמוֹסֵרָי. לְךָ אֶזְבַּח זֶבַח תּוֹדָה, וּבְשֵׁם יהוה אֶקְרָא. נְדָרַי לַיהוה אֲשַׁלֵּם, נֶגְדָה נָּא לְכָל עַמּוֹ. בְּחַצְרוֹת בֵּית יהוה, בְּתוֹכֵכִי יְרוּשָׁלָיִם; הַלְלוּיָהּ.¹

הַלְלוּ אֶת יהוה, כָּל גּוֹיִם; שַׁבְּחוּהוּ כָּל הָאֻמִּים. כִּי גָבַר עָלֵינוּ חַסְדּוֹ, וֶאֱמֶת יהוה לְעוֹלָם; הַלְלוּיָהּ.²

הוֹדוּ לַיהוה כִּי טוֹב,   כִּי לְעוֹלָם חַסְדּוֹ.
יֹאמַר נָא יִשְׂרָאֵל,   כִּי לְעוֹלָם חַסְדּוֹ.
יֹאמְרוּ נָא בֵית אַהֲרֹן,   כִּי לְעוֹלָם חַסְדּוֹ.
יֹאמְרוּ נָא יִרְאֵי יהוה,   כִּי לְעוֹלָם חַסְדּוֹ.

מִן הַמֵּצַר קָרָאתִי יָּהּ, עָנָנִי בַמֶּרְחָב יָהּ. יהוה לִי לֹא אִירָא, מַה יַּעֲשֶׂה לִי אָדָם.

Servants of Hashem

אָנָּה ה' כִּי אֲנִי עַבְדֶּךָ, אֲנִי עַבְדְּךָ בֶּן אֲמָתֶךָ פִּתַּחְתָּ לְמוֹסֵרָי
Please, Hashem — for I am Your servant, I am Your servant, son of Your handmaid — You have released my bonds

The Sfas Emes once told his chassidim that if they concentrate on the words אָנָּה ה', *Please, Hashem*, in Hallel, they would receive tremendous berachah from Hashem. The chassidim had said the phrases אָנָּא ה' הוֹשִׁיעָה נָּא, *O, Hashem, please save us!* and אָנָּא ה' הַצְלִיחָה נָּא, *O, Hashem, please make us prosper!* with intense concentration, yet they didn't feel they had received any special berachah or answers to their tefillos.

The son of the Sfas Emes, the Imrei Emes, explained that his father's chassidim had misunderstood their Rebbe. "When my father said to have special concentration when saying the words אָנָּא ה', he meant you should concentrate particularly on the phrase אָנָּה ה' כִּי אֲנִי עַבְדֶּךָ, *Please, Hashem, for I am Your servant,*

I am Your servant, I am Your servant, son of Your handmaid — You have released my bonds. To You I sacrifice thanksgiving offerings, and the Name of HASHEM I will invoke. My vows to HASHEM I will pay in the presence of His entire people; in the courtyards of the House of HASHEM, in your midst, O Jerusalem, Halleluyah![1]

Praise HASHEM, all you nations; praise Him all you peoples! For His kindness to us was overwhelming, and the truth of HASHEM is eternal, Halleluyah![2]

Give thanks to HASHEM for He is good;
    His kindness endures forever!
Let Israel say: His kindness endures forever!
Let the House of Aharon say:
    His kindness endures forever!
Let those who fear HASHEM say:
    His kindness endures forever!

From the straits did I call to God; God answered me with expansiveness. HASHEM is with me; I have no fear; how can man affect me?

---

1. *Tehillim* 116. 2. Ibid. 117.

---

which appears earlier in Hallel. When we say these words, we're placing ourselves under Hashem's protection. When we relinquish ourselves to His will as a servant does to a master, it brings greater berachah than any possible tefillah (*Likutei Yehudah Haggadah*, p. 124).

Hashem Is With Us

ה' לִי לֹא אִירָא

Hashem is with me; I have no fear

If someone is, God forbid, seriously ill, he will conduct an extensive investigation and research the top doctors and best

יהוה לִי בְּעֹזְרָי, וַאֲנִי אֶרְאֶה בְשֹׂנְאָי. טוֹב לַחֲסוֹת בַּיהוה, מִבְּטֹחַ בָּאָדָם. טוֹב לַחֲסוֹת בַּיהוה, מִבְּטֹחַ בִּנְדִיבִים. כָּל גּוֹיִם סְבָבוּנִי, בְּשֵׁם יהוה כִּי אֲמִילַם. סַבּוּנִי גַם סְבָבוּנִי, בְּשֵׁם יהוה כִּי אֲמִילַם. סַבּוּנִי כִדְבֹרִים, דֹּעֲכוּ כְּאֵשׁ קוֹצִים; בְּשֵׁם יהוה כִּי אֲמִילַם. דָּחֹה דְחִיתַנִי לִנְפֹּל, וַיהוה עֲזָרָנִי. עָזִּי וְזִמְרָת יָהּ, וַיְהִי לִי לִישׁוּעָה. קוֹל רִנָּה וִישׁוּעָה בְּאָהֳלֵי צַדִּיקִים, יְמִין יהוה עֹשָׂה חָיִל. יְמִין יהוה רוֹמֵמָה, יְמִין יהוה עֹשָׂה חָיִל. לֹא אָמוּת כִּי אֶחְיֶה, וַאֲסַפֵּר מַעֲשֵׂי יָהּ. יַסֹּר יִסְּרַנִּי יָּהּ, וְלַמָּוֶת לֹא נְתָנָנִי.

---

hospitals. Once he has recovered, he will go to shul and say *bircas hagomel,* the thanksgiving blessing recited by one who has been saved from danger. Someone who flies on an airplane and arrives safely after crossing over a large body of water also goes to shul and recites the very same *bircas hagomel,* thanking Hashem for saving him from the danger of air travel.

Rav Yechezkel Abramsky, the former *av beis din* of London, asks why people will spend time investigating and researching to find the best doctor, but they never bother to inquire into the credentials and expertise of airplane pilots.

Rav Abramsky explains that people inherently trust another individual when that individual is in the same danger they are in. Since the airplane pilot is also flying on the plane, and, therefore, has a personal interest in seeing that they land safely, we feel we can trust the pilot without looking too closely at his credentials. This is in contrast to the doctor performing surgery on another individual. That doctor is in no physical danger at all, and therefore the individual being operated on has more reason to worry and does what he can to seek out the best possible medical care.

Rav Yaakov Galinsky uses this idea to explain David HaMelech's words: ה' לִי, *Hashem is **together** with me;* therefore, לֹא אִירָא, *I have*

HASHEM is for me through my helpers; therefore I can face my foes. It is better to take refuge in HASHEM than to rely on man. It is better to take refuge in HASHEM than to rely on princes. All the nations encompass me; but in the Name of HASHEM I cut them down! They encompass me; they swarm around me; but in the Name of HASHEM I cut them down! They swarm around me like bees, but they are extinguished as a fire does thorns; in the Name of HASHEM I cut them down! You pushed me hard that I might fall, but HASHEM assisted me. My strength and song is God; He became my salvation. The sound of rejoicing and salvation is in the tents of the righteous: "The right hand of HASHEM does valiantly! The right hand of HASHEM is raised triumphantly! The right hand of HASHEM does valiantly!" I shall not die! I shall live and relate the deeds of God. God chastened me exceedingly but He did not let me die.

---

nothing to fear. Hashem is with the person throughout his distress and pain, so to speak, just like the pilot and passenger who are in danger together. And as the pilot is sure to do everything in his power to keep the plane safe, Hashem is together with each and every one of His children, keeping us safe (*Melech B'Yofyav*, p. 877; *V'Higadeta Haggadah*, p. 393).

True Life

לֹא אָמוּת כִּי אֶחְיֶה. וַאֲסַפֵּר מַעֲשֵׂי יָהּ. יַסֹּר יִסְּרַנִּי יָהּ.
וְלַמָּוֶת לֹא נְתָנָנִי. פִּתְחוּ לִי שַׁעֲרֵי צֶדֶק...

I shall not die! I shall live and relate the deeds of God.
God chastened me exceedingly but He did not let me die.
Open for me the gates of righteousness...

Rav Elazar Menachem Mann Shach delivered a eulogy at the funeral of Rebbetzin Chana Perel, the wife of Rav Aharon

פִּתְחוּ לִי שַׁעֲרֵי צֶדֶק, אָבֹא בָם אוֹדֶה יָהּ. זֶה הַשַּׁעַר לַיהוה, צַדִּיקִים יָבֹאוּ בוֹ. אוֹדְךָ כִּי עֲנִיתָנִי, וַתְּהִי לִי לִישׁוּעָה. אוֹדְךָ כִּי עֲנִיתָנִי, וַתְּהִי לִי לִישׁוּעָה. אֶבֶן מָאֲסוּ הַבּוֹנִים, הָיְתָה לְרֹאשׁ פִּנָּה. אֶבֶן מָאֲסוּ הַבּוֹנִים, הָיְתָה לְרֹאשׁ פִּנָּה. מֵאֵת יהוה הָיְתָה זֹּאת, הִיא נִפְלָאת בְּעֵינֵינוּ. מֵאֵת יהוה הָיְתָה זֹּאת, הִיא נִפְלָאת בְּעֵינֵינוּ. זֶה הַיּוֹם עָשָׂה יהוה, נָגִילָה וְנִשְׂמְחָה בוֹ. זֶה הַיּוֹם עָשָׂה יהוה, נָגִילָה וְנִשְׂמְחָה בוֹ.

אָנָּא יהוה, הוֹשִׁיעָה נָּא.

אָנָּא יהוה, הוֹשִׁיעָה נָּא.

אָנָּא יהוה, הַצְלִיחָה נָּא.

אָנָּא יהוה, הַצְלִיחָה נָּא.

בָּרוּךְ הַבָּא בְּשֵׁם יהוה, בֵּרַכְנוּכֶם מִבֵּית יהוה. בָּרוּךְ הַבָּא בְּשֵׁם יהוה, בֵּרַכְנוּכֶם מִבֵּית יהוה. אֵל יהוה וַיָּאֶר לָנוּ, אִסְרוּ חַג בַּעֲבֹתִים עַד קַרְנוֹת הַמִּזְבֵּחַ. אֵל יהוה וַיָּאֶר לָנוּ, אִסְרוּ חַג בַּעֲבֹתִים עַד קַרְנוֹת הַמִּזְבֵּחַ. אֵלִי אַתָּה וְאוֹדֶךָּ, אֱלֹהַי אֲרוֹמְמֶךָּ. אֵלִי אַתָּה וְאוֹדֶךָּ, אֱלֹהַי אֲרוֹמְמֶךָּ.

Kotler, the rosh yeshivah of Lakewood. He reminded all those in mourning that the rebbetzin was the daughter of Rav Isser Zalman Meltzer, the wife of Rav Aharon Kotler, and the mother of Rav Shneur Kotler and other children and grandchildren who all followed the path of Torah and mitzvos.

"I ask you all present here today," Rav Shach concluded, "has

Open for me the gates of righteousness, I will enter them and thank God. This is the gate of HASHEM; the righteous shall enter through it. I thank You for You answered me and became my salvation! I thank You for You answered me and became my salvation! The stone which the builders despised has become the cornerstone! The stone which the builders despised has become the cornerstone! This has emanated from HASHEM; it is wondrous in our eyes! This has emanated from HASHEM; it is wondrous in our eyes! This is the day HASHEM has made; we will rejoice and be glad in Him! This is the day HASHEM has made; we will rejoice and be glad in Him!

O HASHEM, please save us!
O HASHEM, please save us!
O HASHEM, please make us prosper!
O HASHEM, please make us prosper!

Blessed be he who comes in the Name of HASHEM; we bless you from the House of HASHEM. Blessed be he who comes in the Name of HASHEM; we bless you from the House of HASHEM. HASHEM is God and He illuminated for us; bind the festival offering with cords to the corners of the Altar. HASHEM is God and He illuminated for us; bind the festival offering with cords to the corners of the Altar. You are my God and I shall thank You; my God and I shall exalt You. You are my God, and I shall thank You; my God and I shall exalt You.

Rebbetzin Kotler died? No, for Rebbetzin Kotler is alive! Her children and grandchildren and all that she invested in them continue to be a song of praise and testimony to her great accomplishments!" (Michtavim U'Ma'amarim, Vol. 3, 213).

הוֹדוּ לַיהוה כִּי טוֹב, כִּי לְעוֹלָם חַסְדּוֹ. הוֹדוּ לַיהוה כִּי טוֹב, כִּי לְעוֹלָם חַסְדּוֹ.[1]

יְהַלְלוּךָ יהוה אֱלֹהֵינוּ כָּל מַעֲשֶׂיךָ, וַחֲסִידֶיךָ צַדִּיקִים עוֹשֵׂי רְצוֹנֶךָ, וְכָל עַמְּךָ בֵּית יִשְׂרָאֵל בְּרִנָּה יוֹדוּ וִיבָרְכוּ וִישַׁבְּחוּ וִיפָאֲרוּ וִירוֹמְמוּ וְיַעֲרִיצוּ וְיַקְדִּישׁוּ וְיַמְלִיכוּ אֶת שִׁמְךָ מַלְכֵּנוּ. כִּי לְךָ טוֹב לְהוֹדוֹת וּלְשִׁמְךָ נָאֶה לְזַמֵּר, כִּי מֵעוֹלָם וְעַד עוֹלָם אַתָּה אֵל.

הוֹדוּ לַיהוה כִּי טוֹב, כִּי לְעוֹלָם חַסְדּוֹ.

A Love for Chesed

הוֹדוּ לַה׳ כִּי טוֹב, כִּי לְעוֹלָם חַסְדּוֹ
Give thanks to Hashem for He is good;
His kindness endures forever!

We are charged with following in the ways of Hashem; as the Talmud says, just as Hashem is merciful so should we be merciful (*Shabbos* 133b).

Rav Yaakov Kamenetsky's wife was well known for all the chesed she did. Sometimes her help saved lives; other times it was a small, seemingly trivial act that made a world of difference to someone.

Every Friday young yeshivah boys would knock on the rebbetzin's door, collecting for their yeshivah. The rebbetzin would give them some money, and she always added a candy for each young boy as well.

One year, the rebbetzin was going to Florida for the weeks between Chanukah and Purim, and she didn't want to disappoint her young tzedakah collectors. On the Friday before she traveled, Rebbetzin Kamenetsky gave the boys money to cover every week she was away, and she made sure to count out

Give thanks to HASHEM, for He is good; His kindness endures forever! Give thanks to HASHEM, for He is good; His kindness endures forever![1]

They shall praise You, HASHEM our God, for all Your works, along with Your pious followers, the righteous, who do Your will, and Your entire people, the House of Israel, with joy will thank, bless, praise, glorify, exalt, revere, sanctify, and coronate Your Name, our King! For to You it is fitting to give thanks, and unto Your Name it is proper to sing praises, for from eternity to eternity You are God.

Give thanks to HASHEM, for He is good; His kindness endures forever!

---
1. *Tehillim* 118.

---

enough candy for each of them to have a treat every week until she returned.

This small act of kindness encouraged the boys as they collected tzedakah — and the sweet taste of the candy would remain with the boys for life, as they saw a true demonstration of ahavas chesed, a sincere love of helping others (B'Michtzas Rabbeinu, p. 167).

The Ultimate Praise

הוֹדוּ לַה׳ כִּי טוֹב, כִּי לְעוֹלָם חַסְדּוֹ
Give thanks to Hashem for He is good; His kindness endures forever!

The Talmud tells us that the 26 verses of praises to Hashem in *Tehillim* 136 beginning with הוֹדוּ לַה׳ כִּי טוֹב, *Give thanks to Hashem for He is good*, is called Hallel HaGadol, the "Great Hallel," because we enumerate among the praises the ultimate praise of Hashem (*Pesachim* 118a). What is this ultimate praise? That Hashem sits "above all of creation," and נֹתֵן לֶחֶם לְכָל בָּשָׂר, *He gives*

הוֹדוּ לֵאלֹהֵי הָאֱלֹהִים,	כִּי לְעוֹלָם חַסְדּוֹ.
הוֹדוּ לַאֲדֹנֵי הָאֲדֹנִים,	כִּי לְעוֹלָם חַסְדּוֹ.
לְעֹשֵׂה נִפְלָאוֹת גְּדֹלוֹת לְבַדּוֹ,	כִּי לְעוֹלָם חַסְדּוֹ.
לְעֹשֵׂה הַשָּׁמַיִם בִּתְבוּנָה,	כִּי לְעוֹלָם חַסְדּוֹ.
לְרֹקַע הָאָרֶץ עַל הַמָּיִם,	כִּי לְעוֹלָם חַסְדּוֹ.
לְעֹשֵׂה אוֹרִים גְּדֹלִים,	כִּי לְעוֹלָם חַסְדּוֹ.
אֶת הַשֶּׁמֶשׁ לְמֶמְשֶׁלֶת בַּיּוֹם,	כִּי לְעוֹלָם חַסְדּוֹ.
אֶת הַיָּרֵחַ וְכוֹכָבִים לְמֶמְשְׁלוֹת בַּלָּיְלָה,	
כִּי לְעוֹלָם חַסְדּוֹ.	
לְמַכֵּה מִצְרַיִם בִּבְכוֹרֵיהֶם,	כִּי לְעוֹלָם חַסְדּוֹ.
וַיּוֹצֵא יִשְׂרָאֵל מִתּוֹכָם,	כִּי לְעוֹלָם חַסְדּוֹ.
בְּיָד חֲזָקָה וּבִזְרוֹעַ נְטוּיָה,	כִּי לְעוֹלָם חַסְדּוֹ.

food to all living creatures. Hashem in His glory feeds every single living creature, from the largest elephants to the smallest insects, from a tiny creature of the sea to all of mankind.

We can see *hashgachah pratis* in every aspect of our lives, but perhaps never more clearly than when it comes to *parnassah*.

A *yungerman* decided to return to the States after learning in Israel for several years. He moved with his family to the New York area to find a means of livelihood. Their first Shabbos home, they went to his parents in Queens.

Shabbos morning the *yungerman* asked his father where he would be davening, expecting his father to answer that he would daven in the shul down the block, where he davened most Shabbosos.

"You know what?" his father said. "I'd like to visit our old shul this week." The old shul was a bit of a walk, but if that's where his father wanted to daven, the *yungerman* would go along.

In shul the father met an old friend who had come to Queens from Lakewood that same Shabbos. It was a rare visit to his

Give thanks to the God of gods;
His kindness endures forever!
Give thanks to the Master of masters;
His kindness endures forever!
To Him Who alone does great wonders;
His kindness endures forever!
To Him Who makes the heaven with understanding;
His kindness endures forever!
To Him Who stretched out the earth over the waters;
His kindness endures forever!
To Him Who makes great luminaries;
His kindness endures forever!
The sun for the reign of the day;
His kindness endures forever!
The moon and the stars for the reign of the night;
His kindness endures forever!
To Him Who struck the Egyptians through their firstborn; His kindness endures forever!
And took Israel out from their midst;
His kindness endures forever!
With strong hand and outstretched arm;
His kindness endures forever!

---

parents because of his large family. The two greeted each other after davening and began to chat.

"Your son is just back from Israel?..."

"Beginning to think of parnassah?..."

"Call me after Shabbos..."

A quick phone call after Shabbos, and, yes, the friend from Lakewood knew of a job located near the young man's new home.

A resume sent, an interview conducted, and within a day or two, the young man from Israel was working at a large frum company just five minutes from his house. A trip to Queens for Shabbos, tefillah at the "other shul," a visitor from Lakewood who rarely comes for Shabbos, a business contact — and Hashem has provided a young family with parnassah!

לְגֹזֵר יַם סוּף לִגְזָרִים,	כִּי לְעוֹלָם חַסְדּוֹ.
וְהֶעֱבִיר יִשְׂרָאֵל בְּתוֹכוֹ,	כִּי לְעוֹלָם חַסְדּוֹ.
וְנִעֵר פַּרְעֹה וְחֵילוֹ בְיַם סוּף,	כִּי לְעוֹלָם חַסְדּוֹ.
לְמוֹלִיךְ עַמּוֹ בַּמִּדְבָּר,	כִּי לְעוֹלָם חַסְדּוֹ.
לְמַכֵּה מְלָכִים גְּדֹלִים,	כִּי לְעוֹלָם חַסְדּוֹ.
וַיַּהֲרֹג מְלָכִים אַדִּירִים,	כִּי לְעוֹלָם חַסְדּוֹ.
לְסִיחוֹן מֶלֶךְ הָאֱמֹרִי,	כִּי לְעוֹלָם חַסְדּוֹ.
וּלְעוֹג מֶלֶךְ הַבָּשָׁן,	כִּי לְעוֹלָם חַסְדּוֹ.
וְנָתַן אַרְצָם לְנַחֲלָה,	כִּי לְעוֹלָם חַסְדּוֹ.
נַחֲלָה לְיִשְׂרָאֵל עַבְדּוֹ,	כִּי לְעוֹלָם חַסְדּוֹ.
שֶׁבְּשִׁפְלֵנוּ זָכַר לָנוּ,	כִּי לְעוֹלָם חַסְדּוֹ.
וַיִּפְרְקֵנוּ מִצָּרֵינוּ,	כִּי לְעוֹלָם חַסְדּוֹ.
נֹתֵן לֶחֶם לְכָל בָּשָׂר,	כִּי לְעוֹלָם חַסְדּוֹ.
הוֹדוּ לְאֵל הַשָּׁמָיִם,	כִּי לְעוֹלָם חַסְדּוֹ.[1]

נִשְׁמַת כָּל חַי תְּבָרֵךְ אֶת שִׁמְךָ יהוה אֱלֹהֵינוּ, וְרוּחַ כָּל בָּשָׂר תְּפָאֵר וּתְרוֹמֵם זִכְרְךָ

---

1. Tehillim 136.

— Think About It —

"Nishmas" and the Seder

On Seder night, we explore two related themes: recalling the Exodus from Egypt in all its miraculous details, and giving thanks and praise to Hashem for those miracles. The *tefillah* of "*Nishmas*," which we say after reciting Hallel on Seder night, touches on both motifs, mentioning the Exodus from Egypt and

To Him Who divided the Sea of Reeds into parts;
> His kindness endures forever!

And caused Israel to pass through it;
> His kindness endures forever!

And threw Pharaoh and his army into the Sea of Reeds;
> His kindness endures forever!

To Him Who led His people through the Wilderness;
> His kindness endures forever!

To Him Who smote great kings;
> His kindness endures forever!

And slew mighty kings;
> His kindness endures forever!

Sichon, king of the Emorites;
> His kindness endures forever!

And Og, king of Bashan;
> His kindness endures forever!

And gave their land as an inheritance;
> His kindness endures forever!

An inheritance to Israel His servant;
> His kindness endures forever!

Who remembered us in our lowliness;
> His kindness endures forever!

And released us from our foes;
> His kindness endures forever!

He gives food to all living creatures;
> His kindness endures forever!

Give thanks to God of heaven;
> His kindness endures forever![1]

The soul of every living being shall bless Your Name, Hashem our God; the spirit of all flesh shall always glorify and exalt Your remembrance,

---

1. *Tehillim* 136.

מַלְכֵּנוּ תָּמִיד. מִן הָעוֹלָם וְעַד הָעוֹלָם אַתָּה אֵל, וּמִבַּלְעָדֶיךָ אֵין לָנוּ מֶלֶךְ גּוֹאֵל וּמוֹשִׁיעַ. פּוֹדֶה וּמַצִּיל וּמְפַרְנֵס וּמְרַחֵם, בְּכָל עֵת צָרָה וְצוּקָה, אֵין לָנוּ מֶלֶךְ אֶלָּא אָתָּה. אֱלֹהֵי הָרִאשׁוֹנִים וְהָאַחֲרוֹנִים, אֱלוֹהַּ כָּל בְּרִיּוֹת, אֲדוֹן כָּל תּוֹלָדוֹת, הַמְהֻלָּל בְּרֹב הַתִּשְׁבָּחוֹת, הַמְנַהֵג עוֹלָמוֹ בְּחֶסֶד וּבְרִיּוֹתָיו בְּרַחֲמִים. וַיהוה לֹא יָנוּם וְלֹא יִישָׁן. הַמְעוֹרֵר יְשֵׁנִים, וְהַמֵּקִיץ נִרְדָּמִים, וְהַמֵּשִׂיחַ אִלְּמִים, וְהַמַּתִּיר אֲסוּרִים, וְהַסּוֹמֵךְ נוֹפְלִים, וְהַזּוֹקֵף כְּפוּפִים. לְךָ לְבַדְּךָ אֲנַחְנוּ מוֹדִים. אִלּוּ פִינוּ מָלֵא שִׁירָה כַּיָּם, וּלְשׁוֹנֵנוּ רִנָּה כַּהֲמוֹן גַּלָּיו, וְשִׂפְתוֹתֵינוּ שֶׁבַח כְּמֶרְחֲבֵי רָקִיעַ, וְעֵינֵינוּ מְאִירוֹת כַּשֶּׁמֶשׁ וְכַיָּרֵחַ, וְיָדֵינוּ פְרוּשׂוֹת כְּנִשְׁרֵי שָׁמַיִם, וְרַגְלֵינוּ קַלּוֹת כָּאַיָּלוֹת, אֵין אֲנַחְנוּ מַסְפִּיקִים לְהוֹדוֹת לְךָ, יהוה אֱלֹהֵינוּ וֵאלֹהֵי אֲבוֹתֵינוּ,

giving praise and thanksgiving to Hashem (*Avudraham*).

"*Nishmas*" is a potent *tefillah*, and the Roke'ach writes that one should exert all his strength and concentration when reciting "*Nishmas*." If a person faces an especially difficult situation, he can take upon himself to recite "*Nishmas*," and he will see salvation and *berachah* (*Chanukas HaTorah, Kuntres Acharon; Kaf HaChaim, Orach Chaim* 281:8).

> Rav Yisrael Zev Gustman, who was the youngest dayan on the rabbinical court of Rav Chaim Ozer Grodzensky, recalled his great fears before his appointment to meet with the Russian Army draft board. His rebbi, Rav Shimon Shkop, told him to recite "Nishmas" with tremendous concentration, and through this he would be saved. And indeed, so it was (*Torah Yevakesh MiPihu*, p. 257).

our King. From eternity to eternity You are God, and except for You we have no king, redeemer or helper. O Rescuer, and Redeemer, Sustainer, and Merciful One in every time of trouble and distress. We have no king but You — God of the first and of the last, God of all creatures, Master of all generations, Who is extolled through a multitude of praises, Who guides His world with kindness and His creatures with mercy. HASHEM neither slumbers nor sleeps; He rouses the sleepers and awakens the slumberers; He makes the mute speak and releases the bound; He supports the falling and raises erect the bowed down. To You alone we give thanks. Were our mouth as full of song as the sea, and our tongue as full of jubilation as its multitude of waves, and our lips as full of praise as the breadth of the heavens, and our eyes as brilliant as the sun and the moon, and our hands as outspread as eagles of the sky and our feet as swift as deer — we still could not sufficiently thank You, HASHEM our God and God of our fathers,

The Way We Thank Hashem

אֵין אֲנַחְנוּ מַסְפִּיקִים לְהוֹדוֹת לְךָ ה' אֱלֹהֵינוּ וֵאלֹהֵי אֲבוֹתֵינוּ

*We still could not sufficiently thank You,
Hashem our God and God of our fathers*

Year after year of waiting. The pain of seeing her sisters and even the maidservants giving birth to child after child, while she, Rachel Imeinu, suffers the pain of of being childless. And at last, a son is born to her. Rachel names him Yosef, from the word *asaf*, "to gather in," since Hashem has "gathered" in the humiliation of her childlessness (see *Bereishis* 30:23).

THE EISHES CHAYIL HAGGADAH

Rashi (*Bereishis* 30:23) quotes a midrash to explain the word *asaf*, stating that until a woman has a child she has no one to blame for broken items in the home. However, once a child is born, she can attribute the broken household items to her child. Therefore, the name Yosef evokes Rachel's feelings of thanks to Hashem, who "gathered" in her disgrace by giving her a child she could blame for any accidents that occurred in her home.

Rav Simcha Zissel Broide, the *rosh yeshivah* of Chevron, addresses the glaring question here. Finally, after so many long years of waiting and anguish, Rachel was blessed with a child — and this is what Rachel was thinking about? Broken dishes? For that Rachel gives thanks to Hashem?

Rav Broide sees in this midrash an insight into *hakaras hatov* at its highest level. When one thanks Hashem for the good He has done for him, the level of thanks must be so deep that he even notices and appreciates the smallest, most inconsequential features of the good he has received. Of course, Rachel was overjoyed with the birth of her son Yosef — another tribe born to Yaakov's family — but when thanking Hashem she recognized that proper *hakaras hatov* extends even to the smallest, most trivial good that results from Hashem's *berachah* and *chesed* (*Sam Derech*).

The words of "*Nishmas*" epitomize the feelings of appreciation we must have for the good that Hashem bestows on us — great and small — each and every day.

> *Every night, before he went to sleep, the Chofetz Chaim would thank Hashem for all the good things in his life: his family, his sefarim, his ability to teach Torah, all the big and small blessings of his day.*
>
> *Rav Yechezkel Abramsky recalls once staying at an inn where early in the morning, through the wall, he heard the voice of a Jewish man reciting a stirring "Nishmas" with great emotion and sweetness, expressing his gratitude and thanks for all that Hashem had done for him. Who was this man? Rav Yechezkel discovered later that it was none other than the Chofetz Chaim (Ma'asei L'Melech, p. 175; Tenuos HaMussar, Vol. 4 p. 77; HaMe'oros HaGedolim, p. 318; Chofetz Chaim: Chayav U'Po'alav, Vol. 1, p. 220).*

But the commentators point to an apparent contradiction here in the "*Nishmas*" *tefillah*. We say, *Were our mouth as full of song as the sea, and our tongue as full of jubilation as its multitude of waves, and our lips as full of praise as the breadth of the heavens, and our eyes as brilliant as the sun and the moon, and our hands as outspread as eagles of the sky and our feet as swift as deer — we still could not sufficiently thank You, Hashem our God...for even one of the thousands upon thousands, and myriads upon myriads of favors [miracles, and wonders], that You performed for our ancestors and for us.*

Essentially we're saying that there is no way a living creature, even one endowed with superhuman capabilities, could suitably praise Hashem. But then we say, *Therefore, the limbs that You have set within us, and the spirit and soul that You breathed into our nostrils, and the tongue that You have placed in our mouth — they shall thank and bless, praise and glorify, exalt, be devoted to, sanctify, and pay homage to Your Name...* In other words — we *can* properly praise Hashem! How can we reconcile this apparent contradiction?

Rav Shalom Mordechai Schwadron, the Maharsham, explains that we really do not have the ability to properly praise Hashem, as the praise due to Him is beyond human comprehension and delineation. But our very existence, the organs, muscles, bones, and cells that make up our body and the soul that makes up our spirit, are themselves the greatest possible praise of Hashem's Omnipotence and proof that Hashem is the undisputed Creator and Sustainer of this world and everything that exists within it. Although we can't voice adequate praise to Hashem, our ability to communicate, hear, touch, discern, walk, experience emotions, and the miraculous manner in which our bodies ward off bacteria, grow, adapt, reproduce — in other words, the miraculous functions of our body — are themselves the greatest possible praises to Hashem (see also *Zevach Pesach*; *Rinas Yitzchak, Tefillah L'Shabbos*, p. 145).

Rav Yerucham Levovitz would say that if a person had any idea of the miraculous processes that take place from the time one places food into his mouth to the time it is fully digested and removed from the body, he would send a message home to say that he is *baruch Hashem* fine!

This is why we bless Hashem with the *asher yatzar berachah*,

וּלְבָרֵךְ אֶת שְׁמֶךָ עַל אַחַת מֵאָלֶף אֶלֶף אַלְפֵי אֲלָפִים וְרִבֵּי רְבָבוֹת פְּעָמִים הַטּוֹבוֹת שֶׁעָשִׂיתָ עִם אֲבוֹתֵינוּ וְעִמָּנוּ. מִמִּצְרַיִם גְּאַלְתָּנוּ יהוה אֱלֹהֵינוּ, וּמִבֵּית עֲבָדִים פְּדִיתָנוּ. בְּרָעָב זַנְתָּנוּ, וּבְשָׂבָע כִּלְכַּלְתָּנוּ, מֵחֶרֶב הִצַּלְתָּנוּ, וּמִדֶּבֶר מִלַּטְתָּנוּ, וּמֵחֳלָיִם רָעִים וְנֶאֱמָנִים דִּלִּיתָנוּ. עַד הֵנָּה עֲזָרוּנוּ רַחֲמֶיךָ, וְלֹא עֲזָבוּנוּ חֲסָדֶיךָ. וְאַל תִּטְּשֵׁנוּ יהוה אֱלֹהֵינוּ לָנֶצַח. עַל כֵּן אֵבָרִים

thanking Him for creating and maintaining our digestive systems and being the רוֹפֵא כָל בָּשָׂר וּמַפְלִיא לַעֲשׂוֹת, *the One Who heals all flesh and is wondrous in His acts* (*Tefillas Chanah*, p. 66). Rav Eliyahu Roth used a metaphor to explain the importance of this *berachah*. He would tell his students, "When we say *asher yatzar*, we thank Hashem for performing complicated surgery that rids the body of harmful bacteria and toxins. This 'surgery' is performed gently, without anesthesia, and without pain, by the greatest doctor in the world — and it's free!"

This is what we should be thinking while reciting the *berachah* of *asher yatzar*, as Iyov said, וּמִבְּשָׂרִי אֶחֱזֶה אֱלוֹהַּ, *I see God from my flesh* (*Iyov* 19:26). Our very own bodies, our health, and the *hashgachah pratis* we are witness to throughout our lives are all means of strengthening our *emunah* in Hashem. With a little bit of thought, the wondrous processes that our bodies perform can be used as a tremendous resource in strengthening our *emunah* in Hashem (*HaMevarech Yisbarach*, p. 65).

The Vilna Gaon points out that Hashem's Throne of Glory is specifically mentioned in the *berachah* of *asher yatzar*: גָּלוּי וְיָדוּעַ לִפְנֵי כִסֵּא כְבוֹדֶךָ, *It is obvious and known before Your Throne of Glory*. Even the ministering angels cannot come near Hashem's throne, yet from the highest, holiest place in Heaven, He provides us with the most basic human need (*Avnei Eliyahu, Siddur HaGra*).

> *The more one understands the complexity of the human body, the more one appreciates the miracle of our day-to-day*

and bless Your Name for even one of the thousands upon thousands, and myriads upon myriads of favors [miracles and wonders], that You performed for our ancestors and for us. You redeemed us from Egypt, HASHEM our God, and liberated us from the house of bondage. In famine You nourished us and in plenty You supported us. From the sword You saved us; from the plague You let us escape; and You spared us from severe and enduring diseases. Until now Your mercy has helped us and Your kindness has not forsaken us; do not abandon us, HASHEM our God, to the ultimate end. Therefore, the limbs

---

existence. At Tel HaShomer Hospital in Tel Aviv, a nonobservant doctor would recite the berachah of asher yatzar after leaving the restroom. A fellow doctor who knew he wasn't observant once saw him and, puzzled, asked why someone who didn't observe basic commandments, nevertheless, had taken it upon himself to recite this berachah.

The doctor responded, "I am not observant, but I am a surgeon who sees the miraculous inner workings of the human body moment by moment. How can I not recite this special blessing?" (Birkas Eisan, p. 644).

How We Strengthen Our Bitachon

עַד הֵנָּה עֲזָרוּנוּ רַחֲמֶיךָ, וְלֹא עֲזָבוּנוּ חֲסָדֶיךָ
וְאַל תִּטְּשֵׁנוּ ה' אֱלֹהֵינוּ לָנֶצַח

**Until now Your mercy has helped us
and Your kindness has not forsaken us;
do not abandon us, Hashem our God, to the ultimate end**

The Vilna Gaon explains (to *Mishlei* 25:15) that when we say, עַד הֵנָּה עֲזָרוּנוּ רַחֲמֶיךָ, *Until now Your mercy has helped us*, we're saying that until now You, Hashem, have done so much *chesed* for us, that's what gives us the faith that in the future You will likewise

שֶׁפִּלַּגְתָּ בָּנוּ, וְרוּחַ וּנְשָׁמָה שֶׁנָּפַחְתָּ בְּאַפֵּינוּ, וְלָשׁוֹן אֲשֶׁר שַׂמְתָּ בְּפִינוּ, הֵן הֵם יוֹדוּ וִיבָרְכוּ וִישַׁבְּחוּ וִיפָאֲרוּ וִירוֹמְמוּ וְיַעֲרִיצוּ וְיַקְדִּישׁוּ וְיַמְלִיכוּ אֶת שִׁמְךָ מַלְכֵּנוּ. כִּי כָל פֶּה לְךָ יוֹדֶה, וְכָל לָשׁוֹן לְךָ תִשָּׁבַע, וְכָל בֶּרֶךְ לְךָ תִכְרַע, וְכָל קוֹמָה לְפָנֶיךָ תִשְׁתַּחֲוֶה, וְכָל לְבָבוֹת יִירָאוּךָ, וְכָל קֶרֶב וּכְלָיוֹת יְזַמְּרוּ לִשְׁמֶךָ, כַּדָּבָר שֶׁכָּתוּב: כָּל עַצְמֹתַי תֹּאמַרְנָה, יהוה מִי כָמוֹךָ, מַצִּיל עָנִי מֵחָזָק מִמֶּנּוּ, וְעָנִי וְאֶבְיוֹן מִגֹּזְלוֹ.¹ מִי יִדְמֶה לָּךְ, וּמִי יִשְׁוֶה לָּךְ, וּמִי יַעֲרָךְ לָךְ. הָאֵל הַגָּדוֹל הַגִּבּוֹר וְהַנּוֹרָא, אֵל עֶלְיוֹן, קֹנֵה שָׁמַיִם וָאָרֶץ. נְהַלֶּלְךָ וּנְשַׁבֵּחֲךָ וּנְפָאֶרְךָ וּנְבָרֵךְ אֶת שֵׁם קָדְשֶׁךָ, כָּאָמוּר: לְדָוִד, בָּרְכִי נַפְשִׁי אֶת יהוה, וְכָל קְרָבַי אֶת שֵׁם קָדְשׁוֹ.²

הָאֵל בְּתַעֲצֻמוֹת עֻזֶּךָ, הַגָּדוֹל בִּכְבוֹד שְׁמֶךָ, הַגִּבּוֹר לָנֶצַח וְהַנּוֹרָא בְּנוֹרְאוֹתֶיךָ. הַמֶּלֶךְ הַיּוֹשֵׁב עַל כִּסֵּא רָם וְנִשָּׂא.

---

shower upon us Your *berachah* and never abandon us: וְאַל תִּטְּשֵׁנוּ ה' אֱלֹהֵינוּ לָנֶצַח, *Do not abandon us, Hashem our God, to the ultimate end*. Looking back at all the *chesed* Hashem has done for us gives us the strength and fortitude to continue trusting in Him.

Although we live in times of affluence, many still face financial difficulties and even economic hardship. We can look back to the time of the Chofetz Chaim, when much of Jewry suffered from grueling poverty, to find a way to face our own challenges. The Chofetz Chaim wrote to his fellow Jews, "When the Jewish people strengthen their *bitachon*, they will most certainly bring *berachah* into their homes, as the *pasuk* says, בָּרוּךְ הַגֶּבֶר אֲשֶׁר יִבְטַח

that You have set within us, and the spirit and soul which You breathed into our nostrils, and the tongue that You have placed in our mouth — they shall thank and bless, praise and glorify, exalt, be devoted to, sanctify, and pay homage to Your Name, our King forever. For every mouth shall offer thanks to You; every tongue shall vow allegiance to You; every knee shall bend to You; all who stand erect shall bow before You; all hearts shall fear You; and all men's innermost feelings and thoughts shall sing praises to Your Name, as it is written: "All my bones declare: 'HASHEM, who is like You?' You save the poor man from one stronger than him, the poor and needy from one who would rob him."[1] Who may be likened to You? Who is equal to You? Who can be compared to You? O great, mighty, and awesome God, supreme God, Maker of heaven and earth. We shall praise, acclaim, and glorify You and bless Your holy Name, as it is said:"A psalm of David: Bless HASHEM, O my soul, and let my whole inner being bless His holy Name!"[2]

O God, in the omnipotence of Your strength, great in the honor of Your Name, powerful forever and awesome through Your awesome deeds, O King enthroned upon a high and lofty throne!

---

1. *Tehillim* 35:10. 2. Ibid. 103:1.

בַּה, *Blessed is the man who trusts in Hashem.* Now, when financial hardship is the lot of so many, there is nothing to do but trust in Hashem, and in this merit He will send *berachah* from His holy abode" (*Nefutzos Yisrael*, Ch. 8; *Zechor L'Miriam*, Ch. 20; see also *Me'or Einayim, Va'eschanan*).

THE EISHES CHAYIL HAGGADAH

שׁוֹכֵן עַד מָרוֹם וְקָדוֹשׁ שְׁמוֹ. וְכָתוּב: רַנְּנוּ צַדִּיקִים בַּיהוה לַיְשָׁרִים נָאוָה תְהִלָּה.¹ בְּפִי יְשָׁרִים תִּתְהַלָּל. וּבְדִבְרֵי צַדִּיקִים תִּתְבָּרַךְ. וּבִלְשׁוֹן חֲסִידִים תִּתְרוֹמָם. וּבְקֶרֶב קְדוֹשִׁים תִּתְקַדָּשׁ.

וּבְמַקְהֲלוֹת רִבְבוֹת עַמְּךָ בֵּית יִשְׂרָאֵל, בְּרִנָּה יִתְפָּאַר שִׁמְךָ מַלְכֵּנוּ בְּכָל דּוֹר וָדוֹר. שֶׁכֵּן חוֹבַת כָּל הַיְצוּרִים, לְפָנֶיךָ יהוה אֱלֹהֵינוּ וֵאלֹהֵי אֲבוֹתֵינוּ, לְהוֹדוֹת לְהַלֵּל לְשַׁבֵּחַ לְפָאֵר לְרוֹמֵם לְהַדֵּר לְבָרֵךְ לְעַלֵּה וּלְקַלֵּס, עַל כָּל דִּבְרֵי שִׁירוֹת וְתִשְׁבְּחוֹת דָּוִד בֶּן יִשַׁי עַבְדְּךָ מְשִׁיחֶךָ.

יִשְׁתַּבַּח שִׁמְךָ לָעַד, מַלְכֵּנוּ, הָאֵל הַמֶּלֶךְ הַגָּדוֹל וְהַקָּדוֹשׁ, בַּשָּׁמַיִם וּבָאָרֶץ. כִּי לְךָ נָאֶה, יהוה אֱלֹהֵינוּ וֵאלֹהֵי אֲבוֹתֵינוּ, שִׁיר וּשְׁבָחָה, הַלֵּל וְזִמְרָה, עֹז וּמֶמְשָׁלָה, נֶצַח גְּדֻלָּה וּגְבוּרָה, תְּהִלָּה וְתִפְאֶרֶת, קְדֻשָּׁה וּמַלְכוּת, בְּרָכוֹת וְהוֹדָאוֹת מֵעַתָּה וְעַד עוֹלָם. בָּרוּךְ אַתָּה יהוה, אֵל מֶלֶךְ גָּדוֹל בַּתִּשְׁבָּחוֹת, אֵל הַהוֹדָאוֹת, אֲדוֹן הַנִּפְלָאוֹת, הַבּוֹחֵר בְּשִׁירֵי זִמְרָה, מֶלֶךְ אֵל חֵי הָעוֹלָמִים.

So how exactly can a person strengthen his *bitachon*? The Chofetz Chaim tells us that one can fortify his faith by looking at the past and seeing how Hashem has cared for him each and every day of his life by providing him with food, clothing, a home, and so much more. Through this one can know that Hashem will

He Who abides forever, exalted and holy is His Name. And it is written: "Rejoice in HASHEM, you righteous; for the upright, His praise is pleasant."[1] By the mouth of the upright You shall be praised; by the words of the righteous You shall be praised; by the tongue of the pious You shall be exalted; and amid the holy You shall be sanctified.

And in the assemblies of the myriads of Your people, the House of Israel, with jubilation shall Your Name, our King, be glorified in every generation. For such is the duty of all creatures — before You, HASHEM, our God, and God of our fathers, to thank, praise, laud, glorify, exalt, adore, bless, raise high, and sing praises — even beyond all expressions of the songs and praises of David the son of Jesse, Your servant, Your anointed.

May Your Name be praised forever, our King, the God, and King Who is great and holy in heaven and on earth; for to You, HASHEM, our God, and the God of our fathers, it is fitting to render song and praise, hallel and hymns, power and dominion, victory, greatness and might, praise and glory, holiness and sovereignty, blessings and thanksgivings from now and forever. Blessed are You, HASHEM, God, King, great in praises, God of thanksgivings, Master of wonders, Who favors songs of praise — King, God, Life of all worlds.

---

1. *Tehillim* 33:1.

---

continue to care for him in the future as well (*Nefutzos Yisrael*, Ch. 7).

The blessing over wine is recited and the fourth cup is drunk while reclining to the left side. It is preferable that the entire cup be drunk.
Some recite the following before the fourth cup:

הִנְנִי מוּכָן וּמְזוּמָּן לְקַיֵּם מִצְוַת כּוֹס רְבִיעִי שֶׁל אַרְבַּע כּוֹסוֹת. לְשֵׁם יִחוּד קֻדְשָׁא בְּרִיךְ הוּא וּשְׁכִינְתֵּיהּ, עַל יְדֵי הַהוּא טָמִיר וְנֶעְלָם, בְּשֵׁם כָּל יִשְׂרָאֵל. וִיהִי נֹעַם אֲדֹנָי אֱלֹהֵינוּ עָלֵינוּ, וּמַעֲשֵׂה יָדֵינוּ כּוֹנְנָה עָלֵינוּ, וּמַעֲשֵׂה יָדֵינוּ כּוֹנְנֵהוּ.

בָּרוּךְ אַתָּה יהוה אֱלֹהֵינוּ מֶלֶךְ הָעוֹלָם, בּוֹרֵא פְּרִי הַגָּפֶן.

After drinking the fourth cup, the concluding blessing is recited.
On Shabbos include the passage in parentheses.

בָּרוּךְ אַתָּה יהוה אֱלֹהֵינוּ מֶלֶךְ הָעוֹלָם, עַל הַגֶּפֶן וְעַל פְּרִי הַגֶּפֶן, וְעַל תְּנוּבַת הַשָּׂדֶה, וְעַל אֶרֶץ חֶמְדָּה טוֹבָה וּרְחָבָה, שֶׁרָצִיתָ וְהִנְחַלְתָּ לַאֲבוֹתֵינוּ, לֶאֱכֹל מִפִּרְיָהּ וְלִשְׂבֹּעַ מִטּוּבָהּ. רַחֶם (נָא) יהוה אֱלֹהֵינוּ עַל יִשְׂרָאֵל עַמֶּךָ, וְעַל יְרוּשָׁלַיִם עִירֶךָ, וְעַל צִיּוֹן מִשְׁכַּן כְּבוֹדֶךָ, וְעַל מִזְבְּחֶךָ וְעַל הֵיכָלֶךָ. וּבְנֵה יְרוּשָׁלַיִם עִיר הַקֹּדֶשׁ בִּמְהֵרָה בְיָמֵינוּ, וְהַעֲלֵנוּ לְתוֹכָהּ, וְשַׂמְּחֵנוּ בְּבִנְיָנָהּ, וְנֹאכַל מִפִּרְיָהּ, וְנִשְׂבַּע מִטּוּבָהּ, וּנְבָרֶכְךָ עָלֶיהָ בִּקְדֻשָּׁה וּבְטָהֳרָה [וּרְצֵה וְהַחֲלִיצֵנוּ בְּיוֹם הַשַּׁבָּת הַזֶּה]. וְשַׂמְּחֵנוּ בְּיוֹם חַג הַמַּצּוֹת הַזֶּה. כִּי אַתָּה יהוה טוֹב וּמֵטִיב לַכֹּל, וְנוֹדֶה לְּךָ עַל הָאָרֶץ וְעַל פְּרִי הַגָּפֶן. בָּרוּךְ אַתָּה יהוה, עַל הָאָרֶץ וְעַל פְּרִי הַגָּפֶן.

The blessing over wine is recited and the fourth cup is drunk while reclining to the left side. It is preferable that the entire cup be drunk.

Some recite the following before the fourth cup:

Behold, I am prepared and ready to fulfill the mitzvah of the fourth of the Four Cups. For the sake of the unification of the Holy One, Blessed is He, and His Presence, through Him Who is hidden and inscrutable — [I pray] in the name of all Israel. May the pleasantness of the Lord, our God, be upon us, and may He establish our handiwork for us; our handiwork may He establish.

Blessed are You, HASHEM, our God, King of the universe, Who creates the fruit of the vine.

After drinking the fourth cup, the concluding blessing is recited. On Shabbos include the passage in parentheses.

Blessed are You, HASHEM, our God, King of the universe, for the vine and the fruit of the vine, and for the produce of the field. For the desirable, good, and spacious land that You were pleased to give our forefathers as a heritage, to eat of its fruit and to be satisfied with its goodness. Have mercy, (we beg You,) HASHEM, our God, on Israel Your people; on Jerusalem, Your city; on Zion, resting place of Your glory; Your Altar, and Your Temple. Rebuild Jerusalem the city of holiness, speedily in our days. Bring us up into it and gladden us in its rebuilding, and let us eat from its fruit and be satisfied with its goodness and bless You upon it in holiness and purity. (Favor us and strengthen us on this Shabbos day) and grant us happiness on this Festival of Matzos; for You, HASHEM, are good and do good to all, and we thank You for the land and for the fruit of the vine. Blessed are You, HASHEM, for the land and for the fruit of the vine.

נרצה

חֲסַל סִדּוּר פֶּסַח כְּהִלְכָתוֹ, כְּכָל מִשְׁפָּטוֹ וְחֻקָּתוֹ. כַּאֲשֶׁר זָכִינוּ לְסַדֵּר אוֹתוֹ, כֵּן נִזְכֶּה לַעֲשׂוֹתוֹ. זָךְ שׁוֹכֵן מְעוֹנָה, קוֹמֵם קְהַל עֲדַת מִי מָנָה. בְּקָרוֹב נַהֵל נִטְעֵי כַנָּה, פְּדוּיִם לְצִיּוֹן בְּרִנָּה.

לְשָׁנָה הַבָּאָה בִּירוּשָׁלָיִם.

נרצה / NIRTZAH

Hashem's Tefillin

לְשָׁנָה הַבָּאָה בִּירוּשָׁלָיִם
Next year in Jerusalem

Rav Yisrael Meir Lau, the former chief rabbi of Israel, has made countless visits to wounded Israeli soldiers. After the Yom Kippur War, Rav Lau visited injured soldiers for weeks, many of them suffering from terrible burns, giving comfort and encouragement and davening for their recovery.

One young man he visited regularly in the burn unit of a hospital suffered third-degree burns over the majority of his body when his tank took a direct hit from an Egyptian RPG and exploded. Miraculously, the soldier was pulled out alive and survived, but despite morphine and painkillers he was still in intense pain, and his screams could be heard throughout the hospital ward. Rav Lau and the hospital staff attempted to still the ear-piercing cries of the pain-ridden soldier, but to no avail; in his agony, the soldier continued to scream.

Suddenly, though, the screaming stopped and peace reigned in the burn ward. A feeling of trepidation overcame Rav Lau — had something happened to the young soldier?

Something had: Rav Lau looked into his cubicle and saw the soldier lying calmly as his mother sat beside him stroking a small area of her son's skin that had not been burned. "Sleep,

~NIRTZAH~

The Seder is now concluded in accordance with its laws, with all its ordinances and statutes. Just as we were privileged to arrange it, so may we merit to perform it. O Pure One, Who dwells on high, raise up the countless congregation, soon — guide the offshoots of Your plants, redeemed to Zion with glad song.

NEXT YEAR IN JERUSALEM

---

my child, Ima is here now. No need to worry, sleep now, my child. Ima is here."

Rav Lau saw in this story an explanation of the pasuk describing the ultimate redemption of the Jewish people: כְּאִישׁ אֲשֶׁר אִמּוֹ תְּנַחֲמֶנּוּ כֵּן אָנֹכִי אֲנַחֶמְכֶם וּבִירוּשָׁלַם תְּנֻחָמוּ, *Like a man's mother who comforts him, so too I [Hashem] will comfort them, and Jerusalem will be comforted (Yeshayahu 66:13). Hashem will comfort and heal and restore us like a mother with her special and unique love, with her ability to comfort and restore peace to her children (U'Matok HaOhr, Eichah, p. 415).*

Rav Levi Yitzchak of Berditchev once saw a Jew accidently drop his tefillin. Aghast, the man quickly picked them up off the ground, brushed them off, gave them a kiss, and returned them carefully to their place. Rav Levi Yitzchak lifted his eyes up to Heaven and cried out, "Hashem, see how a simple Jew treats his tefillin, how he picks them up immediately after they fall, brushes them off, and kisses them with such love and care!

"Hashem, what about Your tefillin? It is written within them, מִי כְּעַמְּךָ יִשְׂרָאֵל, *Who is like Your nation, Israel?* Hashem, Your tefillin are on the floor, lying in disgrace, as the nations of the world step on us, exile us, and persecute us! Hashem, have mercy, pick us up from the ground, clean us, and kiss us!" *(Likutei Kedushas HaLevi, p. 204).*

On the first night recite the following.
On the second night continue on page 294.

וּבְכֵן וַיְהִי בַּחֲצִי הַלַּיְלָה.

אָז רוֹב נִסִּים הִפְלֵאתָ בַּלַּיְלָה,
בְּרֹאשׁ אַשְׁמוּרֶת זֶה הַלַּיְלָה,
גֵּר צֶדֶק נִצַּחְתּוֹ כְּנֶחֱלַק לוֹ לַיְלָה,
וַיְהִי בַּחֲצִי הַלַּיְלָה.

דַּנְתָּ מֶלֶךְ גְּרָר בַּחֲלוֹם הַלַּיְלָה,
הִפְחַדְתָּ אֲרַמִּי בְּאֶמֶשׁ לַיְלָה,
וַיָּשַׂר יִשְׂרָאֵל לְמַלְאָךְ וַיּוּכַל לוֹ לַיְלָה,
וַיְהִי בַּחֲצִי הַלַּיְלָה.

זֶרַע בְּכוֹרֵי פַתְרוֹס מָחַצְתָּ בַּחֲצִי הַלַּיְלָה,
חֵילָם לֹא מָצְאוּ בְּקוּמָם בַּלַּיְלָה,
טִיסַת נְגִיד חֲרֹשֶׁת סִלִּיתָ בְּכוֹכְבֵי לַיְלָה,
וַיְהִי בַּחֲצִי הַלַּיְלָה.

יָעַץ מְחָרֵף לְנוֹפֵף אִוּוּי הוֹבַשְׁתָּ פְגָרָיו בַּלַּיְלָה,
כָּרַע בֵּל וּמַצָּבוֹ בְּאִישׁוֹן לַיְלָה,
לְאִישׁ חֲמוּדוֹת נִגְלָה רָז חֲזוֹת לַיְלָה,
וַיְהִי בַּחֲצִי הַלַּיְלָה.

מִשְׁתַּכֵּר בִּכְלֵי קֹדֶשׁ נֶהֱרַג בּוֹ בַּלַּיְלָה,
נוֹשַׁע מִבּוֹר אֲרָיוֹת פּוֹתֵר בִּעֲתוּתֵי לַיְלָה,
שִׂנְאָה נָטַר אֲגָגִי וְכָתַב סְפָרִים בַּלַּיְלָה,
וַיְהִי בַּחֲצִי הַלַּיְלָה.

On the first night recite the following.
On the second night continue on page 294.

It came to pass at midnight.

Y ou have, of old, performed many wonders
                                                        by night.
At the head of the watches of   this night.
To the righteous convert (Avraham)
You gave triumph by dividing for him   the night.
       It came to pass at midnight.
You judged the king of Gerar (Avimelech),
in a dream   by night.
You frightened the Aramean (Lavan),
in the dark   of night.
Yisrael (Yaakov) fought with an angel
and overcame him   by night.
       It came to pass at midnight.
Egypt's firstborn You crushed at   midnight.
Their host they found not upon arising at   night.
The army of the prince of Charoshes (Sisera)
You swept away with stars of   the night.
       It came to pass at midnight.
The blasphemer (Sancheriv) planned to raise
his hand against Jerusalem —
but You withered his corpses   by night.
Bel was overturned with its pedestal,
in the darkness   of night.
To the man of Your delights (Daniel)
was revealed the mystery of the visions of night.
       It came to pass at midnight.
He (Belshazzar) who caroused from the holy
vessels was killed that very   night.
From the lions' den was rescued he (Daniel)
who interpreted the "terrors" of   the night.
The Agagite (Haman) nursed hatred
and wrote decrees   at night.
       It came to pass at midnight.

עוֹרַרְתָּ נִצְחֲךָ עָלָיו בְּנֶדֶד שְׁנַת לַיְלָה,
פּוּרָה תִדְרוֹךְ לְשׁוֹמֵר מַה מִּלַּיְלָה,
צָרַח כַּשּׁוֹמֵר וְשָׂח אָתָא בֹקֶר וְגַם לַיְלָה,
וַיְהִי בַּחֲצִי הַלַּיְלָה.

קָרֵב יוֹם אֲשֶׁר הוּא לֹא יוֹם וְלֹא לַיְלָה,
רָם הוֹדַע כִּי לְךָ הַיּוֹם אַף לְךָ הַלַּיְלָה,
שׁוֹמְרִים הַפְקֵד לְעִירְךָ כָּל הַיּוֹם וְכָל הַלַּיְלָה,
תָּאִיר כְּאוֹר יוֹם חֶשְׁכַת לַיְלָה,
וַיְהִי בַּחֲצִי הַלַּיְלָה.

On the second night recite the following.
On the first night continue on page 298.

וּבְכֵן וַאֲמַרְתֶּם זֶבַח פֶּסַח:

אֹמֶץ גְּבוּרוֹתֶיךָ הִפְלֵאתָ בַּפֶּסַח.
בְּרֹאשׁ כָּל מוֹעֲדוֹת נִשֵּׂאתָ פֶּסַח.
גִּלִּיתָ לְאֶזְרָחִי חֲצוֹת לֵיל פֶּסַח.
וַאֲמַרְתֶּם זֶבַח פֶּסַח.

דְּלָתָיו דָּפַקְתָּ כְּחֹם הַיּוֹם בַּפֶּסַח.
הִסְעִיד נוֹצְצִים עֻגּוֹת מַצּוֹת בַּפֶּסַח.

The "Head" of the Yamim Tovim

בְּרֹאשׁ כָּל מוֹעֲדוֹת נִשֵּׂאתָ פֶּסַח
Ahead of all festivals You elevated Pesach

The liturgist writes here that "ahead of all festivals You elevated Pesach," as it is written regarding Nissan, the month when Pesach falls out, הַחֹדֶשׁ הַזֶּה לָכֶם רֹאשׁ חֳדָשִׁים רִאשׁוֹן הוּא לָכֶם לְחָדְשֵׁי הַשָּׁנָה, *This month shall be for you the beginning [the head] of the months; it shall be for you the first of the months of the year* (Shemos 12:2).

You began Your triumph over him when You disturbed (Achashveirosh's) sleep at night.
Trample the winepress to help those who ask the watchman, "What of the long night?"
He will shout, like a watchman, and say: "Morning shall come after night."
  It came to pass at midnight.

Hasten the day (of Mashiach),
that is neither day nor night.
Most High — make known that Yours
are day and night.
Appoint guards for Your city,
all the day and all the night.
Brighten like the light of day the darkness of night.
  It came to pass at midnight.

On the second night recite the following.
On the first night continue on page 298.

And you shall say: This is the feast of Pesach.

You displayed wondrously Your mighty powers on Pesach.
Ahead of all festivals You elevated Pesach.
To the Oriental (Avraham) You revealed the future midnight of Pesach.
  And you shall say: This is the feast of Pesach.
At his door You knocked in the heat of the day on Pesach;
He satiated the angels with matzah-cakes on Pesach.

The month of Nissan is the first among the months that make up the Jewish calendar.

Rav Yechiel Michel Epstein, author of the *Aruch HaShulchan*, explains why the month of Nissan is considered the head of all months.

The Egyptians worshiped the sheep, ascribing to it godly

וְאֶל הַבָּקָר רָץ זֵכֶר לְשׁוֹר עֵרֶךְ   פֶּסַח.
וַאֲמַרְתֶּם זֶבַח פֶּסַח.

זוֹעֲמוּ סְדוֹמִים וְלוֹהֲטוּ בָּאֵשׁ   בְּפֶסַח.
חוּלַּץ לוֹט מֵהֶם וּמַצּוֹת אָפָה בְּקֵץ   פֶּסַח.
טאטֵאתָ אַדְמַת מוֹף וְנוֹף בְּעָבְרְךָ   בְּפֶסַח.
וַאֲמַרְתֶּם זֶבַח פֶּסַח.

יָהּ רֹאשׁ כָּל אוֹן מָחַצְתָּ בְּלֵיל שִׁמּוּר   פֶּסַח.
כַּבִּיר עַל בֵּן בְּכוֹר פָּסַחְתָּ בְּדַם   פֶּסַח.
לְבִלְתִּי תֵּת מַשְׁחִית לָבֹא בִּפְתָחַי   בְּפֶסַח.
וַאֲמַרְתֶּם זֶבַח פֶּסַח.

מְסֻגֶּרֶת סֻגָּרָה בְּעִתּוֹתֵי   פֶּסַח.
נִשְׁמְדָה מִדְיָן בִּצְלִיל שְׂעוֹרֵי עֹמֶר   פֶּסַח.
שׂוֹרְפוּ מִשְׁמַנֵּי פּוּל וְלוּד בִּיקַד יְקוֹד   פֶּסַח.
וַאֲמַרְתֶּם זֶבַח פֶּסַח.

עוֹד הַיּוֹם בְּנֹב לַעֲמוֹד עַד גָּעָה עוֹנַת   פֶּסַח.
פַּס יָד כָּתְבָה לְקַעֲקֵעַ צוּל   בְּפֶסַח.
צָפֹה הַצָּפִית עָרוֹךְ הַשֻּׁלְחָן   בְּפֶסַח.
וַאֲמַרְתֶּם זֶבַח פֶּסַח.

---

powers. The celestial constellation for the month of Nissan is a *taleh*, a lamb. After enduring nearly a year of incredible suffering from the plagues, Pharaoh still refused to let the Jewish people go. He was waiting for the upcoming month of Nissan, hoping that the month's celestial body, the sheep — his god — would arise and save him. Hashem therefore told Moshe, הַחֹדֶשׁ הַזֶּה לָכֶם רֹאשׁ חֳדָשִׁים, *This month shall be for you the head of the months*: Moshe and the Jews would see how Hashem would punish

And he ran to the herd —
symbolic of the sacrificial beast   of Pesach.
  And you shall say: This is the feast of Pesach.
The Sodomites provoked (God)
and were devoured by fire   on Pesach;
Lot was withdrawn from them —
he had baked matzos at the time   of Pesach.
You swept clean the soil of Mof and Nof (in Egypt)
when You passed through   on Pesach.
  And you shall say: This is the feast of Pesach.
God, You crushed every firstborn of On (in Egypt)
on the watchful night   of Pesach.
But Master — Your own firstborn,
You skipped by merit of the blood   of Pesach,
Not to allow the Destroyer to enter my doors
                                         on Pesach.
  And you shall say: This is the feast   of Pesach.
The beleaguered (Yericho) was besieged
                                         on Pesach.
Midyan was destroyed with a barley cake,
from the Omer   of Pesach.
The mighty nobles of Pul and Lud (Ashur) were
consumed in a great conflagration   on Pesach.
  And you shall say: This is the feast of Pesach.
He (Sancheiriv) would have stood that day
at Nov, but for the advent   of Pesach.
A hand inscribed the destruction of Zul (Bavel)
                                         on Pesach.
As the watch was set, and the royal table decked
                                         on Pesach.
  And you shall say: This is the feast of Pesach.

Pharaoh particularly in Nissan, demonstrating that only Hashem has power and rules the world.
  Since the month of Nissan and the Yom Tov of Pesach instill

קָהָל כְּנִסָּה הֲדַסָּה צוֹם לְשַׁלֵּשׁ בַּפֶּסַח.
רֹאשׁ מִבֵּית רָשָׁע מָחַצְתָּ בְּעֵץ חֲמִשִּׁים בַּפֶּסַח.
שְׁתֵּי אֵלֶּה רֶגַע תָּבִיא לְעוּצִית בַּפֶּסַח.
תָּעֹז יָדְךָ וְתָרוּם יְמִינְךָ כְּלֵיל הִתְקַדֶּשׁ חַג פֶּסַח. וַאֲמַרְתֶּם זֶבַח פֶּסַח.

On both nights continue here:

כִּי לוֹ נָאֶה, כִּי לוֹ יָאֶה:

אַדִּיר בִּמְלוּכָה, בָּחוּר כַּהֲלָכָה, גְּדוּדָיו יֹאמְרוּ לוֹ, לְךָ וּלְךָ, לְךָ כִּי לְךָ, לְךָ אַף לְךָ, לְךָ יהוה הַמַּמְלָכָה, כִּי לוֹ נָאֶה, כִּי לוֹ יָאֶה.

דָּגוּל בִּמְלוּכָה, הָדוּר כַּהֲלָכָה, וָתִיקָיו יֹאמְרוּ לוֹ, לְךָ וּלְךָ, לְךָ כִּי לְךָ, לְךָ אַף לְךָ, לְךָ יהוה הַמַּמְלָכָה, כִּי לוֹ נָאֶה, כִּי לוֹ יָאֶה.

זַכַּאי בִּמְלוּכָה, חָסִין כַּהֲלָכָה, טַפְסְרָיו יֹאמְרוּ לוֹ, לְךָ וּלְךָ, לְךָ כִּי לְךָ, לְךָ אַף לְךָ, לְךָ יהוה הַמַּמְלָכָה, כִּי לוֹ נָאֶה, כִּי לוֹ יָאֶה.

יָחִיד בִּמְלוּכָה, כַּבִּיר כַּהֲלָכָה, לִמּוּדָיו יֹאמְרוּ לוֹ, לְךָ וּלְךָ, לְךָ כִּי לְךָ, לְךָ אַף לְךָ, לְךָ יהוה הַמַּמְלָכָה, כִּי לוֹ נָאֶה, כִּי לוֹ יָאֶה.

מוֹשֵׁל בִּמְלוּכָה, נוֹרָא כַּהֲלָכָה, סְבִיבָיו יֹאמְרוּ לוֹ, לְךָ וּלְךָ, לְךָ כִּי לְךָ, לְךָ אַף לְךָ, לְךָ יהוה הַמַּמְלָכָה, כִּי לוֹ נָאֶה, כִּי לוֹ יָאֶה.

---

within us a clear understanding of Hashem's Godly control over the world, both Nissan and Pesach are the "heads" in the Jewish calendar (*Aruch HaShulchan, Orach Chaim* 429:1–2).

Hadassah (Esther) gathered a congregation
for a three-day fast   on Pesach.
You caused the head of the evil clan (Haman)
to be hanged on a 50-cubit gallows   on Pesach.
Doubly, will You bring in an instant
upon Utzis (Edom)   on Pesach.
Let Your hand be strong, and Your right arm
exalted, as on that night when You hallowed
the festival   of Pesach.
And you shall say: This is the feast of Pesach.

On both nights continue here:

To Him praise is due!
To Him praise is fitting!

Mighty in majesty, perfectly distinguished, His companies of angels say to Him: Yours and only Yours; Yours, yes Yours; Yours, surely Yours; Yours, HASHEM, is the sovereignty. To Him praise is due! To Him praise is fitting!

Supreme in kingship, perfectly glorious, His faithful say to Him: Yours and only Yours; Yours, yes Yours; Yours, surely Yours; Yours, HASHEM, is the sovereignty. To Him praise is due! To Him praise is fitting!

Pure in kingship, perfectly mighty, His angels say to Him: Yours and only Yours; Yours, yes Yours; Yours, surely Yours; Yours, HASHEM, is the sovereignty. To Him praise is due! To Him praise is fitting!

Alone in kingship, perfectly omnipotent, His scholars say to Him: Yours and only Yours; Yours, yes Yours; Yours, surely Yours; Yours, HASHEM, is the sovereignty. To Him praise is due! To Him praise is fitting!

Commanding in kingship, perfectly wondrous, His surrounding (angels) say to Him: Yours and only Yours; Yours, yes Yours; Yours, surely Yours; Yours, HASHEM, is the sovereignty. To Him praise is due! To Him praise is fitting!

עָנָיו בִּמְלוּכָה, פּוֹדֶה כַּהֲלָכָה, צַדִּיקָיו יֹאמְרוּ לוֹ, לְךָ וּלְךָ, לְךָ כִּי לְךָ, לְךָ אַף לְךָ, לְךָ יהוה הַמַּמְלָכָה, כִּי לוֹ נָאֶה, כִּי לוֹ יָאֶה.

קָדוֹשׁ בִּמְלוּכָה, רַחוּם כַּהֲלָכָה, שִׁנְאַנָּיו יֹאמְרוּ לוֹ, לְךָ וּלְךָ, לְךָ כִּי לְךָ, לְךָ אַף לְךָ, לְךָ יהוה הַמַּמְלָכָה, כִּי לוֹ נָאֶה, כִּי לוֹ יָאֶה.

תַּקִּיף בִּמְלוּכָה, תּוֹמֵךְ כַּהֲלָכָה, תְּמִימָיו יֹאמְרוּ לוֹ, לְךָ וּלְךָ, לְךָ כִּי לְךָ, לְךָ אַף לְךָ, לְךָ יהוה הַמַּמְלָכָה, כִּי לוֹ נָאֶה, כִּי לוֹ יָאֶה.

אַדִּיר הוּא יִבְנֶה בֵיתוֹ בְּקָרוֹב, בִּמְהֵרָה, בִּמְהֵרָה, בְּיָמֵינוּ בְּקָרוֹב. אֵל בְּנֵה, אֵל בְּנֵה, בְּנֵה בֵיתְךָ בְּקָרוֹב.

בָּחוּר הוּא. גָּדוֹל הוּא. דָּגוּל הוּא. יִבְנֶה בֵיתוֹ בְּקָרוֹב, בִּמְהֵרָה, בִּמְהֵרָה, בְּיָמֵינוּ בְּקָרוֹב. אֵל בְּנֵה, אֵל בְּנֵה, בְּנֵה בֵיתְךָ בְּקָרוֹב.

הָדוּר הוּא. וָתִיק הוּא. זַכַּאי הוּא. חָסִיד הוּא. יִבְנֶה בֵיתוֹ בְּקָרוֹב, בִּמְהֵרָה, בִּמְהֵרָה, בְּיָמֵינוּ בְּקָרוֹב. אֵל בְּנֵה, אֵל בְּנֵה, בְּנֵה בֵיתְךָ בְּקָרוֹב.

טָהוֹר הוּא. יָחִיד הוּא. כַּבִּיר הוּא. לָמוּד הוּא. מֶלֶךְ הוּא. נוֹרָא הוּא. סַגִּיב הוּא. עִזּוּז הוּא. פּוֹדֶה הוּא. צַדִּיק הוּא. יִבְנֶה בֵיתוֹ בְּקָרוֹב, בִּמְהֵרָה, בִּמְהֵרָה, בְּיָמֵינוּ בְּקָרוֹב. אֵל בְּנֵה, אֵל בְּנֵה, בְּנֵה בֵיתְךָ בְּקָרוֹב.

קָדוֹשׁ הוּא. רַחוּם הוּא. שַׁדַּי הוּא. תַּקִּיף הוּא. יִבְנֶה בֵיתוֹ בְּקָרוֹב, בִּמְהֵרָה, בִּמְהֵרָה, בְּיָמֵינוּ בְּקָרוֹב. אֵל בְּנֵה, אֵל בְּנֵה, בְּנֵה בֵיתְךָ בְּקָרוֹב.

Humble in kingship, perfectly the Redeemer, His righteous say to Him: Yours and only Yours; Yours, yes Yours; Yours, surely Yours; Yours, Hashem, is the sovereignty. To Him praise is due! To Him praise is fitting!

Holy in kingship, perfectly merciful, His troops of angels say to Him: Yours and only Yours; Yours, yes Yours; Yours, surely Yours; Yours, Hashem, is the sovereignty. To Him praise is due! To Him praise is fitting.

Almighty in kingship, perfectly sustaining, His perfect ones say to Him: Yours and only Yours; Yours, yes Yours; Yours, surely Yours; Yours, Hashem, is the sovereignty. To Him praise is due! To Him praise is fitting!

He is most mighty. May He soon rebuild His House, speedily, yes speedily, in our days, soon. God, rebuild, God, rebuild, rebuild Your House soon!

He is distinguished, He is great, He is exalted. May He soon rebuild His House, speedily, yes speedily, in our days, soon. God, rebuild, God, rebuild, rebuild Your House soon!

He is all glorious, He is faithful, He is faultless, He is righteous. May He soon rebuild His House, speedily, yes speedily, in our days, soon. God, rebuild, God, rebuild, rebuild Your House soon!

He is pure, He is unique, He is powerful, He is all-wise, He is King, He is awesome, He is sublime, He is all-powerful, He is the Redeemer, He is the all-righteous. May He soon rebuild His House, speedily, yes speedily, in our days, soon. God, rebuild, God, rebuild, rebuild Your House soon!

He is holy, He is compassionate, He is Almighty, He is omnipotent. May He soon rebuild His House, speedily, yes speedily, in our days, soon. God, rebuild, God, rebuild, rebuild Your House soon!

אֶחָד מִי יוֹדֵעַ? אֶחָד אֲנִי יוֹדֵעַ. אֶחָד אֱלֹהֵינוּ שֶׁבַּשָּׁמַיִם וּבָאָרֶץ.

שְׁנַיִם מִי יוֹדֵעַ? שְׁנַיִם אֲנִי יוֹדֵעַ. שְׁנֵי לֻחוֹת הַבְּרִית, אֶחָד אֱלֹהֵינוּ שֶׁבַּשָּׁמַיִם וּבָאָרֶץ.

שְׁלֹשָׁה מִי יוֹדֵעַ? שְׁלֹשָׁה אֲנִי יוֹדֵעַ. שְׁלֹשָׁה אָבוֹת, שְׁנֵי לֻחוֹת הַבְּרִית, אֶחָד אֱלֹהֵינוּ שֶׁבַּשָּׁמַיִם וּבָאָרֶץ.

אַרְבַּע מִי יוֹדֵעַ? אַרְבַּע אֲנִי יוֹדֵעַ. אַרְבַּע אִמָּהוֹת, שְׁלֹשָׁה אָבוֹת, שְׁנֵי לֻחוֹת הַבְּרִית, אֶחָד אֱלֹהֵינוּ שֶׁבַּשָּׁמַיִם וּבָאָרֶץ.

חֲמִשָּׁה מִי יוֹדֵעַ? חֲמִשָּׁה אֲנִי יוֹדֵעַ. חֲמִשָּׁה חֻמְשֵׁי תוֹרָה, אַרְבַּע אִמָּהוֹת, שְׁלֹשָׁה אָבוֹת, שְׁנֵי לֻחוֹת הַבְּרִית, אֶחָד אֱלֹהֵינוּ שֶׁבַּשָּׁמַיִם וּבָאָרֶץ.

שִׁשָּׁה מִי יוֹדֵעַ? שִׁשָּׁה אֲנִי יוֹדֵעַ. שִׁשָּׁה סִדְרֵי מִשְׁנָה, חֲמִשָּׁה חֻמְשֵׁי תוֹרָה, אַרְבַּע אִמָּהוֹת, שְׁלֹשָׁה אָבוֹת, שְׁנֵי לֻחוֹת הַבְּרִית, אֶחָד אֱלֹהֵינוּ שֶׁבַּשָּׁמַיִם וּבָאָרֶץ.

שִׁבְעָה מִי יוֹדֵעַ? שִׁבְעָה אֲנִי יוֹדֵעַ. שִׁבְעָה יְמֵי שַׁבַּתָּא, שִׁשָּׁה סִדְרֵי מִשְׁנָה, חֲמִשָּׁה חֻמְשֵׁי תוֹרָה, אַרְבַּע אִמָּהוֹת, שְׁלֹשָׁה אָבוֹת, שְׁנֵי לֻחוֹת הַבְּרִית, אֶחָד אֱלֹהֵינוּ שֶׁבַּשָּׁמַיִם וּבָאָרֶץ.

שְׁמוֹנָה מִי יוֹדֵעַ? שְׁמוֹנָה אֲנִי יוֹדֵעַ. שְׁמוֹנָה יְמֵי מִילָה, שִׁבְעָה יְמֵי שַׁבַּתָּא, שִׁשָּׁה סִדְרֵי מִשְׁנָה, חֲמִשָּׁה חֻמְשֵׁי תוֹרָה, אַרְבַּע אִמָּהוֹת, שְׁלֹשָׁה אָבוֹת, שְׁנֵי לֻחוֹת הַבְּרִית, אֶחָד אֱלֹהֵינוּ שֶׁבַּשָּׁמַיִם וּבָאָרֶץ.

Who knows one? I know one: One is our God, in heaven and on earth.

Who knows two? I know two: two are the Tablets of the Covenant; One is our God, in heaven and on earth.

Who knows three? I know three: three are the Patriarchs; two are the Tablets of the Covenant; One is our God, in heaven and on earth.

Who knows four? I know four: four are the Matriarchs; three are the Patriarchs; two are the Tablets of the Covenant; One is our God, in heaven and on earth.

Who knows five? I know five: five are the Books of the Torah; four are the Matriarchs; three are the Patriarchs; two are the Tablets of the Covenant; One is our God, in heaven and on earth.

Who knows six? I know six: six are the Orders of the Mishnah; five are the Books of the Torah; four are the Matriarchs; three are the Patriarchs; two are the Tablets of the Covenant; One is our God, in heaven and on earth.

Who knows seven? I know seven: seven are the days of the week; six are the Orders of the Mishnah; five are the Books of the Torah; four are the Matriarchs; three are the Patriarchs; two are the Tablets of the Covenant; One is our God, in heaven and on earth.

Who knows eight? I know eight: eight are the days of circumcision; seven are the days of the week; six are the Orders of the Mishnah; five are the Books of the Torah; four are the Matriarchs; three are the Patriarchs; two are the Tablets of the Covenant; One is our God, in heaven and on earth.

תִּשְׁעָה מִי יוֹדֵעַ? תִּשְׁעָה אֲנִי יוֹדֵעַ. תִּשְׁעָה יַרְחֵי לֵדָה, שְׁמוֹנָה יְמֵי מִילָה, שִׁבְעָה יְמֵי שַׁבַּתָּא, שִׁשָּׁה סִדְרֵי מִשְׁנָה, חֲמִשָּׁה חֻמְשֵׁי תוֹרָה, אַרְבַּע אִמָּהוֹת, שְׁלֹשָׁה אָבוֹת, שְׁנֵי לֻחוֹת הַבְּרִית, אֶחָד אֱלֹהֵינוּ שֶׁבַּשָּׁמַיִם וּבָאָרֶץ.

עֲשָׂרָה מִי יוֹדֵעַ? עֲשָׂרָה אֲנִי יוֹדֵעַ. עֲשָׂרָה דִבְּרַיָּא, תִּשְׁעָה יַרְחֵי לֵדָה, שְׁמוֹנָה יְמֵי מִילָה, שִׁבְעָה יְמֵי שַׁבַּתָּא, שִׁשָּׁה סִדְרֵי מִשְׁנָה, חֲמִשָּׁה חֻמְשֵׁי תוֹרָה, אַרְבַּע אִמָּהוֹת, שְׁלֹשָׁה אָבוֹת, שְׁנֵי לֻחוֹת הַבְּרִית, אֶחָד אֱלֹהֵינוּ שֶׁבַּשָּׁמַיִם וּבָאָרֶץ.

אַחַד עָשָׂר מִי יוֹדֵעַ? אַחַד עָשָׂר אֲנִי יוֹדֵעַ. אַחַד עָשָׂר כּוֹכְבַיָּא, עֲשָׂרָה דִבְּרַיָּא, תִּשְׁעָה יַרְחֵי לֵדָה, שְׁמוֹנָה יְמֵי מִילָה, שִׁבְעָה יְמֵי שַׁבַּתָּא, שִׁשָּׁה סִדְרֵי מִשְׁנָה, חֲמִשָּׁה חֻמְשֵׁי תוֹרָה, אַרְבַּע אִמָּהוֹת, שְׁלֹשָׁה אָבוֹת, שְׁנֵי לֻחוֹת הַבְּרִית, אֶחָד אֱלֹהֵינוּ שֶׁבַּשָּׁמַיִם וּבָאָרֶץ.

שְׁנֵים עָשָׂר מִי יוֹדֵעַ? שְׁנֵים עָשָׂר אֲנִי יוֹדֵעַ. שְׁנֵים עָשָׂר שִׁבְטַיָּא, אַחַד עָשָׂר כּוֹכְבַיָּא, עֲשָׂרָה דִבְּרַיָּא, תִּשְׁעָה יַרְחֵי לֵדָה, שְׁמוֹנָה יְמֵי מִילָה, שִׁבְעָה יְמֵי שַׁבַּתָּא, שִׁשָּׁה סִדְרֵי מִשְׁנָה, חֲמִשָּׁה חֻמְשֵׁי תוֹרָה, אַרְבַּע אִמָּהוֹת, שְׁלֹשָׁה אָבוֹת, שְׁנֵי לֻחוֹת הַבְּרִית, אֶחָד אֱלֹהֵינוּ שֶׁבַּשָּׁמַיִם וּבָאָרֶץ.

שְׁלֹשָׁה עָשָׂר מִי יוֹדֵעַ? שְׁלֹשָׁה עָשָׂר אֲנִי יוֹדֵעַ. שְׁלֹשָׁה עָשָׂר מִדַּיָּא, שְׁנֵים עָשָׂר שִׁבְטַיָּא,

Who knows nine? I know nine: nine are the months of pregnancy; eight are the days of circumcision; seven are the days of the week; six are the Orders of the Mishnah; five are the Books of the Torah; four are the Matriarchs; three are the Patriarchs; two are the Tablets of the Covenant; One is our God, in heaven and on earth.

Who knows ten? I know ten: ten are the Ten Commandments; nine are the months of pregnancy; eight are the days of circumcision; seven are the days of the week; six are the Orders of the Mishnah; five are the Books of the Torah; four are the Matriarchs; three are the Patriarchs; two are the Tablets of the Covenant; One is our God, in heaven and on earth.

Who knows eleven? I know eleven: eleven are the stars (in Yosef's dream); ten are the Ten Commandments; nine are the months of pregnancy; eight are the days of circumcision; seven are the days of the week; six are the Orders of the Mishnah; five are the Books of the Torah; four are the Matriarchs; three are the Patriarchs; two are the Tablets of the Covenant; One is our God, in heaven and on earth.

Who knows twelve? I know twelve: twelve are the tribes; eleven are the stars (in Yosef's dream); ten are the Ten Commandments; nine are the months of pregnancy; eight are the days of circumcision; seven are the days of the week; six are the Orders of the Mishnah; five are the Books of the Torah; four are the Matriarchs; three are the Patriarchs; two are the Tablets of the Covenant; One is our God, in heaven and on earth.

Who knows thirteen? I know thirteen: thirteen are the attributes of God; twelve are the tribes;

אֶחָד עָשָׂר כּוֹכְבַיָּא, עֲשָׂרָה דִבְּרַיָּא, תִּשְׁעָה יַרְחֵי לֵדָה, שְׁמוֹנָה יְמֵי מִילָה, שִׁבְעָה יְמֵי שַׁבַּתָּא, שִׁשָּׁה סִדְרֵי מִשְׁנָה, חֲמִשָּׁה חֻמְשֵׁי תוֹרָה, אַרְבַּע אִמָּהוֹת, שְׁלֹשָׁה אָבוֹת, שְׁנֵי לֻחוֹת הַבְּרִית, אֶחָד אֱלֹהֵינוּ שֶׁבַּשָּׁמַיִם וּבָאָרֶץ.

חַד גַּדְיָא. חַד גַּדְיָא, דְּזַבִּין אַבָּא בִּתְרֵי זוּזֵי, חַד גַּדְיָא חַד גַּדְיָא.

וְאָתָא **שׁוּנְרָא** וְאָכְלָה לְגַדְיָא, דְּזַבִּין אַבָּא בִּתְרֵי זוּזֵי, חַד גַּדְיָא חַד גַּדְיָא.

וְאָתָא **כַלְבָּא** וְנָשַׁךְ לְשׁוּנְרָא, דְּאָכְלָא לְגַדְיָא, דְּזַבִּין אַבָּא בִּתְרֵי זוּזֵי, חַד גַּדְיָא חַד גַּדְיָא.

וְאָתָא **חוּטְרָא** וְהִכָּה לְכַלְבָּא, דְּנָשַׁךְ לְשׁוּנְרָא, דְּאָכְלָה לְגַדְיָא, דְּזַבִּין אַבָּא בִּתְרֵי זוּזֵי, חַד גַּדְיָא חַד גַּדְיָא.

וְאָתָא **נוּרָא** וְשָׂרַף לְחוּטְרָא, דְּהִכָּה לְכַלְבָּא, דְּנָשַׁךְ לְשׁוּנְרָא, דְּאָכְלָה לְגַדְיָא, דְּזַבִּין אַבָּא בִּתְרֵי זוּזֵי, חַד גַּדְיָא חַד גַּדְיָא.

וְאָתָא **מַיָּא** וְכָבָה לְנוּרָא, דְּשָׂרַף לְחוּטְרָא, דְּהִכָּה לְכַלְבָּא, דְּנָשַׁךְ לְשׁוּנְרָא, דְּאָכְלָה לְגַדְיָא, דְּזַבִּין אַבָּא בִּתְרֵי זוּזֵי, חַד גַּדְיָא חַד גַּדְיָא.

וְאָתָא **תוֹרָא** וְשָׁתָה לְמַיָּא, דְּכָבָה לְנוּרָא, דְּשָׂרַף לְחוּטְרָא, דְּהִכָּה לְכַלְבָּא, דְּנָשַׁךְ לְשׁוּנְרָא, דְּאָכְלָה לְגַדְיָא, דְּזַבִּין אַבָּא בִּתְרֵי זוּזֵי, חַד גַּדְיָא חַד גַּדְיָא.

וְאָתָא **הַשּׁוֹחֵט** וְשָׁחַט לְתוֹרָא, דְּשָׁתָא לְמַיָּא, דְּכָבָה לְנוּרָא, דְּשָׂרַף לְחוּטְרָא, דְּהִכָּה לְכַלְבָּא,

eleven are the stars (in Yosef's dream); ten are the Ten Commandments; nine are the months of pregnancy; eight are the days of circumcision; seven are the days of the week; six are the Orders of the Mishnah; five are the Books of the Torah; four are the Matriarchs; three are the Patriarchs; two are the Tablets of the Covenant; One is our God, in heaven and on earth.

A kid, a kid, that father bought for two zuzim, a kid, a kid.

A cat then came and devoured the kid that father bought for two zuzim, a kid, a kid.

A dog then came and bit the cat, that devoured the kid that father bought for two zuzim, a kid, a kid.

A stick then came and beat the dog, that bit the cat, that devoured the kid that father bought for two zuzim, a kid, a kid.

A fire then came and burnt the stick, that beat the dog, that bit the cat, that devoured the kid that father bought for two zuzim, a kid, a kid.

Water then came and quenched the fire, that burnt the stick, that beat the dog, that bit the cat, that devoured the kid that father bought for two zuzim, a kid, a kid.

An ox then came and drank the water, that quenched the fire, that burnt the stick, that beat the dog, that bit the cat, that devoured the kid that father bought for two zuzim, a kid, a kid.

A slaughterer then came and slaughtered the ox, that drank the water, that quenched the fire, that burnt the stick, that beat the dog,

דְּנָשַׁךְ לְשׁוּנְרָא, דְּאָכְלָה לְגַדְיָא, דְּזַבִּין אַבָּא בִּתְרֵי זוּזֵי, חַד גַּדְיָא חַד גַּדְיָא.

וְאָתָא **מַלְאַךְ הַמָּוֶת** וְשָׁחַט לְשׁוֹחֵט, דְּשָׁחַט לְתוֹרָא, דְּשָׁתָה לְמַיָּא, דְּכָבָה לְנוּרָא, דְּשָׂרַף לְחוּטְרָא, דְּהִכָּה לְכַלְבָּא, דְּנָשַׁךְ לְשׁוּנְרָא, דְּאָכְלָה לְגַדְיָא, דְּזַבִּין אַבָּא בִּתְרֵי זוּזֵי, חַד גַּדְיָא חַד גַּדְיָא.

וְאָתָא **הַקָּדוֹשׁ בָּרוּךְ הוּא** וְשָׁחַט לְמַלְאַךְ הַמָּוֶת, דְּשָׁחַט לְשׁוֹחֵט, דְּשָׁחַט לְתוֹרָא, דְּשָׁתָה לְמַיָּא, דְּכָבָה לְנוּרָא, דְּשָׂרַף לְחוּטְרָא, דְּהִכָּה לְכַלְבָּא, דְּנָשַׁךְ לְשׁוּנְרָא, דְּאָכְלָה לְגַדְיָא, דְּזַבִּין אַבָּא בִּתְרֵי זוּזֵי, חַד גַּדְיָא חַד גַּדְיָא.

Although the Haggadah formally ends at this point, one should continue to occupy himself with the story of the Exodus, and the laws of Pesach, until sleep overtakes him.

── Think About It ──

"Preserving" Pesach for the Coming Year

Walk through any supermarket in Israel, and you'll notice an aisle lined with canned fruits and vegetables marked "*shimurim*." In modern Hebrew, the word *shimurim* refers to canned goods, food that is preserved and can be used far into the future. The Vizhnitzer Rebbe used this sense of the word to explain why the night of Pesach is called *Leil Shimurim*: the word *shimur* means "preserved"; the spiritual nourishment of the Pesach Seder helps a person "preserve" *emunah* for the entire year.

So much goes into preparing for Pesach, and in a few hours the Seder is over. But even after the table has been cleared and the food put away, the floors swept and everyone gone to bed,

that bit the cat, that devoured the kid that father bought for two zuzim, a kid, a kid.

The angel of death then came and killed the slaughterer, who slaughtered the ox, that drank the water, that quenched the fire, that burnt the stick, that beat the dog, that bit the cat, that devoured the kid that father bought for two zuzim, a kid, a kid.

The Holy One, Blessed is He, then came and slew the angel of death, who killed the slaughterer, who slaughtered the ox, that drank the water, that quenched the fire, that burnt the stick, that beat the dog, that bit the cat, that devoured the kid that father bought for two zuzim, a kid, a kid.

<small>Although the Haggadah formally ends at this point, one should continue to occupy himself with the story of the Exodus, and the laws of Pesach, until sleep overtakes him.</small>

---

the message of the Seder is not completed; that message, in fact, is just beginning to follow us throughout the year.

The Seder serves as a platform to teach us many basic principles of Judaism. In these few hours, we feel intensely Hashem's love for every Jew, His attentiveness to our needs and concerns, and His Godly abilities to perform miracles when He sees fit. Throughout the year, if we feel apprehensive about the future, challenged at work, under duress in our home lives, struggling or scared in any way, Pesach and its lessons of *emunah* and *bitachon* are there with us, reassuring, calming, and guiding.

We say in Hallel, אִסְרוּ חַג בַּעֲבֹתִים עַד קַרְנוֹת הַמִּזְבֵּחַ, *Bind the festival [offering] with cords to the corners of the Altar.* The *sefarim* explain these words as meaning that one can "tie" the Yom Tov to himself with thick ropes, keeping it close throughout the year.

Rav Shimshon Pincus writes (*Sichos Succos* p. 198) that a businessman who successfully navigates a business deal reaps the rewards for months and even years to come. The same is true with Yom Tov. When we properly tap into the Yom Tov and its themes, we reap its rewards well into the future as well. After Yom Tov had ended, Rav Yitzchak Hutner wouldn't say, "Yom Tov has passed." He'd say, "Yom Tov has been added to us," as the holiday has become part of us, and its messages continue to resonate throughout the year (*Pachad Yitzchak*, Chanukah, p. 55).

> During World War I, Rav Yerucham Levovitz, the mashgiach of Mir, was in a town when an airstrike struck the electric plant and the city was thrown into utter blackness. In the pitch dark, Rav Yerucham ran to the closest underground cellar, grabbed hold of the banister for support, and quickly ran down the stairs. Later, Rav Yerucham said, "Emunah is like a banister in a blackout: it provides support, guidance, and stability."

Emunah is a life preserver in the stormy sea of life; it is a calming and encouraging presence in an ever-challenging world. We are meant to apply what we have learned during the hours of the Pesach Seder to our everyday lives throughout the year. Real-life challenges require *emunah*. The hours we have spent relating the horrors of Egyptian slavery and our miraculous redemption, the stories we told about the Exodus, from Jewish history, and from our own lives that illustrate Hashem's *hashgachah pratis* go with us throughout the year and help us face whatever challenges we will meet, secure in the knowledge of Hashem's presence and His Hand that guides us (see *Agra D'Kallah*, *Eikev*, which says it is a *segulah* for one in need of any salvation to recall the miracles Hashem has performed for us in the past).

Whenever we are afraid and feel that life's challenges are too great, we should remember how Hashem lovingly redeemed us from Egypt and demonstrated to us His ability to care for us under any circumstances, even defying the laws of nature on behalf of His children, the Jewish nation.

☙ After the Seder
- Since the night of Pesach is *Leil Shimurim*, a guarded night, all the sections of *Krias Shema* said before going to sleep whose primary focus is protection are omitted. Only the first chapter of *Shema* and the *berachah* of "*HaMapil*" are recited (*Rema, Orach Chaim* 481:2; *Mishnah Berurah* 4).

שיר השירים / Song of Songs

Many have the custom to recite *Shir HaShirim* following the Seder.

פרק א

א שִׁיר הַשִּׁירִים אֲשֶׁר לִשְׁלֹמֹה: ב יִשָּׁקֵנִי מִנְּשִׁיקוֹת פִּיהוּ כִּי־טוֹבִים דֹּדֶיךָ מִיָּיִן: ג לְרֵיחַ שְׁמָנֶיךָ טוֹבִים שֶׁמֶן תּוּרַק שְׁמֶךָ עַל־כֵּן עֲלָמוֹת אֲהֵבוּךָ: ד מָשְׁכֵנִי אַחֲרֶיךָ נָּרוּצָה הֱבִיאַנִי הַמֶּלֶךְ חֲדָרָיו נָגִילָה וְנִשְׂמְחָה בָּךְ נַזְכִּירָה דֹדֶיךָ מִיַּיִן מֵישָׁרִים אֲהֵבוּךָ: ה שְׁחוֹרָה אֲנִי וְנָאוָה בְּנוֹת יְרוּשָׁלָםִ כְּאָהֳלֵי קֵדָר כִּירִיעוֹת שְׁלֹמֹה: ו אַל־תִּרְאוּנִי שֶׁאֲנִי שְׁחַרְחֹרֶת שֶׁשֱּׁזָפַתְנִי הַשָּׁמֶשׁ בְּנֵי אִמִּי נִחֲרוּ־בִי שָׂמֻנִי נֹטֵרָה אֶת־הַכְּרָמִים כַּרְמִי שֶׁלִּי לֹא נָטָרְתִּי: ז הַגִּידָה לִּי שֶׁאָהֲבָה נַפְשִׁי אֵיכָה תִרְעֶה אֵיכָה תַּרְבִּיץ בַּצָּהֳרָיִם שַׁלָּמָה אֶהְיֶה כְּעֹטְיָה עַל עֶדְרֵי חֲבֵרֶיךָ: ח אִם־לֹא תֵדְעִי לָךְ הַיָּפָה בַּנָּשִׁים צְאִי־לָךְ בְּעִקְבֵי הַצֹּאן וּרְעִי אֶת־גְּדִיֹּתַיִךְ עַל מִשְׁכְּנוֹת הָרֹעִים: ט לְסֻסָתִי

Reciting Shir HaShirim

After the Seder, it is customary to recite *Shir HaShirim*. Why?

In *Shir HaShirim* we find the *pasuk* קוֹל דּוֹדִי הִנֵּה זֶה בָּא מְדַלֵּג עַל הֶהָרִים מְקַפֵּץ עַל הַגְּבָעוֹת, *The Voice of my Beloved! Behold, it came suddenly to redeem me, as if leaping over mountains, skipping over hills* (*Shir HaShirim* 2:8). This *pasuk* refers to the redemption of Egypt, when Hashem freed *Bnei Yisrael* 190 years early. The Midrash comments that the redemption came in the merit of the patriarchs, who are compared to mountains, and in the merit of the matriarchs, who are compared to the hills (*Shir HaShirim Rabbah* 2:22). Through reciting *Shir HaShirim*, we recall these merits.

Also, on the night of the Seder we recount how Hashem miraculously took us out of Egypt despite our sins due to His overwhelming love for us. Hence, on this night it is only fitting to recite *Shir HaShirim* in which our love for Hashem and His love for us are intimately portrayed.

בְּרִכְבֵי פַרְעֹה דִּמִּיתִיךְ רַעְיָתִי: נָאווּ לְחָיַיִךְ בַּתֹּרִים צַוָּארֵךְ בַּחֲרוּזִים: יא תּוֹרֵי זָהָב נַעֲשֶׂה־לָּךְ עִם נְקֻדּוֹת הַכָּסֶף: יב עַד־שֶׁהַמֶּלֶךְ בִּמְסִבּוֹ נִרְדִּי נָתַן רֵיחוֹ: יג צְרוֹר הַמֹּר | דּוֹדִי לִי בֵּין שָׁדַי יָלִין: יד אֶשְׁכֹּל הַכֹּפֶר | דּוֹדִי לִי בְּכַרְמֵי עֵין גֶּדִי: טו הִנָּךְ יָפָה רַעְיָתִי הִנָּךְ יָפָה עֵינַיִךְ יוֹנִים: טז הִנְּךָ יָפֶה דוֹדִי אַף נָעִים אַף־עַרְשֵׂנוּ רַעֲנָנָה: יז קֹרוֹת בָּתֵּינוּ אֲרָזִים רַהִיטֵנוּ בְּרוֹתִים:

פרק ב

א אֲנִי חֲבַצֶּלֶת הַשָּׁרוֹן שׁוֹשַׁנַּת הָעֲמָקִים: ב כְּשׁוֹשַׁנָּה בֵּין הַחוֹחִים כֵּן רַעְיָתִי בֵּין הַבָּנוֹת: ג כְּתַפּוּחַ בַּעֲצֵי הַיַּעַר כֵּן דּוֹדִי בֵּין הַבָּנִים בְּצִלּוֹ חִמַּדְתִּי וְיָשַׁבְתִּי וּפִרְיוֹ מָתוֹק לְחִכִּי: ד הֱבִיאַנִי אֶל־בֵּית הַיַּיִן וְדִגְלוֹ עָלַי אַהֲבָה: ה סַמְּכוּנִי בָּאֲשִׁישׁוֹת רַפְּדוּנִי בַּתַּפּוּחִים כִּי־חוֹלַת אַהֲבָה אָנִי: ו שְׂמֹאלוֹ תַּחַת לְרֹאשִׁי וִימִינוֹ תְּחַבְּקֵנִי: ז הִשְׁבַּעְתִּי אֶתְכֶם בְּנוֹת יְרוּשָׁלַםִ בִּצְבָאוֹת אוֹ בְּאַיְלוֹת הַשָּׂדֶה אִם־תָּעִירוּ | וְאִם־תְּעוֹרְרוּ אֶת־הָאַהֲבָה עַד שֶׁתֶּחְפָּץ: ח קוֹל דּוֹדִי הִנֵּה־זֶה בָּא מְדַלֵּג עַל־הֶהָרִים מְקַפֵּץ עַל־הַגְּבָעוֹת: ט דּוֹמֶה דוֹדִי לִצְבִי אוֹ לְעֹפֶר הָאַיָּלִים הִנֵּה־זֶה עוֹמֵד אַחַר כָּתְלֵנוּ מַשְׁגִּיחַ מִן־הַחֲלֹּנוֹת מֵצִיץ מִן־הַחֲרַכִּים: י עָנָה דוֹדִי וְאָמַר לִי קוּמִי לָךְ רַעְיָתִי יָפָתִי וּלְכִי־לָךְ: יא כִּי־הִנֵּה הַסְּתָו עָבָר הַגֶּשֶׁם חָלַף הָלַךְ לוֹ: יב הַנִּצָּנִים נִרְאוּ בָאָרֶץ עֵת הַזָּמִיר הִגִּיעַ וְקוֹל הַתּוֹר נִשְׁמַע בְּאַרְצֵנוּ: יג הַתְּאֵנָה חָנְטָה פַגֶּיהָ וְהַגְּפָנִים סְמָדַר נָתְנוּ רֵיחַ קוּמִי לָךְ רַעְיָתִי יָפָתִי וּלְכִי־לָךְ: יד יוֹנָתִי בְּחַגְוֵי הַסֶּלַע בְּסֵתֶר הַמַּדְרֵגָה הַרְאִינִי אֶת־מַרְאַיִךְ הַשְׁמִיעִנִי אֶת־קוֹלֵךְ כִּי־קוֹלֵךְ עָרֵב וּמַרְאֵיךְ נָאוֶה: טו אֶחֱזוּ־לָנוּ שֻׁעָלִים שֻׁעָלִים קְטַנִּים מְחַבְּלִים כְּרָמִים וּכְרָמֵינוּ סְמָדַר: טז דּוֹדִי לִי וַאֲנִי לוֹ הָרֹעֶה בַּשּׁוֹשַׁנִּים: יז עַד שֶׁיָּפוּחַ הַיּוֹם וְנָסוּ הַצְּלָלִים סֹב דְּמֵה־לְךָ דוֹדִי לִצְבִי אוֹ לְעֹפֶר הָאַיָּלִים עַל־הָרֵי בָתֶר:

פרק ג

א עַל־מִשְׁכָּבִי בַּלֵּילוֹת בִּקַּשְׁתִּי אֵת שֶׁאָהֲבָה נַפְשִׁי בִּקַּשְׁתִּיו וְלֹא מְצָאתִיו: ב אָקוּמָה נָּא וַאֲסוֹבְבָה בָעִיר בַּשְּׁוָקִים וּבָרְחֹבוֹת אֲבַקְשָׁה אֵת שֶׁאָהֲבָה נַפְשִׁי בִּקַּשְׁתִּיו וְלֹא מְצָאתִיו: ג מְצָאוּנִי הַשֹּׁמְרִים הַסֹּבְבִים בָּעִיר אֵת שֶׁאָהֲבָה נַפְשִׁי רְאִיתֶם: ד כִּמְעַט שֶׁעָבַרְתִּי מֵהֶם עַד שֶׁמָּצָאתִי אֵת שֶׁאָהֲבָה נַפְשִׁי אֲחַזְתִּיו וְלֹא אַרְפֶּנּוּ עַד־שֶׁהֲבֵיאתִיו אֶל־בֵּית אִמִּי וְאֶל־חֶדֶר הוֹרָתִי: ה הִשְׁבַּעְתִּי אֶתְכֶם בְּנוֹת יְרוּשָׁלַם בִּצְבָאוֹת אוֹ בְּאַיְלוֹת הַשָּׂדֶה אִם־תָּעִירוּ ׀ וְאִם־תְּעוֹרְרוּ אֶת־הָאַהֲבָה עַד שֶׁתֶּחְפָּץ: ו מִי זֹאת עֹלָה מִן־הַמִּדְבָּר כְּתִימֲרוֹת עָשָׁן מְקֻטֶּרֶת מוֹר וּלְבוֹנָה מִכֹּל אַבְקַת רוֹכֵל: ז הִנֵּה מִטָּתוֹ שֶׁלִּשְׁלֹמֹה שִׁשִּׁים גִּבֹּרִים סָבִיב לָהּ מִגִּבֹּרֵי יִשְׂרָאֵל: ח כֻּלָּם אֲחֻזֵי חֶרֶב מְלֻמְּדֵי מִלְחָמָה אִישׁ חַרְבּוֹ עַל־יְרֵכוֹ מִפַּחַד בַּלֵּילוֹת: ט אַפִּרְיוֹן עָשָׂה לוֹ הַמֶּלֶךְ שְׁלֹמֹה מֵעֲצֵי הַלְּבָנוֹן: י עַמּוּדָיו עָשָׂה כֶסֶף רְפִידָתוֹ זָהָב מֶרְכָּבוֹ אַרְגָּמָן תּוֹכוֹ רָצוּף אַהֲבָה מִבְּנוֹת יְרוּשָׁלָם ׀ יא צְאֶינָה וּרְאֶינָה בְּנוֹת צִיּוֹן בַּמֶּלֶךְ שְׁלֹמֹה בָּעֲטָרָה שֶׁעִטְּרָה־לּוֹ אִמּוֹ בְּיוֹם חֲתֻנָּתוֹ וּבְיוֹם שִׂמְחַת לִבּוֹ:

פרק ד

א הִנָּךְ יָפָה רַעְיָתִי הִנָּךְ יָפָה עֵינַיִךְ יוֹנִים מִבַּעַד לְצַמָּתֵךְ שַׂעְרֵךְ כְּעֵדֶר הָעִזִּים שֶׁגָּלְשׁוּ מֵהַר גִּלְעָד: ב שִׁנַּיִךְ כְּעֵדֶר הַקְּצוּבוֹת שֶׁעָלוּ מִן־הָרַחְצָה שֶׁכֻּלָּם מַתְאִימוֹת וְשַׁכֻּלָה אֵין בָּהֶם: ג כְּחוּט הַשָּׁנִי שִׂפְתוֹתַיִךְ וּמִדְבָּרֵךְ נָאוֶה כְּפֶלַח הָרִמּוֹן רַקָּתֵךְ מִבַּעַד לְצַמָּתֵךְ: ד כְּמִגְדַּל דָּוִיד צַוָּארֵךְ בָּנוּי לְתַלְפִּיּוֹת אֶלֶף הַמָּגֵן תָּלוּי עָלָיו כֹּל שִׁלְטֵי הַגִּבֹּרִים: ה שְׁנֵי שָׁדַיִךְ כִּשְׁנֵי עֳפָרִים תְּאוֹמֵי צְבִיָּה הָרוֹעִים בַּשּׁוֹשַׁנִּים: ו עַד שֶׁיָּפוּחַ הַיּוֹם וְנָסוּ הַצְּלָלִים אֵלֶךְ לִי אֶל־הַר הַמּוֹר וְאֶל־גִּבְעַת הַלְּבוֹנָה: ז כֻּלָּךְ יָפָה רַעְיָתִי וּמוּם אֵין בָּךְ: ח אִתִּי מִלְּבָנוֹן כַּלָּה אִתִּי מִלְּבָנוֹן תָּבוֹאִי תָּשׁוּרִי ׀ מֵרֹאשׁ אֲמָנָה

מֵרֹאשׁ שְׂנִיר וְחֶרְמוֹן מִמְּעֹנוֹת אֲרָיוֹת מֵהַרְרֵי נְמֵרִים: ט לִבַּבְתִּנִי אֲחֹתִי כַלָּה לִבַּבְתִּנִי בְּאַחַת מֵעֵינַיִךְ בְּאַחַד עֲנָק מִצַּוְּרֹנָיִךְ: י מַה־יָּפוּ דֹדַיִךְ אֲחֹתִי כַלָּה מַה־טֹּבוּ דֹדַיִךְ מִיַּיִן וְרֵיחַ שְׁמָנַיִךְ מִכָּל־בְּשָׂמִים: יא נֹפֶת תִּטֹּפְנָה שִׂפְתוֹתַיִךְ כַּלָּה דְּבַשׁ וְחָלָב תַּחַת לְשׁוֹנֵךְ וְרֵיחַ שַׂלְמֹתַיִךְ כְּרֵיחַ לְבָנוֹן: יב גַּן | נָעוּל אֲחֹתִי כַלָּה גַּל | נָעוּל מַעְיָן חָתוּם: יג שְׁלָחַיִךְ פַּרְדֵּס רִמּוֹנִים עִם פְּרִי מְגָדִים כְּפָרִים עִם־נְרָדִים: יד נֵרְדְּ | וְכַרְכֹּם קָנֶה וְקִנָּמוֹן עִם כָּל־עֲצֵי לְבוֹנָה מֹר וַאֲהָלוֹת עִם כָּל־רָאשֵׁי בְשָׂמִים: טו מַעְיַן גַּנִּים בְּאֵר מַיִם חַיִּים וְנֹזְלִים מִן־לְבָנוֹן: טז עוּרִי צָפוֹן וּבוֹאִי תֵימָן הָפִיחִי גַנִּי יִזְּלוּ בְשָׂמָיו יָבֹא דוֹדִי לְגַנּוֹ וְיֹאכַל פְּרִי מְגָדָיו:

פרק ה

א בָּאתִי לְגַנִּי אֲחֹתִי כַלָּה אָרִיתִי מוֹרִי עִם־בְּשָׂמִי אָכַלְתִּי יַעְרִי עִם־דִּבְשִׁי שָׁתִיתִי יֵינִי עִם־חֲלָבִי אִכְלוּ רֵעִים שְׁתוּ וְשִׁכְרוּ דּוֹדִים: ב אֲנִי יְשֵׁנָה וְלִבִּי עֵר קוֹל | דּוֹדִי דוֹפֵק פִּתְחִי־לִי אֲחֹתִי רַעְיָתִי יוֹנָתִי תַמָּתִי שֶׁרֹּאשִׁי נִמְלָא־טָל קְוֻצּוֹתַי רְסִיסֵי לָיְלָה: ג פָּשַׁטְתִּי אֶת־כֻּתָּנְתִּי אֵיכָכָה אֶלְבָּשֶׁנָּה רָחַצְתִּי אֶת־רַגְלַי אֵיכָכָה אֲטַנְּפֵם: ד דּוֹדִי שָׁלַח יָדוֹ מִן־הַחֹר וּמֵעַי הָמוּ עָלָיו: ה קַמְתִּי אֲנִי לִפְתֹּחַ לְדוֹדִי וְיָדַי נָטְפוּ־מוֹר וְאֶצְבְּעֹתַי מוֹר עֹבֵר עַל כַּפּוֹת הַמַּנְעוּל: ו פָּתַחְתִּי אֲנִי לְדוֹדִי וְדוֹדִי חָמַק עָבָר נַפְשִׁי יָצְאָה בְדַבְּרוֹ בִּקַּשְׁתִּיהוּ וְלֹא מְצָאתִיהוּ קְרָאתִיו וְלֹא עָנָנִי: ז מְצָאֻנִי הַשֹּׁמְרִים הַסֹּבְבִים בָּעִיר הִכּוּנִי פְצָעוּנִי נָשְׂאוּ אֶת־רְדִידִי מֵעָלַי שֹׁמְרֵי הַחֹמוֹת: ח הִשְׁבַּעְתִּי אֶתְכֶם בְּנוֹת יְרוּשָׁלָ͏ִם אִם־תִּמְצְאוּ אֶת־דּוֹדִי מַה־תַּגִּידוּ לוֹ שֶׁחוֹלַת אַהֲבָה אָנִי: ט מַה־דּוֹדֵךְ מִדּוֹד הַיָּפָה בַּנָּשִׁים מַה־דּוֹדֵךְ מִדּוֹד שֶׁכָּכָה הִשְׁבַּעְתָּנוּ: י דּוֹדִי צַח וְאָדוֹם דָּגוּל מֵרְבָבָה: יא רֹאשׁוֹ כֶּתֶם פָּז קְוֻצּוֹתָיו תַּלְתַּלִּים שְׁחֹרוֹת כָּעוֹרֵב: יב עֵינָיו כְּיוֹנִים עַל־אֲפִיקֵי מָיִם רֹחֲצוֹת בֶּחָלָב יֹשְׁבוֹת עַל־מִלֵּאת: יג לְחָיָו

כַּעֲרוּגַת הַבֹּשֶׂם מִגְדְּלוֹת מֶרְקָחִים שִׂפְתוֹתָיו שׁוֹשַׁנִּים נֹטְפוֹת מוֹר עֹבֵר: יד יָדָיו גְּלִילֵי זָהָב מְמֻלָּאִים בַּתַּרְשִׁישׁ מֵעָיו עֶשֶׁת שֵׁן מְעֻלֶּפֶת סַפִּירִים: טו שׁוֹקָיו עַמּוּדֵי שֵׁשׁ מְיֻסָּדִים עַל־אַדְנֵי־פָז מַרְאֵהוּ כַּלְּבָנוֹן בָּחוּר כָּאֲרָזִים: טז חִכּוֹ מַמְתַקִּים וְכֻלּוֹ מַחֲמַדִּים זֶה דוֹדִי וְזֶה רֵעִי בְּנוֹת יְרוּשָׁלָם:

פרק ו

א אָנָה הָלַךְ דּוֹדֵךְ הַיָּפָה בַּנָּשִׁים אָנָה פָּנָה דוֹדֵךְ וּנְבַקְשֶׁנּוּ עִמָּךְ: ב דּוֹדִי יָרַד לְגַנּוֹ לַעֲרוּגוֹת הַבֹּשֶׂם לִרְעוֹת בַּגַּנִּים וְלִלְקֹט שׁוֹשַׁנִּים: ג אֲנִי לְדוֹדִי וְדוֹדִי לִי הָרֹעֶה בַּשּׁוֹשַׁנִּים: ד יָפָה אַתְּ רַעְיָתִי כְּתִרְצָה נָאוָה כִּירוּשָׁלָם אֲיֻמָּה כַּנִּדְגָּלוֹת: ה הָסֵבִּי עֵינַיִךְ מִנֶּגְדִּי שֶׁהֵם הִרְהִיבֻנִי שַׂעְרֵךְ כְּעֵדֶר הָעִזִּים שֶׁגָּלְשׁוּ מִן־הַגִּלְעָד: ו שִׁנַּיִךְ כְּעֵדֶר הָרְחֵלִים שֶׁעָלוּ מִן־הָרַחְצָה שֶׁכֻּלָּם מַתְאִימוֹת וְשַׁכֻּלָה אֵין בָּהֶם: ז כְּפֶלַח הָרִמּוֹן רַקָּתֵךְ מִבַּעַד לְצַמָּתֵךְ: ח שִׁשִּׁים הֵמָּה מְלָכוֹת וּשְׁמֹנִים פִּילַגְשִׁים וַעֲלָמוֹת אֵין מִסְפָּר: ט אַחַת הִיא יוֹנָתִי תַמָּתִי אַחַת הִיא לְאִמָּהּ בָּרָה הִיא לְיוֹלַדְתָּהּ רָאוּהָ בָנוֹת וַיְאַשְּׁרוּהָ מְלָכוֹת וּפִילַגְשִׁים וַיְהַלְלוּהָ: י מִי־זֹאת הַנִּשְׁקָפָה כְּמוֹ־שָׁחַר יָפָה כַלְּבָנָה בָּרָה כַּחַמָּה אֲיֻמָּה כַּנִּדְגָּלוֹת: יא אֶל־גִּנַּת אֱגוֹז יָרַדְתִּי לִרְאוֹת בְּאִבֵּי הַנָּחַל לִרְאוֹת הֲפָרְחָה הַגֶּפֶן הֵנֵצוּ הָרִמֹּנִים: יב לֹא יָדַעְתִּי נַפְשִׁי שָׂמַתְנִי מַרְכְּבוֹת עַמִּי נָדִיב:

פרק ז

א שׁוּבִי שׁוּבִי הַשּׁוּלַמִּית שׁוּבִי שׁוּבִי וְנֶחֱזֶה־בָּךְ מַה־תֶּחֱזוּ בַּשּׁוּלַמִּית כִּמְחֹלַת הַמַּחֲנָיִם: ב מַה־יָּפוּ פְעָמַיִךְ בַּנְּעָלִים בַּת־נָדִיב חַמּוּקֵי יְרֵכַיִךְ כְּמוֹ חֲלָאִים מַעֲשֵׂה יְדֵי אָמָּן: ג שָׁרְרֵךְ אַגַּן הַסַּהַר אַל־יֶחְסַר הַמָּזֶג בִּטְנֵךְ עֲרֵמַת חִטִּים סוּגָה בַּשּׁוֹשַׁנִּים: ד שְׁנֵי שָׁדַיִךְ כִּשְׁנֵי עֳפָרִים תָּאֳמֵי צְבִיָּה: ה צַוָּארֵךְ כְּמִגְדַּל הַשֵּׁן עֵינַיִךְ בְּרֵכוֹת בְּחֶשְׁבּוֹן עַל־שַׁעַר

בַּתְּרַבִּים אַפֵּךְ כְּמִגְדַּל הַלְּבָנוֹן צוֹפֶה פְּנֵי דַמָּשֶׂק: וְרֹאשֵׁךְ עָלַיִךְ כַּכַּרְמֶל וְדַלַּת רֹאשֵׁךְ כָּאַרְגָּמָן מֶלֶךְ אָסוּר בָּרְהָטִים: זמַה־יָּפִית וּמַה־נָּעַמְתְּ אַהֲבָה בַּתַּעֲנוּגִים: חזֹאת קוֹמָתֵךְ דָּמְתָה לְתָמָר וְשָׁדַיִךְ לְאַשְׁכֹּלוֹת: טאָמַרְתִּי אֶעֱלֶה בְתָמָר אֹחֲזָה בְּסַנְסִנָּיו וְיִהְיוּ־נָא שָׁדַיִךְ כְּאֶשְׁכְּלוֹת הַגֶּפֶן וְרֵיחַ אַפֵּךְ כַּתַּפּוּחִים: יוְחִכֵּךְ כְּיֵין הַטּוֹב הוֹלֵךְ לְדוֹדִי לְמֵישָׁרִים דּוֹבֵב שִׂפְתֵי יְשֵׁנִים: יאאֲנִי לְדוֹדִי וְעָלַי תְּשׁוּקָתוֹ: יבלְכָה דוֹדִי נֵצֵא הַשָּׂדֶה נָלִינָה בַּכְּפָרִים: יגנַשְׁכִּימָה לַכְּרָמִים נִרְאֶה אִם־פָּרְחָה הַגֶּפֶן פִּתַּח הַסְּמָדַר הֵנֵצוּ הָרִמּוֹנִים שָׁם אֶתֵּן אֶת־דֹּדַי לָךְ: ידהַדּוּדָאִים נָתְנוּ־רֵיחַ וְעַל־פְּתָחֵינוּ כָּל־מְגָדִים חֲדָשִׁים גַּם־יְשָׁנִים דּוֹדִי צָפַנְתִּי לָךְ:

פרק ח

אמִי יִתֶּנְךָ כְּאָח לִי יוֹנֵק שְׁדֵי אִמִּי אֶמְצָאֲךָ בַחוּץ אֶשָּׁקְךָ גַּם לֹא־יָבוּזוּ לִי: באֶנְהָגֲךָ אֲבִיאֲךָ אֶל־בֵּית אִמִּי תְּלַמְּדֵנִי אַשְׁקְךָ מִיַּיִן הָרֶקַח מֵעֲסִיס רִמֹּנִי: גשְׂמֹאלוֹ תַּחַת רֹאשִׁי וִימִינוֹ תְּחַבְּקֵנִי: דהִשְׁבַּעְתִּי אֶתְכֶם בְּנוֹת יְרוּשָׁלָםִ מַה־תָּעִירוּ ׀ וּמַה־תְּעֹרְרוּ אֶת־הָאַהֲבָה עַד שֶׁתֶּחְפָּץ: המִי זֹאת עֹלָה מִן־הַמִּדְבָּר מִתְרַפֶּקֶת עַל־דּוֹדָהּ תַּחַת הַתַּפּוּחַ עוֹרַרְתִּיךָ שָׁמָּה חִבְּלַתְךָ אִמֶּךָ שָׁמָּה חִבְּלָה יְלָדַתְךָ: ושִׂימֵנִי כַחוֹתָם עַל־לִבֶּךָ כַּחוֹתָם עַל־זְרוֹעֶךָ כִּי־עַזָּה כַמָּוֶת אַהֲבָה קָשָׁה כִשְׁאוֹל קִנְאָה רְשָׁפֶיהָ רִשְׁפֵּי אֵשׁ שַׁלְהֶבֶתְיָה: זמַיִם רַבִּים לֹא יוּכְלוּ לְכַבּוֹת אֶת־הָאַהֲבָה וּנְהָרוֹת לֹא יִשְׁטְפוּהָ אִם־יִתֵּן אִישׁ אֶת־כָּל־הוֹן בֵּיתוֹ בָּאַהֲבָה בּוֹז יָבוּזוּ לוֹ: חאָחוֹת לָנוּ קְטַנָּה וְשָׁדַיִם אֵין לָהּ מַה־נַּעֲשֶׂה לַאֲחוֹתֵנוּ בַּיּוֹם שֶׁיְּדֻבַּר־בָּהּ: טאִם־חוֹמָה הִיא נִבְנֶה עָלֶיהָ טִירַת כָּסֶף וְאִם־דֶּלֶת הִיא נָצוּר עָלֶיהָ לוּחַ אָרֶז: יאֲנִי חוֹמָה וְשָׁדַי כַּמִּגְדָּלוֹת אָז הָיִיתִי בְעֵינָיו כְּמוֹצְאֵת שָׁלוֹם: יאכֶּרֶם הָיָה לִשְׁלֹמֹה בְּבַעַל הָמוֹן נָתַן אֶת־הַכֶּרֶם לַנֹּטְרִים אִישׁ יָבִא בְּפִרְיוֹ אֶלֶף כָּסֶף: יבכַּרְמִי

שֶׁלִּי לְפָנָי הָאֶלֶף לְךָ שְׁלֹמֹה וּמָאתַיִם לְנֹטְרִים אֶת־פִּרְיוֹ:
יג הַיּוֹשֶׁבֶת בַּגַּנִּים חֲבֵרִים מַקְשִׁיבִים לְקוֹלֵךְ הַשְׁמִיעִנִי:
יד בְּרַח | דּוֹדִי וּדְמֵה־לְךָ לִצְבִי אוֹ לְעֹפֶר הָאַיָּלִים עַל הָרֵי בְשָׂמִים:

GLOSSARY

al kiddush Hashem — for the sake of sanctifying Hashem.

aliyah (pl. *aliyos*) — lit., *going up*. 1. spiritual elevation; 2. act of being called to recite a blessing at the public reading of the Torah; 3. immigration to Israel.

aliyah l'regel — going up to the *Beis HaMikdash* in Jerusalem during the three Festivals of Pesach, Shavuos, and Succos.

Amoraim — Sages whose opinions are cited in the Gemara.

Anshei Knesses HaGedolah — the Men of the Great Assembly.

aron — (cap.) (in Mishkan) Holy Ark that housed the Tablets (*Luchos*); (l.c.) (in shul) ark where the Torah Scrolls are kept.

aron kodesh — holy ark in the synagogue, where the Torah Scrolls are kept.

Asher yatzar — prayer said after performing bodily functions.

av beis din — the head of a religious court.

avodah — lit., *work; task*; the service of Hashem, whether in sacrifice, prayer, or self-refinement.

Avos — the Patriarchs: Avraham, Yitzchak, and Yaakov.

ba'al teshuvah (pl. *ba'alei teshuvah*) — one who repents; one who returns to Torah-true Judaism.

Baruch Hashem — lit., *Blessed is Hashem*; thank Hashem; an expression of appreciation of Hashem's goodness.

batei mikdash — the Holy Temples.

beis midrash — a study hall where Torah is learned, often used as a synagogue as well.

ben bayis — *a person who, though not related, is considered part of the family.*

bentch — (Yiddish) 1. recite Grace after Meals; 2. to bless someone.

berachah (pl. *berachos*) — a blessing recited before performing a mitzvah and before and after eating; a formula for acknowledging a gift from Hashem, whether material or spiritual.

bitachon — lit., *trust*; trust in Hashem.

blech — (Yiddish) a sheet of metal placed over a stovetop above the flame to permit keeping the Shabbos food over the fire.

Bnei Yisrael — lit., *the children of Israel*; the Jewish people.

chag (pl. *chagim*) — a holiday; a festival.

chametz — leavened foods prohibited during the Pesach festival.

chassan — a bridegroom.

chavrusah — a study partner.

chein — grace; charm.

chesed — kindness; acts of beneficence; charitable giving.

chiddushim —Talmudic or halachic novellae.

chinuch — Jewish education; the obligation for a parent to train a child to perform mitzvos.

Chol Hamo'ed — the intermediate days between the first and last days of Pesach and Succos.

chuppah — 1. wedding canopy; 2. the marriage ceremony.

daf yomi — daily study of one folio of the Gemara.

daven — (Yiddish) to pray.

dayan — rabbinical court judge; halachic decisor or judge.

divrei Torah — short speeches on Torah topics.

eiruv tavshilin — a halachic procedure that allows one to cook on a festival ending on Friday for the Shabbos immediately following.

eishes chayil – 1. woman of valor; a worthy wife; 2. (cap.) Proverbs 31:10-31, traditionally recited before the Friday-night Shabbos meal.

emunah — faith.

emunah peshutah — simple, total faith in Hashem.

erev Shabbos — the eve of the Sabbath; Friday.

erev Yom Tov — the eve of a holiday.

gadol (pl. *gedolim*) — 1. an adult according to halachah. 2. an outstanding Torah scholar.

gadol hador (pl. *gedolei hador*) — spiritual leader of the generation.

gemach (pl. *gemachim*) — acronym for *gemilus chasadim*, acts of kindness; system for providing aid of various kinds; e.g., interest-free loans.

Geonim — post-Tamudic Sages; the Sages who lived between approx. 600 C.E. and 1,000 C.E.

geulah — redemption.

hadlakas neiros — candlelighting.

hakafah (pl. *hakafos*) — the encircling of the *bimah* seven times on the holiday of Simchas Torah, while dancing with the Torah Scrolls.

hakaras hatov — gratitude; expressing gratitude.

hashgachah pratis — individual Divine Providence.

hishtadlus — one's own efforts; the required effort.

ishah haShunamis — the woman who hosted the prophet Eliyahu (*II Melachim*, Chapter 4).

kallah — a bride; an engaged girl.

kavod — honor, respect, dignity.

Kedushah — 1. the prayer recited by the angels; 2. a prayer recited during the repetition of the *Shemoneh Esrei* (it may be said only in the presence of a *minyan*); 3. (l.c.) holiness; sanctity.

kibbud av va'eim — honoring one's parents.

kibbudim — lit., *honors*; the honor of being called to the *bimah* during the reading of the Torah or to be a participant at a religious ceremony.

Kiddush — 1. mandatory blessing over wine expressing the sanctity of Shabbos or Festivals; 2. (l.c.) a Shabbos-reception after morning prayers at which Kiddush is recited and refreshments are served; 3. the blessing over wine recited before the Shabbos and Yom Tov meals.

kiddush Hashem — sanctification of Hashem's holy Name.

kittel — long white garment worn by men during the Yom Kippur prayer services and at the Pesach Seder, and, in Ashkenazic tradition, by the groom during the wedding ceremony.

Kodash HaKodashim — Holy of Holies; the inner chamber of the Sanctuary.

kollelim — senior yeshivos, usually for married students.

korbanos — sacrificial offerings.

Krias Yam Suf — the splitting of the Red Sea.

lashon hara — lit., *evil speech*; derogatory speech; slander; gossip.

Leil Hiskadesh Chag — the night of the festival's consecration.

Leil Shimurim — a night of anticipation (the eve of the 15th of Nissan).

limud haTorah — the learning or teaching of the Torah.

ma'asros — tithes.

ma'os chitin — funds collected to help the needy buy provisions for Pesach, esp. matzah.

Makkas Bechoros — the Plague of the Firstborn.

Malachim — heavenly angels.

mashgiach — 1. (cap.) dean of students in a yeshivah who oversees students' spiritual and ethical development; 2. kashrut supervisor.

melamed zechus — give the benefit of the doubt.

menahel — principal; supervisor.

menuchah — rest; peace of mind.

mesader kiddushin — the one who officiates at the marriage ceremony.

mesorah — Jewish heritage; the received tradition.

minhag — custom; practice.

Mishkan — Tabernacle; the portable Temple used by the Jews during their sojourn in the Wilderness.

Mitzrayim — Egypt.

THE EISHES CHAYIL HAGGADAH

Modeh Ani — "I admit in front of You"; prayer upon awakening in the morning, expressing gratitude for life.

mo'ed — festival.

mohel — one who performs a circumcision.

motza'ei Shabbos — Saturday night; the time of the departure of Shabbos.

Mussaf — additional prayer service recited after Shacharis on Shabbos, Rosh Chodesh, and Festivals.

nusach — 1. style of prayer service; 2. melody used during a prayer service.

oneg — joy; pleasure; delight.

oneg Shabbos — lit., *joy of Sabbath*; a gathering to celebrate Shabbos.

parnassah — livelihood.

pasuk — a verse of Scripture.

Pesukei D'Zimrah — Verses of Praise; a section of the morning prayer service.

rasha — an evildoer; a wicked individual.

refuah sheleimah — lit., *a full/complete recovery*; a blessing for a complete/speedy recovery extended to an ailing person.

regalim — lit., *feet*; the three Pilgrimage Festivals.

Rishonim – early commentators on the Talmud, 11th-15th centuries.

rosh yeshivah — the dean of a yeshivah; senior lecturer in a yeshivah.

sefer (pl. *sefarim*) — a book, specifically a book on a holy or learned topic.

Sefer Torah (pl. *Sifrei Torah*) — a Torah Scroll, written on parchment.

segulah (pl. *segulos*) — a spiritual remedy; a valuable tool.

Shacharis — the morning prayer service.

shadchanim — matchmakers.

shalom bayis — peace and harmony in the home; marital harmony.

Shema Yisrael — *Hear O Israel*; this prayer, recited twice daily, expresses the essence of Jewish faith.

shidduch (pl. *shidduchim*) — 1. match, esp. a marriage match; 2. proposed marriage match. 3. one's betrothed.

shiurim — 1. lectures; classes; 2. measurements.

sichos — lectures.

simchah — 1. happiness, joy; a joyous occasion; 2. a happy occasion; a celebration, esp. a celebration of a family milestone such as a wedding, bar mitzvah, or a birth.

siyatta d'Shmaya — Heavenly assistance; help from Hashem.

sugya — (Aramaic) topic; conceptual unit in Talmud study.

talmid chacham — lit., *the student of a wise person*; a person learned in Torah and Talmud.

Tanach — acronym for ***T**orah, **N**eviim, **K**esuvim*; the written Torah, including the Five Books of Moses, the eight books of Prophets, and eleven books of Writings.

Tannaim — the Sages who are quoted in the Mishnah.

tefillah (pl. *tefillos*) — prayer.

Tehillim — 1. the Book of *Psalms*; 2. (l.c.) psalms.

tekias shofar — the sounding of the shofar.

tereifah — not kosher.

terumos — the first portions of the crops that are separated and given to a Kohen.

teshuvah — 1. answer; 2. repentance; 3. rediscovery of Torah Judaism; 4. a response to a halachic query.

tznius – modesty standard in speech, behavior, and dress.

vort — lit., *word*; 1. a Torah thought; 2. an engagement celebration.

yetzer hara — evil inclination; the negative impulse to behave contrary to the Torah's commandments.

yetzer tov — the good inclination.

yichus — lineage.

zechus — merit, privilege.

zeman cheiruseinu — the Time of Our Freedom; i.e., Pesach.